BIBLIOGRAPHY of
DISCOGRAPHIES

BIBLIOGRAPHY
of
DISCOGRAPHIES

Volume 3
POPULAR MUSIC

by
Michael H. Gray

R. R. BOWKER COMPANY
New York and London, 1983

For Dottie, as always

Published by R. R. Bowker Company
1180 Avenue of the Americas, New York, NY 10036
Copyright © 1983 by Xerox Corporation
Printed and bound in the United States of America

Library of Congress Cataloging in Publication Data

Gray, Michael H., 1946–
  Popular music.

  (Bibliography of discographies; v. 3)
  Includes index.
  1. Music, Popular (Songs, etc.)—Discography—
Bibliography.   I. Title.   II. Series.
ML156.2.B49   vol. 3 016.0167899'12s   82-20776
[ML156.4.P6]   [016.0167899'12]
ISBN 0-8352-1683-7 (v. 3)

CONTENTS

PREFACE

This third volume of *Bibliography of Discographies*, encompassing discographies of pop music, rock and country, hillbilly and bluegrass, and motion picture and stage show music, continues a series devoted to discographies in all subject areas. The first volume, containing references to discographies of classical music between 1925 and 1975, was compiled by Michael H. Gray and Gerald D. Gibson and was published by Bowker in 1977. Volume 2, devoted to discographies of jazz and related music, was compiled by Daniel Allen and published in 1981.

The selection of citations for this volume on popular music, as in the previous two, has been guided primarily by the self-description of the item and by its potential usefulness. Some items, such as record company catalogs, have been excluded entirely from citation. Other citations have been included on a selective basis, primarily comparative pricing guides to out-of-print records, which have a clear discographic function, and lists of charted popular records, which can be used discographically.

Some intentional duplication occurs between this volume and Volume 2. Where additional citations to artists or labels found in Volume 2 occur in Volume 3, cross-references have been made to the same headings in Volume 2. In a few cases, citations have been repeated in their entirety when the subject matter of the discography overlapped the boundaries between jazz, related rhythm and blues, and popular music.

RESEARCH METHOD

In gathering citations, there has been a reliance almost exclusively on examination of the discographies themselves. Those not seen by me or my correspondents, but taken from various secondary sources, have been enclosed in double brackets [[ ]]. Citations of monographs are taken as closely as possible from the title page, with interpolations or other alterations enclosed in single brackets. Because of this method, some citations will differ in form from those found in other bibliographies and reference sources. A number of secondary citations that could not be clarified in the time allotted to the research have been omitted.

As part of the examination process, a seven-number annotative code has been adopted to identify elements believed to be of special importance to users. These coded elements appear in double parentheses ((   )) included in or following the citation. The symbol ((—)) is used to signify that no coded elements appear in the discography. The elements and their symbols are:

1 Noncommercial recordings and unissued recordings
2 Personnel
3 Matrix number
4 Index
5 Release dates
6 Take numbers
6a Differing versions of the same song
7 Place and date of recording

ORGANIZATION

The bibliography is divided into two sections: the body, which contains personal names and other subjects arranged in a single-numbered alphabetical sequence, and the index, which contains names of authors, compilers, editors, and series titles. Filing of multiple listings under a given heading is either by the compiler of the discography or the title of the discography.

Forms of personal names in the body generally follow the usage found in the cited sources; when appropriate, cross-references have been made linking variant subjects or name forms to those that have been used. Filing in the main text and in the index follows American Library Association filing rules.

Discographies appear in the following forms:

PRESLEY, ELVIS ARON

(Journal article) P149 JONES, Randall: An Elvis discography *in* Record Exchanger, V/3 (No. 25, January 1978?): 16–19 ((5))

(Title entry) P139 Discographie *in* Elvis Presley. Dreieich: Melzer, 1978: [106]–115 ((5))

(Monograph) P151 JORGENSEN, Ernst; Erik RASMUSSEN; and Johnny MIK-KELSEN: Elvis Presley: recording sessions. 2d ed. Banneringen, Denmark: JEE Publications, 1977. 112 pp. ((1, 2, 3, 4, 5, 6a, 7))

In cases in which the title of the discography fails to provide a complete guide to its contents, notes in brackets have been added that call attention to additional details and references in the discographies.

Because no work of bibliography can ever be complete, readers are invited to submit additions or corrections to the compiler in care of the publisher. Every effort has been made to have citations complete through 1981 and to include citations from 1982 that were available when compiling entries ended. For discographies published after this publication, readers should consult the ongoing annual *Bibliography of Discographies—Annual Cumulation*, published approximately yearly in issues of the *Journal of the Association for*

Recorded Sound Collections (available from the Executive Secretary, Les Waffen, Box 1643, Manassas, VA 22110). Discographic references may also be found in the ARSC *Journal*'s "Current Bibliography," which appears in every issue.

Acknowledgement is gratefully made to the following individuals and institutions who helped in compiling this bibliography: David Ginsburg, who provided advice, citations, and editorial assistance that proved to be invaluable to the compiler; Gerald Gibson, who provided much of the basic material from which the volume evolved; Tim Brooks; Norm Cohen; C. P. Gerald Parker of the National Library of Canada/Bibliotheque nationale du Canada; the staff of the Library of Congress, and especially Sam Brylawski; the staff of the Rodgers and Hammerstein Archives, and especially Gary-Gabriel Gisondi; and contributors, past and present, to the ARSC *Journal* "Bibliography of Discographies."

Michael H. Gray

BIBLIOGRAPHY
OF
DISCOGRAPHIES

A.F.O. label

A1   A.F.O. label listing *in* Shout, No. 94 (April 1974): 6 ((3))

ABBA (musical group)

A2   SHAW, Greg: Bjorn & Benny/Abba discography *in* Who Put the Bomp, No. 16 (Winter 1976/77): 39 ((5))

A-BET label

A3   A-Bet label *in* Hot Buttered Soul, No. 25 (December 1973?): 6–7 ((3))

ACAPPELLA (vocal groups)

A4   KRETZCHMER, Bob: Acappella discography *in* Time Barrier Express, II/5 (March 1976): 30–31; II/6 (April 1976): 24–25 ((5))

A5   OSTROWSKI, R. (Bobby-O): Acappella LP discography *in* Time Barrier Express, I/7 (April 1975): 14 ((—))

ACE, JOHNNY
    See also *Bibliography* Vol. 2, Jazz

A6   [Discography] *in* Shout, No. 45 (July 1969): [6–7] ((2, 3, 6, 7))

A7   PECORARO, Joe: Johnny Ace discography *in* Record Exchanger, No. 14 [April 1973]: [19] ((—))

ACE label

A8   Ace label listing "8000 series" *in* Shout, No. 64 (March 1971): [2–7]; No. 65 (April 1971): [3] ((3))

A9   [Discography] *in* Time Barrier Express, No. 21 (January–February 1977): 21–23 ((—))

THE ACTION (musical group)

A10   HOGG, Brian: The Action *in* Bam Balam, No. 14 (September 1982): 18–23 ((5)) [Includes Mighty Baby, Reg King, and Martin Stone]

A11   The Mods, part IV: The Action *in* Gorilla Beat, No. 5 (1980): 26–28; discography p. 28; addenda in No. 6 (1980): 41 and No. 13 (1982): 71 ((5))

ACUFF, ROY

A12   [Discography] *in* Country Western Express, No. 13 (n.d., 1964?): ? ((—))

A13   [Discography] *in* Disc Collector (No. 7–9, 1952): ? ((—))

A14   [Discography] *in* Disc Collector (No. 1–3, 1953): ? ((—))

A15   SCHLAPPI, E.: [Discography] *in* Disc Collector, No. 23 (January 1966): ? ((3, 5))

A16   SCHLAPPI, Elizabeth: Roy Acuff and his Smoky Mountain Boys: domestic discography. Cheswold, Del.: Disc Collector Publications, 1961. 34 pp. [Revised ed. published *in* Disc Collector, No. 23 (January 1966) 36 pp.] ((1, 3, 7))

A17   Discography *in* SCHLAPPI, Elizabeth: Roy Acuff, the Smoky Mountain Boy. Greta, La.: Pelican Publishing Co., 1978: 251–265 ((1)) [Includes unpublished records but omits record numbers]

ADAMO, SALVATORE

A18   Discographie *in* SALGUES, Yves: Salvatore Adamo. Paris: Seghers, 1975: [187]–188 ((—)) (Collection poesie et chansons Seghers, 31)

ADAMS, JOHNNY, AND THE GONDOLIERS (musical group)

A19 TOPPING, Ray, and Kurt MOHR: [Discography] *in* Shout, No. 71 (November 1971): [7–9] ((2, 3, 6, 7))

ALADDIN label

See also *Bibliography* Vol. 2, Jazz

A20 McGRATH, Bob: Aladdin *in* Record Exchanger, II/6 (January–February 1971): 6–9; additions and corrections in No. 14 [April 1973]: 23

A21 MOONOOGIAN, George A.: [Discography] *in* Goldmine, No. 38 (July 1979): 38–39; No. 39 (August 1979): 34–35 ((—))

A22 PORTER, Bob: Aladdin Records— Unreleased recordings ["from mid-1960's] *in* Record Research, No. 144–145 (March 1977): 11–12 ((—))

A23 TOPPING, Ray: Aladdin label listing *in* Shout, No. 48 (October 1969): [3–8]; No. 49 (November 1969): [4–8] ((—))

THE ALADDINS (musical group)

A24 GOLDBERG, Marv, and Mike RED-MOND: Aladdins discography *in* Record Exchanger, No. 14 [April 1973]: 12 ((5))

ALBIN, JACK

A25 AVERY, Harry E.: Jack Albin research *in* Record Research, No. 139/140 (May–June 1976): 4–7 ((3, 6, 7))

ALEXANDER, ARTHUR

A26 BRYAN, Pete: [Discography] *in* SMG, IV/8 (March 1975): 16 ((—))

A27 MOHR, Kurt: Arthur Alexander discography *in* Shout, No. 108 (April–May 1976): 14 ((3, 5, 7))

ALICE COOPER

A28 Discography *in* Rolling Stone Scrapbook: Alice Cooper. San Francisco: Straight Arrow Publishers, 1975: 70–71 ((—))

ALLAN, JOHNNIE

A29 BOELENS, Milou: Johnnie Allan disc *in* Rock & Roll International Magazine (Dutch) (August 1976): 12 ((—))

A30 MILLAR, Bill: Johnnie Allan: a swamp fox special *in* New Kommotion, No. 20 (Summer 1978): 15–19; discography pp. 18–19 ((2, 3, 7))

A31 TOPPING, Ray: Johnnie Allan discography *in* Goldmine, No. 73 (June 1982): 15 ((2, 3, 7))

ALLEN, AUSTIN

A32 [RUSSELL, Tony]: Lee and Austin Allen *in* Old Time Music, No. 4 (Spring 1972): 13–14 ((1, 6, 7))

ALLEN, JULES VERNE

A33 RUSSELL, Tony, and Frank MARE: Jules Allen *in* Old Time Music, No. 10 (Autumn 1973): 18 ((3, 6, 7))

ALLEN, LEE

A34 STAGG, Tom: Lee Allen discography *in* Footnote, VII/6 (August–September 1976): 29–30 ((3, 6, 7))

ALLEN, RAY

A35 Discography *in* Paul's Record Magazine, No. 17–18: 30 ((3, 5))

ALLEN, RED

A36 BRASSINGTON, Dave: Red Allen record listing *in* Country & Western Roundabout, IV (No. 16, January–March 1968): 19–20 ((—))

ALLEN, REX

A37 [Discography] *in* Country Western Express, No. 20 (August 1958): ? ((—))

ALLEN, WARD

A38 [Discography] *in* Country Western Express, No. 17 (January–March 1958): ? ((—))

ALLEN BROTHERS

A39   [Discography] *in* Disc Collector (No. 13): ? ((3, 7))

ALLEY, SHELLY LEE

A40   HEALY, Bob, et al.: Shelly Lee Alley *in* JEMF Quarterly, IX (No. 29, Spring 1973): 33-34 ((3, 6, 7))

ALLISON, KEITH

A41   MILLER, Billy: Keith Allison *in* Kicks, No. 1 (Spring 1979): 32-36; discography pp. 35-36 ((—)) [Includes the work of the Raiders and others]

THE ALLISONS (musical group)

A42   Discography *in* Whole Lotta Rockin', No. 18 (1976): 16 ((5))

AMBROSE, BERT

A43   BARTER, Roy: Ambrose *in* Commodore, No. 3 (Autumn 1971): 15+ ((—))

A44   RUST, Brian: Bert Ambrose: a discography *in* Recorded Sound, No. 21 (January 1966): 26-29; No. 22-23 (April–July 1966): 79-87 ((2, 3, 6, 7))

AMERICAN BREAD (musical group)

A45   LIND, Jeff, and Rod HEIDEN: American Bread discography *in* Goldmine, No. 52 (September 1980): 23 ((5))

AMON DUUL (musical group)

A46   Amon Duul II: Discographie in SCHOBER, Ingeborg: Tanz der Lemminge. Reinbek bei Hamburg: Rowohlt, 1979: 258-260 ((5))

ANDERSON, AL

A47   BEZANKER, Paul: Interview: Al Anderson *in* Paul's Record Magazine, II/5 (November 1975): 11-23 ((3))

ANDERSON, ANDY

A48   TOPPING, Ray: Andy Anderson discography *in* New Kommotion, No. 14 (Winter 1977): 10 ((1, 2, 3, 7))

ANDERSON, BILL

A49   [[Discography *in* Country Corner, No. 14: 4; No. 15: 9]]

A50   STRUBING, Hauke: Bill Anderson [discography] *in* Country Corner, No. 44 (May 1975): 18-24 ((3, 7))

ANDERSON, LYNN

A51   KUHN, Wolfgang: Lynn Anderson— LP Diskographie in Country Corner, No. 52 (December 1976): 19-22 ((—))

ANDIE label

A52   Andie label *in* Time Barrier Express, No. 22 (March–April 1977): 19 ((—))

A53   Discography *in* Paul's Record Magazine, No. 12 (January–April 1976): 30 ((3))

ANDREOLI, PETER (aka Peter Anders)

A54   GARI, Brian: The Anders & Poncia story *in* The Rock Marketplace, No. 10 (June 1975): 26-29; discography p. 29 [Anders and Poncia as performers, writers, and producers, including recordings by the Videls, the Tradewinds, and the Innocents] ((5))

ANDREWS, LEE

A55   Lee Andrews/Hearts discography *in* Music World, No. 86 (June 1981): 14 ((—))

THE ANGELS (musical group)

A56   GONZALEZ, Fernando L., and Ken CLEE: Angels discography *in* Goldmine No. 45 (February 1980): 9 ((3, 5, 7))

ANGLIN, JACK

A57   [Discography] *in* Country Western Spotlight, No. 42 (June 1963): ? ((—))

ANGRUM, STEVE

A58   Steve Angrum's recordings *in* Footnote, IX/4 (May–June 1978): 15 ((2, 7))

THE ANIMALS (musical group)

A59   FRICKE, David: The Animals *in* Trans-Oceanic Trouser Press, II/1 (February–March 1975): 3–6; II/2 (April–May 1975): 29–31; II/3 (June–August 1975): 36–39 ((—))

A60   HEBING, Alfred: Animalization *in* Gorilla Beat, No. 10 (1981): 46–57; discography pp. 52–57; addenda in No. 11 (1981): 49–52 and No. 13 (1982): 72–73 ((5, 6a))

A61   HOGG, Brian: The Animals *in* Bam Balam, No. 13 (August 1981): 3–10; discography pp. 6–10; addendum in No. 14 (September 1982): 15 ((5)) [Includes Barry Jenkins with the Nashville Teens, Dave Rowberry with the Mike Cotten Sound, and the Alan Price Set]

A62   Retrospective rock: The Animals *in* Rock It with Aware, II/4 (1976): 5–8; additions [and] correxions [sic] in II/5 (c1977): 30 ((5))

ANNA label

A63   BEZANKER, Paul: Anna [discography] *in* Paul's Record Magazine, III/2 (February 1976): 21 ((3, 4))

A64   CALTA, Gary A.: Diggin' up discographies: Anna records *in* Goldmine, No. 12 (September–October 1976): 4 ((—))

A65   TOPPING, Ray: Anna label listing *in* Shout, No. 100 (December 1974): 1–2 ((3, 5))

ANTITUA, FANNY

A66   [[WILSON, W. J.: Fanny Antitua discography *in* Hobbies, LXIV/28 (August 1959): ?]]

ANTON, ARTHUR

A67   [[UPTON, Stuart: Anton and the Paramount Theatre Orchestra: a discography. West Wickham, England: Commodore Society: n.d.]]

APOLLO label

A68   Apollo discography *in* Big Town Review, I/3 (July–August 1972): 26–[33] ((3))

A69   LEGERE, Will: [Discography] *in* Disc Collector, No. 17 (May 1961): ? ((—))

APPLE label [England]

A70   KOLANJIAN, Steve, and Keith SLUCHANSKY: British Apple discography *in* Rock It with Aware, II/2 [1975?]: 3, 10–14; additions and corrections in II/4 (1976): 6; II/5 (1977): 3–4 ((5))

APPLE label [U.S.]

A71   KOLANJIAN, Steve: American Apple singles [and] American Apple albums *in* Rock It with Aware, II/1 (1973): 6–[9] [singles] and 10–[1] [albums]; additions and corrections in II/2 [1975?]: 2–3; II/3 (1976): 3–4; II/4 (1976): 3; II/5 (1977): 3–4 ((3, 5))

THE APPLEJACKS (musical group)

A72   HEBING, Alfred: The Applejacks *in* Gorilla Beat, No. 11 (1981): 64–66; discography pp. 65–66; addenda in No. 13 (1982): 71 ((5))

ARAWAK label

A73   FAULL, Trev: Arawak Records *in* Outlet, No. 16 (January 1980): 9–10 ((—))

ARCADE label

A74   ROBERTSON, Paul: Arcade label *in* New Kommotion, No. 15 (Spring 1977): 9, 11; addenda in No. 19 (Spring 1978): 12 and No. 22 (1979): 66 ((—))

ARCH label

A75   Arch label *in* Hot Buttered Soul, No. 27 (February 1974): 6 ((3))

ARDENT label

A76   GUTCH, Frank, and Lance Wade
ANDERSON: Ardent discography *in*
Bomp, No. 18 (March 1978): 66
((—))

ARGO label [Australia]

A77   PERKINS, Ken: Discography of
Chess/Checker/Argo releases 78 rpm
and 45 rpm *in* Big Beat of the 50's,
No. 27 (May 1981): 34–36 ((5))

ARNOLD, EDDY

A78   [Discography] *in* Disc Collector, No.
11 and 13 [n.d.]: ? ((—))

A79   [Discography] *in* Hillbilly Folk Record
Journal, II/1 (January–March 1955): ?
((—))

A80   HEALY, R.: [Discography] *in* Country Western Spotlight, No. 34 (June
1961) and No. 35 (September 1961): ?
((2, 7))

ARNOLD, LLOYD

A81   KINDER, Bob: Lloyd Arnold discography *in* Goldmine, No. 54 (November 1980): 160 ((—))

ARTIS, RAY

A82   Discography *in* Paul's Record Magazine, No. 17–18: 40 ((—))

THE ARTISTICS (musical group)

A83   PRUTER, Robert: The Artistics discography *in* It Will Stand, No. 12/13
(c1980): 16 ((5))

ASHLEY, CLARENCE T.

A84   [Discography] *in* notes for Folkways
FA 2355 [sound recording] (1961): ?
((3, 7))

ASHLOCK, JESSE

A85   [COHEN, Norm]: Jesse Ashlock *in*
JEMF Quarterly, VIII (No. 27,
Autumn 1972): 121 ((3, 5, 6, 7))

**ASHTON, GARDNER & DYKE
(musical group)**

A86   Ashton, Gardner & Dyke *in* Jamz,
No. 4 (May 1972): 47–48; discography
p. 48 ((—))

ASHWORTH, ERNEST

A87   [[Discography *in* Country Corner, No.
5: 12]]

ASLEEP AT THE WHEEL (musical group)

A88   Asleep at the Wheel discography *in*
Down Beat, XLIII (June 17, 1976): 17
((—))

A89   GONZALEZ, Fernando L.: Asleep at
the Wheel discography *in* Goldmine,
No. 41 (October 1979): [131] ((5))

A90   GONZALEZ, Fernando L.: Asleep at
the Wheel discography *in* Goldmine,
No. 58 (March 1981): 190 ((5))

THE ASSOCIATION (musical group)

A91   CLEE, Ken: The Association discography *in* Goldmine, No. 49 (June
1980): 11 ((—))

ASTAIRE, FRED

A92   [[[Discography] *in* GREEN, Benny:
Fred Astaire. New York: Hamlyn,
1979: 169–173]]

A93   LARSEN, John B., and Jim HAYES:
Fred Astaire on 78's *in* Gunn Report,
No. 43 (December 1973): 37; No. 44
(January–February 1974): 41; No. 45
(March–April 1974): 8; No. 48 (Sep-
tember–October 1974): 4; No. 50
(January–February 1975): 10; No. 53
(July–August 1975): 13-14 ((3, 6, 7))

A94   LEVINE, Howard: Discography *in*
GREEN, Stanley: Starring Fred
Astaire. Garden City, N.Y.: Double-
day, 1977: 470–[475] ((7))

ATKINS, CHET

A95   [Discography] *in* Country Western
Spotlight, No. 22 (April–June 1958): ?
((—))

A96   PYMM, Brian: Chet Atkins discography *in* Rumble, II/4 (Winter
1974/75): 2–5 ((5))

A97 ROMIN, Ole: Chet Atkins LP disco *in* Kountry Korral, XI/6 (1978): 11 ((—))

A98 WELCH, Paul D., and Jere R. UNCHAPHER: Chet Atkins discography *in* Goldmine, No. 64 (September 1981): 17–18; No. 65 (October 1981): 174 ((1, 5, 7))

ATLANTIC label
See also *Bibliography* Vol. 2, Jazz

A99 Atlantic 45 rpm *in* Record Exchanger, II/2 [Summer 1971]: 18–22 ((3))

A100 MARTIN, Tony, and Chris SAVORY: Atlantic oldies *in* Hot Buttered Soul, No. 15 (February 1973): 8–9 ((3))

A101 RUPPLI, Michel: Atlantic Records: a discography. Westport, Conn: Greenwood Press, 1979. 4 vols. ((2, 3, 4, 7))

THE ATLANTICS (musical group)

A102 DUFF, Colin, and Frank CAMPBELL: The Atlantics discography *in* Big Beat of the 50's, No. 22 (November 1979): 50–52 ((—))

ATLEE, JOHN YORKE

A103 LORENZ, Kenneth M.: [Discography] *in* Kastlemusik Monthly Bulletin, III/9 (E-46; September 1978): 11–14 ((3))

ATOMIC BOMB—SONGS AND MUSIC

A104 Checklist of atomic bomb songs in country music *in* WOLFE, Charles K.: Nuclear country: the atomic bomb in country music *in* Journal of Country Music, VI/4 (January 1978): 4–[21] ((7))

ATTRIX label

A105 FAULL, Trev: Attrix discography *in* Outlet, No. 15 (November 1979): 18 ((—))

AUDITION label

A106 Audition label *in* Time Barrier Express, No. 22 (March–April 1977): 20 ((—))

AURORA label
See also *Bibliography* Vol. 2, Jazz

A107 HEARNE, Will Roy: Aurora 22000 numerical *in* JEMF Newsletter, II/2 (February 1967): 36–40 ((3))

AUSTIN, GENE

A108 [[McANDREW, J.: Star studded shellac (Gene Austin) *in* Record Changer, XIV/3 (1955): 16]]

A109 MAGNUSSON, Tor: The Gene Austin recordings *in* Matrix, No. 92–104 (April 1971–August 1974): continuously paginated; 27 pp. ((1, 2, 3, 7))

AUTRY, GENE

A110 [[[Discography] *in* AUTRY, Gene: Back in the saddle again. Garden City, N.Y.: Doubleday, 1978: [191]–206]]

A111 [Discography] *in* Country Western Spotlight (Special issue, September 1962): ? ((—))

A112 [Discography] *in* Disc Collector, II/2 (April–June 1952): ?; II/3 (July–September 1952): ? ((—))

A113 EDWARDS, J.: [Discography] *in* Country Western Spotlight, No. 14 (December 1956): ? ((—))

A114 STOTEN, John: Gene Autry record listing *in* Country & Western Roundabout, III/11 (May–June–July 1965): 10–13; III/12 (November–December 1965): 14–17; IV/13 (March–June 1966): 13–16; IV/14 (October–December 1966): 13–17; additions in IV/16 (January–March 1968): 5 ((—))

AUTUMN label

A115 HARRISON, John: Autumn: singles listing *in* SMG, V/4 (January–February 1977): 23 ((5))

A116 SHAW, Greg: Autumn discography *in* Who Put the Bomp, No. 12 (Summer 1974): 14–15 ((—))

AVALON, FRANKIE

A117 Frankie Avalon checklist *in* Goldmine, No. 28 (September 1978): 13 ((—))

THE AVALONS (musical group)

A118 AMAL, Jason: The Avalons [Groove label only] *in* Big Town Review, I/1 (February–March 1972): 28 ((3))

AVERAGE WHITE BAND (musical group)

A119 Average White Band discography *in* Down Beat, XLIII (April 8, 1976): 12 ((−))

THE AVONS (musical group)

A120 LAVATELLI, George: [Discography] *in* Bim Bam Boom, I/3 (December 1971–January 1972): 12 ((3, 5))

AXTON, HOYT

A121 Hoyt Axton discography *in* Goldmine, No. 63 (August 1981): 149 ((5))

AYERS, KEVIN

A122 BRETHOLZ, Myron: Putting on Ayers *in* Trouser Press, No. 16 (October–November 1976): 3–7; discography p. 7 [Includes recordings with the Soft Machine] ((5))

A123 [Discography] *in* Zig Zag, V/6 (No. 46, October 1974): [36] ((2))

AZNAVOUR, CHARLES

A124 Discographie *in* SALGUES, Yves: Charles Aznavour. Paris: Seghers, 1971, c1964: [185]–188 (Collection poesie et chansons, 121) ((−))

BBC WIRELESS SYMPHONY ORCHESTRA

B1 UPTON, Stuart: [Discography] *in* Commodore, No. 9 (Spring 1973): 11+ ((−))

B.T. PUPPY label

B2 ENGEL, Ed: B. T. Puppy records discography *in* Bim Bam Boom, III/1 (No. 13, August–September 1974): 20 ((−))

BABS, ALICE
See also *Bibliography* Vol. 2, Jazz

B3 HEDMAN, Frank; Karleric LILIE-DAHL; and Lars ZAKRISSON: Alice Babs. Stockholm: Kungliga biblioteket, 1973. 48 pp. ((7)) (Nationalfonotekets discografier, 505)

BABY HUEY AND THE BABYSITTERS (musical group)
See also *Bibliography* Vol. 2, Jazz

B4 [[[Discography] *in* Shout (No. 71): 6]]

BACHELORS (musical group)

B5 GOLDBERG, Marv: The Bachelors *in* Yesterday's Memories, II/4 (1976): 5 ((7))

BACHMAN-TURNER OVERDRIVE (musical group)

B6 Discography *in* MELHUISH, Martin: Bachman-Turner Overdrive. Toronto: Methuen; New York: Two Continents, 1976: [174]–178 ((−))

BADDELEY, HERMIONE

B7 LYNCH, Richard: The two Hermiones *in* Kastlemusik Monthly Bulletin, VII/9 (September 1982): 1, 8 ((5))

BADFINGER (musical group)

B8 OLAFSON, Peter, and Dan MATOVINE: Iveys/Badfinger discography *in* Trouser Press Collector's Magazine, I/6 (January–April 1979): [3] ((5))

B9 RAY, Larry: Badfinger and related discography *in* Goldmine, No. 65 (October 1981): 20 ((5))

BADIA, CONCHITA

B10 [[[Discography] *in* ALAVEDRA, Juan: Conxita Badia: una vida d'artista. Barcelona: Editorial Portic, 1975: 239–243]]

BAEZ, JOAN

B11 Discographie oficial *in* FEITO, Alvaro: Joan Baez. Madrid: Jucar, 1976: 143–153 ((5))

B12   Discogrophy [sic] *in* Country & Western Express, No. 18 [n.d.]: 3 ((—))

B13   Discography—including cassettes *in* SWAN, Peter: Joan Baez, a bio-disco-bibliography. Brighton, England: Noyce, 1977: 18–21 ((4, 5))

B14   SWANEKAMP, Joan: Diamonds and rust: a bibliography and discography on Joan Baez. Ann Arbor, Mich.: Pierian Press, 1980. 75 pp. ((5))

BAGLIONI, CLAUDIO

B15   Discografia *in* his Il romanzo de un cantante. Rome: Lato side, 1978: 71–73 ((5))

BAILEY, DEFORD

B16   OLSSON, Bengt: The Grand Ole Opry's DeFord Bailey *in* Living Blues, No. 21 (May–June 1975): 14 ((7))

BAILEY BROTHERS (musical group)

B17   HENDERSON, Gary A., and Walter V. SAUNDERS: The Bailey Brothers discography *in* Bluegrass Unlimited, V/8 (February 1971): 7 ((1, 2, 3, 7))

BAKER, BILL

B18   PEARLIN, Victor: [Discography] *in* Paul's Record Magazine, II/2 (August 1975): 14; additions and corrections in II/4 (October 1975): 16 ((3))

BAKER, LAVERN

B19   MOONOOGIAN, George: Early Lavern Baker discography *in* Goldmine, No. 48 (May 1980): 143 ((3, 7))

BAKER, SAM

B20   MOHR, Kurt: [Baker] discography *in* Soul Bag, No. 72–73 (June–July 1979): 4–5 ((2, 7))

BALDRY, LONG JOHN

B21   HOGG, Brian: Boom boom: British blue-eyed R&B *in* Bam Balam, No. 13 (August 1981): 26–27 ((5))

BALLARD, HANK, AND THE MIDNIGHTERS (musical group)

B22   FUCHS, Aaron: Hank Ballard and the Midnighters *in* Goldmine, No. 61 (November 1981): 13 ((5))

B23   GOLDBERG, Marv: The Midnighters *in* Big Town Review, I/3 (July–August 1972): 48 ((5))

B24   TOPPING, Ray: Midnighters discography *in* Shout, No. 62 (January 1971): [5–7]; additions and corrections in No. 65 (April 1971): [1] ((2, 3, 7))

BALLEW, SMITH

B25   KINKLE, Roger D.: Numerical list of Smith Ballew recordings *in* his Checksheet (project #1). Evansville, Ind.?: n.d.: 1–7; additions and corrections in Checksheet #2: 7; New ed. in Checksheet #7. (Evansville, Ind.?: n.d.: 1–12 ((—))

B26   ORR, Geoffrey: Jazz Discographies Unlimited presents Smith Ballew. Laurel, Md.: Jazz Discographies Unlimited, 1972. 63 l. ((3, 4, 6, 7))

BANDY, MOE

B27   Moe Bandy album discography *in* Country Corner, XIII (No. 57, December 1977): 19 ((—))

BANG label

B28   LAZELL, Barry: Bang Records *in* SMG, VI/1 (May 1977): 4–5; Part 2 in VI/2 (September 1977): 13–14 ((3))

BAR X COWBOYS (musical group)

B29   [Discography] *in* Country Directory, No. 4 [n.d.]: ? ((2, 3, 7))

B30   [Discography] *in* Country Western Spotlight (Special issue, September 1962): ? ((—))

B31   EDWARDS, J.: [Discography] *in* Country Western Spotlight, No. 20 (September–December 1957): ? ((—))

BARBARA

B32   EVANS, Colin: Selected recordings *in* Recorded Sound, No. 79 (January 1981): 11–22 ((—))

BARDENS, PETER

B33 ROBBINS, Ira: Peter Bardens: the company he's kept *in* Trouser Press, No. 16 (October–November 1976): 16–18; discography p. 18; addenda in No. 19 (April–May 1977): 26 [Includes recordings with Camel, the Cheynes, Them, Shotgun Express, and Village] ((5))

BARE, BOBBY

B34 Bobby Bare LP discography *in* Kountry Korral (No. 2, 1979): 9 ((—))

B35 KARLSSON, Sture: Bobby Bare LP disco *in* Kountry Korral (No. 2, 1980): [32]–33 ((5))

B36 McCONCHIE, Ray: Bobby Bare discography *in* Goldmine, No. 51 (August 1980): 164–165 ((5))

BARFIELD, JOHNNY

B37 [Discography] *in* Country Western Spotlight, No. 34 (June 1961): ? ((—))

B38 EDWARDS, J.: [Discography] *in* Country Western Spotlight, No. 18 (April 1957): ? ((—))

BARLOW, DEAN

B39 GOLDBERG, Marv: The Dean Barlow story *in* Yesterday's Memories, II/1 (1976): 20 ((7))

BARNES, MAX D.

B40 NAUCLER, Erik: Max D. Barnes discography *in* Kountry Korral, XI/6 (1978): 13 ((—))

BARRETT, RICHARD

B41 [[[Discography] *in* Soul Music (No. 27)]]

BARRON, LONNIE

B42 RUSSELL, Wayne, and John MORRIS: The Lonnie Barron story *in* New Kommotion, No. 16 (Summer 1977): 17 ((7))

BARRY, JOE

B43 BROVEN, John: Joe Barry *in* New Kommotion, No. 26 (1982): 18–20; discography (by Ray TOPPING): 20 ((2, 3, 7))

BARRY, JOHN

B44 SMART, Peter: Discography *in* Rumble, III/2 (Winter 1975/6): 5–8 ((5))

B45 WOOD, Robert: John Barry: filmography/discography *in* Soundtrack Collector's Newsletter, III/14 (June 1978): 13–[17] ((5))

BARRY, LEN

B46 CARELLA, Vinny J., and Ed ENGEL: Discography *in* Paul's Record Magazine, IV/1 (No. 12, August 1976): 12–14 ((5))

BATON label

B47 [[[Discography] *in* Soul Music (No. 12)]]

B48 GOLDBERG, Marv: The Baton story *in* Yesterday's Memories, III/1 (No. 9, 1976): 26–28 ((3, 5, 7))

BAXTER, PHIL

B49 KUNSTADT, Len: Phil Baxter—exploratory discography in Record Research, No. 92 (September 1968): 3; corrections in No. 98 (May 1969): 5 ((3, 6, 7))

BAY CITY ROLLERS (musical group)

B50 Diskographie *in* THURMAIR, Elisabeth: Die Bay City Rollers. Bergisch Gladbach: Lubbe, 1978: 236 ((—))

BAYES, NORA

B51 ALLEN, Barbara: Nora Bayes; a discography *in* Discographer, I/1: 63–68 ((3, 7))

B52 COLTON, Bob: Nora Bayes—her discography *in* Recorded Americana; Bulletin of Record Research, No. 2 (March 1958): [3–5]; additions in No. 3 (May 1958): [3] ((3, 6, 7))

THE BEACH BOYS (musical group)
See also WILSON, BRIAN

B53 BETROCK, Alan, and Gene SCULAT-
TI: The Beach Boys *in* The Rock Marketplace, No. 7 (October 1974): 3–5, 8;
discography pp. 5 and 8; addenda in
No. 8 (December 1974): 42 ((1, 3, 5))

B54 CALLAHAN, Mike: Beach Boys discography *in* Goldmine, No. 54 (November 1980): 20–22; No. 55 (December
1980): 175 [bootleg records] ((1, 5))

B55 ELLIOTT, Brad: Surf's up!: the
Beach Boys on record. Ann Arbor,
Mich.: Pierian Press, 1982. 494 pp.
((1, 2, 4, 5, 6a, 7))

B56 GELFAND, Steve: A Beach Boys
album discography *in* Goldmine, No.
33 (February 1979): 10 ((5))

B57 Discography *in* GOLDEN, Bruce: The
Beach Boys: Southern California pas-
toral. San Bernardino, Calif. R.
Reginald; Borgo Press, 1976: 40–52
((5))

B58 HOGG, Brian: The Beach Boys *in*
Bam Balam, No. 12 (November 1980):
8–16; discography pp. 12–16; addendum in No. 14 (September 1982):
14–15 ((5))

B59 The Beach Boys: a chronological discography *in* PREISS, Byron: The
Beach Boys: the authorized illustrated
biography. New York: Ballantine
Books, 1978: 154–160 ((5)) [Includes
unpublished records]

B60 REUM, Peter: Beach Boys discography *in* Time Barrier Express, III/4
(No. 24, April–May 1979): 44–52
((5))

B61 U.S. discography *in* TOBLER, John:
The Beach Boys. London; New York:
Hamlyn, Phoebus, 1977: 95–96 ((5))

THE BEALE STREETERS (musical group)

B62 PEARLIN, Victor: The Beale
Streeters *in* Paul's Record Magazine,
II/5 (November 1975): 9–10 ((3))

BEART, GUY

B63 Discography *in* BEART, Guy: Cou-
leurs et coleres du temps: l'integrale
des poemes et chansons. Paris:
Seghers, 1976: 269–270 ((—))

THE BEATLES (musical group)

B64 Discographie in Das Album der
Beatles. Hamburg: Gruner & Jahr,
1981: 371–382 ((5))

B65 [[[Discography] *in* ANTONI, Roberto:
Il viaggio dei cuori solitari: un libro
sui Beatles. Milan: Il formichiere,
1979: 121–125]]

B66 BAKKER, Erik, and Koss JANSSEN:
Dig it: the Beatles bootleg book: Vol.
1. Alphen ann de Rijn, Netherlands:
Micrography, 1974. ((1, 4, 7))

B67 BARNES, Ken: The weird world of
Beatle novelties *in* Who Put the
Bomp, No. 13 (Spring 1975): 13–15;
addenda in No. 14 (Fall 1975): 44;
No. 15 (Spring 1976): 44; No. 16 (Oc-
tober 1976): 60 ((—))

B68 BETROCK, Alan: Beatle-rock *in*
Jamz, No. 4 (May 1972): 36–42; discography pp. 41–42; addenda in No. 5
(1972): 41 [Beatle sound-alikes, e.g.,
Grapefruit and Badfinger] ((5))

B69 Discographies *in* CARR, Roy: The
Beatles: an illustrated record. New
York: Harmony Books, 1975, 1978:
118–126 ((1, 5, 7))

B70 CASTLEMAN, Harry, and Walter J.
PODRAZIK: All together now: the
first complete Beatles discography,
1961–1975. Ann Arbor, Mich.: Pierian
Press, 1975. 379 pp. ((1, 4, 5, 7))

B71 CASTLEMAN, Harry, and Walter J.
PODRAZIK: All together now: the
first complete Beatles discography,
1961–1975. Ann Arbor, Mich.: Pierian
Press, 1976. 385 pp. ((1, 4, 5, 7))
[Also issued by Ballantine Books, New
York, 1976; 2nd parts of the above;
reflects changes and additions]

B72 CASTLEMAN, Harry, and Walter J.
PODRAZIK: The Beatles again? Ann
Arbor, Mich.: Pierian Press, 1977. 280
pp. ((1, 4, 5, 7))

B73 Discography *in* COWAN, Philip:
Behind the Beatles songs. London:
Polytantric Press, 1978: 50–59 ((1,
5))

B74 Discography *in* DAVIES, Hunter: The
Beatles. Rev. ed. New York: McGraw-
Hill, 1978: 354–381; 1st ed., New
York: McGraw-Hill, 1968; New York:
Dell, 1969: discography pp. 389–400
((—))

B75 Discography *in* DAVIS, Edward E.: The Beatles book. New York: Cowles, 1968: 202–213 ((5))

B76 A Beatle discography *in* DILELLO, Richard: The longest cocktail party; an insider's diary of the Beatles. Chicago: Playboy Press, 1972: 309–322 ((—))

B77 Discography *in* DISTER, Alain: Les Beatles. Paris: A. Michel, 1978: [173]–185 ((5))

B78 FONVIELLE, Chris: Songs they never sang *in* Who Put the Bomp, No. 14 (Fall 1975): 21; additions and corrections in No. 15 (Spring 1976): 44 ((5))

B79 GUZEK, Arno: Beatles discography. Copenhagen: Guzek: Eksp., C. P. Wulff Co., 1976. 72 pp. ((1, 2, 4, 7))

B80 GUZEK, A., and C. MARTIN: The recordings of John, Paul, George, and Ringo. Portland, Oregon: Guzek and Martin, 1977. ((1, 2, 4, 7))

B81 HANSEN, Jeppe: Beatles-diskografi, 1961–1972. Slagelse: Slagelse Central-bibliotek; Eksp.: Musikafdelingen, Stenstuegade 3, 1973. 33 pp. ((4, 5, 7))

B82 KOLANJIAN, Steve: The Beatles: part one, one disc *in* Aware, No. 7 (Spring 1981): 3–20; No. 8 (Winter 1981–82): 3–6 ((5, 7))

B83 John Lennon/Beatles discography *in* Schwann-2 Record & Tape Guide, No. 34 (Spring–Summer 1981): 4–5 ((7))

B84 Discografia *in* LUQUI, Joaquin: Los Beatles que amo. Madrid: Nuevos ediciones, 1977: [173]–186 ((—))

B85 McGEARY, Mitchell: The Beatles complete discography. 5th rev. ed. Olympia, Wash.: McGeary, 1975. 18 pp. ((1, 5))

B86 McGEARY, Mitchell: The Beatles discography. 9th ed. Lacey, Wash.: Ticket to Ryde, Ltd., 1976. 33 pp. ((5))

B87 Grammofoonplaten van de Beatles *in* MEIJDEN, Henk van der: Yeah, yeah, yeah, zo zijn de Beatles! Amsterdam: Strengholt, 1964: 159–160 ((—))

B88 Discography *in* MELLERS, Wilfrid: Twilight of the gods; the Beatles in retrospect. London: Faber & Faber; New York: Viking Press, 1973: [208]–209 ((—))

B89 Discografia *in* PASTONESI, Marco: Beatles. Milan: Gammalibri, 1980: 153–164 ((—))

B90 QUINONES, Mario: Beatle boots *in* Trans-Oceanic Trouser Press, No. 1 (March 1974): 13–16 ((1))

B91 REINHART, Charles F.: Beatles novelty discography. Lancaster, Pa.: Reinhart, 1977. 24 pp. ((1, 4))

B92 REINHART, Charles: You can't do that!: Beatles bootlegs & novelty records, 1963–1980. Ann Arbor, Mich.: Pierian Press, 1981. 411 pp. ((1, 4, 7))

B93 [[Discography *in* ROMBECK, Hans: Die Beatles. Bergish Gladbach: Lubbe, 1981: 330–355]]

B94 [[RUSSELL, J. P.: The Beatles on record. New York: Scribners, 1982. Previously published as The Beatles album file and complete discography]]

B95 An international Beatles discography *in* SCHAFFNER, Nicholas: The Beatles forever. Harrisonburg, Pa.: Stackpole Co., 1977: 202–211 ((5))

B96 Discographie *in* SELORON, Francoise: Les Beatles. Paris: Nouvelles Editions Polaires, 1972: [121]–129 ((5))

B97 Cronologia discografica *in* SIERRA I FABRA, Jordi: The Beatles, musicos del siglo XX. Barcelona: Musica de Nuestro Tiempo, 1976: 148–156 ((1, 5, 7))

B98 Diszkografia *in* UNGVARI, Tamas: Beatles biblia. Budapest: Gondolat, 1969: [300–305] ((5))

B99 [[WALLGREN, Mark: The Beatles, for the record. New York: Simon & Schuster, 1982]]

THE BEAU BRUMMELS (musical group)

B100 HANEL, Ed: Snappy, smart and Americans: the Beau Brummels *in* Trans-Oceanic Trouser Press, II/4 (September–October 1975): 26–27, 30 ((5)); Brummelgems in II/5 (November–December 1975): 32 ((—))

B101 HOGG, Brian: Psychotic reaction: San Francisco begins [Brummels discography] *in* Bam Balam, No. 10 (November 1979): 17–19 ((5))

B102 SMALL, Bill: Beau Brummels discography *in* Who Put the Bomp, No. 12 (Summer 1974): 15 ((—))

BEAUCARNE, JULOS

B103 Discographie *in* his Julos Beaucarne. Paris: Seghers, 1977: [167]–170 (Collection poesie et chansons Seghers, 39)

THE BEAU-MARKS (musical group)

B104 RUSSELL, Wayne: Disco *in* SMG, VI/1 (May 1977): 9 ((—))

THE BEAVERS (musical group)

B105 GOLDBERG, Marv: The Beavers *in* Yesterday's Memories, I/2 (1975): 27 ((7))

B106 RUSSELL, Wayne: Disco *in* SMG, VI/1 (May 1977): 9 ((—))

BE-BOP label

B107 ROBBINS, Ira, and Dave SCHULPS: The poop on Be-Bop *in* Trans-Oceanic Trouser Press, II/5 (November–December 1975): 19–20 ((—))

BECAUD, GILBERT (pseud.)

B108 Discographie *in* IZARD, Christophe: Gilbert Becaud. Paris: Seghers, 1972: [166]–170 ((—))

B109 Discographie de Louis Amade *in* SPRENGERS, Robert: Ton frere le poete. Louvin: A. Rossels Printing, 1968: 255–259 ((—))

B110 Gilbert Becaud na deskach Supraphon *in* TATEROVA, Milada: Gilbert Becaud. Praha: Supraphon, 1969: [36–37] ((—))

BECK, JEFF

B111 BETROCK, Alan: Discography *in* Jamz, No. 2 (October 1971): 17; addenda in No. 3 (February 1972): 23 ((2, 5))

BEE GEES (musical group)

B112 The Bee Gees discography (U.S. releases only) *in* Billboard, XC/35 (September 2, 1978): Sec. 2: 16–17 ((5))

B113 Bee-Gee rock *in* Jamz, No. 4 (May 1972): 43–44 [Bee-Gees sound-alikes] ((—))

B114 Langspielplatten der Bee Gees *in* HENKELS, Michael: Bee Gees. Hamburg: Taurus-Press, 1979: 216–240 ((—))

B115 KOLANJIAN, Steve: 15 years of Bee Gees fever *in* Rockin' with Aware Research Magazine, [no. 6?] (1979): 24–34 ((1, 5))

B116 Discographie *in* SAHNER, Paul: Bee Gees. Bergisch Gladbach: Lubbe, 1979: 121–122 ((—))

B117 Discography *in* STEVENS, Kim: The Bee Gees. New York: Quick Fox, 1978: 88–92 ((5))

BELA, DAJOS

B118 GARNER, Clive: Dajos Orchestra *in* Commodore, No. 15 (Autumn 1974): 3+ ((—))

BELAFONTE, HARRY

B119 Discography *in* SHAW, Arnold: Belafonte, an unauthorized biography. Philadelphia: Chilton, 1960: ix–xi ((5))

B120 Discografie *in* WELIS, Jos: De weg van Harry Belafonte. Tielt: Lennoo, 1961: 109–110 ((—))

BELL, ARCHIE, AND THE DRELLS (musical group)

B121 Archie Bell & the Drells discography *in* It Will Stand, No. 4 (c1979): 5 ((—))

B122 MOHR, Kurt: Archie Bell & Drells discography *in* Shout, No. 84 (February–March 1973): [1–3] ((2, 3, 7))

BELLAMY BROTHERS

B123 ERIKSSON, Carl Eric: Bellamy Brothers LP disco *in* Kountry Korral Magazine (No. 2, 1980): 34 ((—))

THE BELMONTS (musical group)

B124   McDOWELL, Mike: Belmonts discography in Blitz, No. 29 (November–December 1978): 21–23 [Includes recordings with and without Dion] ((5))

BENEKE, GORDON LEE (TEX)

B125   Tex Beneke [1946–1965] in EDWARDS, Ernie, ed.: Glenn Miller alumni; a discography. Whittier, Calif.: Ernegeobil Publications, [1966?] 2 vols.: 21 pp. in vol. 2 ((3, 6, 7))

B126   GARROD, Charles: Tex Beneke and his orchestra. Spottswood, N.J.: Joyce Music Publications, 1973: 37, 71. ((1, 2, 3, 4, 6, 7))

BENNATO, EDOARDO

B127   Discografia in GRANETTO, Luigi: Edoardo Bennato. Rome: Lato side, 1980: 124–125 ((—))

BENNETT, BOYD

B128   Boyd Bennett in Rock 'n' Roll International Magazine (Danish), No. 107 (July–August 1977): 23 ((—))

B129   RUSSELL, Wayne: "Move on Boyd Bennett": follow up to last issue in SMG, V/4 (January–February 1977): 15 ((3))

B130   SMART, Peter: Discography in SMG, V/3 (Summer 1976): 23 ((—))

BENNETT, CLIFF

B131   BLAND, Malcolm: Cliff Bennett and the Rebel Rousers in SMG, VI/4 (October 1980): 22–26; discography pp. 25–26 ((—))

BENNETT, JOE, AND THE SPARKLE TONES (musical group)

B132   BLAIR, John: Discography in Goldmine, No. 63 (August 1981): 13 ((5))

B133   RUSSELL, Wayne: Joe Bennett & the Sparkle Tones in Kommotion, No. 10/11 (Winter 1975–76): 23–24 ((—))

BENNETT, RICHARD RODNEY

B134   CAPS, John, and Thomas DEMARY: Filmography and discography of Richard Rodney Bennett in SCN, Soundtrack Collector's Newsletter, II/8 (October 1976): [13–16] ((5))

BENSON ORCHESTRA OF CHICAGO

B135   RUST, Brian: The Benson Orchestra of Chicago; a discography in Recorded Sound, No. 31 (July 1968): 322–324 ((1, 2, 3, 6, 7))

BERLIN, IRVING

B136   Discographies in JAY, Dave: The Irving Berlin songography; 1907–1966. New Rochelle, N.Y.: Arlington House, 1969. 172 pp. ((—))

B137   Selected discography in program notes for The vintage Irving Berlin [sound recording], New World Records NW 238, 1977: 2 ((—))

BERLINER label

B138   RUST, Brian: (British) Berliner, G & T and Zonophone 7-inch records in Talking Machine Review, No. 63–64 (Autumn 1981): 1726–1758 ((2, 3, 7))

BERMAN, SHELLY

B139   SMITH, Ronald L.: The original Shelly Berman albums in Goldmine, No. 46 (March 1980): 144 ((—))

BERNHARDT, CLYDE

B140   GRIFFITHS, David: Clyde Bernhardt discography in Record Research, No. 181–182 (April 1981): 13 ((2, 3, 6, 7))

BERNSTEIN, ELMER

B141   MARSHALL, James, et al.: Elmer Bernstein: filmography/discography in Soundtrack!, No. 26 (Summer 1981): 7–12; No. 27 (December 1981): 5–7 ((7))

BERRY, CHUCK

B142   A Chuck Berry discography in Rock It with Aware Magazine, II/4 (1976): 2–24 ((5))

B143 Chuck Berry discography; pt. 1—
Singles *in* R-O-C-K, No. 4 (1981):
8-27 ((1, 7))

B144 CLEE, Ken: Chuck Berry discography
in Goldmine, No. 42 (November
1979): 8 ((5, 7))

B145 [Discography] *in* DeWITT, Howard
A.: Chuck Berry: Rock 'n' roll music.
Fremont, Calif.: Horizon, 1981:
173-213 ((1, 5, 7)) [Includes 45's,
albums, records for the Chess label,
Berry's hits and cover records]

B146 [Discography] *in* Mojo-Navigator
Rock & Roll News, No. 14 (August
1967): 26-27 ((—))

B147 Discography—Chuck Berry (1955-
1963) *in* Record Finder, I/2 (July
1978): [15] ((5))

B148 REFF, Morten: Chuck Berry discography—Part 2 *in* Whole Lotta
Rockin', No. 9 (February 1974): 23
((—))

B149 VERA, Billy: The Chess sessions *in*
Time Barrier Express, IV/1 (No. 27,
April-May 1980): 48-49 ((7))

BERRY, MIKE

B150 BLAND, Malcolm: The annotated discography *in* SMG, V/3 (Summer
1976): 5-10 ((—))

B151 BRUNO, Bill: The preservation of
rock & roll *in* Music World, No. 82
(February 1981): 43 ((—))

BERRY, RICHARD

B152 BARNEVELD, Archie: Richard Berry
single disco till 1959 *in* Rockville International (January-February 1977):
17 ((5))

THE BEVERLY HILL BILLIES
(musical group, not TV stars)

B153 GRIFFIS, Ken: Beverly Hill Billies
discography *in* JEMF Quarterly, XVI
(No. 57, Spring 1980): 15-17 ((3, 6,
7))

B154 HEALY, Bob: [Discography] *in*
Country Directory, No. 3 (1962): 7
((3, 7))

BIESE, PAUL

B155 JONES, David L.: Paul Biese (Early
U.S. dance orchestras, part 3) *in* New
Amberola Graphic, No. 20 (Winter
1977): 3-5 ((7))

BIG "J" & THE SEPIA REEFERS
(musical group)

B156 GONZALEZ, Ferdie L.: Big "J" and
the Reefers discography *in* Goldmine,
No. 25 (April 1978): 21 ((3, 5, 7))

BIG STAR (musical group)

B157 HOGG, Brian: Big Star *in* Bam
Balam, No. 5 (February 1977): 12-13;
discography p. 13; addenda in No. 6
(November 1977): 23 and No. 7
(c1978): 2, 9 ((1, 2, 5))

THE BIG THREE (musical group)

B158 Always some other guy . . . *in* Gorilla
Beat, No. 1 (1979): 9-13, 23; discog-
raphy pp. 12-13, 23; addendum in
No. 2 (1979): 21 ((—))

B159 SCHACHT, Janis: Big 3 *in* The Rock
Marketplace, No. 9 (March 1975): 41
((5))

BIG TOP label

B160 Big Top records *in* Paul's Record
Magazine, IV/1 (No. 12, August
1976): 31; IV/2 (No. 13-14): 43-45;
additions and corrections in No. 15
(January-February 1977): 39 ((3))

BIG YOUTH (musical performer)

B161 HALASA, Malu: Big Youth discography *in* Goldmine, No. 58 (March
1981): 196 ((—))

BIHARI label

B162 [[[Discography] *in* Blues Research,
No. 74: ?]]

BILLQUIST, ULLA

B163 BREDEVIK, Gunnar: Ulla Billquist.
Stockholm: Kungliga biblioteket,
1070. 56 l. (Nationalfonoteks diskografier, 502) ((2, 3, 6, 7))

BIOGRAPH label

B164   Our favorite 40 from Biograph *in* Tarakan Music Letter, II/5 (May–June 1981): 3 ((—))

BITTER BLOOD STREET THEATRE (musical group)

B165   KLITSCH, Hans Jurgen: Bitter Blood *in* Gorilla Beat, No. 15 (1982): 61–64; discography p. 64 ((5))

BLACK, BILL, COMBO (musical group)

B166   JANCIK, Wayne: Bill Black Combo discography *in* Goldmine, No. 58 (March 1981): 17 ((—))

BLACKBYRDS (musical group)

B167   Selected Blackbyrds discography *in* Down Beat, XLIV (April 7, 1977): 16 ((—))

BLACKFACE COMEDY GROUPS

B168   COGSWELL, Robert: A discography of blackface comedy dialogs *in* JEMF Quarterly, XV (No. 55, Fall 1979): 166–179 ((2, 3, 4, 5, 6, 7))

BLAKE, CICERO

See also *Bibliography* Vol. 2, Jazz

B169   PRUTER, Robert: Cicero Blake discography *in* Goldmine, No. 65 (October 1981): 189 ((5))

BLAKE, TOMMY

B170   KOMOROWSKI, Adam, and Dick GRANT: Tommy Blake *in* New Kommotion, No. 22 (1979): 7 ((2, 3, 7))

BLANC, MEL

B171   [[[Discography] *in* Memory Lane, No. 25 (January 1973)]]

THE BLENDERS (musical group)

B172   GOLDBERG, Marv, and Mike REDMOND: The Blenders *in* Yesterday's Memories, I/2 (1975): 24 ((7))

BLOOD, SWEAT AND TEARS (musical group)

B173   [[[Discography] *in* Hi Fi Stereophonie, No. 10 (October 1972): 944]]

BLOODWYN PIG (musical group)

B174   ABRAHAMS, Mick: Bloodwyn Pig *in* Bedloe's Island, No. 5 (c1972): 13–14; discography p. 14 ((—))

BLOSSOM TOES (musical group)

B175   FLEURY, Joseph: Blossom Toes . . . a big blunder? *in* Jamz, No. 4 (May 1972): 44–46; discography p. 46 [Includes offshoots Stud, B.B. Blunder, etc.] ((—))

THE BLUE LYRES (musical group)

B176   ﹍BES, Sandy: Amendments and additions to "British Dance Bands 1912–1939" by Brian Rust and Edward S. Walker: Part 14 *in* Gunn Report, No. 67 (March–April 1978): 17–18 ((3, 6))

BLUE MOON label

B177   TOPPING, Ray: Blue Moon label *in* New Kommotion, No. 15 (Spring 1977): 17 ((—))

THE BLUE RIDGE PLAYBOYS (musical group)

B178   HEALY, Bob: [Discography] *in* Country Directory, No. 4 [n.d.]: ? ((2, 3, 7))

B179   HEALY, Bob: The Blue Ridge Playboys (Leon Selph) *in* Music Memories and Jazz Report, III/6 (Winter 1963): 8–9 ((2, 3, 7))

THE BLUE RIDGE RAMBLERS (musical group)

B180   RUSSELL, Tony: H. M. Barnes' Blue Ridge Ramblers *in* Old Time Music, No. 17 (Summer 1975): 11 ((3, 7))

BLUE SKY BOYS (musical group)

B181   [Discography] *in* Country News & Views, III/1 (July 1964): 12–15 ((—))

B182   [Discography] *in* Country Western Express [New series], No. 19 [n.d.]: ? ((—))

B183   McCUEN, B.: [Discography] *in* Country Directory, No. 1 (November 1960): ? ((3, 6, 7))

B184   McCUEN, Brad: Blue Sky Boys (Bill and Earl Bolick) *in* Disc Collector, No. 24 (May 1973): 1-6 ((3, 6, 7)) [Reprinted from Country Directory, November 1960]

B185   McCUEN, Brad: Blue Sky Boys discography *in* Hillbilly, No. 50 (March 1977): 21-28 ((2, 3, 6, 7))

B186   PASSANTINO, Sal: For collectors only *in* Bim Bam Boom, II/3 (No. 9, 1973): 50 ((3))

BLUE SUEDE SHOES (song title)

B187   RUSSELL, Wayne: "Blue suede shoes" *in* SMG, V/4 (January–February 1977): 18 ((—))

BLUEBEAT label

B188   FAULL, Trev: Bluebeat *in* Outlet, No. 10 (March 1979): 22-31; addenda in No. 12 (July 1979): 7 ((—))

BLUEBIRD Label
  See also *Bibliography* Vol. 2, Jazz

B189   HEARNE, Will Roy: [Discography] *in* Country Western Spotlight, No. 24 (December 1958) thru No. 41 (March 1963): various paginations ((—))

B190   WADIN, Eric, and Bob HEALY: Bluebird 33-0500 numerical series *in* Disc Collector, No. 24 (May 1973): 25-26 ((4))

BLUEBONNET label

B191   SCHUMANN, E. Reinald: [Label list] *in* Hillbilly, No. 28 (December 1968): 7-9 ((—))

BLUEBONNET label (rock)

B192   GRANT, Dick: Bluebonnet & associated labels *in* New Kommotion, No. 21 (1979): 45 ((3))

BLUEGRASS MUSIC—Australia

B193   BIRT, Eddie: A listing of Australasian bluegrass on record *in* Country & Western Spotlight, No. 9 (December 1976): 27-29 ((—))

BLUEGRASS MUSIC—UNITED STATES

B194   HAGLUND, Urban: A listing of bluegrass LP's. Vasteras: Kountry Korral Productions, 1971. 71 pp. ((5))

B195   Appendix *in* PRICE, Steven D.: Old as the hills: the story of bluegrass music. New York: Viking Press, 1975: [97]-110 ((—))

BLUES PROJECT (musical group)

B196   TAMARKIN, Jeff: The Blues Project discography *in* Goldmine, No. 62 (July 1981): 13 ((—))

BLUESTOWN label

B197   KOCHAKIAN, Dan: Bluestown *in* Whiskey, Women, and . . . II: 15 ((3, 7))

B198   KOCHAKIAN, Dan: Bluestown label *in* Goldmine, No. 51 (August 1980): 161-162 ((1, 3))

BOAG, MAX

B199   BRETHOUR, Ross: A Max Boag discography. Aurora, Ont.: Brethour, 1978.

BOB AND LUCILLE (LUCILLE STARR/ FERN REGAN AND BOB REGAN)

B200   KIBBLE, Doug: Bob & Lucille: Canadian sweethearts *in* New Kommotion, No. 16 (Summer 1977): 34-35; discography p. 35; addenda in No. 17 (Autumn 1977): 38 and No. 22 (1979): 64 ((—))

BOBBETTES (musical group)

B201   [[[Discography] *in* Soul Music (No. 12)]]

B202   GOLDBERG, Marv: One, two, three . . . here comes the Bobbettes *in* Yesterday's Memories, II/3 (1976): 16 ((7))

B203 GONZALEZ, Fernando L.: [Discography] *in* Goldmine, No. 64 (September 1981): 8 ((3, 5))

BOERO, FELIPE

B204 Discografia *in* BOERO DE IZETA, Carlota: Felipe Boero. Buenos Aires: Ediciones Culturales Argentinas, 1978: 205-206 ((—))

BOLAN, MARC

B205 BETROCK, Alan: T. Rex discography *in* Jamz, No. 3 (February 1972): 32–33, addenda in No. 4 (May 1972): 35 and No. 5 (c1972): 43 ((5))

B206 Discography *in* Marc Bolan: a tribute. London: Essex House Publishing, , Springwood Books, 1978: [124–125] ((5))

B207 HOGG, Brian: Tyrannosaurus Rex [Marc Bolan] *in* Bam Balam, No. 2 (June 1975): 13–16; discography pp. 14–16 ((—)) [pre-T. Rex]

B208 Marc Bolan: original British 45's *in* Trouser Press Collector's Magazine, II/6 (January–April 1979): [3] ((—))

B209 MILLER, Kathy: Roly Poly Boly *in* Trans-Oceanic Trouser Press, II/2 (April–May 1975): 5–10 ((—))

B210 WELCH, Chris, and Simon NAPIER-BELL: Discography *in* program notes for You scare me to death [sound recording], Cherry Berry Records ERED 20, 1981 ((5)) [English label]

BOLING, CARL, AND HIS FOUR ACES (musical group)

B211 [Discography] *in* Country Western Spotlight (Special issue, September 1962): ? ((—))

B212 EDWARDS, J.: [Discography] *in* Country Western Spotlight, No. 20 (September–December 1957): ? ((—))

BOMP label

B213 Bompin' records on the people in your town *in* Gorilla Beat, No. 8 (1980): 22–26 ((5))

BOND, EDDIE

B214 Discographies *in* GRANT, Dick, and Adam KOMOROWSKI: The Eddie Bond story. n.p.: Misty Mountain Music/New Kommotion/Enkay Productions, 1982. ((1, 2, 3, 5, 7)) [Includes compositions]

B215 THOMPSON, Gary: Discography *in* Goldmine, No. 30 (November 1978): 25 ((5))

B216 The ultimate Eddie Bond—discography *in* Rockville International, No. 92 (August–September 1974): 30, 38 ((—))

BOND, JAMES (fictional character)

B217 [Discography of records inspired by James Bond or by other fictional spy characters] *in* Nostalgia World, No. 16 (Winter 1981): [25] ((—))

BOND, JOHNNY

B218 A preliminary Johnny Bond discography *in* JEMF Quarterly, VI/3 (No. 19, Autumn 1970): 102–106; VII/4 (No. 24, Winter 1971): 186–191 ((2, 3, 6, 7))

BOND, LUTHER

B219 [[[Discography] *in* Soul Music (No. 32)]]

BONDS, GARY "U.S."

B220 CARA, Holly: Gary "U.S." Bonds discography *in* Goldmine, No. 63 (August 1981): 15 ((—))

B221 JONES, Wayne: Gary "U.S." Bonds discography *in* Goldmine, No. 32 (January 1979): 13 ((—))

BONO, SONNY

B222 BETROCK, Alan: Sonny Bono: the early years, 1957-1963 *in* Time Barrier Express, IV/1 (No. 27, April–May 1981): 65–67 ((5))

BOO label

B223 Boo label *in* Hot Buttered Soul, No. 42 (November 1975?): 4 ((3))

BOOKER T. AND THE M.G.'s
(musical group)
See also *Bibliography* Vol. 2, Jazz

B224 [[Discography *in* Black Wax Magazine, No. 2 (February 1973) and No. 3 (March 1973): ?]]

BOONE, PAT

B225 CLEE, Ken: Pat Boone discography *in* Goldmine, No. 27 (January–April 1978): 19 ((—))

THE BOOTS (musical group)

B226 KLITSCH, Hans Jurgen: Boot-stretchers *in* Gorilla Beat, No. 14 (1982): 22–41; discography pp. 35, 38; family tree p. 41 ((2))

BOSTIC, EARL

B227 Earl Bostic discography *in* It Will Stand, No. 11 (c1980): 9–10 ((—))

BOWEN, JIMMY

B228 [[Discography *in* New Kommotion, No. 13 (c1976): addenda in No. 19 (Spring 1978): 12]]

BOWIE, DAVID

B229 CARR, Roy: David Bowie: an illustrated record. New York; London: Eel Pie Publishers, 1981. 120 pp. [Discographic information throughout] ((1, 5))

B230 The compleat David Bowie *in* The Rock Marketplace, No. 1 (May 1973): 6, 26 ((5))

B231 Davie Bowie *in* Hifi Stereo (May 1978): 129–130 ((—))

B232 David Bowie discography *in* Sounds Fine, No. 18 (July 1977): 11 ((5))

B233 FLETCHER, David Jeffrey: David Bowie discography *in* Goldmine, No. 46 (March 1980): 14–16 ((5))

B234 FLETCHER, David Jeffrey: David Robert Jones Bowie: the discography of a generalist, 1962–1979. 3rd ed. Chicago: F. Fergeson Productions, 1979. 123 pp. ((1, 5, 7))

B235 HINMAN, Doug: Epherma: Bowie *in* New Haven Rock Press, IV/4 (No. 18, c1972/3): 8 ((—))

B236 Records of David Bowie *in* KELLEHER, Ed: David Bowie: a biography in words & pictures. New York: Sire Books, Chappell Music Co., 1977: 60–63 ((1, 5))

B237 Bowie a traves de sus discos *in* SIERRA I FABRA, Jordi: David Bowie. Barcelona: Musica de nuestro tiempo, 1977: 39–77 ((—))

B238 WALKER, John: Rare Bowie for fun and profit *in* Trouser Press, No. 19 (April–May 1977): 8–11, 34; No. 20: ? ((5, 6a))

BOWLLY, AL

B239 FENTON, Alasdair: Al Bowlly *in* Street Singer, No. 21 (March–April 1971): 12+ ((—)) [LP's only]

B240 HARVEY, Clifford M., and Brian RUST: The Al Bowlly discography. Hatch End, Middlesex: Rust's Rare Records, 1964. 52 pp. ((3, 4, 6, 7))

B241 PATTISON, Albert: Al Bowlly: the micro-groove discography. Strensall, York, England: Pattison, 1976. 27 pp. ((—))

B242 RUST, Brian, and Clifford HARVEY: Al Bowlly discography *in* COLIN, Sid: Al Bowlly. London: Elm Tree Books, 1979: 111–160 ((3, 6, 7))

BOWN, ANDY

B243 Andy Bown interview *in* The Rock Marketplace, No. 2 (July 1973): 24–26; discography p. 26 [Includes the Herd, Judas Jump, and Storyteller] ((5))

BOYD, BILL, AND HIS COWBOY RAMBLERS (musical group)

B244 McCUEN, B.: [Discography] *in* Country Directory, No. 3 (1962): ? ((3, 7))

BOYD, JIM, AND HIS MEN OF THE WEST (musical group)

B245 McCUEN, B.: [Discography] *in* Country Directory, No. 3 (1962): ? ((2, 3, 7))

BRANCH, ERNEST

B246 [COHEN, Norm,] and Guthrie MEADE: Ernest Branch and Bernice

Coleman *in* JEMF Quarterly, VIII/2 (No. 26, Summer 1972): 103 ((3, 6, 7))

BRANDELIUS, HARRY

B247   LILIEDAHL, Karleric: Harry Brandelius. Stockholm: Kungliga biblioteket, 1975. 48 l. (Nationfonotekets diskografier, 506) ((2, 3, 6, 7))

BRANDSTRUP, LUDVIG

B248   ANDREASEN, Axel: Ludvig Brandstrup og grammofonen; en discografi. Kobenhavn: Andreasen, 1974. 34 l. ((3, 4, 6, 7))

BRASSENS, GEORGES

B249   Discographie *in* BARLOW, Michel: Chanson, Georges Brassens. Paris: Hatier, 1981: 17–22 ((5))

B250   Discographie *in* BRIAL, Jean-Michel: Georges Brassens. Paris: PAC, 1981: 241–251 ((—))

B251   Discography *in* HANTRAIS, Linda: Le vocabulaire de Georges Brassens. Paris: Klincksieck, 1976: 241 ((—))

BREAKOUT (musical group)

B252   Breakout LP-discography *in* Jazz Press, No. 34 (March 18, 1977): 15 ((—))

BREL, JACQUES

B253   Discographie *in* BARLATIER, Pierre: Jacques Brel. Paris: Solar, 1978: 73–78 ((—))

B254   Discographie des 33 tours 30 cm disponibles *in* BOLAND, Bernard: Le retour de Brel *in* Hifi Stereo, No. 34 (January 1978): 178–181 ((—))

B255   Discographie *in* DAMPENON, Philippe: Jacques Brel. Wissous: G. Cottreau, 1978: 81–84 ((7))

B256   Discographie *in* HONGRE, Brunot: "Chansons," Jacques Brel: analyse critique. Paris: Hatier, 1976: 79 ((—))

B257   Discographie *in* Jacques Brel. Bruxelles: Edition des Archers, 1978: 116–118 ((—))

B258   Discographie *in* Jacques Brel: Liberte oblige. Paris: Societe internationale de presse et d'edition, 1978: 91–96 ((7))

B259   [[[Discography] *in* MAILLARD, Jean Claude: Jacques Brel. Paris: J. P. Delville, 1978: [88–91]]]

B260   Discographie *in* MONESTIER, Martin: Jacques Brel: le livre du souvenir. Paris: Tchou, 1978: [251]–253 ((7))

B261   [[[Discography] *in* MONSERRAT, Joelle: Jacques Brel. Paris: PAC, 1982: 217–227]]

B262   Discographie *in* RICHARD, Jean Yves: Jacques Brel. Montreal: Editions France-Quebec, 1968: 115–116 ((—))

BRENT label

B263   [[Discography *in* New Kommotion, No. 12 (c1976); addenda in No. 16 (Summer 1977): 42 and No. 14 (Winter 1977): 31]]

BRICE, FANNY

B264   [[DEBUS, A. G.: The records of Fanny Brice *in* Hobbies, LXI (March 1956): 34–35]]

B265   FREIND, Marc, and Jim BEDOIAN: Fanny Brice; a bio-discography *in* Discographer (II/4): 201–210 ((3, 6, 7))

BRIDGES, CAS

B266   MONDRONE, Sal: Rare sounds *in* Bim Bam Boom, No. 7 (September 1972): 41 ((3))

BRIDGES, CHARLES

B267   SEROFF, Doug: Charles Bridges discography *in* Goldmine, No. 45 (February 1980): 16–17 ((1, 2, 3, 6, 7))

BRINSLEY SCHWARZ (musical group)

B268   Brinsley Schwarz discography *in* Trouser Press Press, No. 3 (1976): 66 [Includes group recordings under its own name and session work plus Kippington Lodge and Limelight, and solo work by Brinsley Schwarz, Nick Lowe, Bob Andrews, and Billy Rankin] ((5))

B269 ROSENSTEIN, Bruce: Brinsley Schwarz *in* Trans-Oceanic Trouser Press, II/3 (June–August 1975): 13–17 ((—))

BRISSON, CARL

B270 ENGLUND, B.: Carl Brisson *in* Talking Machine Review International, No. 38 (February 1976): 566–567 ((3, 6, 7))

BRITANNIA label

B271 ANDREWS, F.: Britannia Records *in* Talking Machine Review, No. 34 (June 1975): 361–365 ((5))

BRITT, TINA

B272 PETARD, Gilles: Tina Britt discography *in* Shout, No. 88 (August 1973): [3–4] ((3, 7))

BROADCAST label

B273 [Discography] *in* Folk Style, No. 2 (April 1958): ? ((—)) [English series]

B274 HAYES, Jim: Broadcast [8" 78 rpm series, July 1927–July 1931] *in* Gunn Report, No. 30 (October–November 1971): [35]–39 ((3, 6))

B275 HAYES, Jim: "Broadcast" Twelve super dance *in* Gunn Report, No. 26 (February–March 1971): [29]–31 ((3, 6))

B276 HAYES, Jim: 1928 vintage light music on "Broadcast" Twelve records: a new series for the record collector *in* Vintage Light Music, No. 15 (Summer 1978): 7; 1929 vintage light music . . . in No. 16 (Autumn 1978): 14–15; 1930 vintage light music . . . in No. 17 (Winter 1979): 18–19; 1931 vintage light music . . . in No. 18 (Spring 1979): 12–13; 1932 vintage light music . . . in No. 19 (Summer 1979): 23 ((3, 5))

BROADCAST FOUR-TUNE label

B277 HAYES, Jim: Disc research England: Broadcast Four-Tune *in* Gunn Report, No. 66 (January–February 1978): 9–11 ((3, 6))

BROADWAY BELLHOPS (musical group)

B278 BACKENSTO, Woody, and John R. NELSON: Paging the Bellhops *in* Record Exchanger, IV (February 1951): [2–7] ((2, 3, 6, 7))

BROOKS, DONNIE

B279 MYERS, Gary: Donnie Brooks discography *in* Record Exchanger, VI/2 (No. 29, [1980]): 20 ((5))

BROOKS, LONNIE
See also *Bibliography* Vol. 2, Jazz

B280 STRUM, Adriaan: Lonnie Brooks discography *in* Goldmine, No. 59 (April 1981): 18 ((5))

THE BROTHERS FOUR (musical group)

B281 Brothers Four discography *in* Goldmine, No. 43 (December 1979): 126 ((5))

BROWN, ARTHUR

B282 TELL, Pontus von: The god of hellfire: the crazy world of Arthur Brown *in* Gorilla Beat, No. 15 (1982): 22–31; discography p. 31 ((5))

BROWN, BILLY

B283 RUSSELL, Wayne: The Columbia rockabilly sounds of Billy Brown *in* New Kommotion, No. 17 (Autumn 1977): 16; addenda in No. 19 (Spring 1978): 12 and No. 22 (1979): 64 ((3, 7))

BROWN, BUSTER

B284 POGGI, P. J.: "I'm goin', but I'll be back": the Buster Brown story *in* Who Put the Bomp, No. 7 (Summer 1971): 29–30; discography p. 30 ((1))

BROWN, CLARENCE "GATEMOUTH"
See also *Bibliography* Vol. 2, Jazz

B285 TOPPING, Ray: Clarence "Gatemouth" Brown discography *in* Goldmine, No. 58 (March 1981): 10–11, 15 ((2, 3, 6, 7))

BROWN, DURWOOD

B286 PINSON, Bob: [Discography] *in* Country Directory, No. 4 [n.d.]: ? ((2, 3, 7))

BROWN, JAMES

B287 Discography *in* Goldmine, No. 27 (January–April 1978): 25 ((—))

B288 GROSSWEINER, Bob: James Brown discography *in* Goldmine, No. 66 (November 1981): 9–10 ((5))

BROWN, JIM

B289 [Discography] *in* Country Western Express, No. 21 (December 1958): ? ((—))

BROWN, MICHAEL

B290 HOGG, Brian: Michael Brown *in* Bam Balam, No. 4 (June 1976): 16–19; addenda in No. 7 (c1978): 9 ((2)) [Leader of the Left Banke and Stories]

B291 SCHULPS, Dave: The Michael Brown scrapbook *in* Trouser Press, No. 14 (June–July 1976): 18, 23–25; discography p. 25 [Includes recordings with the Left Banke, Montage, and Stories] ((—))

BROWN, MILTON

B292 PINSON, Bob: [Discography] *in* Country Directory, No. 4 (1962?): ? ((2, 3, 7))

B293 PINSON, Bob: Milton Brown and his musical Brownies *in* Old Time Music, No. 5 (Summer 1972): 21–22 ((3, 6, 7))

BROWN, PETER

B294 Brown, Ornamwents, Spedding & Piblokto *in* Jamz, No. 4 (May 1972): 28–31; discography p. 31 ((3, 5))

BROWN, RUTH

B295 GRENDYSA, Peter: Ruth Brown discography *in* Goldmine, No. 54 (November 1980): 9 ((1, 3, 5, 7))

B296 GRENDYSA, Peter: Ruth Brown discography *in* It Will Stand, No. 12/13 (c1980): 5–6 ((5))

THE BROWN DOTS (musical group)

B297 GOLDBERG, Marv, and Mike REDMOND: The Brown Dots & The Four Tunes *in* Yesterday's Memories, I/1 (1975): 18 ((7))

BROWNSVILLE STATION (musical group)

B298 BROWN, Warren: Brownsville Station discography *in* Ballroom Blitz, No. 24 (January 1978): 18 ((5))

BRUCE, ED

B299 KARTHE, Peter: [Discography] *in* Kountry Korral, XIV/5 (1981): 14 ((7))

BRUCE, LENNY

B300 HANBY, Bob: Albums *in* Goldmine, No. 32 (January 1979): 29–30 ((—))

BRUNSWICK label

B301 Brunswick 100 series *in* JEMF Quarterly, IX (No. 31, Autumn 1973): 103–108; IX (No. 32, Winter 1973): 174–179; X (No. 33, Spring 1974): 26–27; X (No. 34, Summer 1974): 78–82 ((3))

BRUNSWICK label [England]

B302 BAYLY, E.: Brunswick picture labels *in* Talking Machine Review, No. 56–57 (February–April 1979): 1469–1473 ((3))

B303 [[PELLETIER, Paul M.: Brunswick complete singles listing: 1952–1967. London: Record Information Services. Brunswick Supplement. London: Record Information Services. (Publication Nos. 14 and 14a)]]

BUCHANAN AND GOODMAN (musical group)

B304 WELTMAN, Shelly: [Discography] *in* Record Exchanger, No. 8 [Fall 1971]: 18 ((—))

THE BUCKINGHAMS (musical group)

B305 LIND, Jeff, and Rod HEIDEN: Buckinghams discography *in* Goldmine, No. 62 (July 1981): 19; addi-

tions and corrections in No. 65
(October 1981): 17 ((5))

BUCKLEY, TIM

B306 Complete Buckley discography *in*
Down Beat, XLIV (June 16, 1977): 27
((—))

BUD AND TRAVIS (musical duo)

B307 Bud and Travis discography *in* Goldmine, No. 58 (March 1981): 201
((—))

BUFFALO SPRINGFIELD (musical group)

B308 HOGG, Brian: Buffalo Springfield *in*
Bam Balam, No. 12 (November 1980):
2, 3–7; discography pp. 2, 6–7;
addenda in No. 14 (September 1982):
15 ((1, 5)) [Includes predecessors]

BUFFETT, JIMMY

B309 GRAMER, Ilrich: Jimmy Buffett:
Troubadour auf Reisen *in* Country
Corner (June 1981): 48 ((—))

BULLET label

B310 HAWKINS, Martin: Bullet discography *in* Goldmine, No. 53 (October
1980): 170–171 ((—))

BULLET label [Country recordings]

B311 ANDERSON, Sharon, and Alan
CACKETT: The Bullet label *in* Coun-
try Record Exchanger, II (No. 17,
July 1968): 5–6 ((—))

BUMBLE, B. AND THE STINGERS (musical group)

B312 [Discography] *in* Rockville International, No. 92 (August–September
1974): [22] ((6))

B313 KENNETT, Robert: B. Bumble & the
Stingers *in* Not Fade Away, No. 6
(March 1975): 4–5 ((5))

BUNGARNER, SAMANTHA

B314 CRISP, David L.: Discography *in*
Country & Western Spotlight, No. 25
(November 1980): 14 ((1, 3, 6, 7))

BUNKER HILL label

B315 [[[Discography] *in* Shout (No. 63):
12]]

BURKE, MICKEY

B316 NAUCLER, Mickey: Skivor *in* Kountry Korral (June 1971): 15 ((—))

BURNETT, RICHARD

B317 WOLFE, Charles K.: Richard Burnett
discography *in* Old Time Music, No.
12 (Spring 1974): 32 ((3, 5, 6, 7))

BURNETTE, DORSEY

B318 [[Discography *in* New Kommotion
(c1976); addenda in No. 14 (Winter
1977): 31 and No. 22 (1979): 64]]

BURNETTE, JOHNNY
See also *Bibliography* Vol. 2, Jazz

B319 BLAIR, John: Johnny Burnette Trio
discography *in* Time Barrier Express,
IV/1 (No. 27, April–May 1980): 23–25
((3, 5, 7))

B320 JONES, Pete: The Johnny Burnette
R&R Trio: details from the Coral session files *in* Kommotion, No. 9
(Spring–Summer 1975): 16–17 ((3, 5,
7))

B321 SMART, Peter, and Bob WEST-
FALL: Johnny Burnette on disc *in*
Kommotion, No. 8 (Winter 1975):
6–8, 16; addenda in No. 9 (Spring–
Summer 1975): 5 and No. 10/11
(Winter 1975-76): 26–27 ((5))

B322 WEST, Dennis, and John BLAIR:
Johnny Burnette Trio & related dis-
cography *in* Record Exchanger, V/5
(No. 27, 1978): [20–26] ((5))

BURNETTE, "SMILEY"

B323 [Discography] *in* Disc Collector, No.
17 (May 1961): ? ((—))

BURTON, JAMES

B324 TOBLER, John: Discography *in* Zig
Zag, No. 59 (April 1976): [21] ((—))

BURY, MIKE

B325 The complete Mike Bury discography *in* Rock 'n' Roll International Magazine (Danish), No. 105 (April 1977): 7–8 ((5))

BUSH, JOHNNY

B326 LUNDGREN, Lars, and Erik NAUCLER: Johnny Bush record listing *in* Kountry Korral (No. 1, 1979): 13 ((—))

BUTCHER, DWIGHT

B327 EARLE, Gene: Dwight Butcher discography *in* JEMF Quarterly, V/1 (No. 13, Spring 1969): 17–22; addenda in VI/2 (No. 18, Summer 1970): 90 ((2, 3, 4, 6, 7))

BUTLER, BILLY

B328 PRUTER, Robert: Billy Butler discography *in* It Will Stand, No. 19 (c1981): 17–18 ((5, 6a))

B329 PRUTER, Robert: The Billy Butler story *in* Record Exchanger, IV/5 (December 1975): 20–21 ((—))

BUTLER, CARL

B330 BENSON, Charles: Carl Butler record listing (titles A to I) *in* Country & Western Roundabout, I/4 (May 1963): 23; titles J to Z in II/2 (August 1963): 16 ((—))

BUTLER, JERRY

B331 PRUTER, Robert, and John CORDELL: Jerry Butler discography *in* It Will Stand, No. 27–28 (c1982): 8–10 ((5))

B332 RICHARDSON, Clive: Discography *in* program notes for The Impressions [sound recording], Sire SASH-3717-2, 1976. ((5))

BUTTS, BUDDY

B333 SEROFF, Doug: Buddy Butts/Norfolk Jazz Quartet discography *in* Goldmine, No. 40 (September 1979): 15A ((3, 7))

THE BYRDS (musical group)

B334 HOGG, Brian: Byrds *in* Bam Balam, No. 8 (December 1978): 22–31; discography pp. 28–31; addenda in No. 10 (November 1979): 10 and No. 12 (November 1980): 32 ((1, 5)) [Includes pre-Byrds recordings and Gene Clark solo]

BYRNE, JERRY

B335 SMART, Peter: Jerry Byrne *in* Kommotion, No. 10–11 (Winter 1975–76): 24–25 ((3))

CBS-CORONET label
See CORONET label

C.J. label
See also *Bibliography* Vol. 2, Jazz

C1 MOHR, Kurt, and Emmanuel CHOISNEL: C. J. label *in* Soul Bag (No. 17): 7–9 ((—))

CADENCE label

C2 CALLAHAN, Mike: Cadence label discography *in* Goldmine, No. 66 (November 1981): 185–186 ((5))

THE CADETS (musical group)

C3 FILETI, Donn: The Jacks/Cadets *in* Yesterday's Memories, I/2 (1975): 8–9 ((7))

C4 MONDRONE, Sal: Rare sounds *in* Bim Bam Boom, I/2 (October–November 1971): 18; additions and corrections in I/3 (December 1971–January 1972): 21 ((—))

THE CADILLACS (musical group)

C5 MONDRONE, Sal, et al.: The Cadillacs *in* Bim Bam Boom, I/5 (April–May 1972): 5 ((3, 5))

CAESAR, SHIRLEY

C6 SACRE, Bob: Young, gifted, and underrated *in* Blues-Link, No. 3 (January–February 1974): 14–16 ((3, 7))

CAGLE, AUBREY

C7 GLENISTER, Derek: Aubrey Cagle *in* New Kommotion, No. 19 (Spring 1978): 25 ((2, 3, 7))

CAIN, BENNY

C8 Benny & Vallie Cain discographie *in* Country Corner, No. 37 (December 1973): 25–26 ((7))

C9 SAUNDERS , Walter V.: Benny Cain and Vallie *in* Bluegrass Unlimited, VI/11 (May 1972): 12 ((2, 3, 5, 7))

CALE, J. J.

C10 ROHRIG, Steffi: J. J. Cale: country blues *in* Country Corner, XVI/6 (June 1981): 44 ((—))

CALE, JOHN

C11 BRETHOLZ, Myron: John Cale: knight of fear *in* Trans-Oceanic Trouser Press, II/4 (September–October 1975): 13–17 ((—))

C12 Discography *in* Zig Zag, III/8 (No. 32): [14] ((5))

C13 John Cale discography *in* Trouser Press Press, No. 3 (1976): 62 [Solo, production session work; reprinted from Trouser Press No. 10] ((5))

CALIFORNIA label

C14 California Records CEP-300 series discography *in* Kountry Korral (No. 3, 1979): 29 ((—))

CALLAHAN BROTHERS (musical duet)

C15 PINSON, Bob: Bill & Joe Callahan: a great brother duet *in* Old Time Music, No. 16 (Spring 1975): 19–22 ((3, 6, 7))

C16 PINSON, Bob: [Discography] *in* Country Directory, No. [n.d.]: ? ((2, 3, 7))

C17 Pinson, Bob: [Discography] *in* Disc Collector, No. 13 [n.d.]: ? ((—))

THE CALVANES (musical group)

C18 HINCKLEY, Dave: The Calvanes *in* Yesterday's Memories, III/3 (1977): 7 ((7))

CALVE, PIERRE

C19 Discographie *in* his Vivre en ce pays . . . ou ailleurs. Montreal: Lemeac, 1977: 129–131 ((—))

CAMEO label

C20 The Cameo Records story *in* Who Put the Bomp, No. 13 (Spring 1975): 33–36; addenda in No. 15 (Fall 1975): 44 ((5))

CAMPBELL, JO ANN

C21 BIG BOPPER BILL: Discography: Jo Ann Campbell 45 rpm *in* Paul's Record Magazine, III/3 (April 1976): 5–7 ((5))

CAMPI, RAY

C22 DRUST, Greg: Ray Campi discography *in* Goldmine, No. 15 (March–April 1977): 10–11 ((5))

C23 KOMOROWSKI, Adam: Ray Campi: rockabilly rebel *in* New Kommotion, No. 26 (1982): 32–33, 36, 39–40, 42; discography (by Ray TOPPING and Adam KOMOROWSKI): 39–40, 42 ((1, 2, 3, 7))

C24 STRUM, Adri: Ray Campi disco *in* Rockville International (June–July 1974): 28–29 ((5))

CANNON, FREDDY

C25 CLEE, Ken: Freddy Cannon discography *in* Goldmine, No. 42 (November 1979): 15 ((—))

C26 McDOWELL, Mike: Freddy Cannon discography *in* Blitz, No. 28 (September–October 1978): 25–26 ((5))

CANTOR, EDDIE

C27 BEDOIAN, James: The Eddie Cantor discography *in* Discographer, I/4 (1st Quarter, 1969): 333–342 ((3, 7))

CAPITOL label [Australia]

C28 SUTTCLIFFE, Mike: Discography of Australian Capitol discs *in* Gunn Report, No. 75 (November–December 1979): 12; No. 76 (January–February 1980): 15 ((3))

CAPITOL label [England]

C29 [[PELLETIER, Paul M.: British Capitol complete singles & EP's: 1948–1955. London: Record Information Services. (Publication No. 12)]]

C30 PELLETIER, Paul M.: British Capitol 45 rpm singles catalog: 1954–1981. Chessington: Record Information Services, 1982. 72 pp. ((5)) (British Popular Series, No. 1)

CAPITOL label [Netherlands]

C31 [[MORGAN, Alun: Classics on [Dutch] Capitol *in* Jazz & Blues, II (August 1972): 22–24]]

CAPITOL label [U.S.]
See also *Bibliography* Vol. 2, Jazz

C32 BENNETT, Bill: Capitol research (1942 to 1949 & beyond) *in* Record Research, No. 183–184 (July 1981): 11; No. 185–186 (October 1981): 12; No. 187–188 (December 1981): 12 ((3))

THE CAPITOLS (musical group)

C33 [[[Discography] *in* Soul Music (No. 29)]]

THE CAP-TANS (musical group)

C34 HINCKLEY, Dave: The Cap-Tans *in* Yesterday's Memories, II/4 (1976): 11 ((7))

CARAVAN (musical group)

C35 Caravan discography *in* Zig Zag, VI/2 (No. 52, 1975): 21 ((—))

THE CARDINALS (musical group)

C36 CHANEY, Phil: The Cardinals *in* Yesterday's Memories, I/4 (1975): [21] ((3, 5, 7))

C37 GRENDYSA, Peter, and Chris BEACHLEY: Cardinals discography *in* It Will Stand, No. 22–23 (c1981): 26 ((5))

CARLISLE, CLIFF

C38 FUCHS, Walter W.: Aufnahmen-Sitzungen *in* Hillbilly, No. 28 (December 1968): 31–33; No. 29 (March 1969): 29–30; No. 30 (June 1969): 17–18 ((3, 6, 7))

CARLISLE BROTHERS

C39 [Discography] *in* Country Western Spotlight (Special issue, September 1962): ? ((—))

C40 [Discography] *in* Folk Style, No. 7 [n.d.]: ? ((2, 3, 7))

C41 EDWARDS, J.: [Discography] *in* Country Western Spotlight, No. 2 (December 1955): ? ((—))

C42 EDWARDS, JOHN: [Discography] *in* Country & Western Spotlight, No. 8 (September 1976): 10 ((—)) [Reprinted from Country Western Spotlight, No. 2 (December 1955)]

CARLTON label

C43 BEZANKER, Paul: Carlton records *in* Paul's Record Magazine, IV/1 (August 1976): 32; IV/2 (No. 13/14): 46–48; additions and corrections in No. 15 (January–February 1977): 39 ((3))

C44 Carlton and Guaranteed label listings *in* SMG, V/3 (Summer 1976): 27–28; V/4 (January–February 1977): 17 ((—))

CARNEY, KATE

C45 BARKER, Tony: Kate Carney discography *in* Music-Hall Records, No. 4 (December 1978): 64–71; additions in No. 5 (February 1979): 83 ((3, 7))

CARNIVAL label

C46 MOHR, Kurt: Carnival label listing *in* Shout, No. 69 (September 1971): [5–6] ((3))

CAROLINA TARHEELS (musical group)

C47 EARLE, E.: [Discography] *in* notes for Folk Legacy FSA-24 [sound recording], 1965: ? ((2, 3, 7))

THE CAROLS (musical group)

C48 GOLDBERG, Marv, and Mike REDMOND: Interview with the Carols *in*

Bim Bam Boom, III/1 (No. 13, August–September 1974): [52] ((3, 5))

CARROLL, JOHNNY

C49 BLAIR, John: Johnny Carroll discograpy *in* Goldmine, No. 50 (July 1980): 15 ((5))

CARSON, FIDDLIN' JOHN

C50 [COHEN, Norm]: Fiddlin' John Carson discography *in* JEMF Quarterly, X/4 (No. 36, Winter 1974): 144–156 ((3, 4, 5, 6, 7))

C51 GRESS, Reinhard: Fiddlin' John Carson diskographie *in* Hillbilly, No. 58 (March 1979): 16–19 ((—))

CARSON, JAMES

C52 [COHEN, Norm]: James Carson [Roberts] and Martha, on Capitol *in* JEMF Quarterly, VIII (No. 27, Autumn 1972): 132 ((3, 5, 6, 7))

CARSTE, HANS

C53 GARNER, Clive: Hans Carste *in* Commodore, No. 5 (Spring 1972): 10 ((—))

CARTER, BUSTER

C54 RUSSELL, Tony: Buster Carter and Preston Young *in* Old Time Music, No. 7 (Winter 1972/3): 7 ((3, 7))

CARTER, MAYBELLE

C55 Kleine Auswahl—Discographie *in* Country Corner, XII (No. 53, February 1977): 26 ((—))

CARTER, WILF

C56 CLEARY, Don: Wilf Carter discography. n.p.: Cleary, n.d. 32 pp. ((2, 3, 4, 6, 7))

C57 [[Discography *in* Country Corner, No. 16: 3]]

C58 [Discography] *in* Country News & Views, I/2 (October 1962): 9–11; I/4 (April 1963): 16–17; II/2 (October 1963): 17 ((—))

C59 [Discography] *in* Country Western Express, No. 17 (January–March 1958): ? ((—))

C60 [Discography] *in* Disc Collector (No. 12 and 13, 1957): ? ((—))

C61 SCHUMANN, E. R.: [Song index] *in* Hillbilly, No. 12 (December 1964): 6–10; LP index in No. 13 (March 1965): 9 ((—))

C62 WADIN, E.: [Discography] *in* Country Western Spotlight, No. 50 (June 1965): ? ((3))

C63 WADIN, E.: [Discography] *in* Country Western Spotlight, No. 52 (December 1965): ?; No. 53 (March 1966): ? ((—))

CARTER FAMILY (musical group)

C64 [[[Discography] *in* ATKINS, John: The Carter Family. London: Old Time Music, 1973: 36–59]]

C65 BENSON, Charles: The original Carter Family complete record listing title A to D *in* Country & Western Roundabout, IV (No. 16, January–March 1968): 15–16 ((—))

C66 Carter Family (A.P., Sara, Joe and Janette) *in* Country Music Times (Australia), VII/1 (February 1973): 19–21 ((7))

C67 CHRISTIE, Keith G.: Carter Family discography. Nashville: Records' Associates (issued July 1963) ((2, 3, 6, 7))

C68 Discography *in* DAVIDSON, Alec: The Carter Family. London: Old Time Music, 1973: 36–59 ((3, 6, 7))

C69 [Discography] *in* Disc Collector, I/1 (April–June 1951): ? ((—))

C70 [Discography] *in* Folk Style, No. 8 [n.d., 1960?]: ? ((—))

C71 EDWARDS, John: The Carter Family: a discography *in* Sunny Side Sentinel; Carter Family Fan Club Journal, Series 2, No. 3 (October 1963) ((1, 3, 6, 7))

C72 EDWARDS, J.: [Discography] *in* Hillbilly Folk Record Journal, II/2 (March–June 1955): ?; II/3 (July–September 1955): ? ((—))

C73 EDWARDS, J.: [Discography] *in* Hillbilly Folk Record Journal, II/3 (July–Sept. 1955): ? ((—))

C74   FUCHS, Walter W.: Acme diskographie *in* Hillbilly, No. 24 (December 1967): 7–8 ((—))

C75   Recordings of the Carter Family *in* KRISHEF, Robert K.: The Carter Family. Minneapolis: Lerner Publications Co., 1978: 63 ((—))

C76   LEGERE, B.: [Discography] *in* Country Western Spotlight, No. 34 (June 1961): ? ((—))

C77   MALONEY, T.: [Discography] *in* Disc Collector, I/4 (October–December 1951): ? ((—))

C78   MORRIS, John: Carter Family (A.P., Sara, Maybelle) *in* Country Music Times (Australia), VI/7 (August 1972): 12–17; VI/8 (October 1972): 18–24; VI/9 (December 1972): ? ((3, 6, 7))

CARTWRIGHT BROTHERS
(musical group)

C79   RUSSELL, Tony: Cartwright Brothers (Bernard and Jack) *in* Old Time Music, No. 9 (Summer 1973): 14 ((3, 6, 7))

CASA-GRANDE label

C80   MOONOOGIAN, George: Casa-Grande discography *in* Goldmine, No. 44 (January 1980): 133 ((—))

CASANI CLUB ORCHESTRA

C81   HAYES, Jim: The Casani Club Orchestra, directed by Charlie Kunz (1935–1937) on Rex 78's *in* Vintage Light Music, No. 8 (Autumn 1976): 10–11 ((3, 5, 7)); . . . on Sterno 78s (1933 to 1935) in No. 10 (Spring 1977): 11–12 ((3, 5))

CASEY, AL

C82   [[Discography] *in* New Kommotion, No. 12 (c1976); addenda in No. 16 (Summer 1977): 42]]

CASH, ALVIN
See also *Bibliography* Vol. 2, Jazz

C83   PRUTER, Robert: Alvin Cash discography *in* Goldmine, No. 51 (August 1980): 169 ((5))

C84   PRUTER, Robert: Discography *in* Goldmine, No. 23 (February 1978): 24 ((5))

CASH, JOHNNY

C85   ANDERL, Peter: Johnny Cash Tribut—Diskographie *in* Hillbilly, No. 53 (December 1977): 24–27 ((—))

C86   BENSON, Charles; Margaret BENSON; and Ivor WALTON: [Discography] *in* Country & Western Roundabout, III (No. 10, February–March–April 1965): 16–18; addenda in III (No. 11, May–June–July 1965): 45 ((—))

C87   CHRISTENSEN, Erik: Johnny Cash disco: kompletteringar [completion] *in* Kountry Korral, XI/3–4 (1978): 10, 12 ((5))

C88   [Discography] *in* Country News and Views, IV/1 (July 1965): ? ((—))

C89   [Discography] *in* Country Western Spotlight, No. 49 (March 1965): ? ((—))

C90   Johnny Cash discography *in* GOVONI, Albert: A boy named Cash. New York: Lancer Books, 1970: 187–190 ((—))

C91   Johnny Cash discography *in* Strictly Cash, No. 10 (April 1967) thru No. 19 (January 1968): various paginations ((—))

C92   Johnny Cash: Langspielplatten *in* Hillbilly, No. 32 (December 1969): 9–12 ((—))

C93   ROKITTA, Kurt: Johnny Cash; seine Sun-Disco *in* Country Corner, No. 45 (July 1975): 44–46 ((3, 5, 7))

C94   [[SMITH, John L.: Johnny Cash discography and recording history (1955–1968). Los Angeles: John Edwards Memorial Foundation, 1969]]

C95   [[SMITH, John L.: [Discography updates] *in* JEMF Quarterly, VII/2 (No. 22, Summer 1971): 59–?; VII/3 (No. 23, Autumn 1971): 130–?]]

C96   SMITH, John L.: Johnny Cash discography update: 1972–1975 *in* JEMF Quarterly, XII/4 (No. 44, Winter 1976): 196–201 ((3, 7))

C97   SMITH, John L.: Johnny Cash, 1971–72 discography *in* JEMF Quarterly, IX/3 (No. 31, Autumn 1973): 118–127 ((3, 7))

C98 SMITH, John L.: The Johnny Cash Sun sessions revisited *in* JEMF Quarterly, X/3 (No. 35, Autumn 1974): 97–104 ((3, 6, 7))

CASH label

C99 GIBBON, Peter, and Tony TISO-VEC: [Discography] *in* Yesterday's Memories, III/3 (1977): 25 ((7))

CASHMAN, PISTILLI AND WEST (musical group)

C100 WOODWARD, Rex: Cashman, Pistilli & West discography *in* Goldmine, No. 67 (December 1981): 161–162 ((5))

THE CASTELLES (musical group)

C101 HORNER, Charlie, and Steve APPLE-BAUM: The Castelles *in* Bim Bam Boom, II/6 (No. 12, 1974): 29 ((—))

THE CATALINAS (musical group)

C102 BEACHLEY, Chris: The Catalinas discography *in* It Will Stand, No. 14–15 (c1980): 7 ((—))

CATS AND THE FIDDLE (musical group)

C103 GRENDYSA, Pete, et al.: The Cats and the Fiddle *in* Yesterday's Memories, II/2 (1976): ? ((3, 5, 7))

CHAFFIN, CLEVE

C104 [COHEN, Norm]: A preliminary Cleve Chaffin discography *in* JEMF Quarterly, X/1 (No. 33, Spring 1974): 29 ((—))

CHALLENGE label

C105 [Discography] *in* Disc Collector, No. 15 (November 1960) thru No. 17 (June 1961): ? ((—))

C106 WOLFE, Charles K.: Challenges: old time numerical *in* Devil's Box, X/2 (June 1976): 28–30; X/3 (September 1976): 38–41; X/4 (December 1976): 29–33; additions and corrections in XI/2 (June 1977): 19–21 ((—))

CHALMERS, THOMAS

C107 WILE, RAYMOND: The recording career of Thomas Chalmers *in* Talking Machine Review, No. 45 (April 1977): 946–953 and No. 46 (June 1977): 1039–1044, 1062 ((3, 5, 6, 7))

CHAMPION label

See also *Bibliography* Vol. 2, Jazz

C108 PEARLIN, Victor: Champion/Cherokee discography *in* Record Digest, I/16 (May 1, 1978): 24 ((3))

THE CHAMPS (musical group)

C109 Discography *in* MYERS, Gary: The Champs *in* Record Exchanger, V/1 (No. 23): [24–25] ((—))

CHANCE, NOLAN

C110 PRUTER, Robert: Discography *in* Goldmine, No. 27 (January–April 1978): 23 ((5))

CHANCELLOR label

C111 Chancellor label *in* Paul's Record Magazine, IV/2 (No. 13–14, September–December 1976): 33; additions and corrections in No. 15 (January–February 1977): 39 ((—))

CHANDLER, GENE

C112 PRUTER, Robert: Gene Chandler discography *in* Goldmine, No. 44 (January 1980): 17 ((5))

THE CHANTAYS (musical group)

C113 DALLEY, Robert J.: Discography *in* Goldmine, No. 52 (September 1980): 27 ((5))

C114 LAZELL, Barry: Chantays discography *in* Rumble, III/2 (Winter 1975/6): 13 ((—))

THE CHANTELS (musical group)

C115 GROIA, Phil: Discography *in* Bim Bam Boom, II/3 (No. 9, 1973): 20 ((3))

THE CHANTERS (musical group)

C116 GOLDBERG, Marv: The Chanters *in* Goldmine, No. 35 (April 1979): 43 ((5))

CHAPIN, HARRY

C117 BRADLEY, Alan: [Discography] *in* Rock It with Aware, II/2 (1975?): 22; additions and corrections in II/4 (1976): 4 and II/5 (1977): 4 ((—))

THE CHARADES (musical group)

C118 CLARK, Ian: Charades discography *in* Goldmine, No. 49 (June 1980): 17 ((5))

THE CHARIOTEERS (musical group)

C119 GRENDYSA, Peter A., and George MOONOOGIAN: Charioteers discography *in* Record Exchanger (No. 16): 18 ((5))

C120 GRENDYSA, Peter A., and Rick WHITESELL: The Charioteers discography *in* Goldmine, No. 49 (June 1980): 15–16 ((1, 3, 5, 7))

CHARISMA label

C121 Charisma Records discography *in* Trouser Press Collector's Magazine, I/3 (January–February 1979): [3]; I/4 (March–April 1979): 8 ((—))

THE CHARLATANS (musical group)

C122 [Discography] *in* HOGG, Brian: Psychotic reaction: San Francisco begins *in* Bam Balam, No. 10 (November 1979): 19–20; addenda in No. 14 (September 1982): 16 ((1, 5))

CHARLEBOIS, ROBERT

C123 Discographie *in* Robert Charlebois. Paris: Seghers, 1973: [175–176] ((—)) (Collection poesie et chansons Seghers, 22)

CHARLES, BOBBY

C124 [[Discography *in* New Kommotion, No. 12 (c1976); addenda in No. 16 (Summer 1977): 42]]

CHARLES, RAY

See also *Bibliography* Vol. 2, Jazz

C125 MOONOOGIAN, G. A.: Ray Charles discography *in* Goldmine, No. 45 (February 1980): 11 ((5))

CHARLIE AND RAY (musical duo)

C126 MOHR, Kurt: Discography *in* Shout, No. 53 (March 1970): [7–9] ((1, 3, 7))

CHARLY label

C127 Singles on the Charly label *in* Not Fade Away, No. 10 (1977): 16 ((—))

THE CHARMERS (musical group)

C128 MOHR, Kurt: Charmers/Thrashers discography *in* Shout, No. 87 (July 1973): [3–4] ((3, 7))

THE CHARTS (musical group)

C129 VANCE, Marcia: The Charts *in* Bim Bam Boom, I/3 (December 1971– January 1972): 15 ((5))

THE CHATEAUS (musical group)

C130 GOLDBERG, Marv, and Mike REDMOND: The Chateaus *in* Yesterday's Memories, II/4 (1977): 26 ((7))

CHECKER, CHUBBY

C131 AMBER, Arnie: Chubby Checker discography *in* Goldmine, No. 65 (October 1981): 177, 190 ((—))

CHECKER label

C132 AIRLIE, Bob: Chess/Checker white rock & roll recordings *in* Kommotion, No. 10–11 (Winter 1975–76): 37 ((3))

CHECKER label [Australia]

C133 PERKINS, Ken: Discography of Chess/Checker/Argo releases 78 rpm and 45 rpm *in* Big Beat of the 50's, No. 27 (May 1981): 34–36 ((5))

CHECKER label [U.S.]

C134 LAVATELLI, George: Checker *in* Time Barrier Express, II/6 (April 1976): 36–48 ((3, 4))

THE CHEERS (musical group)

C135 PRUTER, Robert: Cheers discography *in* Goldmine, No. 34 (March 1979): 29 ((5))

THE CHEETAHS (musical group)

C136 The Cheetahs *in* Gorilla Beat, No. 6 (1980): 41–44; discography p. 44; addenda in No. 7 (1980): 16 and No. 13 (1982): 71 ((5))

CHEROKEE RAMBLERS (musical group)

C137 DANIEL, Wayne W.: Cherokee Ramblers discography *in* Old Time Music, No. 37 (Autumn 1981–Spring 1982): 13 ((3, 6, 7))

CHESS label
See also *Bibliography* Vol. 2, Jazz

C138 AIRLIE, Bob: Chess/Checker white rock & roll recordings *in* Kommotion, No. 10–11 (Winter 1975-76): 37 ((3))

C139 LAVATELLI, George: Chess *in* Time Barrier Express, II/7 (No. 17, May–June 1976): 22-30; II/9 (October 1976): [17]–20 ((3))

CHESS label [Australia]

C140 PERKINS, Ken: Discography of Chess/Checker/Argo releases 78 rpm and 45 rpm *in* Big Beat of the 50's, No. 27 (May 1981): 34–36 ((5))

THE CHESSMEN (musical group)

C141 Chessmen discography *in* Time Barrier Express, II/3 (December 1975): 11 ((—))

C142 LEE, Alan: [Discography] *in* Yesterday's Memories, II/4 (1976): 24 ((—))

THE CHESTERFIELD KINGS (musical group)

C143 KLITSCH, Hans Jurgen: Chesterfield Kings *in* Gorilla Beat, No. 15 (1982): 50–52; discography p. 52 ((—))

THE CHESTNUTS (musical group)

C144 GALGANO, Bob, and Tom LUCIANI: The Chestnuts *in* Bim Bam Boom, I/2 (October–November 1971): 26 ((—))

CHEVALIER, ALBERT

C145 [[[Discography] *in* Record Advertiser, III/6 (September–October 1973): ?]]

CHEVALIER, MAURICE

C146 PEREZ, Michel: Maurice Chevalier discographie *in* Diapason, No. 164 (February 1972): 10 ((—))

C147 ROTANTE, Anthony: Maurice Chevalier. Part 3: Post-Hollywood Victor (HMV) 1935–1947 *in* Record Research, No. 137–138 (February–March 1976): 6 ((3, 6, 7)); Part 4: French Decca 1948 [and beyond] in No. 139–140 (May–June 1976): 15 ((3)); Part 5: on LP in No. 141 (July 1976): 10 ((—)); No. 142 (September 1976): 9 ((—)); No. 143 (December 1976): 10 ((—))

C148 Maurice Chevalier na deskach Supraphon *in* TATEROVA, Milada: Maurice Chevalier. Praha: Supraphon, 1970: [41–42] ((—))

C149 Enregistrements realisés par Maurice Chevalier *in* WILLEMETZ, Albert: Maurice Chevalier. Geneva: Kister, 1954: [40] ((—))

CHEYNES (musical group)

C150 The Cheynes *in* The Rock Marketplace, No. 7 (October 1974): 37 ((5))

CHIRGWIN, G. H.

C151 BARKER, Tony: G. H. Chirgwin discography *in* Music-Hall Records, No. 2 (August 1979): 3-7; addition in No. 5 (February 1980): 83 ((3, 5, 7))

CHISWICK label

C152 FAULL, Trev: The Chiswick story *in* Outlet, No. 4 (July 1978): 1–8; discography pp. 4–8; addenda in No. 11 (May 1979): 24–25 ((1))

CHOATES, HARRY

C153 LEADBITTER, Mike: Harry Choates *in* Old Time Music, No. 6 (Autumn 1972): 21–22 ((3, 6, 7))

CHOCOLATE WATCH BAND (musical group)

C154 Discography *in* Bam Balam, No. 10 (November 1979): 22–23; addendum in No. 12 (November 1980): 33 ((—))

C155 McDOWELL, Mike: Chocolate Watch Band discography *in* Blitz, No. 39 (March–April 1981): 12 ((5))

C156 SHAW, Greg: Discography *in* Who Put the Bomp, No. 12 (Summer 1974): 29 ((—))

THE CHORDS (musical group)

C157 GOLDBERG, Marv, and Mike REDMOND: The Chords *in* Yesterday's Memories, II/3 (1976): 6 ((7))

CHRISTIE, LOU

C158 ENGEL, Edward R.: Lou Christie discography *in* Time Barrier Express, IV/1 (No. 27, April–May 1980): 32–33 ((1, 5))

C159 YOUNG, Harry: Lou Christie discography *in* Goldmine, No. 41 (October 1979): 16 ((5))

CHRISTMAS MUSIC

C160 DOYLE, Jim: Wax Christmas *in* Goldmine, No. 21 (December 1977): 11 ((5))

C161 R & B Christmas records *in* Record Exchanger, V/5 (No. 27, 1978): 18–19 ((5))

CHRISTOPHER, HOMER

C162 RUSSELL, Tony: Homer Christopher discography *in* Old Time Music, No. 33 (Summer 1979–Spring 1980): 17 ((2, 3, 6, 7))

CHROME (musical group)

C163 FAULL, Trev: The march of the C-H-R-O-M-E police *in* Outlet, No. 16 (January 1980): 2–4 ((5))

CHURCHILL, SAVANNAH

C164 ANDERSON, Will, and John CORRADO: [Discography] *in* Record Exchanger, IV/3 (May 1975): 5–7 ((—))

CHY-TOWNS label

C165 BAKER, Cary: Chy-Towns label listing *in* Shout, No. 88 (August 1973): [7] ((—))

CINDY label

C166 TRABOSCI, Tom: [Discography] *in* Bim Bam Boom, No. 8 (December 1972): [24] ((—))

CINECORD label

C167 FORBES, Sandy: The Cinecord story *in* Collecta, No. 24 (December 1975): 11–15 ((3, 6, 7))

CINECYDE (musical group)

C168 McDOWELL, Mike: Cinecyde discography *in* Blitz, No. 27 (July 1978): 24 ((1, 5))

CITY label

C169 City Records discography *in* Gorilla Beat, No. 2 (1979): 14 ((—))

CLANTON, JIMMY

C170 SCHWARTZ, Phil: Discography: Jimmy Clanton *in* Goldmine, No. 14 (January–February 1977): 13 ((5))

CLAPTON, ERIC

C171 Discography *in* PIDGEON, John: Eric Clapton: biography. St. Albans: Panther, 1976: 139–144 ((5))

C172 Discography *in* TURNER, Steve: Conversations with Eric Clapton. London: Abacus, 1976: 112–116 ((5))

CLARION label

See also *Bibliography* Vol. 2, Jazz

C173   CARTER, Sydney H.: A catalogue of "Clarion" & Eberoid records. Bournemouth, England: Talking Machine Review, 1977. unpaged. ((5))

CLARK, ALICE

C174   MOHR, Kurt: [Discography] *in* Shout, No. 95 (May 1974): 1 ((—))

CLARK, BUDDY

C175   GOTTLIEB, R.E.M.: Buddy Clark 'discography' *in* Record Research, No. 149–150 (October 1977): 10 [Part 1, 1934–36]; No. 151–152 (January 1978): 16; No. 153–154 (April 1978): 14; No. 155–156 (July 1978): 15; No. 157–158 (September 1978): 16; No. 161–162 (February–March 1979): 16; No. 163–164 (May–June 1979): 16 ((1, 3, 6, 7))

CLARK, DAVE

See DAVE CLARK FIVE

CLARK, DEE

C176   PERKINS, Ken: Additions to previously published discographies *in* Big Beat of the 50's, No. 20 (May 1979): 62 ((—))

C171   PRUTER, Robert: The Dee Clark discography *in* Goldmine, No. 60 (May 1981): 21 ((5))

CLARK, PETULA

C178   KOTZKY, Bruce: Petula Clark U.S. discography *in* Goldmine, No. 38 (July 1979): 20–21 ((5))

CLARK, SANFORD

C179   GARBUTT, Bob: Sanford Clark discography *in* Goldmine, No. 62 (July 1981): 112, 165 ((3, 5, 6))

C180   HINK, Bernward: Discographie von Sanford Clark *in* Country Corner, VII (No. 31, April 1972): 25–26 ((—))

C181   SMART, Peter: A portrait of the fool (or the man Lee Lazlewood built) *in*

Kommotion, No. 4 (Winter 1974): 5–8; discography pp. 7–8 ((5))

CLARK, YODELING SLIM

C182   CLEARY, Don: Yodeling Slim Clark discography. n.p.: Cleary (?), 1980. 24 pp. ((3))

CLARKE, LADDIE

C183   HAYES, Jim: Laddie Clarke's Imperial Orchestra *in* Vintage Light Music, No. 14 (Spring 1978): 5 ((3))

THE CLASSICS (musical group)

C184   FLAM, Steve: Classics discography *in* Bim Bam Boom, I (No. 6, July 1972): 22 ((5))

CLAY, OTIS

See also *Bibliography* Vol. 2, Jazz

C185   PRUTER, Robert: Otis Clay discography *in* Goldmine, No. 45 (February 1980): 19–20 ((5))

THE CLEFS (musical group)

C186   GOLDBERG, Marv: The Clefs *in* Yesterday's Memories, I/4 (1975): [25] ((7))

THE CLEFTONES (musical group)

C187   [Discography] *in* Bim Bam Boom, I/1 (August–September 1971): 7 ((—))

C188   GONZALEZ, Fernando L.: Cleftones discography *in* Goldmine, No. 48 (May 1980): 13 ((3))

CLERC, JULIEN

C189   Discographie *in* HEYMANN, Daniele: Julien Clerc. Paris: Seghers, 1972: [167]–170 ((5))

THE CLIFTERS (musical group)

C190   FAULL, Trev: Cliff hangin' with the Clifters *in* Instrumental Obscurities Unlimited, No. 20 (c1978): 7–8 ((5))

CLIFTON, BILL

C191 [[Discography *in* Country Corner, No. 2: 5–9]]

C192 [Discography] *in* Country Western Express, No. 17 (January–March 1958): ? ((—))

C193 [Discography] *in* Disc Collector, No. 20 [n.d.]: ? ((—))

C194 [Discography] *in* Disc Collector, No. 22 [n.d., 1966?]: ? ((—))

C195 FUCHS, Walter W.: Bill Clifton Aufnahmen-Sitzungen *in* Hillbilly, No. 19 (September 1966): 5–6, 34; No. 20 (December 1966): 11–12 ((7))

C196 RONALD, R.: [Discography] *in* Country News & Views, III/3 (January 1965): 9–14 ((1, 2, 7))

C197 RONALD, R. J.: Bill Clifton & the Dixie Mountain Boys; a discography *in* Bluegrass Unlimited, III/1 (July 1968): 5–8; III/2 (August 1968): 8–13; additions and corrections in III/5 (November 1968): 12–13 ((1, 3, 5, 7)) [Originally appeared in Country News & Views]

C198 RONALD, R. J., ed. and rev. by Ron PETRONKO: Discography *in* Bluegrass Unlimited, VI/4 (October 1971): 13–15 ((1, 2, 3, 6, 7))

CLINCH MOUNTAIN BOYS (musical group)

C199 DEIJFEN, Lars: Ralph Stanley and the Clinch Mountain Boys LP-disco *in* Kountry Korral, XIV/1 (1981): 47–49 ((—))

CLINE, PATSY

C200 [Discography] *in* Country Western Express, No. 10 [New series]: 6 ((—))

THE CLOVERS (musical group)

C201 The Clovers—Atlantic—Disco in Rocking Regards, No. 5 (December 1976): 11 ((5))

C202 GOLDBERG, Marv, and Mike REDMOND: Clovers discography *in* Record Exchanger, No. 15 [June 1973]: 6 ((3, 5))

THE CLOWNS (musical group)

C203 [[[Discography] *in* Shout (No. 70): 4–10]]

COAKLEY, TOM

C204 DAVENPORT, Bob: Tom Coakley—discography *in* After Beat, I/8 (May 1971): 10 ((7))

THE COASTERS

C205 BOYAT, Bernard: Discographie *in* Big Beat, No. 16 (June 1978): 24 ((—))

C206 GOLDBERG, Marv, and Mike REDMOND: Discography *in* Record Exchanger, III/2 (No. 13 [June 1973]): 9 ((—))

C207 Discography *in* MILLAR, Bill: The Coasters. London: Star Books, 1975: 189–204 ((1, 2, 3, 6, 7))

COCHRAN, EDDIE

C208 BEARD, Will: Eddie Cochran: British E.P. discography *in* New Rockpile, No. 11 (Summer 1974): [2] ((—))

C209 Discographie d'Eddie Cochran *in* Immortal Eddie Cochran. Paris: Horus, 1979: 79–89 ((—))

C210 Eddie Cochran disko *in* Kountry Korral (December 1970): 32 ((7))

C211 Eddie Cochran recording file: Part 1 *in* New Kommotion, No. 19 (Spring 1978): 49–50 ((3, 4, 7))

C212 Eddie Cochran Goldstar file: Part 2 *in* New Kommotion, No. 20 (Summer 1978): 21 ((3, 4, 7))

C213 TOPPING, Ray, and Derek GLENISTER: An Eddie Cochran discography *in* MURI, Eddie, and Tony SCOTT: Something else: a tribute to Eddie Cochran. Prescot, England: A.V.R.R.A.S., 1979: 32–42 ((2, 3, 6a, 7))

COCHRAN, JACK WAUKEEN

C214 [Discography] *in* Big Beat, No. 14 (November 1976): 15 ((—))

C215 WEISER, Ronny: !!Rockabilly uprising!!; Jack Waukeen Cochran *in* Goldmine, No. 12 (September–October 1976): 5 ((—))

COCHRANE, PEGGY

C216 [Discography] *in* Commodore, No. 4 (Winter 1971): 7 and No. 5 (Spring 1972): 15+ ((—))

COCHRANE, TEX

C217 MILLER, Don: Tex Cochrane *in* Disc Collector, No. 24 (May 1973): 24 ((—))

COE, DAVID ALLAN

C218 OLSSON, Tomas: David Allen Coe LP disco *in* Kountry Korral, XI/5 (1978): 13 ((7))

COHEN, LEONARD

C219 [[[Discography] *in* MANZANO, Lizandro Alberto: Leonard Cohen. Barcelona: Unilibro, 1978: 157–160]]

COLDER, BEN

C220 STIDOM, Larry: Ben Colder discography *in* Goldmine, No. 65 (October 1981): 179 ((5))

COLEMAN BROTHERS (musical group)

C221 GRENDYSA, Peter A., et al.: The Coleman Brothers discography *in* Goldmine, No. 36 (May 1979): 32 ((3, 5))

COLLIER, MITTY

C222 PRUTER, Robert: [Discography] *in* Goldmine, No. 66 (November 1981): 26 ((5))

COLLINS, JUDY

C223 Discography *in* CLAIRE, Vivian: Judy Collins. New York: Flash Books, 1977: [72]–77 ((5))

C224 Judy Collins—album discography *in* Goldmine, No. 62 (July 1981): 169 ((5))

COLLINS, TOMMY

C225 ATKINS, John: Tommy Collins record listing *in* Country & Western Roundabout, IV (No. 15, March–June 1967): 15–17 ((—))

C226 [Discography] *in* Country News & Views, IV/3 (January 1966): ? ((—))

C227 [Discography] *in* Country Western Express, No. 16 (October–December 1957): ? ((—))

C228 Tommy Collins Langspielplatten *in* Country Corner, No. 44 (May 1975): 36 ((—))

C229 WEIZE, Richard A.: Tommy Collins Diskographie *in* Hillbilly, No. 44 (September 1975): 7–11; additions and corrections in No. 48 (September 1976): 28 ((—))

COLLINS, UNCLE TOM

C230 [COHEN, Norm]: Uncle Tom Collins *in* JEMF Quarterly, VIII/2 (No. 26, Summer 1972): 72 ((3, 6, 7))

COLLINS KIDS (LARRY AND LORRIE COLLINS)

C231 PERKINS, Ken: Collins Kids: additions to previously published discographies *in* Big Beat of the 50's, No. 20 (May 1979): 61 ((—))

C232 SWAN, Johnny: The Collins Kids biography/discography *in* Kommotion, No. 9 (Spring–Summer 1975): 18–19 ((3, 5))

COLOMBO, EMILIO

C233 FENTON, Alasdair: Emilio Colombo & his Orchestra *in* Vintage Light Music, No. 8 (Autumn 1976): 4–6 ((3, 5, 6, 7))

THE COLTS (musical group)

C234 OSTROWSKI, Bob: The Colts *in* Bim Bam Boom, I/3 (December 1971–January 1972): 18 ((—))

COLUMBIA label
See also *Bibliography* Vol. 2, Jazz

C235 ANDREWS, Frank: The Columbia Bubble Books *in* Hillandale News, No. 92 (October 1976): 46–49 ((—))

C236 BRYAN, Martin: Columbia 'BC' half foot long records *in* New Amberola Graphic, XII/1 (No. 41, Summer 1982): 3–9 ((7))

C237 [Discography, 100-D series] *in* Record Research, No. 56 (October 1963): ? ((—))

C238 [Discography, 15000-D series] *in* Folk Style, No. 13-15 [n.d.]: ? ((—))

C239 [Discography, 15000-D series] *in* Hillbilly Folk Record Journal, II/2 (April 1955); III/1 (January 1956); III/4 (October 1956): ? ((—))

C240 [[RANDLE, Bill: American popular music discography. Vol. 3. The Columbia 1-D series: 1923-1929. Bowling Green, Ohio: Bowling Green University Press, 1974. 411 pp.]]

C241 WICKHAM, Graham: [Columbia 40500-F, "Cajun" series] *in* Blue Yodeler, No. 10 (September 1966): ? ((—))

COLUMBO, RUSS

C242 LIQUORI, John: Russ Columbo: his golden voice lives on and on *in* Jazz Discounter, II (March 1949): 5 ((7))

COMBER, CHRIS

C243 [Record listing] *in* Country Western Express, No. 24 [n.d.]: 6-8 ((—))

COMBO label

C244 GIBBON, Peter, and Tony TISOVEC: [Discography] *in* Yesterday's Memories, III/3 (1977): 28-30 ((7))

COMETS (musical group)

C245 AIRLIE, Bob: Instrumentals by the Comets *in* Rumble (Spring 1977): 14-15 ((—))

COMMANDER CODY

C246 Commander Cody LP disco *in* Kountry Korral Magazine (No. 2, 1980): 15 ((—))

COMSTOCK, BOBBY

C247 BEZANKER, Paul: Discography *in* Paul's Record Magazine, IV/2 (1976): 15, 68; additions and corrections in No. 15 (January-February 1977): 41-42 ((5, 7))

C248 Discography *in* JONES, Wayne: Bobby Comstock: Goldmine interview *in* Goldmine, No. 17 (July-August 1977): 5 ((—))

THE CONCORDS (musical group)

C249 GOLDBERG, Marv, and Mike REDMOND: Concords discography *in* Record Exchanger, III/5 (No. 16 [Fall 1973]: 10 ((3, 5))

CONNOLLY, DOLLY

C250 KUNSTADT, Len, and Bob COLTON: Dolly Connolly *in* Record Research, No. 84 (June 1967): 7 ((3, 6, 7))

CONNORS, CAROL

C251 BARNES, Ken: Who is Carol Connors? *in* The Rock Marketplace, No. 8 (December 1974): 6, 34-35; discography p. 6; addenda in No. 9 (March 1975): 46 [As writer and performer] ((5))

CONNORS, STOMPIN' TOM

C252 FUCHS, Walter W.: Diskographie *in* Hillbilly, No. 37 (March 1971): 6; No. 38 (June 1971): 38 ((—))

CONQUEROR label

C253 [Discography] *in* Disc Collector, No. 15 (November 1960) thru No. 17 (May 1961): various paginations ((—))

COOKE, SAM

C254 Discography *in* McEWEN, Joe: Sam Cooke: a biography in words & pictures. [s.l.]: Sire Books, New York: Distributed by Chappell Music Co., 1977: 40-45 ((5))

C255 SEROFF, Doug: Sam Cooke discography *in* Record Exchanger, IV/1 (No. 17): [15] ((5))

THE COOL CREEK MARCH (song title)

C256 [[WOLFE, Charles K.: New light on the Cool Creek March *in* JEMF Quarterly, XII/1 (No. 41, Spring 1976): 1-8]]

THE COOLBREEZERS (musical group)

C257 LEE, Alan: [Discography] *in* Yesterday's Memories, II/4 (1976): 24 ((7))

COOPER, ALICE
See ALICE COOPER

COOPER, WILMA LEE

C258 COGSWELL, Robert: Wilma Lee and Stoney Cooper discography *in* JEMF Quarterly, XI/2 (No. 38, Summer 1975): 89–94 ((2, 3, 5, 6, 7))

C259 [Discography] *in* Country Western Express, No. 29 (May 1960): ? ((—))

COPAS, COWBOY

C260 [Discography] *in* Country Western Express, No. 10 [New series]: 6–7 ((—))

C261 [Discography] *in* Country Western Spotlight, No. 42 (June 1963): ? ((—))

CORONA DANCE ORCHESTRA
See also *Bibliography* Vol. 2, Jazz

C262 The Corona Dance Orchestra *in* Rhythm Rag, No. 4 (Spring 1977): 17–18 ((3, 7))

CORONET label

C263 The Coronet label (Western series) Australia *in* Country & Western Roundabout, I/2 (November 1962): 23 ((—))

C264 CRISP, David, and Hedley CHARLES: [Coronet label list] *in* Country & Western Spotlight, No. 12 (June 1977): 30–32 ((—))

C265 PERKINS, Ken, and Denys WILLIAMS: CBS-Coronet discography *in* Big Beat of the 50's, No. 22 (November 1979): 34–39; No. 25 (September 1980): 40–50; No. 26 (February 1981): 12–16; No. 27 (May 1981): 53–54 ((—))

CORSINI, IGNACIO

C266 Discografia *in* his Ignacio Corsini. Buenos Aires: Todo Es Historia, 1979: 69–94 ((3,6,7))

CORTEZ, DAVE

C267 MOHR, Kurt: Dave "Baby" Cortez discography *in* Shout, No. 104 (August 1975): 4–8; additions and corrections in No. 107 (February–March 1976): 22 and No. 108 (April–May 1976): 20 ((2, 3, 5, 7))

COSLOW, SAM

C268 Selective discography of Sam Coslow songs *in* his Cocktails for two: the many lives of giant songwriter Sam Coslow. New Rochelle, N.Y.: Arlington House, 1977: 273–285 ((5))

COSMA, VLADIMIR

C269 PECQUERIAUX, Jean-Pierre: Vladimir Cosma: filmography/discography *in* Soundtrack!, No. 27 (December 1981): 9–11; I/1 [New series?] (March 1982): 9–11 ((7))

COSMOS label

C270 TAYLOR, Barry: Cosmos discography *in* Trouser Press, No. 19 (April–May 1977): 23 ((—))

COSTELLO, ELVIS

C271 O'MALLEY, Michael, and Hans Jurgen KLITSCH: Costello so far! *in* Gorilla Beat, No. 9 (1981): 11–16; addendum in No. 11 (1981): 52–54 ((5, 7))

C272 SLUCHANSKY, Keith, et al.: Discovering Elvis Costello *in* Aware, No. 8 (Winter 1981–82): 8–26 ((7))

COSTELLO, TOM

C273 BARKER, Tony: Tom Costello discography *in* Music-Hall Records, No. 7 (June 1979): 12–13 ((3, 7))

COUNT FIVE (musical group)

C274 Discography *in* Bam Balam, No. 10 (November 1979): 21–22 ((5))

C275 SHAW, Greg: Discography *in* Who Put the Bomp, No. 12 (Summer 1974): 29 ((—))

COUNTRY GENTLEMEN (musical group)

C276 [Discography] *in* Country Western Express, No. 28 (March–April 1960): ? ((—))

COUNTRY JIM (pseud. of James Bledsoe)

C277 Country Jim discography *in* R & B Magazine, No. 8 (Fall 1971): [16a] ((3, 7))

COUNTRY JOE AND THE FISH
See also McDONALD, COUNTRY JOE

C278 HOGG, Brian: Country Joe and the Fish *in* Bam Balam, No. 10 (November 1979): 26–30; discography pp. 29–30 ((5))

COUNTRY MUSIC

C279 BRONNER, Simon J.: Old-time tunes on Edison records 1899–1923 *in* Journal of Country Music, VIII/1 (May 1979): 95–100 ((5))

C280 Discographies *in* FUCHS, Walter: Die Geschichte der Country Music. Bergisch Gladbach: Lubbe, 1980. 544 pp. ((—))

C281 Discographies *in* JEIER, Thomas: Lexicon der Country Music. Munich: Heyne, 1980. 623 pp. ((—))

C282 OSBORNE, Jerry: 55 years of recorded country/western Music. Phoenix: O'Sullivan, Woodside & Co., 1976 ((—))

C283 RUSSELL, Tony: Cowboys on record *in* Old Time Music, No. 8 (Spring 1973): 22 ((3, 6, 7))

C284 WHITBURN, Joel: Top Country & Western records: 1949–1971. Menomonee Falls, Wisc.: Record Research, 1972. 152 pp. ((4))

Country Music—Australia

C285 Discography *in* WATSON, Eric: Country music in Australia. Kensington, N.S.W.: Rodeo Publications, 1975: 131–172 ((3, 7))

Country Music—Japan

C286 SUZUKI, Katsushiko: A list of C & W 78 RPM records in early Japan. Tokyo: Suzuki, 1972. 44 pp. ((5))

Country Music—United States

C287 Discographies *in* FABER, Charles F.: The country music almanac. Lexington, Ky.: 1978– : vol. 1: 17–27; 34–91 ((—))

C288 Discography *in* GREEN, Douglas B.: Country roots: the origins of country music. New York: Hawthorn Books, 1976: 215–220 ((—))

C289 [[[Discography] *in* HORTSMAN, Dorothy A.: Sing your heart, country boy: an anthology of country lyrics. New York: Dutton, 1975]]

C290 [[Discography *in* MALONE, Bill: Country music U.S.A.: a fifty-year history. Austin: University of Texas Press, 1968: 367–374]]

C291 Discography *in* PRICE, Steven D.: Take me home; the rise of country and western music. New York: Praeger, 1974: [169]–176 ((—))

C292 Discography *in* SHESTACK, Melvin: The country music encyclopedia. New York: T. Y. Crowell Co., 1974: 325–375 ((—))

C293 Discographies *in* Stars of country music. Urbana: University of Illinois Press, 1975. 476 pp. ((—))

COUNTRY SNAKES (musical group)

C294 JOHANSSON, Thomas: LP disco Country Snakes *in* Kountry Korral Magazine (No. 2, 1980): 18 ((5))

COURTNEY, LOU

C295 MOHR, Kurt: Lou Courtney discography *in* Shout, No. 99 (October 1974): 1–2 ((3, 5, 6, 7))

COVAY, DON
See also *Bibliography* Vol. 2, Jazz

C296 TOPPING, Ray, and Clive RICHARDSON: Don Covay discography *in* Shout, No. 76 (May 1972): [3–8] ((2, 7))

COVENTRY HIPPODROME ORCHESTRA

C297   UPTON, Stuart: Coventry Hippodrome Orchestra *in* Commodore, No.
2 (Summer 1971): 3 + ((—))

COWBOY CARL

C298   WHITESELL, Rick: Cowboy Carl
discography *in* Goldmine, No. 49
(June 1980): 180 ((5))

COX, BILL

C299   EARLE, E.: [Discography] *in* Disc
Collector, No. 13–15 [n.d., 1960?]: ?
((2, 3, 6, 7))

COYNE, KEVIN

C300   Kevin Coyne discography *in* Trouser
Press, No. 25 (January 1978): 28
((—))

CRADDOCK, BILLY "CRASH"

C301   Billy "Crash" Craddock discography
in Music World and Record Digest
Weekly News, No. 52 (July 4, 1979):
[6] ((—))

C302   SMART, Peter: Crashing in at last *in*
Kommotion, No. 10–11 (Winter 1975–
76): 14–17; discography pp. 16–17
((5))

CRAMER, FLOYD

C303   Floyd Cramer discography *in* Kountry
Korral (No. 2, 1979): 10 ((—))

CRAWFORD, JESSE

C304   List of all phonograph records known
to have been made by Jesse Crawford
. . . transcriptions . . . *in* LANDON,
John W.: Jesse Crawford—poet of the
organ, wizard of the mighty Wurlit-
zer. Vestal, N.Y.: Vestal Press, 1974:
251–273 ((1, 7))

CREAM (musical group)

C305   MUIRHEAD, Bert: BCC—the power
trio *in* Trans-Oceanic Trouser Press,
II/1 (February–March 1975): 11–16
((—)) [Reprinted from Hot Wacks
magazine]

THE CREATION (musical group)

C306   ALDRIDGE, W. Lynne: The history
of the Creation: an interview with
Kenny Picket *in* Blitz, No. 42 (March–
April 1980): 10–13; No. 43 (July–
August 1982): 8–10; discography in
No. 42, p. 13 [Includes the Birds and
Mark 4] ((2, 5))

C307   Creation *in* The Rock Marketplace,
No. 5 (April 1974): 26–29, 35; discography pp. 29 and 35; addenda in No.
6 (July 1974): 43; No. 7 (October
1974): 43; No. 9 (March 1975): 46 [In-
cludes the Birds and Mark 4] ((5))

C308   Creation discography *in* Jamz, No. 4
(May 1972): 8 ((5))

C309   HOGG, Brian: Creation *in* Bam
Balam, No. 4 (June 1976): 3–6, 19;
addenda in No. 12 (November 1980):
33 and No. 14 (September 1982): 17
((2, 6a)) [Includes Mark 4 and the
Birds]

C310   The mods, pt. 4: painterman: the
Creation *in* Gorilla Beat, No. 6
(1980): 4–10; discography pp. 8–10;
addenda in No. 7 (1980): 16; No. 9
(1981): 48; No. 13 (1982): 71 ((5))
[Includes Mark 4]

CREST label

C311   [[Discography *in* New Kommotion,
No. 13 (c1976); addenda in No. 16
(Summer 1977): 42]]

CREWE, BOB

C312   Discography *in* INGRAM, George A.:
Producer of hits: the man behind the
Four Seasons: part one of the Bob
Crewe story *in* SMG, VI/2 (September
1977): 8–9 ((5))

THE CRICKETS (musical group)
See also HOLLY, BUDDY

C313   BLAND, Malcolm, comp.: Crickets:
individual discographies [of Sonny
Curtis, Jerry Naylor, Buzz Cason,
Tommy Allsup, Divid [sic] Box, Earl
Sinks, Jerry Allison, Nikki Sullivan,
and Keith Allison] *in* SMG, V/4 (January–February 1977): 6–9 ((—))

C314   CLEE, Ken: Buddy Holly/Crickets
discographies *in* Music World, No. 3
(March 1981): 34–37 ((—))

C315 Crickets discography *in* SMG, V/2 (Spring 1976): 7–14 ((—))

THE CRICKETS [black musical group, 1953–1955]

C316 GOLDBERG, Marv: The sweetest chirping in the world: the Crickets *in* Yesterday's Memories, I/2 (1975): 13 ((3, 7))

CROCKETT, HOWARD

C317 Discography *in* Kountry Korral, X/2 (April 1977): 38–39 ((3, 5))

CROSBY, BING

C318 Discography *in* BARNES, Ken: The Crosby years. New York: St. Martin's Press, 1980: 103–157 ((7))

C319 [[Bing Crosby discography 1950–1977. Ladd Publications: ?]]

C320 Complete list of Bing Crosby records *in* CROSBY, Ted: The story of Bing Crosby. Cleveland and New York: World Publishing Co., 1937: [206–207]; 1946 ed. has discography entitled "List of Bing Crosby's recordings": 229–239 ((—))

C321 HARDING, Ralph S., and Derek C. PARKER: The road to Bing Crosby *in* Vintage Jazz Mart/Palaver, No. 5 (September 1961): ? ((1, 3, 6, 7))

C322 MELLO, Edward J., and Tom McBRIDE: Crosby on record, 1926–1950. San Francisco: Mello's Music, 1950. 101 pp. ((1, 3, 4))

C323 Bing Crosby discography *in* MIZE, J. T. H.: Bing Crosby and the Crosby style. Chicago: Who is who in music, 1946: [143]–170; 1948 ed. has discography pp. 147–[168] ((—))

C324 A Crosby discography *in* ULANOV, Barry: The incredible Crosby. New York: Whittlesey House, 1948: 297–321 ((—))

C325 The complete recordings of Bing Crosby *in* ZWISOHN, Laurence J.: Bing Crosby: a lifetime of music. Los Angeles: Palm Tree Library, 1978: 65–142 ((1, 4, 7))

THE CROSSFIRES (musical group)

C326 DALLEY, Robert: Discography *in* Goldmine, No. 67 (December 1981): 168 ((1))

THE CROWNS (musical group)

C327 LAY, Rip: Arthur Lee Maye and the Crowns *in* Big Town Review, I/1 (February–March 1972): 7 ((3))

THE CROWS (musical group)

C328 BECKMAN, Jeff, and Hank FEIGENBAUM: Gee, it's the Crows *in* Big Town Review, I/2 (April–May 1972): 34 ((3))

CRUDUP, ARTHUR
See also *Bibliography* Vol. 2, Jazz

C329 GRAY, Mike: [Selected] list of his albums *in* Big Beat of the 50's, No. 21 (August 1979): 55–56 ((—))

THE CRUISERS (musical group)

C330 LEE, Alan: [Discography] *in* Yesterday's Memories, II/4 (1976): 24 ((7))

CRUMIT, FRANK

C331 EDWARDS, J.: [Discography] *in* Country Western Spotlight, No. 1 (November 1955): ?; No. 18 (April 1957): ? ((—))

C332 EDWARDS, J.: [Discography] *in* Country Western Spotlight (Special issue, September 1962): ? ((—))

C333 EDWARDS, John: [Discography] *in* Country & Western Spotlight, No. 7 (June 1976): 9–10; additions and corrections in No. 8 (September 1976): 10 ((—)) [Reprinted from Country Western Spotlight, No. 1 and 18]

C334 Frank Crumit; a discography *in* Discographer, I/2 (4th Quarter 1967): 1-141–1-151 ((3, 5, 7))

CRYING IN THE CHAPEL (song title)

C335 REDMOND, Mike: Crying in the chapel *in* Record Exchanger, IV/5 (December 1975): 26–27 ((5))

CRYSTAL label

C336   LEGERE, Will: [Discography] *in* Disc Collector, No. 16 (February 1961) and No. 17 (May 1961): various paginations ((—))

CRYSTAL SPRINGS RAMBLERS (musical group)

C337   [Discography] *in* Blue Yodler, No. 14 (1967): ? ((2, 3, 6, 7))

THE CRYSTALS (musical group)

C338   GONZALEZ, Fernando L.: The Crystals discography *in* Goldmine, No. 55 (December 1980): 17 ((1, 3, 5, 7))

THE CUES (musical group)

C339   GOLDBERG, Marv, and Mike REDMOND: On cue: the story of the Cues *in* Yesterday's Memories, I/3 (1975): 31–32 ((7))

CUMBERLAND MOUNTAIN FOLKS (musical group)

C340   Molly O'Day, Lynn Davis, and the Cumberland Mountain Folks: a biodiscography. Los Angeles: John Edwards Memorial Foundation, 1975. 35 pp. ((2, 3, 6, 7))

THE CUMBERLAND THREE (musical group)

C341   The Cumberland Three discography *in* Goldmine, No. 46 (March 1980): 152 ((—))

CURTIS, JIMMY

C342   Jimmy Curtis discography *in* Paul's Record Magazine (No. 16): 15 ((—))

CURTIS, LEE

C343   Liverpool beat *in* Gorilla Beat, No. 3 (1979): 29–33; discography pp. 32–33 ((—))

CURTIS, MAC

C344   BOYAT, Bernard: [Discography] *in* Big Beat, No. 10 (March–April–May 1974): 25 ((—))

C345   MILLAR, Bill: Mac Curtis *in* New Kommotion, No. 19 (Spring 1978): 4–11; discography pp. 10–11; addenda in No. 22 (1979): 64 ((1, 2, 3, 7))

C346   STRUM, Adri: Mac Curtis discography *in* Rockville/Roaring Sixties (March–April 1975): 30 ((1))

C347   TREUDE, Helmut: Mac Curtis disco *in* Country Corner, No. 51 (October 1976): 40–41 ((—))

CURVED AIR (musical group)

C348   FARBER, Jim: Curved Air: a brief blast *in* Trans-Oceanic Trouser Press, II/3 (June–August 1975): 34–35 ((—))

DJO label

D1   BAKER, Cary: Daran/Ja-Wes/DJO label listing *in* Shout, No. 83 (January 1973): [8–9]; additions and corrections in No. 95 (May 1974): 6 ((—))

DAB label

D2   SILVERMAN, Mike: Dab discography *in* Goldmine, No. 39 (August 1979): 6 ((—))

DA CAPO label

D3   LILIEDAHL, Karleric: Da Capo. Stockholm: Kungliga biblioteket, 1969. 23 l. (Nationalfonotekets diskografier, 10) ((3, 4, 6, 7))

DAFFAN, TED

D4   HEALY, R.: [Discography] *in* Country Directory, No. 4 [n.d., 1962?]: ? ((2, 3, 7))

DAKAS, WES, AND THE CLUB 93 REBELS (musical group)

D5   RUSSELL, Wayne: Discography *in* Rumble, III/2 (Winter 1975/6): 8–9 ((5))

DALE, DICK

D6   Dick Dale—disco *in* Rocking Regards, No. 6 (February 1977): 10–11 ((5))

D7   GEDEN, Robert: Dick Dale: king of the surf guitar *in* The Rock Marketplace, No. 9 (March 1975): 18–21; discography p. 21; addenda in No. 10 (June 1975): 50 ((5))

DALE, LARRY

D8   PEARLIN, Victor: Larry Dale: discography *in* Paul's Record Magazine, III/2 (February 1976): 16 ((3, 5))

DALHART, VERNON

D9   [COHEN, Norm], et al.: Vernon Dalhart preliminary discography *in* JEMF Quarterly, VI/4 (No. 20, Winter 1970) thru XIII/1 (No. 45, Spring 1977): various paginations ((3, 6, 7))

D10   [Discography] *in* Disc Collector, No. 17 (May 1961): ? ((—)) [Edison cylinders only]

D11   [Discography] *in* Folk Style, No. 13 [n.d., 1966?]: ? ((—))

D12   EDWARDS, J.: [Discography] *in* Country Western Spotlight, No. 3 (January 1956): ? ((—))

D13   EDWARDS, J.: [Discography] *in* Country Western Spotlight (Special issue, September 1962): ? ((—))

D14   HOFFMANN, M.: [Discography] *in* Disc Collector, II/1 thru III/16 (January–March 1952 on): ? ((—))

DALIDA

D15   Discographie francaise *in* PAGE, Christian: Dalida. Paris: PAC, 1981: 99–121 ((5))

DALLA, LUCIO

D16   Discografia *in* Lucio Dalla: il futuro dell'automobile, dell'anidride solforosa e di altre cose. Rome: Savelli, 1977: [155]–159 ((5))

DANA, VIC

D17   MASOTTI, Fred: Vic Dana discography *in* Goldmine, No. 22 (January 1978): 19 ((—))

DANCE ORCHESTRAS

D18   Discography *in* McCARTHY, Albert J.: The dance band era. London: Studio Vista, 1971; Spring Books, 1974; Philadelphia: Chilton, 1971: 171–173 ((—)) [A new ed. published under the title Big band jazz (London: Barrie and Jenkins, 1974; New York: Berkley Publishing Co., 1977) has a discography on pp. 356–360 ((—))]

D19   RUST, Brian: American dance band discography, 1917–1942. New Rochelle, N.Y.: Arlington House, 1975. 2 vols., 2,066 pp. ((1, 2, 3, 4, 6, 7)); FRASE, Bill: Corrections and additions *in* Record Research, No. 157–158 (September 1978): 8–9; No. 159–160 (December 1978): 15–16 ((3))

D20   RUST, Brian, and Edward S. WALKER: British dance bands 1912–1939. London: Storyville, 1973. 458 pp. ((2, 3, 6, 7)); FORBES, Sandy, and Jim HAYES: Dance band research: amendments & additions to "British dance bands 1912–1939" *in* Gunn Report, No. 49 (November–December 1974) thru No. 69 (August–September 1979): various paginations

D21   SCHUTTE, Joachim: Discographie des RBT-Orchesters und der anderen Formationen des Berliner Rundfunks. Menden: Der Jazzfreund, 1977. 80 pp. ((3, 7))

THE DANDELIERS (musical group)

D22   SURLEY, Ralph: The Dandeliers *in* Bim Bam Boom, No. 8 (December 1972): [39] ((—))

DANLEERS

D23   GOLDBERG, Marv: Danleers discography *in* Record Exchanger, V/2 (No. 24, October(?) 1977): 27 ((—))

DANN TRIO

D24   WILE, Ray: The Edison recordings of the Dann Trio (violin, cornet, piano) *in* Record Research, No. 146–147 (May–June 1977): 8–9 ((7))

DANNY & THE JUNIORS (musical group)

D25 VANCE, Marcia: Danny & the Juniors *in* Bim Bam Boom, II/6 (No. 12, 1974): 33 ((5))

THE DAPPERS (musical group)

D26 GOLDBERG, Marv, and Mike REDMOND: The Dappers *in* Yesterday's Memories, III/4 (1977): 33 ((7))

DARAN label

D27 BAKER, Cary: Daran/Ja-Wes/DJO label listing *in* Shout, No. 83 (January 1973): [8–9]; additions and corrections in No. 95 (May 1974): 6 ((—))

DARBY, TOM

D28 EDWARDS, J., et al.: [Discography] *in* Blue Yodler (Special edition, 1967): ? ((2, 3, 6, 7))

D29 EDWARDS, J., et al.: [Discography] *in* program notes for Testament Record T-3302, 1967[?]: ? ((2, 3, 6, 7))

THE DARELYCKS (musical group)

D30 PROVOST, Greg: The Darelycks history *in* Gorilla Beat, No. 6 (1980): 15–17; discography p. 17 ((1, 5))

DAREWSKI, HERMAN

D31 HAYES, Jim: Herman Darewski on 78s *in* Vintage Light Music, No. 9 (Winter 1977): 8 ((3, 7))

DARIN, BOBBY

D32 Darin on records *in* DIORIO, Al: Borrowed time: the 37 years of Bobby Darin. Philadelphia: Running Press, 1981: 236–246 ((5))

D33 GOVAARD, Stan: Bobby Darin USA Decca/Atco disco *in* Rockville International (January–February 1974): 7 ((3))

D34 MARTENS, Paul F.: Bobby Darin discography *in* Goldmine, No. 58 (March 1981): 23–24 ((—))

D35 TOD, Margaret: Bobby Darin discography, Part 1: singles *in* SMG, III/5

(April–May 1973): 2–5; Part 2: EP's and LP's in III/6 (June–July 1973): 4–9 ((3)) [Notes full album track listings and singles not issued on albums]

DARNELL, LARRY

D36 GRENDYSA, Peter: Larry Darnell discography *in* Goldmine, No. 50 (July 1980): 151 ((5))

THE DAVE CLARK FIVE (musical group)

D37 DE STIJL, Stu: It's glad over again *in* Outlet, No. 23 (June 1981): 38–41 ((5))

D38 KOLANJIAN, Steve: Rock retrospective: the Dave Clark Five *in* Rock It with Aware [no. 6?] (1979): 8–11 ((5))

D39 KORNMAN, Bill: The Dave Clark Five discography *in* Goldmine, No. 61 (June 1981): 10–13 ((1, 5))

DAVE DEE, DOZY, BEAKY, MICH & TICH (musical group)

D40 BANDS, Michel, and Hans Jurgen KLITSCH: Deedeedeebeeem'n'tee *in* Gorilla Beat, No. 11 (1981): 4–14; discography pp. 8–14; addenda in No. 13 (1982): 70 ((5))

D41 FLEURY, Joseph: DD, D, B, M&T (+ co.) discography *in* Jamz, No. 5 (c1972): 54, 90 ((5))

DAVIDSON, HARRY

D42 UPTON, Stuart: Harry Davidson and his Orchestra on 78 rpm (1944–1955) *in* Vintage Light Music, No. 19 (Summer 1979): 9–13 ((3))

D43 UPTON, Stuart: Harry Davidson organ records *in* Commodore, No. 10 (Summer 1973): 15 ((—))

DAVIES, CYRIL

D44 HOGG, Brian: Boom boom; British blue-eyed R&B [Davies discography] *in* Bam Balam, No. 13 (August 1981): 18 ((5))

DAVIES, RAY

D45 BETROCK, Alan: Ray Davies discography *in* Zig Zag, V/9 (No. 49,

January–February 1977): 23 ((5))
[Reprinted from Rock Marketplace]

D46   . . . by Ray Davies *in* The Rock Marketplace, No. 8 (December 1974): 26–28; discography p. 28; addenda in No. 9 (March 1975): 46 [Non-Kinks writing and production efforts] ((5))

DAVIS, JIMMIE

D47   [Discography] *in* Country & Western Spotlight, No. 27 (May 1981): 14–18 ((—))

D48   EDWARDS, J.: [Discography] *in* Country Western Spotlight, No. 5 (March 1956): ? ((—))

D49   EDWARDS, J.: [Discography] *in* Country Western Spotlight (Special issue, September 1962): ? ((—))

D50   WADIN, E.: [Discography] *in* Country Western Spotlight, No. 41 (March 1963): ? ((—))

DAVIS, LINK

D51   TOPPING, Ray: Link Davis: The man with the buzzin' sax *in* New Kommotion, No. 21 (1979): 18–19; addendum in No. 22 (1979): 64 ((1, 2, 3, 7))

DAVIS, LYNN
See CUMBERLAND MOUNTAIN FOLKS

DAVIS, PEE WEE

D52   Pee Wee Davis discography *in* Bluegrass Unlimited, VI/8 (February 1972): 15 ((3, 7))

THE SPENCER DAVIS GROUP

D53   HOGG, Brian: Spencer Davis Group *in* Bam Balam, No. 12 (November 1980): 18–21; discography pp. 20–21 ((5)) [Includes the Hellions, a predecessor of Traffic]

DAVIS, TYRONE
See also *Bibliography* Vol. 2, Jazz

D54   PRUTER, Robert: Tyrone Davis discography *in* Goldmine, No. 55 (December 1980): 24–25 ((5))

DAVIS label

D55   FLAM, Steve, et al.: Davis discography *in* Bim Bam Boom, I/2 (October–November 1971): 25; additions and corrections in I/3 (December 1971–January 1972): 21 ((—))

THE DAVIS SISTERS (musical group)

D56   Discography *in* Rocking Regards, No. 19 (March 1981): 4–7 ((—))

DAWKINS, JIMMY

D57   ARNIAC, Jean-Pierre, et al.: Jimmy Dawkins discographie *in* Soul Bag, XII/81–82 (1981): 10–11 ((2, 7))

BILLY DAWN QUARTETTE (musical group)

D58   MONDRONE, Sal: Rare sounds *in* Bim Bam Boom, No. 7 (September 1972): 41 ((3))

D59   WHITESELL, Rick, and Marv GOLDBERG: The Billy Dawn Quartette *in* Yesterday's Memories, III/4 (1977): 23 ((7))

DAWSON, SMOKY

D60   [Discography] *in* Country Western Spotlight, No. 51 (September 1965): ? ((—))

DAYLIGHTERS (musical group)

D61   PRUTER, Robert: Daylighters discography *in* Goldmine, No. 57 (February 1981): 13–14 ((5))

D62   PRUTER, Robert: Discography *in* Goldmine, No. 31 (December 1978): 26 ((5))

DEAN, EDDIE

D63   [COHEN, Norm]: Eddie and Jimmie Dean for American Record Corporation *in* JEMF Quarterly, VIII/2 (No. 26, Summer 1972): 69 ((3, 6, 7))

DEAN, JAMES

D64   James Dean on discs [records inspired by Dean or from motion picture soundtracks starring the actor] *in*

Nostalgia World, No. 3 (March 1979): 7 ((—))

D65 JONES, Wayne: Records relating to James Dean in Goldmine, No. 56 (January 1981): 21–22 ((—))

D66 McAULIFFE, Jon: Feast your eyes in Music World, No. 78 (September 1980): 6–7 ((—))

DEAN AND MARK (musical group)

D67 RUSSELL, Wayne: Dean and Mark in SMG, VI/2 (September 1977): 21 ((—))

DEB label

D68 FAULL, Trev: The Deb releases in Outlet, No. 12 (July 1979): 5–6; addenda in No. 16 (January 1980): 11 ((—))

THE DEBONAIRES (musical group)

D69 MOHR, Kurt: Debonaires discography in Hot Buttered Soul, No. 32 (July 1974): 6–7 ((3, 6, 7))

De CASTRO SISTERS (musical group)

D70 Discography in Paul's Record Magazine (No. 16): 22 ((5))

DECCA label
See also Bibliography Vol. 2, Jazz

D71 BENSON, Charles: Decca (red label) FM series. 1952 (78 rpm discs) in Country & Western Roundabout, II (No. 8, May–June–July 1964): 13–14 ((—))

D72 CRISP, Dave: Decca "Y" series 1949–1958 in Country & Western Spotlight, No. 13 (December 1977): 29–30 ((3, 5))

D73 CRISP, David: [Discography, X1000 Australian series] in Country Western Spotlight, No. 53 (March 1966): ? ((—))

D74 CRISP, David L.: Numerical list of hillbilly releases [in the Australian X1000 series] in Devil's Box, X/1 (March 1976): 4–8; X/2 (June 1976): 31–36 ((3))

D75 [Discography, 5000 U.S. Decca series] in Record Research, No. 23 (November 1960); No. 24 (December 1960); No. 72–74 (April thru June 1965): various paginations ((—))

D76 [Discography, South African Decca] in Folk Style, No. 10–11 [n.d.]: various paginations ((—))

D77 HAYES, Jim: [Label list, U.S. Decca] in Street Singer, No. 23 (July–August 1976):· 18–32 ((3, 6))

D78 HEARNE, Will Roy: [Discography, 5000 U.S. Decca series] in Country Western Spotlight, No. 42 (June 1963); No. 44 (December 1963) thru No. 51 (December 1965): various paginations ((—))

D79 PEARLIN, Victor: Decca's 48000 series in Paul's Record Magazine, III/3 (April 1976): [14–26]; additions and corrections in III/4 (May 1976): 4; III/5 (June 1976): 4 ((3, 4))

DEE, JOEY

D80 Joey Dee discography in Goldmine, No. 20 (November 1977): 6–7 ((5))

DEENE, CAROLE

D81 HOLLIE, Jon: Girls, girls, girls in Outlet, No. 8 (Xmas 1978): 24 ((—))

DEEP PURPLE (musical group)

D82 A Deep Purple discography in Rock It with Aware, II/4 (1976): 16–18 ((—)); Deeper into Deep Purple in II/5 (1977): 28–29 ((5))

DEEP RIVER BOYS (musical group)

D83 GRENDYSA, Peter: The Deep River Boys in Goldmine, No. 38 (July 1979): 10–11 ((3, 6, 7))

De GREGORI, FRANCESCO

D84 Discografia in his Francesco de Gregori, un mito. Rome: Lato side, 1980: 106–107 ((5))

De GROOT

D85 De Groot and the New Victoria Orchestra in Vintage Light Music, No. 24 (Autumn 1980): 6–7 ((—))

D86   MURRAY, Alastair: De Groot and
the Piccadilly Orchestra *in* Commodore, No. 11 (Autumn 1973): 2+
((—))

De JOHN SISTERS (musical group)

D87   Discography *in* Paul's Record Magazine (No. 16): 22 ((5))

DELERUE, GEORGES

D88   PECQUERIAUX, Jean-Pierre:
Georges Delerue: filmography/discog-
raphy *in* SCN (Soundtrack Collector's
Newsletter), V (No. 21, April 1980):
12–16; No. 22 (August 1980): 13–17;
No. 23 (Fall 1980): 13–15 ((—))

THE DELLS (musical group)

D89   [[[Discography] *in* Shout (No. 50 and
No. 61); additions and corrections in
No. 65 (April 1971): [2]]]

D90   SBARBORI, Jack: The Dells . . . 23
years later *in* Record Exchanger, IV/6
(No. 22, August 1975): 10–11 ((3, 5,
7))

DELMORE, ALTON

D91   WOLFE, Charles K.: Discography *in*
DELMORE, Alton: Truth is stranger
than publicity. Nashville: Country
Music Foundation Press, 1977:
179–188 ((2, 3, 6, 7))

DELMORE BROTHERS (musical group)

D92   EDWARDS, J.: [Discography] *in*
Country Western Spotlight, No. 4
(February 1956): ? ((—))

D93   EDWARDS, J.: [Discography] *in*
Country Western Spotlight (Special
issue, September 1962): ? ((—))

D94   GARBUTT, Bob: [Discography] *in*
Goldmine, No. 65 (October 1981):
16–17 ((—))

D95   WOLFE, Charles K.: The Delmore
Brothers: a pre-War discography *in*
Journal of Country Music, No. 6
(Spring 1975): [2]–11 ((3, 6, 7))

DELPHS, JIMMY

D96   MOHR, Kurt: [Discography] *in*
Shout, No. 34 (October 1968): [8–9]
((2, 3, 7))

DELPORTE, CHARLES

D97   Musique-enregistrement *in*
COGNIAT, Raymond: Delporte.
Paris: F. Hazan, 1977: 62 ((—))

THE DEL SATINS (musical group)

D98   KRAMER, Arlene: The Del Satins *in*
Bim Bam Boom, I/3 (December 1971–
January 1972): 9 ((—))

DELTA label

D99   KUDLACEK, Kerry: Delta *in* Blues
Research, No. 16: 11 ((3))

DELTA RHYTHM BOYS (musical group)

D100   GRENDYSA, Peter: Discography—
the Delta Rhythm Boys *in* Goldmine,
No. 34 (March 1979): 20–22; additions
and corrections in No. 38 (July 1979):
42 ((1, 3, 5, 7))

DELUXE label
See also *Bibliography* Vol. 2, Jazz

D101   HORLICK, Dick: Deluxe *in* Big Town
Review, I/1 (February–March 1972):
30–36 ((3, 5))

D102   ROTANTE, Tony: Deluxe label *in*
Record Research, No. 124 (November
1973): 10; No. 125/126 (February
1974): 14; No. 127 (May 1974): 8
((3))

THE DEL-VETTS (musical group)

D103   LIND, Jeff: The Del-Vetts *in* Kicks,
No. 2 (Winter 1979): 20 ((5))

THE DEL VIKINGS (musical group)

D104   PINGEL, Stefan: The Del Vikings *in*
Rocking Regards, No. 19 (March
1981): 14–20 ((3, 5))

THE DEL-VONS (musical group)

D105 GOLDBERG, Marv: [Discography] *in* Goldmine, No. 35 (April 1979): 43 ((5))

De MASI, FRANCESCO

D106 MARSHALL, James, et al.: Francesco De Masi; filmography/discography *in* Soundtrack!, No. 25 (Spring 1981): 15–20 ((5))

THE DEMENS (musical group)

D107 HINCKLEY, Dave: The Demens *in* Yesterday's Memories, III/1 (No. 9, 1976): 29–30 ((5))

DEMON label

D108 [Label list] *in* Paul's Record Magazine, IV/2 (No. 13/14, 1976): 54 ((—))

THE DENNISONS (musical group)

D109 SCHACHT, Janis: Dennisons *in* The Rock Marketplace, No. 9 (March 1975): 41 ((5))

DENVER, JOHN

D110 Discography, songbooks, TV, films, awards *in* DACHS, David: John Denver. New York: Pyramid Books, 1976: 89–93 ((—))

D111 Discography *in* FLEISCHER, Leonore: John Denver. New York: Flash, 1976: 76–79 ((5))

D112 PETER, Manfred: Discographie *in* Country Corner (March 1981): 41 ((55))

DERAM label

D113 American Deram *in* Rock It with Aware Magazine, II/4 (1976): 11–12 ((—))

D114 BETROCK, Alan: Early Deram singles *in* Jamz, No. 5 (c1972): 33–34 ((—)) [U.S. and U.K.]

D115 British Deram *in* Rock It with Aware Magazine, II/4 (1976): 9–11 ((5))

De SHANNON, JACKIE

D116 LEIGH, Spencer: Albums [and] singles by Jackie de Shannon *in* Who Put the Bomp, No. 15 (Spring 1976): 15; additions and corrections in No. 16 (October 1976): 60 and No. 17 (November 1976): 60, 62 ((5))

THE DESIRES (musical group)

D117 [Discography] *in* Time Barrier Express, No. 21 (January–February 1977): [13] ((5))

D118 SICURELLA, Joe: Discography *in* Bim Bam Boom, II/3 (No. 11, 1973): 39 ((—))

THE DETROIT EMERALDS
(musical group)

D119 MOHR, Kurt: The Detroit Emeralds: discography *in* Black Wax, No. 4 (May 1973): 3 ((2, 3, 6, 7))

DEVLIN, JOHNNY

D120 Discography *in* Big Beat of the 50's, No. 29 (October 1981): 9–11 ((—))

DEXTER, AL

D121 [Discography] *in* Disc Collector, No. 11 [n.d.]: ? ((—))

THE DIAMONDS (musical group)

D122 GONZALEZ, Fernando: Diamonds discography *in* Paul's Record Magazine (No. 16): 20 ((3, 5, 7))

D123 MINTER, Robert: Diamonds discography *in* Big Beat of the 50's, No. 20 (May 1979): 51–54 ((—))

D124 MONDRONE, Sal: Rare sounds *in* Bim Bam Boom, I/4 (February–March 1972): 23 ((3))

DICKENS, "LITTLE" JIMMY

D125 Little Jimmy Dickens record listing *in* Country Record Exchange, II (No. 11, January 1968): 4–10 ((—))

D126 MONCH, Edward K.: Jimmy Dickens [discography] *in* Hillbilly, No. 53 (December 1977): 8–14 ((7))

DIETRICH, MARLENE

D127 LYNCH, Richard C.: A Dietrich discography in Kastlemusik Monthly Bulletin, III/12 (E-49; December 1978): 1, 24; IV/1 (January 1979): 6-7 ((7))

DIG label

See also ULTRA label in Bibliography Vol. 2, Jazz

D128 Dig label in Hot Buttered Soul, No. 27 (February 1974): 6 ((3))

D129 PECORARO, Joe 'Jivin': Dig discography in Time Barrier Express, I/1 (September 1974): 25 [Includes Ultra] ((1))

D130 TOPPING, Ray: Dig label listing in Shout, No. 57 (July 1970): [6-8]; additions and corrections in No. 59 (October 1970): [8]; No. 65 (April 1971): [2] ((—))

DILL, DANNY

D131 Danny Dill discography in Kountry Korral, X/4 (August 1977): 27 ((3))

DILLESHAW, JOHN

D132 RUSSELL, Tony: Discography in Old Time Music, No. 36 (Summer 1981): 17 ((1, 2, 3, 6, 7))

DIMENSION label

D133 The Dimension label story in The Rock Marketplace, No. 6 (July 1974): 23; addendum in No. 7 (October 1974): 43 ((5))

DION

D134 WESTFALL, Bob, and Barry LAZELL: Dion discography in SMG, V/2 (Spring 1976): 15-18; additions and corrections in V/3 (Summer 1976): 17 ((5))

DIONN label

D135 Dionn label in Paul's Record Magazine, IV/2 (No. 13-14, 1976): 33; additions and corrections in No. 15 (January-February 1977): 40 ((—))

THE DIPLOMATS (musical group)

D136 [[[Discography] in Soul Music (No. 22): ?]]

DIRE STRAITS (musical group)

D137 Die Platten in DEWES, Klaus: Dire Straits. Munich: Heyne, 1980: 156-159 ((—))

DIRECT label

D138 FAULL, Trev: The Direct label detail of Nov 66 to Mar 67 period in Outlet, No. 16 (January 1980): 37 ((—))

DISCO MUSIC

D139 Discographies in BARONI, Sandro: Disco music. Rome: Arcana editrice, 1979. 173 pp. ((—))

D140 Discographies in HEIER, Thomas: Disco-Stars. Munich: Heyne, 1979 ((—))

D141 [[[Discography] in NEISSER, Horst F.: Jugend in Trance?: Diskotehken in Deutschland. Heidelberg: Quelle und Meyer, 1979: 118-127]]

LES DISQUES DU CREPUSCULE label

D142 FAULL, Trev: Les Disques du Crepuscule in Outlet, No. 24 (c1981/2): 24-25 ((—))

THE DIXIE CUPS (musical group)

D143 [[[Discography] in Shout, No. 105 (October-November 1975); additions and corrections in No. 108 (April-May 1976): 21]]

DIXON BROTHERS

D144 McELREA, R.: [Discography] in Country News and Views, II/1 (July 1963): 9-12 ((2, 3, 7)) [Dorsey Dixon and Beatrice Dixon]

D145 PARIS, Mike: Dixon Brothers (Dorsey and Howard) in Old Time Music, No. 10 (Autumn 1973): 15-16 ((3, 6, 7))

DO IT label

D146 FAULL, Trev: Do it—then do it some more *in* Outlet, No. 24 (c1981/2): 32–33 ((—))

DOBKINS, CARL, JR.

D147 Carl Dobkins Jr. discography *in* Goldmine, No. 51 (August 1980): 167 ((—))

DOCKETT, JIMMY

D148 MOHR, Kurt: [Further discographical information on the Interiors and Jimmy Dockett] *in* Shout, No. 83 (January 1973): [3–4] ((2, 3, 7))

DOCTOR BIRD label

D149 FAULL, Trev: Doctor Bird records: 1000 series, Jan–Dec 1966 *in* Outlet, No. 16 (January 1980): 30–33 ((—))

DR. HOOK (musical group)

D150 CORTESE, Bob: Dr. Hook album discography *in* Goldmine, No. 59 (April 1981): 21 ((—))

DOGGETT, BILL

D151 GRENDYSA, Peter: Bill Doggett discography *in* Goldmine, No. 39 (August 1979): 23–26 ((3, 5))

D152 MOHR, Kurt: Discography *in* Soul Bag (No. 17): 20–26 ((2, 3, 6, 7))

DOLENZ, MICKY

D153 CLAYTON, John: Micky Dolenz solo discography *in* Blitz, No. 26 (May 1978): 24; addenda in No. 28 (September–October 1978): 26 [Pre- and post-Monkees recordings] ((5))

DOMINION label

D154 [[BADROCK, Arthur: Dominion Records: a catalogue and history. Bournemouth, England: Talking Machine Review, 1976. 31 pp.]]

D155 Dominion label (pt. 3) *in* Gunn Report, No. 44 (January–February 1974): 37–38 ((3))

D156 HAYES, Jim: Dominion versus Piccadilly *in* Vintage Light Music, No. 14 (Spring 1978): 4–5 ((3))

DOMINO, FATS

See also *Bibliography* Vol. 2, Jazz

D157 Discography *in* Record Finder, I/2 (July 1978): [15] ((5))

D158 Discography: Fats Domino *in* Rock 'n' Roll International Magazine (Danish), No. 105 (April 1977): 23–24 ((—))

D159 Discography: Fats Domino (Imperial singles) *in* Record Exchanger, I/3 (No. 3, June 1970): 10–11 ((3))

THE DOMINOES (musical group)

D160 BECKMAN, Jeff: Billy Ward and the Dominoes *in* Big Town Review, I/1 (February–March 1972): 18 ((—))

DON & DEWEY (musical duo)

See also *Bibliography* Vol. 2, Jazz

D161 BARNEVELD, Archie: Don & Dewey disco *in* Rockville International (June–July 1974): 15–17 ((2, 3, 7))

D162 [[[Discography] *in* Shout, No. 107 (February–March 1976): 21–22]]

D163 HINCKLEY, Dave: Don and Dewey and . . . the Squires *in* Yesterday's Memories, III/2 (1977): 5 ((7))

DON AND JUAN (musical duo)

D164 MOHR, Kurt: [Discography] *in* Shout, No. 34 (October 1968): [8–9] ((2, 3, 7))

DONEGAN, LONNIE

D165 [Discography] *in* Disc Collector, No. 10 and 11 [n.d.]: ? ((—))

DONNER, RAL

D166 KOMOROWSKI, Adam: You don't know what you've got until you lose it: the Ral Donner story *in* New Kommotion, No. 21 (1979): 4–9; discography pp. 7, 9; addenda in No. 22 (1979): 64 ((1, 2, 3, 7))

D167 LAY, Rip: Ral Donner discography *in* Goldmine, No. 42 (November 1979): 10 ((5))

D168 WILSON, Terry: Ral Donner: Chicago's Elvis *in* Kommotion, No. 8 (Winter 1975): 23; addenda in No. 9 (Spring–Summer 1975): 5 and No. 10–11 (Winter 1975–76): 26 ((3, 5))

DONOVAN

D169 [[Discography *in* Country Corner, No. 5: 23]]

THE DOORS (musical group)

D170 HOGG, Brian: The Doors *in* Bam Balam, No. 9 (July 1979): 3–10; discography pp. 8–10 ((1, 5))

D171 Discography *in* HOPKINS, Jerry: No one gets out alive. New York: Warner Books, 1980: 383–386 ((5))

D172 MODDEMANN, Rainer: Let's open the Doors *in* Gorilla Beat, No. 8 (1980): 27–37; discography pp. 35–36; addenda in No. 9 (1981): 49–50 ((5))

D173 Discographie *in* MULLER, Herve: Jim Morrison au-dela des Doors. Paris: A. Michel, 1973: [184]–185 ((—))

DOOTO label

See also *Bibliography* Vol. 2, Jazz

D174 . . . discography *in* Record Exchanger, No. 4 (August–September 1970): [9–11] ((—))

DOOTONE label

D175 Dootone . . . discography *in* Record Exchanger, No. 4 (August–September) 1970): [9–11] ((—))

THE DOOTONES (musical group)

D176 GOLDBERG, Marv, and Rick WHITESELL: The Dootones *in* Yesterday's Memories, III/3 (1977): 20 ((7))

EL DORADOS (musical group)

D177 GALGANO, Bob: El Dorados and Kool Gents *in* Bim Bam Boom, I/2 (October–November 1971): 8 ((5))

D178 HINCKLEY, Dave: The El Dorados *in* Goldmine, No. 35 (April 1979): 36, 43 ((5))

DORE label

D179 BLAIR, John: Dore Records discography *in* Goldmine, No. 31 (December 1978): 14–16 ((5))

DO RE MI TRIO

D180 WHITESELL, Rick, and Marv GOLDBERG: The Do Re Mi Trio *in* Yesterday's Memories, III/4 (1977): 13 ((7))

DORSEY, LEE

See also *Bibliography* Vol. 2, Jazz

D181 Lee Dorsey discography *in* Hot Buttered Soul, No. 25 [n.d.]: 2–4 ((2, 3, 7))

DOUAI, JACQUES

D182 Discographie *in* Jacques Douai. Paris: Seghers, 1974: [147]–159 ((5)) (Collection poesie et chansons Seghers, 28)

DOUBLE SHOT label

D183 [[Double Shot label *in* Black Wax, No. 1 and 2]]

THE DOVELLS (musical group)

D184 CARELLA, Vinny J., and Ed ENGEL: Discography *in* Paul's Record Magazine, IV/1 (No. 12, August 1976): 12–14 ((5))

DOWN label

D185 Discography *in* Paul's Record Magazine, II/2 (August 1975): 10 ((1, 5))

DOWNING, AL

D186 TOPPING, Ray: Big Al Downing discography *in* Shout, No. 86 (June 1973): [2–4]; additions and corrections in No. 90 (November 1973): [8] ((2, 3, 5, 7))

THE DOWNLINERS SECT (musical group)

D187 Downliners Sect *in* Gorilla Beat, No. 2 (1979): 23–25; discography pp. 33–35; addenda in No. 8 (1980): 45; No. 9 (1981): 48; No. 13 (1982): 72 ((—))

D188 The Downliners Sect *in* The Rock Marketplace, No. 7 (October 1974): 35 ((5))

D189 HOGG, Brian: Downliners Sect *in* Bam Balam, No. 6 (November 1977): 20–21; addenda in No. 7 (c1978): 2 and No. 12 (November 1980): 33 ((2, 5))

DRAKE, JIMMY

D190 SMART, Peter: Nervous Norvus on disc *in* SMG, V/4 (January–February 1977): 19 ((5))

THE DREAMTONES (musical group)

D191 NASSAR, Ray, and Ken WICKMAN: Discography *in* Paul's Record Magazine (No. 17–18): 36 ((3))

DREW, PATTI

D192 PRUTER, Robert: Evanston soul: Patti Drew and the Drew-vels *in* Record Exchanger, V/4 (No. 26, 1978): 22–24 ((5))

D193 PRUTER, Robert: Patti Drew discography *in* It Will Stand, No. 20 (c1981): 15 ((5))

DREW label

D194 Drew label *in* Hot Buttered Soul, No. 27 (February 1974): 9 ((3))

DREXEL label

D195 STALLWORTH, Bob: The Gems and the Drexel label *in* Yesterday's Memories, II/2 (1976): 10 ((3, 7))

DRIEU LA ROCHELLE, PIERRE

D196 [[[Discography] *in* DESANTI, Dominique: Drieu La Rochelle: le seducteur mystifie. Paris: Flammarion, 1978: 459–460]]

THE DRIFTERS (musical group)

See also *Bibliography* Vol. 2, Jazz

D197 BEACHLEY, Chris: The Drifters: 1959–1971 *in* It Will Stand, No. 6 (c1979): 6–7; addenda in No. 7 (c1979): 3 and No. 24–25 (c1981): 22–23 ((1, 2, 5, 7))

D198 BEACHLEY, Chris, and Marv GOLDBERG: The Drifters: 1971–present *in* It Will Stand, No. 7 (c1979): 6–7; addenda in No. 24–25 (c1981): 6–7 ((2, 5))

D199 DAVIS, Jim, and Chris BEACHLEY: The Drifters 1953–1959 *in* It Will Stand, No. 5 (c1979): 6–7; addenda in No. 7 (c1979): 3 ((1, 2, 5, 7))

D200 GOLDBERG, Marv, and Mike REDMOND: Drifters discography *in* Record Exchanger, IV/2 (December 1974): 14–[24] ((3, 5))

D201 Discography *in* MILLAR, Bill: The Drifters. London: Studio Vista, 1971: 105–110; New York: Macmillan, 1971: 169–179 ((2, 3, 6, 7))

DRIFTWOOD, JIMMY

D202 HUNKEL, Georg: Discographie *in* Country Corner, No. 23 (March–April 1970): 4–6 ((—))

D203 Jimmy Driftwood discographie *in* Country Corner (September 1979): 5 ((—))

THE DROOGS (musical group)

D204 HOGG, Brian: The Droogs *in* Bam Balam, No. 4 (June 1976): 22–23 ((2))

DUBAS, MARIE

D205 Discographie *in* LAROCHE, Robert de: Marie Dubas. Paris: Candeau, 1980: 303–305 ((1, 3, 5))

D206 Discographie de Marie Dubas *in* Bulletin de la Phonotheque nationale, X/1–2 (1972): 17–20 ((—))

THE DUBS (musical group)

D207 NASSAR, Ray: The magic lingers on *in* Paul's Record Magazine, II/5 (November 1975): 7–8 ((—))

DUCKS DELUXE (musical group)

D208 SILVESTER, Pete: Ducks Deluxe
R.I.P. *in* Trans-Oceanic Trouser
Press, II/5 (November–December
1975): 21–23 ((5))

THE DUDES (musical group)

D209 The Dudes family tree *in* Who Put the
Bomp, No. 14 (Fall 1975): 31; addi-
tions and corrections in No. 15
(Spring 1976): 44 ((—))

DUDLEY, DAVE

D210 ROSENDAHL, Kjell: Dave Dudley:
Six days on the road: discografi *in*
Kountry Korral, X/1 (February 1977):
6 ((—))

THE DU DROPPERS (musical group)

D211 [Discography] *in* Yesterday's
Memories, III/4 (1977): 47 ((3, 7))

D212 GOLDBERG, Marv, and Mike RED-
MOND: Interview with the Du
Droppers *in* Bim Bam Boom, III/1
(No. 13, August–September 1974): 50,
52 ((3, 5))

DUFRESNE, DIANE

D213 [Discography] *in* Diane Dufresne:
album. Montreal: L'Aurore, 1976: 89
((—))

THE DUKAYS (musical group)

D214 Dukays' discography *in* PRUTER,
Robert: The Dukays *in* Record Exchanger, V/5 (No. 27, 1978): 4–7
((5))

DUMONT, CHARLES

D215 Discographie de Charles Dumont *in*
his Non, je ne regrette rien. Paris: G.
Authier, 1977: 215 ((—))

DUNCAN, JOHNNY

D216 [Discography] *in* Country Western Express, No. 18 (March 1958): ? ((—))

DUNCAN AND GODFREY (musical group)

D217 BARKER, Tony: Duncan and God-
frey *in* Music-Hall Records, No. 4
(December 1978): 79–[81] ((3, 7))

DUNES label

D218 MASOTTI, Fred, and Barry LAZELL:
Dunes label listing *in* SMG, IV/11
(June 1975): 6 ((—))

DUNHAM, MELLIE

D219 Mellie Dunham discography *in* JEMF
Quarterly, XII/3 (No. 43, Autumn
1976): 116–117 ((3, 6, 7))

DURANTE, JIMMY

D220 KUMM, Robert: Schnozzola in the
groove: a happy legacy of Jimmy
Durante recordings *in* Kastlemusik
Monthly Bulletin, V/6 (June 1980): 1,
12–13 ((5, 7))

DURBIN, DEANNA

D221 HAYES, Jim: Deanne Durbin on
English 78's *in* Commodore, No. 14
(Summer 1974): 6 ((—))

DURUTTI COLUMN (VINNI REILLY)

D222 FAULL, Trev: The new sound guitar
for the eighties *in* Outlet, No. 25
(April 1982): 14–15 ((2, 7))

DUSTY, SLIM

D223 BENSON, Charles: Slim Dusty record
listing; titles A to F *in* Country &
Western Roundabout, II (No. 6,
December 1963): 17; titles G to Q in
II (No. 7, February–March–April
1964): 15–16; titles R to T in II (No.
8, May–June–July 1964): 44–45; titles
U to Z in II (No. 9, November–December 1964): 19 ((—))

D224 Recordings released *in* his Slim Dusty.
Adelaide: Rigby, 1979: 195–206
((—))

D225 PRICE, A.: [Discography] *in* Country
Western Spotlight, No. 44 (December
1963): ? ((—))

DUTEIL, YVES

D226   Discographie *in* CHANDET, Elisabeth: Yves Duteil. Paris: Seghers, 1981: 173 (Collection poesie et chansons Seghers, 44) ((—))

DUVAL, AIME

D227   Discographie *in* ROEY, Johan de: Aime Duval en het religieuze chanson. Tielt: Lannoo, 1960: 112–118 ((—))

DYLAN, BOB

D228   BARTH, Mitchell: Dylan discography *in* Goldmine, No. 48 (May 1980): 15 ((5))

D229   CABLE, Paul: Bob Dylan; his unreleased recordings. London: Scorpion Press/Dark Star, 1978; New York: Schirmer Books, 1980. 192 pp. ((1, 2, 3, 4, 7))

D230   Discographie officiele [et] enregistrements pirates *in* DUCRAY, Francois: Dylan. Paris: A. Michel, 1975: [174–189] ((1, 5, 7))

D231   GENT, Sandy: A discography of Bob Dylan. Brooklyn, N.Y.: Gent, 1975. 17 pp. [Computer printout available from the compiler]

D232   Discography *in* GRAY, Michael: Song & dance man; the art of Bob Dylan. New York: Dutton, 1972: 305–327 ((—))

D233   HEYLIN, Clinton M.: Rain unravelled tales (the nightingale's code examined): A rumorography. 2nd ed. Cheshire, England: Heylin, 1982. 135 pp. ((1, 7))

D234   HOGGARD, Stuart: Bob Dylan: an illustrated discography. Oxford: Transmedia Express, 1978. 108 + 23 pp. ((1, 2, 4, 7))

D235   KROGSGAARD, Michael: Twenty years of recording: the Bob Dylan reference book. Copenhagen: Scandinavian Institute for Rock Research, 1981. 608 pp. ((1, 2, 4, 7))

D236   McAULIFFE, Jon: The Dylan collectibles *in* Music World and Record Digest Weekly News, No. 59 (August 22, 1979): 10–11; No. 60 (August 29, 1979): 12; No. 70 (January 1980): [14–15] ((—))

D237   Discografia oficial *in* ORDOVAS, Jesus: Bob Dylan. vol. 1 Madrid: Jucar, 1972: 103–107; vol. 2 Bob Dylan, 2. Madrid: Jucar, 1975: 243–246 ((—))

D238   Plattenhinweise *in* HiFi Stereophonie, XV/3 (March 1976): 270 ((—))

D239   Discographie *in* REDMOND, Alain: Les chemins de Bob Dylan. Paris: Epi, 1971: 179–182 ((—))

D240   RINZLER, Alan: Bob Dylan: the illustrated record. New York: Harmony, 1978. 120 pp. ((5))

D241   ROQUES, Dominique: The great white answers: the Bob Dylan bootleg records. Paris: Live Oak Productions, 1980. 200 pp. ((1, 3, 7))

D242   A Dylan discography *in* SCADUTO, Anthony: Bob Dylan. New York: Grosset & Dunlap, 1972: 275–276 ((5))

D243   A Dylan discography *in* SCADUTO, Anthony: Bob Dylan. New York: New American Library, 1979: 352–361 ((1, 5, 7))

D244   Discographies *in* SCHMITT, Walter: Bob Dylan halb & halb. Trier: Editions Treves, 1978: 2 vols.: vol. 1: 110–112; vol. 2: 207 ((1, 5, 7))

D245   Diskografie *in* STROOP, Jan: Bob Dylan bij benadering. Hoorn: West-Friesland, 1973: 183–189 ((1, 4, 5, 7))

D246   Discografi *in* TANG, Jesper: Bob Dylan smiler! Kobenhavn: Borgen, 1972: 227–[231] ((5))

D247   [[WILSON, Keith: Bob Dylan: a listing. Toronto: Wilson, 1977. 55 pp.]]

THE DYNAMICS (musical group)

D248   [[[Discography] *in* Soul Music (No. 27): ?]]

DYNAMITE label

D249   DAVELAAR, Gerard: Light on Dynamite! *in* Gorilla Beat, No. 11 (1981): 25–38; discography pp. 32–38 ((5)) [Includes the Skydog label]

E-TYPES (musical group)

E1   Discographie *in* Jazz Hot, No. 360 (April 1979): 51 ((—))

E2   SHAW, Greg: Discography *in* Who Put the Bomp, No. 12 (Summer 1974): 29 ((—))

EAGLE label

E3   LEGERE, Will: [Discography] *in* Disc Collector, No. 16 (February 1961): ? ((—))

EARLS, JACK

E4   BIG AL: Jack Earls *in* New Kommotion, No. 22 (1979): 15 ((1, 2, 3, 7))

E5   Jack Earls (Legendary Sun performers) *in* Big Beat of the 50's, No. 31 (May 1982): 39–41 ((—))

EARTH, WIND AND FIRE (musical group)

E6   Discographie *in* Jazz Hot, No. 360 (April 1979): 51 ((—))

E7   Earth, Wind and Fire discography *in* Down Beat, XLII (June 19, 1975): 15 ((—))

EAST TEXAS SERENADERS (musical group)

E8   HOEPTNER, F.: [Discography] *in* Disc Collector, No. 17 (May 1961): ? ((3, 7))

THE EASYBEATS (musical group)

E9   FLEURY, Joseph: Easybeats on my mind *in* The Rock Marketplace, No. 3 (October 1973): 3–5; discography p. 8 plus unnumbered leaf of addenda; further addenda in No. 5 (April 1974): 34; No. 6 (July 1974): 39; No. 9 (March 1975): 46 ((5))

E10   HOGG, Brian: The Easybeats *in* Bam Balam, No. 11 (June 1980): 24–30; discography pp. 27–30; addenda in No. 12 (November 1980): 33 ((5, 6a)) [Includes Vanda/Young compositions and post-Easybeats recordings]

EATON, ROLAND

E11   Roland Eaton disco *in* Kountry Korral, X/3 (June 1977): 17 ((3))

EBERLE, RAY

E12   Ray Eberle and his Orchestra *in* EDWARDS, Ernie, ed.: Glenn Miller alumni; a discography . . . Whittier, Calif.: Erngeobil Publications, 1966. 2 vols.; 2 pp. in vol. 1 ((7))

EBEROID label

E13   CARTER, Sydney H.: A catalogue of "Clarion" and Eberoid records. Bournemouth, England: Talking Machine Review, 1977. unpaged. ((5))

THE ECHOES (musical group)

E14   FAULL, Trev: Flashback to the early sixties with the Echoes *in* Instrumental Obscurities Unlimited, No. 18–19 (Winter 1977): 23–24 ((5))

ECLIPSE label

E15   HAYES, Jim: Eclipse *in* Gunn Report, No. 32 (February–March 1972): [34]–35; No. 34 (June–July 1972): [33–35] ((3))

EDDIE AND ERNIE (musical duo)

E16   SUZUKI, Hiroshi: Eddie & Ernie discography *in* Hot Buttered Soul, No. 36 (December 1974?): 3 ((2, 3, 6, 7))

EDDIE AND THE SHOWMEN (musical group)

E17   DALLEY, Robert J.: Eddie and the Showmen discography *in* Goldmine, No. 65 (October 1981): 173 ((5))

EDDY, DUANE

E18   Duane Eddy LP disco *in* Kountry Korral, XI/6 (1978): 61 ((—))

E19   GRANT, Jim: Twangs for the memories *in* New Kommotion, No. 20 (Summer 1978): 4–14; discography pp. 13–14; addenda in No. 22 (1979): 64 ((2, 3, 7))

E20   STRETTON, John, and Barry LA-ZELL: Duane Eddy discography *in* Rumble, III/3 (Spring 1976): 11-12 and III/4 (Summer-Autumn 1976): 6-11 ((5))

EDDY, NELSON
See also McDONALD, JEANETTE

E21   BERGMAN, J. Peter: Discography *in* KNOWLES, Eleanor: The films of Jeanette McDonald and Nelson Eddy. South Brunswick, N.J.: Barnes, 1975: 396-443 ((1, 3, 5, 6, 7))

E22   Nelson Eddy discography *in* CASTANZA, Philip: The films of Jeanette McDonald. Secaucus, N.J.: Citadel Press, 1978: 222-[224] ((—))

EDISON label
See also *Bibliography* Vol. 2, Jazz

E23   BETZ, Peter: Edison concert cylinder records; a catalogue of the series issued 1899-1901. London: City of London Phonograph & Gramophone Society, 1968. 22 pp. ((—))

E24   CARTER, Sydney H.: Blue Amberol cylinders. [n.p.]: Talking Machine Review. 130 pp. ((4))

E25   DETHLEFSON, Ronald: Edison Blue Amberol recordings, 1912-1914. Brooklyn, N.Y.: APM Press, 1980. 206 pp. ((4, 5))

E26   Edison Amberol records *in* New Amberola Graphic, No. 5-6, 8-12, 17-21 (Spring 1973 thru Spring 1977): various paginations ((—))

E27   HEALY, Bob: [Discography] *in* Disc Collector, No. 19 (November 1961): ? ((—))

E28   KARLIN, Fred J.: Edison Diamond discs, 50001-52651. Santa Monica, Calif.: Bona Fide Publications, 1972. 160 pp. ((—))

E29   WILE, Ray: [Discography, long-playing records] *in* Record Research, No. 88 (January 1968): 8; No. 90 (May 1968): 9 ((3, 6, 7))

E30   WILE, Raymond: Edison disc masters *in* Talking Machine Review, No. 5, 11-14, 16-18, 22-23, 25, 28, 30-31, 38-39, 42, 44, 54-55, 60-61 (August 1971 thru October-November 1979): various paginations ((3, 6, 7))

E31   WILE, Raymond R.: Edison disc recordings. Philadelphia: Eastern National Park and Monument Association, 1978. 427 pp. ((3, 5, 6))

EDISON BELL RADIO label

E32   ENGLUND, Bjorn: Swedish Edison Bell Radio *in* Talking Machine Review, No. 28 (June 1974): 122B-122D ((3, 6))

EDISON BELL WINNER label

E33   ADRIAN, Karlo: Numerical listing of Edison Bell Winner. Bournemouth, England: Talking Machine Review, 1975. 9 vols. ((3, 6))

EDMONDS, NORMAN S.

E34   DAVIS, Stephen F., and Robert E. NOBLEY: Norman Edmonds *in* Old Time Music, No. 9 (Summer 1973): 23 ((3, 6, 7))

EDMUNDS, DAVE

E35   Dave Edmunds discography *in* Trouser Press Press, No. 3 (1976): 63; addenda in Trouser Press, No. 19 (April-May 1977): 26 [Includes Love Sculpture and production work] [Revised version of discography in Trouser Press, No. 12] ((5))

E36   Dave Edmunds discography *in* Who Put the Bomp, No. 15 (Spring 1976): 21 ((5))

E37   SCHULPS, Dave, and Alan BET-ROCK: [Discography] *in* Trans-Oceanic Trouser Press, II/6 (No. 12, February-March 1976): 14-15 ((5))

E38   WAGSTAFF, John: The story of Dai & Basher, part 1: Dave Edmunds *in* Gorilla Beat, No. 13 (1982): 55-67; discography pp. 56-57 ((1, 5)) [Includes Rockpile, Love Sculpture, Image, Human Beans, solo recordings, productions, and session work]

EDWARDS, TIBBY

E39   MILNE, Rick: Tibby Edwards discography *in* Big Beat of the 50's, No. 23 (March 1980): 21-22 ((—))

ELECTRIC LIGHT ORCHESTRA
(musical group)

E40 BELLMAN, Joel: Electric Light Orchestra discography *in* Trouser Press, III/5 (No. 17, December 1976–January 1977): 7; additions and corrections in No. 18 (February–March 1977): 2 ((—))

ELECTROLA label

E41 "Goldene Trichter" series *in* Talking Machine Review, No. 59 (August 1979): 1585 ((—))

THE ELEGANTS (musical group)

E42 The Elegants *in* Time Barrier Express, No. 21 (January–February 1977): [11] ((—))

E43 Elegants discography *in* Paul's Record Magazine, No. 15 (January–February 1977): 7 ((5))

ELEKTRA label

E44 An Elektra Records disco: part 1 *in* Rock It with Aware Magazine, II/3 (no date; 1976?): 10–14 [numerical listings]; additions & correxions [sic] in II/4 (1976): 4 ((—))

ELEKTRADISK label

E45 HEALY, Bob: [Discography] *in* Disc Collector, No. 15 (November 1960): No. 16 (February 1961): ? ((—))

ELEN, GUS

E46 BARKER, Tony: Gus Elen *in* Music-Hall Records, No. 5 (February 1979): [84]–95 ((3, 7)); additions in No. 6 (April 1979): 103

THE ELGINS (musical group)

E47 MOHR, Kurt: Elgins discography *in* Black Wax, No. 5 (May 1973): 12, 18 ((2, 3, 6))

ELLIOTT, JACK

E48 FEUSS, Jurgen: Jack Elliott—disco *in* Country Corner, No. 26 (December

1970): 4–5; No. 30 (December 1971): 28 ((—))

E49 MARSHALL, Jim, and John DODDS: Jack Elliott disc listing *in* Country News & Views, II/4 (April 1964): 24–25 ((—))

ELLISON, ANDY

E50 Andy Ellison discography *in* Trouser Press Press, No. 3 (1976): 63; addendum in No. 19 (April–May 1977): 26 [Solo work, John's Children, and Jet] [Revised version of discography in Trouser Press, No. 12] ((5))

E51 BETROCK, Alan: Discography *in* Trans-Oceanic Trouser Press, II/6 (February–March 1976): 15 ((5))

ELLISON, LORRAINE

E52 MOHR, Kurt, and Rob HUGHES: Lorraine Ellison discography *in* Shout, No. 103 (June 1975): 6–7; additions and corrections in No. 107 (February–March 1976): 22 ((2, 3, 5, 7))

THE EMANORS (musical group)

E53 BERGER, Ken: Emanors discography *in* Record Exchanger, III/5 (No. 16 [Fall 1973]): 14 ((—))

EMBASSY label

E54 FAULL, Trev: An introduction to the Embassy label *in* Outlet, No. 26 (July 1982): 29–31 ((—))

EMBER label

E55 TISOVEC, Tony, and Steve FLAM: Ember discography *in* Bim Bam Boom, I/6 (July 1972): 27 ((3))

E56 TOPPING, Ray: Ember label listing *in* Shout, No. 51 (January 1970): [1–6] ((—))

THE EMBERS (musical group)

E57 MOHR, Kurt: Discography *in* Shout, No. 95 (May 1974): 4 ((3, 5, 7))

THE EMPIRES (musical group)

E58 HINCKLEY, Dave: The Empires *in* Yesterday's Memories, III/4 (1977): 29 ((7))

EMSLAND HILLBILLIES (musical group)

E59 SCHUMANN, E. Reinald: Emsland Hillbillies *in* Hillbilly, No. 60 (September 1979): 26 ((—))

THE ENCHANTERS (musical group)

E60 WILSON, Jim: The Enchanters *in* Hot Buttered Soul, No. 29 (April 1974): 9; No. 31 (June 1974): 2–3 ((2, 3, 7))

END label

E61 TOPPING, Ray: End label listing *in* Shout, No. 67 (June 1971): [2, 5–7] ((3))

E62 TRABOSCI, Tom: End discography *in* Bim Bam Boom, No. 7 (September 1972): 33 ((3))

ENDSLEY, MELVIN

E63 SWAN, Johnny: Melvin Endsley: singin' blues *in* Kommotion, No. 10–11 (Winter 1975–76): 11–13 ((3))

ENJOY label

E64 [Discography] *in* Record Exchanger, III/1 (No. 12 [Winter 1972]): [12–13] ((3))

ENO, BRIAN

E65 Eno discography *in* Trouser Press, No. 3 (1976): 64 [Includes Roxy Music, solo records, productions, and session work] ( )—))

ENTWHISTLE, JOHN

E66 SCHULPS, David: Ox tales *in* Trans-Oceanic Trouser Press, II/5 (June–August 1975): 20–23 ((—))

ERA label

E67 BEZANKER, Paul: ERA Records *in* Paul's Record Magazine, IV/1 (August 1976): 33; IV/2 (No. 13–14, 1976): 49–51; No. 16: 31–35; additions and corrections in No. 15 (January–February 1977): 39 ((3))

E68 MARTIN, Tony: ERA label listing *in* Hot Buttered Soul, No. 15 (February 1973): 7 ((—))

ESCHER, RUDOLF

E69 Discography *in* Key Notes, No. 5 (No. 1, 1977): 17 ((—))

THE ESCORTS (musical group)

E70 SCHACHT, Janis: Escorts *in* The Rock Marketplace, No. 9 (March 1975): 37–38 ((5))

ESCUDERO, LENY

E71 Discographie *in* Leny Escudero. Paris: Seghers, 1973: [187]–190 ((—)) (Collection poesie et chansons Seghers, 20)

ESQUERITA (ESKEW REEDER)

E72 TOPPING, Ray: Esquerita discography *in* New Kommotion, No. 21 (1979): 15–16 ((2, 3, 7))

THE ETERNALS (musical group)

E73 Eternals discography *in* Time Barrier Express, II/8 (No. 18, August–September 1976): 15 ((5))

E74 SICURELLA, Joe: Evolution of a group; the Eternals *in* Big Town Review, I/3 (July–August 1972): 7 ((5))

ETIQUETTE label

E75 Etiquette discography *in* Kicks, No. 2 (Winter 1979): 25 ((—))

EVANS, PAUL

E76 VANCE, Marcia: Paul Evans: discography *in* Paul's Record Magazine, II/6 (December 1975): 15 ((—))

EVERLAST label

E77 Discography *in* Record Exchanger, III/1 (No. 12 [Winter 1972]): [12–13] ((3))

EVERLY, DON

E78 Don Everly LP disco *in* Kountry Korral Magazine (No. 2, 1980): 16 ((—))

THE EVERLY BROTHERS (musical group)

E79 FOURNIER, Alain: Discographie *in* Big Beat, No. 14 (November 1976): 11 ((5))

E80 MILLER, Billy: The beat 'n sound of the Everly Brothers *in* Kicks, No. 1 (Spring 1979): 5–13; discography pp. 10–13 ((1)) [Includes solo recordings]

E81 MUSKEWITZ, Jim: Everly Brothers discography *in* Record Exchanger, VI/2 (No. 29, 1980): 10–11 ((5))

EXCLUSIVE label

E82 PEARLIN, Victor: Exclusive Records discography *in* Paul's Record Magazine (No. 17–18): 46–50 ((3))

FABIAN

F1 Discography (U.S. and U.K.) *in* SMG, III/12 (April–May 1974): 4–6 ((—))

F2 HANDEL, Rob van den: Fabian *in* Rock 'n' Roll International Magazine, No. 107 (July–August 1977): 23 ((—))

FACENDA, TOMMY

F3 DUNHAM, Bob: Tommy Facenda: ring! ring! goes the bell: school is in! *in* New Kommotion, No. 15 (Spring 1977): 27–28; discography p. 28 ((3, 5))

F4 FACENDA, Tommy: Discography *in* Goldmine, No. 28 (September 1978): 21 ((—))

FACES (musical group)

See also SMALL FACES

F5 Discography *in* PIDGEON, John: Rod Stewart and the changing Faces. St. Albans: Panther, 1976: 135–142 ((1, 5))

FACTORY label

F6 FAULL, Trev: Factory Records *in* Outlet, No. 19 (June 1980): 2–4; plus updates in subsequent issues ((1, 5))

FACTORY-BENELUX label

F7 FAULL, Trev: Factory-Benelux *in* Outlet, No. 24 (c1981–82): 25 ((—))

FAIRBURN, WERLEY

F8 MASOTTI, Fred, and Peter SMART: Werley Fairburn on disc *in* Kommotion, No. 10–11 (Winter 1975– 76): 40 ((—))

FAIRPORT CONVENTION (musical group)

F9 FARBER, Jim: Fairport Convention *in* Trans-Oceanic Trouser Press, II/5 (November–December 1975): 6–7 ((—))

FALKENBURG, FRANZ

See listing for STEVENS, ERNEST L.

FAME, GEORGE

F10 Discography *in* HOGG, Brian: Boom boom: British blue-eyed R&B *in* Bam Balam, No. 13 (August 1981): 30–32 ((5)) [Covers Fame and the Blue Flames]

F11 WILLMORE, Mike: Georgie Fame— English discography *in* Who Put the Bomp, No. 8 (Fall–Winter 1971): 12–13 ((—))

FAMILY (musical group)

F12 Family history *in* Bedloe's Island, No. 4 (Spring 1972): 4, 15 ((—))

F13 SEEBACHER, Karl: Family *in* Trans-Oceanic Trouser Press, II/2 (April–May 1975): 20–23 ((—))

FARLOWE, CHRIS

F14 [Discography] *in* HOGG, Brian: Boom boom: British blue-eyed R&B *in* Bam Balam, No. 13 (August 1981): 27–29 ((5))

FARON'S FLAMINGOS (musical group)

F15 Liverpool beat *in* Gorilla Beat, No. 2 (1979): 36–37 ((5))

FARR, GARY & THE T-BONES
(musical group)

F16   Gary Farr & the T-Bones *in* The Rock
Marketplace, No. 7 (October 1974): 38
((5))

THE FASCINATORS (musical group)

F17   NEWMAN, Ralph M.: Tony Passal-
acque and "The" Fascinators *in* Bim
Bam Boom, No. 7 (September 1972):
22 ((3))

FAST label

F18   Fast product *in* Gorilla Beat, No. 2
(1979): 15 ((—))

FAYE, ALICE

F19   [[Discography *in* MOSHIER, W.
Franklyn: The Alice Faye movie book.
Harrisburg, Pa.: A & W Visual
Library, 1974: 185]]

FAYRUZ

F20   Discography *in* Fayrouz, legend and
legacy. Washington, D.C.: Forum for
International Art and Culture, 1981:
96–102 ((5))

FEATHERS, CHARLIE

F21   Charlie Feathers discografi *in* Kountry
Korral (December 1973): 33 ((—))

F22   The greatest rocker of all time . . .
Charlie Feathers *in* Bim Bam Boom,
III/1 (No. 13, August–September
1974): 42 ((5))

F23   KOMOROWSKI, Adam: Charlie
Feathers discography *in* New Kommotion, No. 22 (1979): 36–37 ((1, 2, 3,
7))

F24   STRUM, Adri, et al.: Charlie Feathers
(on wax) *in* Rockville International,
No. 95 (November–December 1974):
16–17 ((1, 2, 3, 6, 7))

F25   TREUDE, Helmut: Charlie Feathers
disco *in* Country Corner, No. 50 (July
1976): 16–20 ((7))

FEDERAL label

F26   ROTANTE, Tony: Federal label
[F12000 series] *in* Record Research,
No. 111 (July 1971) thru No. 117
(August 1972), No. 121 (March 1973),
No. 122 (June 1973): various pagina-
tions ((3))

FELU, EDUARDO

F27   Discografia *in* SABATO Y LEON
BERNAROS, Ernesto: Eduardo Felu.
Madrid: Jucar, 1974: [183]–190 ((—))

FENDER, FREDDY

F28   [[Discography *in* New Kommotion,
No. 13 (c1976); addenda in No. 14
(Winter 1977): 31 and No. 22 (1979):
64]]

THE FENDERMEN (musical group)

F29   BETZ, Olaf: The Fendermen *in* Rocking Regards, No. 16 ([July?] 1979): 22
((—))

F30   RUSSELL, Wayne: Discography *in*
SMG, V/3 (Summer 1976): 26 ((3))

FENTON, SHANE & THE FENTONES
(musical group)

F31   TOMRLEY, Alan, and Barbara
TOMRLEY: Discography *in* SMG,
VI/4 (October 1980): 6 ((5))

FENTON label

F32   WAGENAAR, Al: Western Michigan
rock in the sixties *in* Ballroom Blitz,
No. 23 (November 1977): 24–26;
discography p. 26 [Includes other
western Michigan small labels] ((—))

FERGUSON, ROBERT

F33   PEARLIN, Victor: H-Bomb Ferguson
in Music World and Record Digest
Weekly News, No. 44 (May 9, 1979):
6 ((—))

FERNWOOD label

F34   [[Discography *in* New Kommotion
(c1976); addenda in No. 14 (Winter
1977): 31]]

F35   HAWKINS, Martin: Fernwood label
discography *in* Goldmine, No. 64
(September 1981): 196 ((5))

FERRY, BRYAN

F36 Discography *in* BALFOUR, Rex: The Bryan Ferry story. London: Michael Dempsey, 1976: 126–128 ((—))

FESTIVAL label [Australia]

F37 BENSON, Charles: [Festival label] *in* Country & Western Roundabout, II/7 (February–March–April 1964): 8 ((—))

FICTION label

F38 FAULL, Trev: Discography so far: Fiction label *in* Outlet, No. 15 (November 1979): 13 ((—))

FIELDS, ARABELLA

F39 LOTZ, Rainer E.: Arabella Fields *in* Storyville, No. 89 (June–July 1980): 171–177 ((3))

FIELDS, HAPPY FANNY

F40 Discography *in* BARKER, Tony: Happy Fanny Fields *in* Music-Hall Records, No. 8 (August 1979): [36]–40 ((3, 7))

FIELDS, LILY

F41 Lily Fields discography *in* Shout, No. 89 (September 1973): [6–7] ((2, 3, 7))

THE FIFTH ESTATE (musical group)

F42 The Fifth Estate discography *in* Goldmine, No. 57 (February 1981): 20 ((3, 5))

FILLIS, LEN

F43 FENTON, Alasdair: Len Fillis, master guitarist *in* Vintage Light Music, No. 31 (Summer 1982): 5–6 ((3))

FINCK, HERMAN

F44 [Discography] *in* Commodore, No. 4 (Winter 1971): 10 ((—))

FISHER, SHUG

F45 [COHEN, Norm, and Ken GRIFFIS]: Preliminary notes to a Shug Fisher discography *in* JEMF Quarterly, X/2 (No. 34, Summer 1974): 60–61 ((1, 3, 6, 7))

FISHER, SONNY

F46 MILLAR, Bill: That rockin' daddy *in* New Kommotion, No. 25 (1980): 15–16; discography (by Ray TOPPING): 16 ((2, 3, 7))

FISHER, TOM

F47 CALLAHAN, Mike: Tom Fisher discography *in* Goldmine, No. 49 (June 1980): 174–175 ((—))

THE FI-TONES (musical group)

F48 GROIA, Phil: The Fi-Tones *in* Bim Bam Boom, I/5 (April–May 1972): 37 ((3))

THE FIVE AMERICANS (musical group)

F49 THOM, Mike: Five Americans discography *in* Full Blast, I/1 (Winter 1979): 38–42 ((7))

THE FIVE BLUE NOTES (musical group)

F50 GOLDBERG, Marv, and Mike REDMOND: The 5 Blue Notes *in* Yesterday's Memories, I/4 (1975): [16] ((7))

THE FIVE CHIMES (musical group)

F51 VANCE, Marcia, and Marv GOLDBERG: The Arthur Crier story *in* Yesterday's Memories, III/4 (1977): 10 ((7))

THE FIVE CROWNS (musical group)

F52 GOLDBERG, Marv: The Five Crowns *in* Big Town Review, I/2 (April–May 1972): 14 ((3))

F53 SILVANI, Louie: Discography *in* Bim Bam Boom, I/4 (February–March 1972): 28 ((3))

THE FIVE DISCS (musical group)

F54 FLAM, Steve: The Five Discs *in* Bim Bam Boom, I/4 (February–March 1972): 10 ((3))

THE FIVE ECHOES (musical group)

F55   PRUTER, Robert: Five Echoes discography *in* Goldmine, No. 35 (April 1979): 38 ((5))

THE FIVE JADES (musical group)

F56   Five Jades discography *in* Time Barrier Express, II/4 (January–February 1976): [7] ((—))

THE FIVE KEYS (musical group)

F57   Discography: The Five Keys *in* Record Exchanger, No. 1 (December 1969): 6–11 ((3, 6, 7))

F58   The Five Keys [discography] *in* Shout, No. 105 (October–November 1975): 13–16; additions and corrections in No. 108 (April–May 1976): 105 ((3, 5, 6))

THE FIVE PENNIES (musical group)

F59   GOLDBERG, Marv: The Five Pennies *in* Yesterday's Memories, II/2 (1976): 22 ((7))

THE FIVE RED CAPS (musical group)

F60   GRENDYSA, Pete: The Red Caps *in* Yesterday's Memories, II/1 (1976): 9–10 ((7))

F61   GRENDYSA, Pete: Sneakin' back *in* Bim Bam Boom, III/1 (No. 13, August–September 1974): 59–60 ((3))

THE FIVE SATINS (musical group)

F62   GALGANO, Bob, et al.: [Discography] *in* Bim Bam Boom, I/3 (December 1971–January 1972): 6 ((—))

F63   NASSAR, Ray: Discography *in* Paul's Record Magazine, II/3 (September 1975): 11–12; additions and corrections in II/4 (October 1975): 11–12 ((5))

THE FIVE WILLOWS (musical group)

F64   MOHR, Kurt, et al.: Discography *in* Shout, No. 37 (November 1968): [8–9] ((2, 3, 6, 7))

THE FLAIRS (musical group)

F65   GOLDBERG, Marv, and Mike REDMOND: Discography *in* Record Exchanger, III/2 (No. 13 [February 1973]): ((—))

F66   GOLDBERG, Marv, and Rick WHITESELL: The Flairs *in* Yesterday's Memories, III/2 (1977): 8–10 ((7))

F67   McCUTCHEON, Lynn: The Flairs *in* Bim Bam Boom, I/6 (July 1972): 13 ((3))

FLAMIN' GROOVIES (musical group)

F68   HOGG, Brian: Flamin' Groovies *in* Bam Balam, No. 5 (February 1977): 17–23; discography pp. 18–23; addenda in No. 7 (c1978): 2 and No. 12 (November 1980): 33–34 ((2, 3, 6a)) [Includes the Charlatans, Loose Gravel, and Hot Knives]

F69   ISLER, Scott: Flamin' Groovies discography *in* Trans-Oceanic Trouser Press, No. 13 (April–May 1976): 22 ((5))

F70   SHAW, Greg: Flamin' Groovies discography *in* Who Put the Bomp, No. 13 (Spring 1975): 12; addenda in No. 15 (Fall 1975): 44 ((5))

THE FLAMINGOS (musical group)

See also *Bibliography* Vol. 2, Jazz

F71   GONZALEZ, Fernando L.: Flamingos 45 discography *in* Goldmine, No. 24 (March 1978): 13 ((1, 5, 7))

F72   TANDREDI, Carl: Chance recordings of the Flamingos *in* Bim Bam Boom, I/4 (February–March 1972): 6 ((3, 5, 7))

FLANAGAN, RALPH

F73   Ralph Flanagan Orchestra *in* EDWARDS, Ernie, ed.: Glenn Miller alumni; a discography . . . Whittier, Calif.: Erngeobil Publications, 1966. 2 vols.: 13 pp. in vol. 2 ((3, 6, 7))

F74   MYRICK, Thomas: Ralph Flanagan and his Orchestra: discography *in* The Record Finder, I/7 (June 1979): 6, 16–17 ((3, 7))

FLASH label

F75 TISOVEC, Tony: Flash label listing *in* Shout, No. 63 (February 1971): [6–7]; additions and corrections in No. 65 (April 1971): [2] ((3))

FLATT, LESTER

F76 [Discography] *in* Country News & Views, V/2 (October 1966): ? ((2, 3, 7))

F77 [Discography] *in* Country Western Express, No. 16 (October–December 1957): ? ((—))

F78 KUYKENDALL, Pete: Discography *in* Disc Collector, No. 14 (June 1960): 37–44 ((2, 3, 7))

F79 RONALD, R. J.: Discography *in* Bluegrass Unlimited, II/7 (January 1968): [2]–4; II/8 (February 1968): 5–10 ((2, 3, 7)) [Reprinted from Country News & Views, V/2 (October 1966)]

FLEETWOOD MAC (musical group)

F80 Discographic information *in* CARR, Roy: Fleetwood Mac. New York: Harmony Books, 1978. 120 pp. ((5))

F81 Fleetwood Mac *in* Jamz, No. 4 (May 1972): 15–17; discography pp. 16–17 ((5))

F82 GOODMAN, Arnie: Fleetwood Mac discography *in* Fleetwood Mac: #1 then (U.K.) and #1 now (U.S.) *in* Aware Magazine, II/5 (1977): 18–23, 30 ((5))

FLETCHER, DARROW

F83 PRUTER, Robert: Darrow Fletcher discography *in* Goldmine, No. 63 (August 1981): 144 ((5))

F84 PRUTER, Robert: Discography *in* Goldmine, No. 47 (April 1980): 160 ((5))

FLING label

F85 Discography *in* Record Exchanger, III/1 (No. 12 [Winter 1972]): [12–13] ((3))

FLIP label

F86 TISOVEC, Tony: Flip label listing *in* Shout, No. 62 (January 1971): [8–10]; additions and corrections in No. 65 (April 1971): [2] ((5))

FLOYD, FRANK
(aka HARMONIKA FRANK)

F87 Discographie *in* Big Beat, No. 13 [n.d.]: 23 ((1, 2, 3, 6, 7))

F88 LAVERE, Steve: Frank Floyd disco *in* Rockville International (June–July 1974): 54–55 ((1, 3, 5, 7))

FLYRIGHT label

F89 HAWKINS, Martin: Flyright label discography, 500-series *in* Goldmine, No. 62 (July 1981): 157, 169 ((—))

FOG CITY label

F90 STANTON, Roy: Fog City label list *in* Shout, No. 99 (October 1974): 6 ((3))

FOGERTY, JOHN

F91 SANDE, Tor M.: Diskografi *in* R-O-C-K, No. 5/6 (February 1981): 16–17 ((5))

FOLK-STAR label

F92 KUYKENDALL, Pete: [Discography] *in* Disc Collector, No. 14 (August 1960): ? ((—))

FONANDERN, GUSTAV

F93 LILIEDAHL, Karleric: Gustav Fonandern (1880–1960). Stockholm: Kungliga biblioteket, 1978. 30 l. (Nationalfonotekets diskografier, 511) ((3, 4, 6, 7))

FONOTIPIA label

F94 ANDREWS, H. Frank: A Fonotipia fragmentia—part 5: "Food for thought"—an interjection *in* Talking Machine Review, No. 45 (April 1977): 963–982 ((—))

FONTAINE, EDDIE

F95 BOELENS, Milou: Eddie Fontaine *in* Rock 'n' Roll International Magazine (Danish), No. 104 (February 1977): [2] ((5))

F96 Discography *in* Eddie Fontaine: a voice of the fifties *in* SMG, VI/3 (January 1978): 25, 27 ((3, 5))

F97 SMART, Peter: Eddie Fontaine discography *in* Goldmine, No. 58 (March 1981): 19 ((1, 3, 5, 7))

FONTANA label

F98 [Discography] Fontana Records *in* Bomp! No. 21 (March 1979): 41, 44, 46 ((—))

FONVILLE, BOB

F99 SKURZEWSKI, Bob, and Terry SKURZEWSKI: Fonville/Hernandez discography *in* Goldmine, No. 62 (July 1981): 156 ((—))

FORD, FRANKIE

F100 BOELENS, Milou: Discography *in* Rock 'n' Roll International Magazine (Danish), No. 103 (November 1976): [8] ((5))

F101 KINDER, Bob: Frankie Ford discography *in* Record Exchanger, VI/1 (No. 28 [December 1979?]): 24–25 ((—))

FORD, TENNESSEE ERNIE

F102 [Discography] *in* Disc Collector, II/3 (July–September 1952): ? ((—))

FORMBY, GEORGE

F103 HAYES, Jim: George Formby on English 78s *in* Street Singer, No. 33 (October–November–December 1973): 47–49; No. 34 (January–February–March 1974): 57–61 ((3))

F104 Discography *in* RANDALL, Alan, and Ray SEATON: George Formby. London: Allen, 1974: 187–192 ((—))

FORREST, HELEN

F105 SIXSMITH, Robert A.: Discography *in* FORREST, Helen: I had the craz-

iest dream. New York: Coward, Mc-Cann & Geoghegan, 1982: 245–306 ((1, 2, 3, 5, 6, 7))

FORTUNE, JOHNNY

F106 DALLEY, Robert J.: Johnny Fortune record discography *in* Goldmine No. 55 (December 1980): 168–169 ((5))

FORTUNE label

F107 Fortune Records: their story *in* Paul's Record Magazine, II/5 (November 1975): 25, 32–37 ((3, 5))

F108 TISOVEC, Tony: Fortune discography *in* Bim Bam Boom, I/5 (April–May 1972): 21–22 ((3, 5))

THE FORTUNES (musical group)

F109 TIBBS, Gary: The Fortunes: they've had their troubles *in* Blitz, No. 35 (March–April 1980): 16–17; discography p. 17 ((5))

FOSTER, CHUCK, AND HIS ORCHESTRA

F110 SALAS, Frank: Recordings by Chuck Foster and his Orchestra *in* Afterbeat, I/5 (February 1971): 7 ((—))

FOSTER, GARLEY
See entry for CAROLINA TARHEELS

THE FOUR ARISTOCRATS (musical group)

F111 RUST, Brian: Discography *in* Gunn Report, No. 76 (January–March 1981): 16 ((2, 3, 6, 7))

THE FOUR BARS (musical group)

F112 WHITESELL, Rick, and Marv GOLDBERG: The Four Bars *in* Yesterday's Memories, III/3 (1977): ? ((7))

THE FOUR BEL-AIRES (musical group)

F113 LEE, Alan: [Discography] *in* Yesterday's Memories, II/4 (1976): 22 ((7))

THE FOUR BUDDIES (musical group)

F114 Four Buddies discography *in* Record Exchanger, III/1 (No. 12 [Winter 1972]): [15] ((1, 5))

F115 HINCKLEY, Dave: Four Buddies discography *in* Goldmine, No. 35 (April 1979): 39 ((—))

THE FOUR FRESHMEN (musical group)

F116 The Four Freshmen *in* Classic Wax, No. 3 (May 1981): 9 ((5))

THE FOUR IMPERIALS (musical group)

F117 Four Imperials discography *in* Goldmine, No. 12 (September-October 1976): 30 ((5))

4 in 1 label

F118 HAYES, Jim: Toward a numerical catalogue, serial 00 to serial 90, August 1932 to April 1934, part 3 *in* Gunn Report, GR 56 (January-February 1976): 4; part 4 in GR 57 (May-June 1976): 15; part 5 in GR 58 (July-August 1976): 14; part 6 in GR 59 (September-October 1976): 10-11; part 7 in No. 62 (March-April 1977): 7-[9]; part 8 in No. 63 (May-June-July 1977): 5-7; part 9 in No. 64 (August-September-October 1977): 5-6; part 10 in No. 65 (November-December 1977): 5-6 ((3))

THE FOUR J'S (musical group)

F119 VANCE, Marcia: Danny and the Juniors *in* Bim Bam Boom, II/6 (No. 12, 1974): 33 ((5))

THE FOUR JEWELS (musical group)

F120 LEE, Alan: [Discography] *in* Yesterday's Memories, II/4 (1976): 22 ((7))

THE FOUR KNIGHTS (musical group)

F121 WHITESELL, Rick: Discography— the Four Knights *in* Goldmine, No. 40 (September 1979): 28A ((3, 5, 7))

F122 WHITESELL, Rick: Discography: the Four Knights *in* Goldmine, No. 58 (March 1981): 187 ((3, 5, 7))

THE FOUR NEONS (musical group)

F123 [Discography] *in* Record Exchanger, III/1 (No. 12 [Winter 1972]): [28] ((3))

THE FOUR PHARAOHS (musical group)

F124 ARDIT, Dave: The Four Pharaohs *in* Bim Bam Boom, III/1 (No. 13, August-September 1974): 55 ((5))

THE FOUR PREPS (musical group)

F125 McDOWELL, Mike: The Four Preps discography *in* Blitz, No. 38 (November-December 1980): 20 ((5))

THE FOUR SEASONS (musical group)

F126 INGRAM, George: Discography, 1970-1975 *in* SMG, IV/11 (June 1975): 4-5 ((5))

F127 INGRAM, George A.: The Four Seasons' early careers, part 1: 1953-1956 *in* SMG, III/10 (January-February 1974): 8-9; part 2: the Four Lovers, 1956-1959 in III/11 (March 1974): 5-7; part 3: from the Romans to the Seasons, 1960-1962 in IV/1 (June 1974): 2-4 ((5))

F128 VANCE, Marcia, and Ralph M. NEWMAN: The Four Seasons *in* Bim Bam Boom, II/3 (No. 9, 1973): 58 ((—))

F129 WOODWARD, Rex: Four Seasons discography 1970-1980 *in* Goldmine, No. 63 (August 1981): 22 ((5))

THE FOUR TOPS (musical group)

F130 GONZALEZ, Fernando L.: The Four Tops discography *in* Goldmine, No. 63 (August 1981): 8 ((3, 5, 7))

THE FOUR TUNES (musical group)

F131 GOLDBERG, Marv, and Mike REDMOND: The Brown Dots & the Four Tunes *in* Yesterday's Memories, I/1 (1975): 18-20 ((7))

THE FOUR VAGABONDS (musical group)

F132 WHITESELL, Rick, et al.: The Four Vagabonds *in* Yesterday's Memories, II/3 (1976): 10 ((7))

THE FOUR VIRGINIANS (musical group)

F133 RORRER, Kinney: The Four Virginians *in* Old Time Music, No. 14 (Autumn 1974): 18 ((3, 7))

FOX, CURLEY

F134 A preliminary Curley Fox discography *in* Bluegrass Unlimited (April 1977): 16 ((2, 3, 5, 7))

F135 A preliminary Curley Fox discography *in* Devil's Box, No. 27 (December 1974): 18–21; additions and corrections in IX/1 (March 1975): 5 and IX/2 (June 1975): 56 ((2, 3, 7))

FOXX, INEZ AND CHARLIE

F136 CUMMINGS, Tony: Inez & Charlie Foxx discography *in* Shout, No. 37 (November 1968): [5–7] ((2, 3, 6, 7))

FRAMPTON, PETER

F137 Discography *in* ADLER, Irene: Peter Frampton. New York: Quick Fox, 1979: 94–96 ((5))

F138 Discography *in* DALY, Marsha: Peter Frampton. New York: Grosset & Dunlap, 1978: 167 ((5))

F139 Chronological discography of recordings by Peter Frampton *in* KATZ, Susan: Frampton!: an unauthorized biography. New York: Jove Publications, 1978: 188–190 ((5))

F140 Peter Frampton discography *in* Trouser Press Press, No. 3 (1976): 64 [The Herd, Humble Pie, and solo] ((5))

F141 Chronologia de canciones *in* SIERRA I FABRA, Jordi: Peter Frampton: . . . alive! Barcelona: Musica de Nuestro Tiempo, 1977: 103–109 ((—))

FRANCOIS, CLAUDE

F142 Claude Francois, 1939–1978 Hifi Stereo (May 1978): 131–132 ((—))

F143 Discographie *in* GOISE, Denis: Claude Francois: le bien-aime. Paris: Menges, 1978: [155]–167 ((5, 7))

FRANKLIN, ARETHA

F144 Discography *in* JONES, Hettie: Big star fallin' mama; five women in black music. New York: Viking Press, 1974: [139]–140 ((—)) [Includes listings for Ma Rainey, Bessie Smith, Mahalia Jackson, Billie Holiday, and Aretha Franklin]

FRANKLIN, BOBBY

F145 MOHR, Kurt, and Tony CUMMINGS: Bobby Franklin *in* Black Wax, No. 6 (July 1973): 13 ((2, 3, 6, 7))

FRANKLIN, IRENE

F146 DEBUS, Allen G.: Irene Franklin, vaudeville headliner *in* New Amberola Graphic, No. 37 (Summer 1981): 4–9 ((—))

FRANKLIN, REX

F147 [[Discography *in* Country Corner, No. 1: 19]]

F148 [Discography] *in* Country Western Spotlight, No. 43 (September 1963): ? ((—))

F149 FRANKLIN, Rex: Rex and Noelene diskographie *in* Hillbilly, No. 60 (September 1979): 20–22 ((5, 7))

FRAZIER, AL

F150 Al Frazier discography *in* Al Frazier & his groups *in* Record Exchanger, VI/1 (No. 28 [December 1979?]): 4–11 ((5))

FREBERG, STAN

F151 Discography—Stan Freberg *in* Record Finder, I/2 (July 1978): [3] ((5))

THE FREDERIC (musical group)

F152 WAGENAAR, Al: Frederic discography *in* Blitz!, No. 32 (September–October 1979): 9–12 ((—))

FREEMAN, BOBBY

F153 MOHR, Kurt: Bobby Freeman discography *in* Shout, No. 51 (January

1970): [6–8]; additions and corrections in No. 55 (May 1970): [5] ((2, 3, 6, 7))

FREEMAN, "PORKY" HUGH

F154 BEAR, Gene, and Ken GRIFFIS: A preliminary Porky Freeman discography *in* JEMF Quarterly, XI (Spring 1975): 35, 37 ((3))

FREENY HARMONIZERS (musical group)

F155 RUSSELL, Tony: Freeny Harmonizers *in* Old Time Music, No. 8 (Spring 1973): 18 ((3, 7))

FREENY'S BARN DANCE BAND

F156 RUSSELL, Tony: Freeny's Barn Dance Band *in* Old Time Music, No. 8 (Spring 1973): 15 ((3, 6, 7))

FRICKE, JANIE

F157 LANEHED, Stefan: Janie Fricke LP disco *in* Kountry Korral Magazine (No. 2, 1980): 24–25 ((5))

FRIED, GERALD

F158 MARSHALL, James: Gerald Fried: filmography/discography *in* Soundtrack Collector's Newsletter, IV (No. 18, July 1979): 13–16; HAMMONDS, Roger: additions in No. 20 (January 1980): 8 ((5))

FRIPP, ROBERT

F159 Robert Fripp *in* Trouser Press Collector's Magazine, IV/2 (November–December 1981): 5 ((—))

F160 SLABICKY, Ihor: Fripp: the finale *in* Trans-Oceanic Trouser Press, II/2 (April–May 1975): 32–34 ((—))

FRIZZELL, LEFTY

F161 BINGE, Reimar, et al.: Lefty Frizzell-Disco *in* Country Corner, No. 46 (October 1975): 14–15 ((—))

F162 WEIZE, Richard A.: Lefty Frizzell diskographie *in* Hillbilly, No. 45 (December 1975): 9–15; additions and corrections in No. 48 (September 1976): 29–31 ((1))

FUGI (real name Ellington Jordan)

F163 Fugi *in* Black Wax, No. 3 (March–April 1973): 6 ((2, 3, 6, 7))

FUGS (musical group)

F164 Platten *in* KAISER, Rolf-Ulrich: Fuck the fugs. Cologne: Kinder d. Geburtstagspresse, 1969: 28–29 ((—))

THE BOBBY FULLER FOUR (musical group)

F165 HOGG, Brian: Bobby Fuller Four *in* Bam Balam, No. 14 (September 1982): 29–32, 39 ((5))

FUNICELLO, ANNETTE

F166 [Discography] *in* Goldmine, No. 28 (September 1978): 21 ((—))

F167 KUHN, Donald: Annette discography *in* Goldmine, No. 17 (July– August 1977): 68 ((—))

F168 YOKITIS, Vince: Annette Funicello *in* Kastlemusik Monthly Bulletin, IV/9 (September 1979): 22 ((—))

F169 YOKITIS, Vince J.: Annette Funicello discography *in* Record Finder, I/2 (July 1978): [13] ((—))

FURY label

F170 Fury discography *in* Record Exchanger, II/6 (No. 11 [Fall 1972]): 12; additions and corrections in III/3 (No. 14, April 1973): 23 ((3))

G & T label

G1 RUST, Brian: (British) Berliner, G & T and Zonophone 7-inch records *in* Talking Machine Review, No. 63–64 (Autumn 1981): 1726–1758 ((2, 3, 7))

GNP CRESCENDO label

G2 SHAW, Greg: GNP Crescendo discography *in* Who Put the Bomp, No. 12 (Summer 1974): 11 ((—))

GABRIEL, PETER

G3 Peter Gabriel discography *in* Trouser Press, No. 20 (July 1977): 14 ((—))

GAGNON, ANDRE

G4   Discography in ROZON, Lucie:
Andre Gagnon. Montreal: Libre Expression, 1978: 203–205

GAINSBOURG, SERGE

G5   Discographie in his Serge Gainsbourg.
Paris: Seghers, 1969: [185]–[186]
((—))

G6   Discographie in PIERREFEU,
Micheline de: Gainsbourg.
Paris: Brea, 1980: [133]–137
((—))

GALA label

G7   Gala . . . and all that jazz in Matrix,
No. 60 (August 1965): 9+; No. 71
(June 1967): 11+ ((—))

GALORE, MAMIE

G8   MOHR, Kurt, and Gilles PETARD:
Mamie Galore discography in Shout,
No. 83 (January 1973): [2–3] ((2, 3,
7))

GAMBLE label

G9   Gamble label in Paul's Record Magazine, No. 13–14 (September–December
1976): 33; additions and corrections in
No. 15 (January–February 1977): 40–
41 ((—))

GANDINO, LEONELLI

G10   HAYES, Jim: The "Imperial" Gandino in Commodore, No. 11 (Autumn
1973): 8 ((—))

GARDEL, CARLOS

G11   Discografia in ANGEL MORENA,
Miguel: Historia artistica de Carlos
Gardel: estudio cronologico. Buenos
Aires: Editorial Freeland, 1976:
163–217 ((—))

G12   Discografia in CONSUELO, Jorge
Miguel: Gardel, mito-realidad. Buenos
Aires: Pena Lillo, 1964: 91–100
((—))

G13   Discografia in DEFINO, Armando:
Carlos Gardel. Buenos Aires: Fabril,
1968: 221–237 ((—))

G14   Lista discografia completa de Carlos
Gardel in FERNANDEZ, Augusto:
Por siempre, Carlos Gardel. Buenos
Aires: Ediciones Latinprens Latinoamericanas, 1973: 199–209 ((—))

G15   Discografia in MATAMORO, Blas:
Carlos Gardel. Buenos Aires: Centro
Editor de America latina, 1971: 106–
111 ((—))

G16   Discografia original completa e
revisada in SILVA, Federico: Informe sobre Gardel. Montevideo:
Alfa, 1971: 87–107 ((—))

GARLAND, JUDY

G17   Judy on records in DIORIO, Al: Little girl lost. New Rochelle, N.Y.:
Arlington House, 1974: 229–267 ((7))

G18   LYNCH, Richard C.: A Judy Garland
movie songbook in Kastlemusik
Monthly Bulletin, V/9 (September
1980): 1, 12–13 ((4))

GARRETT, JO ANN

G19   Jo Ann Garrett discography in
Goldmine, No. 24 (March 1978): 15
((5))

G20   PRUTER, Robert: Jo Ann Garrett
discography in Goldmine, No. 56
(January 1981): 173 ((5))

GASKIN, GEORGE JEFFERSON

G21   LORENZ, Kenneth M.: George J.
Gaskin (1863–1920) in Kastlemusik
Monthly Bulletin, III/10 (E-47; October 1978): 9–11; III/11 (E-48,
November 1978): 9–11 ((5, 7))

GATEWAY SINGERS (musical group)

G22   Gateway Singers album discography in
Goldmine, No. 45 (February 1980):
130 ((—))

GATKINS, BILL

G23   Cherokee Ramblers discography in
DANIEL, Wayne W.: Bill Gatkins &
his jug band in Old Time Music, No.
37 (Autumn 1981–Spring 1982): 13
((3, 6, 7))

GATLIN, LARRY

G24 ANDERL, Peter: Larry Gatlin diskographie *in* Hillbilly, No. 49 (December 1976): 39 ((5))

GAYE, MARVIN

G25 Discographie *in* Jazz Hot, No. 332 (November 1976): 17 ((—))

GAYLE, CRYSTAL

G26 Crystal Gayle LP discography *in* Kountry Korral (No. 2, 1979): 15 ((—))

GEE label

G27 TOPPING, Ray, et al.: Gee label listing *in* Shout, No. 66 (May 1971): [2–5] ((3))

G28 TRABOSCI, Tom: Gee discography *in* Bim Bam Boom, No. 7 (September 1972): 31–32 ((3))

GEM label

G29 GONZALEZ, F.: [Discography] *in* Yesterday's Memories, III/4 (1977): 35 ((3, 7))

THE GEMS (musical group)

G30 PRUTER, Robert: Gems discography *in* Goldmine, No. 43 (December 1979): 26 ((5))

G31 STALLWORTH, Bob: The Gems and the Drexel label *in* Yesterday's Memories, II/2 (1976): 10 ((3, 7))

GENESIS (musical group)

G32 [[[Discography] *in* Genesis lyrics. London: Sidgwick & Jackson, 1979: 93]]

G33 [Discography] *in* GALLO, Armando: Genesis: the evolution of a rock band. London: Sidgwick & Jackson, 1978: on end papers ((—))

G34 Discography *in* GALLO, Armando: Genesis, I know what I like. Los Angeles: D.I.Y., 1980: 158–163 ((5, 7))

G35 Genesis . . . discography *in* Trouser Press, No. 20 (July 1977): 14 ((—))

G36 [[Discography *in* VOGORITO, Giampiero: Genesis. Milan: Gammalibri, 1981: 101–128]]

THE GERMAN BLUE FLAMES (musical group)

G37 HEBING, Alfred: The German Blue Flames *in* Gorilla Beat, No. 9 (1981): 27–35; discography p. 32 ((—))

THE GERMAN BONDS (musical group)

G38 Beat in Germany, pt. 2 *in* Gorilla Beat, No. 2 (1979): 18–19 ((5))

GERRY AND THE PACEMAKERS

G39 Gerry and the Pacemakers LP discography *in* Kountry Korral (No. 1, 1979): 20 ((—))

G40 KOLANJIAN, Steve: Rock retrospective: Gerry and the Pacemakers *in* Aware Magazine, II/5 (1977): 8–9 ((5))

G41 SOAP, Joe: Gerry & the Pacemakers *in* Outlet, No. 26 (July 1982): 11–14 ((5))

GHETTO label

G42 Ghetto label *in* Hot Buttered Soul, No. 26 (January 1974): 11 ((3))

GIANT label

G43 Giant label *in* Hot Buttered Soul, No. 25 (December 1973?): 11 ((3))

GIBB, ANDY

G44 KOLANJIAN, Steve: Andy Gibb discography *in* Rock It with Aware, [no. 6?] 1979: 36 ((1, 5))

GIBBONS, STEVE

G45 BAJEMA, Roaland: Gibbons *in* Gorilla Beat, No. 14 (1982): 14–21; discography pp. 18–20; Uglies/Balls family tree p. 21 ((5))

GIBSON, BOB

G46 Bob Gibson album discography *in* Goldmine, No. 65 (October 1981): 186 ((—))

GIBSON, DON

G47 Don Gibson LP discography *in* Kountry Korral (No. 2, 1979): 17 ((—))

G48 SELLERS, Morgan: Don Gibson LP listing *in* Country Record Exchange, I/8 (September 1967): 5-6 ((—))

GIGI (musical group)

G49 MOHR, Kurt: Gigi discography *in* Black Wax, No. 6 (July 1973): 17 ((2, 3, 6, 7))

GILKYSON, TERRY AND THE EASY RIDERS (musical group)

G50 WEIZE, Richard A.: Terry Gilkyson and the Easy Riders diskographie *in* Hillbilly, No. 58 (March 1979): 8-12 ((—))

GILLEY, MICKEY

G51 COFFEY, Dan: The complete Mickey Gilley discography *in* The Big Beat of the 50's, No. 20 (May 1979): 26-33 ((2, 3, 7))

G52 GRANT, Dick, and Adam KOMOROWSKI: Mickey Gilley: the urban cowboy *in* New Kommotion, No. 25 (1980): 18-25; discography pp. 23-25 ((1, 2, 3, 7))

G53 OLOFSSON, Claes-Hakan: Mickey Gilley collection *in* Kountry Korral, X/1 (February 1977): 20-21 ((5))

G54 SMART, Peter: Mickey Gilley on disc *in* Kommotion, No. 8 (Winter 1975): 26-28; addenda in No. 9 (Spring-Summer 1975): 4 and No. 10-11 (Winter 1975-76): 26 ((—))

GINGOLD, HERMIONE

G55 LYNCH, Richard: The two Hermiones *in* Kastlemusik Monthly Bulletin, VII/9 (September 1982): 1, 8 ((5))

GLAD label

G56 MOHR, Kurt: Glad label listing *in* Shout, No. 41 (February 1969): [8] ((3))

THE GLADIOLAS (musical group)

G57 BEACHLEY, Chris: The Gladiolas/ Zodiacs *in* Yesterday's Memories, I/3 (1975): 16 ((7))

THE GLASER BROTHERS (musical group)

G58 [Glaser Brothers discography] *in* Kountry Korral, XIV/1 (1981): 61 ((—))

GODZILLA label

G59 TIVEN, Jon: Bootlegs: Godzilla Records *in* New Haven Rock Press, IV/1 (No. 15, early 1972): 21-22 ((—))

GOINS BROTHERS

G60 Schallplattenaufnahmen *in* Country Corner, No. 36 (October 1973): 19 ((—))

GOLDDISC label

G61 TRABOSCI, Tom: [Discography] *in* Bim Bam Boom, No. 8 (December 1972): [24] ((—))

GOLDEN WORLD label

G62 Golden World label *in* Hot Buttered Soul, No. 29 (April 1974): 2-3 ((3))

GOLDIES 45 label

G63 LAZELL, Barry: Goldies 45: the latest of the U.S. reissue lines *in* SMG, III/8 (October-November 1973): 4-10 ((—))

GOLDSMITH, JERRY

G64 BOHN, Ronald, et al.: Jerry Goldsmith: filmography/discography *in* Soundtrack!, I/2 (June 1982): 3-8; I/3 (September 1982): 7-11 ((5))

G65 Filmodiscografia essenziale *in* Discoteca, XX (No. 192, March 1979): [128] ((5))

G66 LEVENSON, C. H.: This and that: Goldsmith gold revisited *in* Kastlemusik Monthly Bulletin, V/9 (September 1980): 3 ((7))

GOLLIWOGS (musical group)

G67 [Discography] *in* HOGG, Brian:
Psychotic reaction: San Francisco
begins *in* Bam Balam, No. 10
(November 1979): 20–21 ((—)) [pre-
Creedence Clearwater]

GONE label

G68 TOPPING, Ray: Discography *in*
Shout, No. 68 (August 1971): [6–10]
((3))

G69 TRABOSCI, Tom: Gone discography
in Bim Bam Boom, No. 7 (September
1972): 32–33 ((3))

GONG (musical group)

G70 CORNYETZ, Danny: Gong *in* Trans-
Oceanic Trouser Press, II/3 (June–
August 1975): 29–33 ((1))

GOODMAN, DICKIE

G71 ROGERS, Michael C.: Dickie Good-
man discography *in* Flying saucers to
Start warts: an interview with Dickie
Goodman *in* Record Exchanger, V/2
(No. 24, October [?] 1977): 20–23
((5))

GOODMAN, SHIRLEY

See also SHIRLEY & LEE

G72 MOHR, Kurt: A Shirley Goodman
discography *in* Shout, No. 106 (December 1975–January 1976): 5–7 ((2,
3, 5, 7))

GOODRICK, MICK

G73 Ausgewahlte Diskografie *in* Blue
Notes (No. 3, 1979): 40 ((—))

GOODSON label

G74 BADROCK, Arthur, and Derek
SPRUCE: The Goodson label *in*
Matrix, No. 51 (February 1964): 7 + ;
No. 55 (October 1964): 10 ((—))

GORDON, JIMMIE

G75 ROWE, Mike: Mike Rowe's numer-
ology guide *in* Blues Unlimited, No.
116 (November–December 1975): 19
((3, 6, 7))

GORDON, LUKE

G76 NAUCLER, Erik: Diskografi *in* Kountry Korral (June 1970): 6 ((—))

GORDON, ROBERT

G77 NEWMAN, Ralph M.: Robert Gordon discography *in* Time Barrier Express, No. 25 (July–August 1979): 39
((5))

GORDON, ROBERT W.

G78 RUSSELL, Tony: Afterword: the
Gordon recordings *in* Old Time
Music, No. 31 (Winter 1979–80):
11–12 ((7))

GORDY label

G79 CALTA, Gary A.: Gordy Records,
part 1 *in* Goldmine, No. 13 (November–December 1976): 4; part 2 in No.
14 (January–February 1977): 17
((—))

GORE, JOE

G80 [COHEN, Norm]: Joe Gore and
Oliver Pettrey *in* JEMF Quarterly,
VIII (No. 26, Summer 1972): 104 ((3,
6, 7))

GORE, LESLEY

G81 FITZPATRICK, Jack: Lesley Gore
discography *in* SMG, V/2 (Spring
1976): 4–5 ((5))

G82 Lesley Gore discography *in* Who Put
the Bomp, No. 15 (Spring 1976): 46;
additions and corrections in No. 16
(October 1976): 60 ((5))

G83 NATOLI, Jack: Lesley Gore discography *in* Goldmine, No. 34 (March
1979): 9 ((5))

GOSPEL TRUTH label

G84 Gospel Truth label *in* Hot Buttered
Soul, No. 26 (January 1974): 8–9
((3))

GOTT, KAREL

G85 Discographie *in* FISCHER, Trixi:
Karel Gott: Musik unserer Zeit. Wem-
ding: Wirkner, 1981: 125 ((—))

GOULDMAN, GRAHAM
    See also 10cc

G86 HOGG, Brian: The Mockingbirds *in* Bam Balam, No. 14 (September 1982): 24–28 ((5)) [Pre-10cc]

GRACIE, CHARLIE

G87 BOELENS, Milou: Discography *in* Rockville/Roaring Sixties (March– April 1975): 35 ((5))

G88 Charlie Gracie discography *in* Goldmine, No. 24 (March 1978): 18– 19 ((7))

G89 Charlie Gracie discography *in* Rock 'n' Roll International Magazine (Danish), No. 103 (November 1976): [3] ((—))

GRAETZ, PAUL

G90 CARTHASER, Friedrich, and Manfred WEIHERMULLER: Discographie: Paul Graetz *in* Anschlage, No. 7 (April 1981): 83–93 ((2, 3, 4, 5, 6, 7))

THE GRAHAM BOND ORGANIZATION

G91 [Discography] *in* HOGG, Brian: Boom boom: British blue-eyed R&B *in* Bam Balam, No. 13 (August 1981): 22–23 ((5))

GRAMOPHONE COMPANY, LTD.

G92 LILIEDAHL, Karleric: The Gramophone Co. Trelleborg: Liliedahl, 1973. ((3, 4, 6, 7))

GRAND OLE OPRY (radio program)

G93 Discography *in* HURST, Jack: Grand Ole Opry. New York: Abrams, 1975: 393–396 ((—))

GRATEFUL DEAD (musical group)

G94 Appendix A *in* HARRISON, Hank: The Dead. Millbrae, Calif. Celestial Arts, 1980: 313–314 ((5))

GRAY, JERRY

G95 Jerry Gray [1946–1965] *in* EDWARDS, Ernie, ed.: Glenn Miller alumni; a discography. Whittier, Calif.: Erngeobil Publications, 1966. 2 vols.: 12 pp. in vol. 1 ((3, 6, 7))

GRAY, TOM

G96 Tom Gray on records *in* Bluegrass Unlimited (February 1977): 46 ((—))

GRAYSON, C. B.

G97 Discography *in* Old Time Music, No. 35 (Winter 1980–Spring 1981): 13–14 ((2, 3, 6, 7))

GRAYZELL, RUDY "TUTTI"

G98 RUSSELL, Wayne: Rudy "Tutti" Grayzell *in* SMG, V/4 (January–February 1977): 19 ((—))

GRECO, JULIETTE

G99 Discographie essentialle *in* GRISOLIA, Michel: Juliette Greco. Paris: Seghers, 1975: 163–166 ((—)) (Collection poesie et chansons Seghers, 35)

GREEN, GARLAND

G100 PRUTER, Robert: Discography *in* Goldmine, No. 38 (July 1979): 29 ((5))

GREENE, CLARENCE

G101 Clarence Greene discography *in* JEMF Quarterly, VII/4 (No. 24, Winter 1971): 168–170 ((2, 3, 6, 7))

GREENWICH, ELLIE

G102 BETROCK, Alan: Ellie Greenwich *in* The Rock Marketplace, No. 9 (March 1975): 3–7, 32–33; discography pp. 32–33; addenda in No. 10 (June 1975): 15, 50 [Greenwich as performer, writer, and producer, including recordings by the Raindrops and Neil Diamond, as well as recordings of collaborator and husband Jeff Barry] ((3, 5))

GREGORY, BOBBY

G103 [Discography] *in* Country Western Express, No. 26 (December 1959): ? ((—))

GRIFFIN, BUCK

G104 RUSSELL, Wayne: Buck Griffin discography *in* New Kommotion, No. 14 (Winter 1977): 13; addenda in No. 16 (Summer 1977): 42 and No. 19 (Spring 1982): 12 ((3, 7))

GRIMES, TINY

G105 GRENDYSA, Peter: The Tiny Grimes story *in* Yesterday's Memories, II/2 (1976): 29 ((3, 7))

THE GRIMMS (musical group)

G106 REID, Tom: Grimms LP discography *in* Trouser Press, II/5 (No. 17, December 1976–January 1977): 12 ((—))

GRISMAN, DAVID

See also *Bibliography* Vol. 2, Jazz

G107 Dave Grisman discography *in* Goldmine, No. 32 (January 1979): 23 ((5))

G108 LABORIE, Tim: Dawg's best friend: the music of David Grisman *in* Tarakan Music Letter, II/4 (March–April 1981): [1], 5 ((—))

GRONBERG, AKE

G109 KARLSSON, Kjell-Ake: Ake Gronberg. Stockholm: Kungliga Biblioteket, 1976. 26 l. (Nationalfonotekets diskografier, 507) ((3, 4, 6, 7))

GROOVE label

See also *Bibliography* Vol. 2, Jazz

G110 Discography *in* Hot Buttered Soul, No. 25 (December 1973): 11 ((3))

G111 MILNE, Rick: Groove discography *in* Big Beat of the 50's, No. 21 (August 1979): 40–48 ((2, 3))

GROSS-BART, EDDIE

G112 WALKER, Steve, et al.: Eddie Gross-Bart *in* Gunn Report, No. 30 (October–November 1971): [40–41] ((3, 6, 7))

GROSVENOR, LUTHER

G113 LAUL, Bob: Luther Grosvenor discography *in* Trouser Press, III/5 (No. 17, December 1976–January 1977): 24; update in No. 19 (April–May 1977): 26 ((5))

THE GROUND HOGS (musical group)

G114 McPHEE, Tony: Who will save the world—the mighty Groundhogs *in* Trans-Oceanic Trouser Press, II/5 (November–December 1975): 26–28 ((—))

GUARANTEED label

G115 Carlton and Guaranteed label listings *in* SMG, V/3 (Summer 1976): 27–28; V/4 (January–February 1977): 17 ((—))

GUARDSMAN label

G116 BADROCK, Arthur, and Derek SPRUCE: Guardsman label; dance band issues only *in* RSVP, No. 1 (May 1965?) to No. 11 (April 1966): various paginations ((2, 6))

GUCCINI, FRANCESCO

G117 [[Discography *in* Francesco Guccini. Rome: Lato side, 1981: 129–[133]]]

THE GUESS WHO (musical group)

G118 Guess Who and Roots: discography: the early recordings (all Canadian releases) *in* Chad Allan and the Expressions, or the Guess Who *in* SMG, VI/3 (January 1978): 7 ((—))

GUITAR SLIM (real name Eddie Jones)

See also *Bibliography* Vol. 2, Jazz

G119 HANSEN, Barry: Discographie de Guitar Slim *in* Soul Bag, No. 77 (1980): 29–30 ((3, 7))

GUNTER, ARTHUR

G120 REIF, Fred: Arthur Gunter discography *in* Goldmine, No. 43 (December 1979): 19 ((2, 7))

GUNTER, HARDROCK

G121   BIG AL: The Hardrock Gunter story, part 2 *in* New Kommotion, No. 25 (1980): 27–32; discography (based on an original in New Kommotion, No. 17 by Ray TOPPING): 31–32 ((1, 2, 3, 7))

G122   TOPPING, Ray: Hardrock Gunter discography *in* New Kommotion, No. 17 (Autumn 1977): 22–23; addenda in No. 19 (Spring 1978): 14–15 and No. 22 (1979): 65 ((3, 7))

GUTHRIE, WOODY

G123   [Discography] *in* Country Directory, No. 1 (November 1960): ? ((—)) [Library of Congress recordings only]

G124   KWESKIN, Jim: Exploratory research of Woody Guthrie's Asch-Folkways recordings *in* Record Research, No. 161–162 (February–March 1979): 13; No. 163–164 (May–June 1979): 13 ((3, 7))

G125   [Discography] *in* PORTELLI, Alessandro: La canzone populare in America: le rivoluzione musicale di Woody Guthrie. Bari: De Donato, 1975: 311–[315] ((—))

G126   Discography *in* YURCHENCO, Henrietta: A mighty hard road; the Woody Guthrie story. New York: McGraw-Hill, 1970: 155–156 ((—))

GUY, BUDDY

G127   ARNIAC, Jean-Pierre: Discographie Buddy Guy *in* Soul Bag, XI/75–76 (1981): 11–15 ((2, 3, 7))

HAAS, GABY

H1   [[Discography *in* Country Corner, No. 17: 3]]

HAGGARD, MERLE

H2   Discography *in* Country & Western Spotlight, No. 8 (September 1976): 6–8 ((—))

H3   Merle Haggard discography *in* JEMF Quarterly, VII/1 (No. 21, Spring 1971): 18–22; VII/2 (No. 22, Summer 1971): 97–   ((5))

H4   ROKITTA, Kurt: Merle Haggard—singles *in* Country Corner, No. 43 (February 1975): 20 ((—))

H5   Selected Merle Haggard discography *in* Down Beat, XL (May 1980): 18 ((—))

HALEY, BILL

H6   Discographie: Bill Haley *in* Anschlage, No. 7 (April 1981): 66–70 ((1, 5, 7))

H7   ELLIOTT, Brad, and Denise GREGOIRE: Bill Haley discography *in* Goldmine, No. 59 (April 1981): 9–10 ((5))

H8   GREGOIRE, Denise: Discography of Bill Haley's Mexican records *in* Goldmine, No. 47 (April 1980): 147 ((5))

H9   KLOSTER, Jan: Discography *in* R-O-C-K (May 1981): 22–29 ((5))

H10   TAYLOR, Kevin, and John MARSHALL: Bill Haley: the Decca years and later *in* Big Beat of the 50's, No. 27 (May 1981): 4–15 ((5))

H11   TAYLOR, Kevin, and John MARSHALL: Discography *in* Big Beat of the 50's, No. 22 (November 1979): 12–14 ((5))

H12   WEIZE, Richard: Discographie: Bill Haley *in* Anschlage, No. 1 (March 1978): 140–143; No. 2 (June 1978): 117–133 ((1, 4, 5, 7))

H13   WHITESELL, Rick, and Stan MAYO: Discography *in* Record Exchanger, IV/6 (No. 20): 9; additions and corrections in Paul's Record Magazine, III/2 (February 1976): 4 ((5))

HALL, ROY

H14   [Discography] *in* Country News & Views, II/3 (January 1964): 23–24, 26; additions in IV/1: ? ((2, 3, 7)) [Includes listing for Hugh Hall]

HALL, TOM T.

H15   ERIKSSON, Carl-Eric: Tom T. Hall LP disco *in* Kountry Korral Magazine, XIV/2 (1981): 28 ((—))

H16   Tom T. Hall—Langspielplatten—Disco *in* Country Corner, No. 41 (October 1974): 20 ((—))

HALLYDAY, JOHNNY

H17 Discographie *in* HEMERET, Georges: Rock & twist. [Nancy?, 1962]: 141–[142] ((—))

H18 Index *in* LAMPARD, Bob: Johnny: la premiere discographie complete de Johnny Hallyday. Paris: Delville, 1977: 84–[93] ((5))

HALVIK, FERDINAND

G19 CONRAD, Gerhard: [Discography] *in* Jazz Freund, XVI (September 1974): 30 ((7))

HAMBLEN, STUART

H20 Stuart Hamblen discography *in* JEMF Quarterly, XIV (No. 49, Spring 1978): 13–22 ((1, 3, 6, 7))

THE HAMBONE KIDS (musical group)

H21 Hambone Kids discography *in* Goldmine, No. 52 (September 1980): 181 ((5))

HAMILTON, GEORGE, IV

H22 Discography *in* Kountry Korral, X/2 (April 1977): 13 ((—))

H23 George Hamilton IV LP discography *in* Kountry Korral (No. 2, 1979): 13 ((—))

H24 SCHUMANN, E. Reinald: Langspielplatten von George Hamilton IV *in* Hillbilly, No. 28 (December 1968): 6, 30 ((—))

H25 STRUBING, Hauke: George Hamilton IV auf Langspielplatten *in* Country Corner, No. 45 (July 1975): 3 ((—))

HAMILTON, PATTI, AND THE LOVELITES (musical group)

H26 PRUTER, Robert: [Discography] *in* Goldmine, No. 61 (June 1981): 161 ((5))

HAMILTON, ROY

H27 GRENDYSA, Peter: Roy Hamilton discography *in* Goldmine, No. 35 (April 1979): 13, 15 ((3, 5, 6))

HAMMILL, PETE
See VAN DER GRAAF GENERATOR

THE HAMPTONS (musical group)

H28 [[[Discography] *in* Soul Music (No. 20)]]

HANDLEY, TOMMY

H29 Partial discography *in* GOSLIN, John: Off the record: Tommy Handley *in* Talking Machine Review, No. 56–57 (February–April 1979): 1474–1478 ((3, 7))

H30 The recordings of Tommy Handley *in* Collecta, No. 25 (September 1976): 12 ((—))

HANNA-BARBERA label

H31 H.B.R. records *in* Who Put the Bomp, No. 13 (Spring 1975): 16 ((5))

HANSEN BROTHERS (musical group)

H32 BINGHAM, Tom: Hansen Brothers discography *in* Goldmine, No. 45 (February 1980): 119 ((5))

THE HAPPENINGS (musical group)

H33 ENGEL, Ed: The Happenings *in* Record Exchanger, V/4 (No. 26, 1978): 18–20 ((—))

HARDESTY, HERB

H34 TOPPING, Ray: Herb Hardesty discography *in* Goldmine, No. 49 (June 1980): 176 ((2, 7))

HARDY, FRANCOISE

H35 Discography (partial) *in* SIMONS, Andy: Francoise Hardy *in* Bomp!, No. 21 (March 1979): 42–43 ((—))

HARKREADER, SID

H36 [COHEN, Norm]: Sid Harkreader on Paramount *in* JEMF Quarterly, VII (No. 28, Winter 1972): 193 ((3, 7))

H37 Sid Harkreader discography *in* his Fiddlin' Sid's memoirs. Los Angeles:

John Edwards Memorial Foundation, 1976: 35–37 ((1, 3, 6, 7))

HARLEY, STEVE, AND COCKNEY REBEL (musical group)

H38 Steve Harley/Cockney Rebel discography *in* Trouser Press Press, No. 3 (1976): 68; addendum in No. 19 (April–May 1977): 26 ((—))

HARMOGRAPH label

H39 WHYATT, Bert: Harmograph label *in* Storyville, No. 92 (December 1980–January 1981): 54–58; No. 93 (February–March 1981): 88–89 ((2, 3))

HARMONICA FRANK
See FLOYD, FRANK

HARMONY-VELVET label

H40 The Harmony-Velvet Tone-Viva numerical lists *in* Discographer, II/3 (3rd Quarter, 1971): [2-159]-1-284; II/4 2-227–2-242 ((3))

HAROLD, RICHARD

H41 [COHEN, Norm,] and Guthrie MEADE: Richard Harold *in* JEMF Quarterly, VII (No. 26, Summer 1972): 104 ((3, 6, 7))

THE HARPTONES (musical group)

H42 ARDOLINO, Art: Harptones singles *in* Shout, No. 93 (February 1974): 4–5 ((5))

H43 MARCUS, Ed: The Harptones *in* Stormy Weather, No. 3 (January 1970): 7 ((5))

H44 VANCE, Marcia, and Steve FLAM: Harptones discographie *in* Bim Bam Boom, I/2 (October–November 1971): 6 ((—))

HARRELL, KELLY

H45 LEVERETT, W.: [Discography] *in* Disc Collector, No. 11 [n.d.]: ? ((—))

HARRIS, BARBARA JO

H46 MOHR, Kurt: Barbara Jo Harris discography *in* Black Wax, No. 6 (July 1973): 7 ((2, 3, 7))

HARRIS, DON

H47 HESS, Norbert: Don Harris & Dewey Terry discography *in* Shout, No. 102 (April 1975): 5–10 ((3, 6, 7))

HARRIS, EMMYLOU

H48 Emmylou Harris disco *in* Kountry Korral, X/2 (April 1977): 32 ((—))

H49 HOLMQUIST, Goran: Emmylou Harris LP disco *in* Kountry Korral Magazine (No. 2, 1980): 20–24 ((5))

H50 CLEE, Ken: Emmylou Harris singles discography *in* Music World, No. 76 (July 1980): 8–9 ((—))

HARRIS, WEE WILLIE

H51 Discography *in* Not Fade Away, No. 14 (1979): 7 ((5))

HARRIS, WYNONIE

H52 GOLDMAN, John: Wynonie Harris singles *in* New Kommotion, No. 14 (Winter 1977): 21 ((—))

H53 MOONOOGIAN, George: Wynonie Harris discography *in* Goldmine, No. 41 (October 1979): 13–14 ((3, 5, 6, 7))

HARRISON, GEORGE

H54 Discography *in* MICHAELS, Ross: George Harrison: yesterday and to-day. New York: Flash Books, 1977: [90]–96 ((5))

HARRISON, WILBERT

H55 GRENDYSA, Peter: Wilbert Harrison discography *in* Goldmine, No. 37 (January 1979): 24 ((5))

HARRISON BROTHERS (musical group)

H56 TOPPING, Ray: Discography *in* Shout, No. 60 (November 1970): [1–2] ((3, 7))

HART, FREDDIE

H57 Freddie Hart auf Langspielplatten (Auswahl) *in* Country Corner, XII (No. 53, February 1977): 18 ((—))

H58 Freddie Harts LP *in* Kountry Korral (December 1973): 12 ((—))

HART, LARRY

H59 [[Discography *in* New Kommotion, No. 11 (c1976); addenda in No. 16 (Summer 1977): 42]]

HARTLEY, FRED

H60 Fred Hartley *in* Commodore, No. 4 (Winter 1971): 10 ((—))

H61 HAYES, Jim: Fred Hartley on 78's *in* Commodore, No. 10 (Summer 1973): 17 ((—))

HARVEST label

H62 Harvest discography *in* Jamz, No. 4 (May 1972): 33 [Singles only] ((—))

HARVEY, ALEX

H63 Alex Harvey discography *in* Trouser Press Press, No. 3 (1976): 65; addenda in No. 19 (April–May 1977): 26 ((—))

H64 HOGG, Brian: Alex Harvey soul band *in* Bam Balam, No. 14 (September 1982): 36–39 ((5))

H65 ROBBINS, Ira, and Dave SCHULPS: Alex Harvey in Hot City *in* Trans-Oceanic Trouser Press, II/5 (November–December 1975): 2–5 ((—))

HARVEY label

H66 TOPPING, Ray: Harvey label listing *in* Shout, No. 77 (June 1972): 8 ((3, 5))

HASTINGS MUNICIPAL ORCHESTRA

H67 UPTON, Stuart: The Hastings Municipal Orchestra *in* Vintage Light Music, No. 4 (Autumn 1975): 7 ((—))

HATHAWAY, DONNY

H68 DAGUERRE, Pierre: Discographie de Donny Hathaway *in* Soul Bag, No. 78–79 (November 1980): [7–11] ((2, 3, 7))

HAWKING BROTHERS (musical group)

H69 CHARLES, H.: [Discography] *in* Country News and Views, II/1 (July 1963): 17–18 ((3, 7))

H70 [Discography] *in* Country Western Spotlight, No. 45 (March 1964): ? ((—))

HAWKINS, DALE

H71 BOELENS, Milou: Dale Hawkins discography *in* Rock 'n' Roll International Magazine (Dutch), No. 107 (July–August 1977): extra 2–extra 3 ((5))

H72 GOVAARD, Stan: Dale Hawkins discography *in* Rockville International (December 1973): 6–8 ((2, 3, 7))

H73 MILLAR, Bill: Dale Hawkins *in* New Kommotion, No. 16 (Summer 1977): 8–15; discography pp. 14–15; addenda in No. 22 (1979): 65 ((2, 3, 7))

H74 WESTFALL, Bob, and Bob AIRLIE: Dale Hawkins on disc *in* Kommotion, No. 10–11 (Winter 1975–76): 38–39 ((3))

HAWKINS, HANKSHAW

H75 [Discography] *in* Country Western Express, No. 10 [New series]: ? ((—))

H76 [Discography] *in* Country Western Spotlight, No. 42 (June 1963): ? ((—))

H77 WEIZE, Richard, and Edvard MONCH: Hankshaw Hawkins diskographie *in* Hillbilly, No. 60 (September 1979): 10–16 ((5))

HAWKINS, RONNIE

H78 ESCOTT, Brian, and Wile Willie JEFFREY: Rockin' with Ronnie *in* New Kommotion, No. 18 (Winter 1978): 4–8; discography pp. 6–7; addenda in No. 19 (Spring 1978): 12 and No. 22 (1979): 65 ((1, 2, 3, 7))

HAWKINS, SCREAMIN' JAY
See also *Bibliography* Vol. 2, Jazz

H79 Discography *in* Goldmine, No. 30 (November 1978): 9 ((5))

H80 NEWMAN, Ralph M.: Screamin' Jay Hawkins *in* Bim Bam Boom, No. 7 (September 1972): 36 ((—))

H81 TOPPING, Ray, and Kurt MOHR: Screamin' Jay Hawkins discography *in* Shout, No. 56 (June 1970): [2–6] ((—))

THE HAWKS (musical group)

H82 WHITESELL, Rick, and Marv GOLDBERG: The Hawks *in* Yesterday's Memories, III/3 (1977): 17 ((7))

HAWKWIND (musical group)

H83 LEGRAND, Vince, and Ira ROBBINS: Hawkwind! *in* Trans-Oceanic Trouser Press, II/4 (September–October 1975): 28–30 ((—))

HAYWARD, RICHARD

H84 [Discography] *in* Hillbilly Folk Record Journal, IV/1 (January–March 1957): ? ((—))

HAZLEWOOD, LEE

H85 SMART, Peter: A genius called Lee *in* Kommotion, No. 10–11 (Winter 1975–76): 6–11; discography pp. 8–11 ((5))

HEART (musical group)

H86 THOM, Teresa: Heart discography *in* Full Blast, I/1 (Winter 1979): 11–13 ((7))

THE HEARTBEATS (musical group)

H87 GRENDYSA, Peter: The Heartbeats discography *in* Goldmine, No. 55 (December 1980): 20–21 ((3, 5))

H88 RASCIO, Mike: [Discography] *in* Big Town Review, I/2 (April–May 1972): [9] ((3))

THE HEARTBREAKERS (musical group) [New York City]

H89 LEVY, Ray: The other heartbreakers *in* Yesterday's Memories, II/3 (1976): 20 ((7))

THE HEARTBREAKERS (musical group) [Washington, D.C.]

H90 LEE, Alan, et al.: Heartbreak for the Heartbreakers *in* Bim Bam Boom, II/3 (No. 11, 1973): [27] ((3))

HEARTS (musical group)

H91 Lee Andrews/Hearts discography *in* Music World, No. 86 (June 1981): 14 ((—))

HEIDI label

H92 TOPPING, Ray: Heidi label listing *in* Shout, No. 51 (January 1970): [14] ((3, 5))

HELMS, BOBBY

H93 [Discography] *in* Goldmine, No. 28 (September 1978): 10 ((—))

HENDERSON, DICK

H94 HAYES, Jim: The records of Dick Henderson and the Henderson Twins *in* Gunn Report, No. 40 (June–July 1973): [38] ((3, 5))

HENDRICKS, BOBBY

H95 GOLDBERG, Marv, and Mike REDMOND: The Bobby Hendricks story *in* Yesterday's Memories, III/4 (1977): 20 ((7))

HENDRIX, JIMI

H96 Discographie *in* FELLER, Benoit: Jimi Hendrix. Paris: A. Michel, 1976: [188]–190 ((—))

H97 Jimi Hendrix (1942–1970) *in* New Haven Rock Press, II/4 (Fall 1970): 16 ((1))

H98 McKELLAR, John: A Jimi Hendrix discography *in* KNIGHT, Curtis: Jimi: an intimate biography. New York:

Praeger; London: Allen, 1974: [209]–218 ((1, 7))

H99 Records by Jimi Hendrix/Jimi Hendrix Experience *in* NOLAN, Tom: Jimi Hendrix: a biography in words & pictures. [s.l.]: Sire Books; New York: distributed by Chappell Music Co., 1977: 52–55 ((1, 5))

H100 Discografia *in* ORDOVAS, Jesus: Jimi Hendrix. Madrid: Jucar, 1974: [269]–273 ((7))

H101 THE PURPLE HAZE ARCHIVES and Dave ARMSTRONG: Jimi Hendrix: a discography. Tucson: Purple Haze Archives, 1981. 46 pp. ((1, 2, 5, 7))

H102 Discography *in* WELCH, Chris: Hendrix: a biography. London: Ocean Books, 1972; New York: Flash Books, 1973: 102–103 ((1))

HENRIQUE, WALDEMAR

H103 Discografia *in* CLAVER FILHO, Jose: Waldemar Henrique: o canto da Amazonia. Rio de Janeiro: Edicao Funarte, 1978: 116–121 ((5))

HENRY, CLARENCE "FROGMAN"

H104 GARBUTT, Bob, and Dan NOOGEN: Clarence "Frogman" Henry discography *in* Goldmine, No. 52 (September 1981): 17 ((—))

H105 HANDEL, Rob van den: Clarence "Frogman" Henry *in* Rock 'n' Roll International Magazine (Danish), No. 109 (January 1978): 10 ((—))

HENSLEE, GENE

H106 Discography *in* Kountry Korral, X/2 (April 1977): 36 ((3, 5))

HENSLEY, HAROLD

H107 Harold Hensley discography *in* JEMF Quarterly, VI/4 (No. 20, Winter 1970): 151 ((7))

HEPPENER, ROBERT

H108 Discography *in* Key Notes, No. 5 (No. 1, 1977): 31 ((—))

HERALD label

See also *Bibliography* Vol. 2, Jazz

H109 Herald label listing *in* Shout, No. 58 (August 1970): [4–8]; No. 59 (October 1970): [4–8]; No. 60 (November 1970): [2–5]; additions and corrections in No. 65 (April 1971): [2] ((3))

H110 TISOVEC, Tony, and Steve FLAM: Herald discography *in* Bim Bam Boom, I/6 (July 1972): 26–27 ((3))

THE HERD (musical group)

H111 BETROCK, Alan: The Herd & Judas Jump *in* Jamz, No. 2 (October 1971): 18–19; discography p. 19; addenda in No. 3 (February 1972): 22; No. 4 (May 1972): 34; No. 5 (c1972): 75 ((2, 5))

HERITAGE label

H112 Heritage label *in* Paul's Record Magazine, IV/2 (No. 13–14, September–December 1976): 33 ((—))

HERMAN'S HERMITS (musical group)

H113 CLEE, Ken, and Ken PAULSON: Herman's Hermits discography *in* Goldmine, No. 44 (January 1980): 19 ((—))

H114 Herman's Hermits discography *in* Ballroom Blitz!, No. 25 (March 1978): 23–24, [35]; additions in No. 36 (May–June 1980): 17; No. 41 (November–December 1981): 13 ((5))

HERNANDEZ, RALPH

H115 SKURZEWSKI, Bob, and Terry SKURZEWSKI: Fonville/Hernandez discography *in* Goldmine, No. 62 (July 1981): 156 ((—))

HEROLD, TED

H116 WEIZE, Richard: Discographie: Ted Herold *in* Anschlage, No. 6 (January 1980): 66–79; No. 7 (April 1981): 70–71 ((3, 4, 5))

HERRMANN, BERNARD

H117 DOHERTY, Jim: The overlooked Bernard Herrmann *in* Soundtrack!, No. 25 (Spring 1981): 22–28 ((5))

H118   Discography *in* JOHNSON, Edward:
Bernard Herrmann, Hollywood's music-
dramatist. Rickmansworth, England:
Triad Press, 1977: 43–56 ((1, 5, 7))

HERSCHEL GOLD SEAL label

H119   HENRIKSEN, Henry: Herschel Gold
Seal label *in* Record Research, No.
131 (January 1975): 5 ((3))

HEWITT, BEN

H120   BRYAN, Pete, and Peter SMART:
Ben Hewitt on Mercury *in* Kommotion, No. 8 (Winter 1975): 26 ((3))

HEWLETT, JOHN

H121   ZEPEDA, Stephen: John Hewlett discography *in* Bomp, No. 18 (February
1978): 47 ((5))

HICKEY, ERSEL

H122   WESTFALL, Bob: Ersel Hickey discography *in* Goldmine, No. 12 (September–October 1976): 32 ((5))

H123   WESTFALL, Bob: Ersel Hickey discography *in* SMG, V/3 (Summer
1976): 32 ((—))

HICKMAN, ART

H124   CAMP, J. H.: Art Hickman . . . discography *in* After Beat, I/1 (October
1970): 5 ((2, 7))

HICKORY label

H125   TAYLOR, Brian, and Ray TOP-
PING: Hickory label: part one *in* New
Kommotion, No. 14 (Winter 1977):
20–21; part 2 by David YEATS in No.
16 (Summer 1977): 5 ((—))

THE HI FIVES (musical group)

H126   ITALIANO, Ronnie: The Hi Fives *in*
Time Barrier Express, I/10 (July
1975): 21–24, 50; discography p. 50
((5))

HIGELIN, JACQUES

H127   Discographie *in* WATHELET,
Michele: Jacques Higelin. Paris:

Seghers, 1980: 185–[187] (Collection
poesie et chansons Seghers, 43) ((—))

HIGH SCHOOL USA (song title)

H128   BIG BOPPER BILL: Discography *in*
Paul's Record Magazine, III/2 (February 1976): 23 ((—))

HIGHNIGHT, LUKE

H129   [RUSSELL, Tony]: Luke Highnight *in*
Old Time Music, No. 11 (Winter
1973/4): 24 ((3, 7))

HIGHTOWER, ROSETTA

H130   MOHR, Kurt: Orlons & Rosetta Hightower discography *in* Shout, No. 66
(May 1971): [6–9] ((3, 7))

THE HIGHWAYMEN (musical group)

H131   The Highwaymen discography *in*
Goldmine, No. 49 (June 1980): 181
((—))

HILDER, TONY

H132   BLAIR, John, and Bill SMART:
Tony Hilder discography *in* Who Put
the Bomp, No. 14 (Fall 1975): 13
((—))

HILL, BUNKER

H133   MOHR, Kurt: Bunker Hill discography *in* Shout, No. 63 (February
1971): [12] ((3, 7))

HILL, DAVID

H134   WESTFALL, Bob: David Hill: New
York's best pop rocker? *in* Kommotion, No. 9 (Spring–Summer 1975):
19; addenda in No. 10–11 (Winter
1975–76): 26 ((—))

HILLAGE, STEVE

H135   GREEN, Jim: Hillage rising: a former
gongster spills the karmic beans *in*
Trouser Press, No. 16 (October–November 1976): 19–21; discography p.
21 ((—))

HI-Q label

H136 TISOVEC, Tony: Hi-Q discography *in* Bim Bam Boom, I/5 (April–May 1972): 22 ((3))

HIS MASTER'S VOICE label

H137 HAYES, Jim: Disc research England: HMV B8000 series. Liverpool: Hayes, 1975. 55 pp. ((3, 5))

H138 HAYES, Jim: HMV BD 100 series. Liverpool: Hayes, 1974. 26 l. ((3, 5))

H139 LAZELL, Barry: HMV pop singles listing 1955-1967 [pt. 3] *in* SMG, IV/8 (March 1975) thru V/3 (Summer 1976): various paginations ((—))

HIS MASTER'S VOICE label [Australia]

H140 [Discography, EA series] *in* Folk Style, No. 12 [n.d.]: ? ((—))

HIS MASTER'S VOICE label [India]

H141 STOTEN, John: Old time music in India *in* Old Time Music, No. 13 (Summer 1974): 17-18; No. 14 (Autumn 1974): 19-20, 22 ((5))

HOGAN, CARL

H142 GROIA, Phil: Carl Hogan, the Valentines *in* Bim Bam Boom, No. 7 (September 1972): 39 ((3))

HOLIDAY label

H143 Discography *in* Record Exchanger, III/1 (No. 12 [Winter 1972]): [12-13] ((3))

H144 TISOVEC, Tony: Holiday label listing *in* Shout, No. 80 (September 1972): [4] ((—))

THE HOLLIES (musical group)

H145 BETROCK, Alan: Hollies discography *in* Jamz, No. 5 (c1972): 64, 69 ((5))

H146 FAULL, Trev: The Hollies' discography: the first ten years *in* Outlet, No. 5 (August 1978): 15-18 ((5))

H147 HOGAN, Richard: Hollies *in* Trans-Oceanic Trouser Press, II/4 (September-October 1975): 33-35 ((—))

H148 Hollies *in* Gorilla Beat, No. 7 (1980): 31-47; discography pp. 39-47; addenda in No. 8 (1980): 47-48 and No. 9 (1981): 48 and No. 10 (1981): 43 ((5))

H149 KOLANJIAN, Steve, and Gary ROSENWITZ: The Hollies *in* Rock It with Aware, II/2 (1975?): 4-9; additions and corrections in II/3 (1976?): 5; II/4 (1976): 4 ((—))

H150 LORBER, Steve: The Hollies—a brief appreciation, part 1 *in* Trans-Oceanic Trouser Press, II/4 (September-October 1975): 31-32 ((—))

H151 RIJUNDT, Jan: Diskografie *in* Rockville/Roaring Sixties (March–April 1975): 15-16 ((5))

HOLLY, BUDDY

See also THE CRICKETS

H152 BEECHER, John, and Malcolm JONES: Master list *in* notes "The Buddy Holly Story" *in* The complete Buddy Holly [sound recording], MCA [England] CDMSP 807, 1979: [58-61] ((5, 7))

H153 BIG BOPPER BILL: Buddy Holly: discography *in* Paul's Record Magazine, II/6 (December 1975): 7-8 ((—))

H154 BRAULT, Patrick, and Xavier MARIE: 1950-1959: L'oeuvre enregistree *in* Big Beat, No. 17-18 (June 1979): 22-34 ((1, 2, 3, 6, 7))

H155 Buddy Holly discography *in* Stormy Weather, No. 5 (January 1973): 7, 14 ((—))

H156 Buddy Holly diskografi *in* Kountry Korral (August 1971): 16-17 ((5))

H157 CLEE, Ken: Buddy Holly/Crickets discographies *in* Music World, No. 3 (March 1981): 34-37 ((—))

H158 Discography *in* GOLDROSEN, John: Buddy Holly: his life and music. Bowling Green, Ohio: Popular Press, 1975: 230-236 ((1, 5, 7))

H159 Discography *in* GOLDROSEN, John: The Buddy Holly story. New York: Quick Fox, 1979: 244-250 ((1, 2, 5, 7))

H160 GONZALEZ, Fernando L.: Buddy Holly discography *in* Goldmine, No. 19 (October 1977): 14-17 ((3, 7))

H161 INGRAM, John: Buddy Holly: the original versions *in* New Kommotion, No. 19 (Spring 1978): 16–17; addenda in No. 22 (1979): 65 ((5)) [Original recordings that Holly covered]

H162 [[INGRAM, John, and Brian SHEP-HERD: Buddy Holly discography *in* New Kommotion, No. 23 (1980): 34–36]]

H163 Discography *in* LAING, Dave: Buddy Holly. London: Macmillan, 1971: 109–111; New York: Macmillan, 1971: 141–144 ((7))

H164 Discography *in* PEER, Elizabeth, comp.: Buddy Holly. New York: Peer International Corp., 1972: 135–144 ((7))

H165 SMITH, Clyde: Buddy Holly singles *in* Record Exchanger, No. 5 (November–December 1970): 9 ((—))

H166 Discography *in* TOBLER, John: The Buddy Holly story. London: Plexus, 1979: 93–96 ((5))

THE HOLLYWOOD FLAMES (musical group)

H167 BYRD, Bobby: The Flames *in* Yesterday's Memories, I/2 (1975): 7–8; III/2 (1977): 27–29 ((7))

THE HOLLYWOOD SAXONS (musical group)

H168 GOLDBERG, Marv, and Rick WHITESELL: The Hollywood Saxons *in* Yesterday's Memories, III/3 (1977): 15 ((7))

HOLLYWOOD STARS (musical group)

H169 FOWLEY, Kim: Hollywood Stars *in* Who Put the Bomp, No. 13 (September 1975): 17–21 ((7))

HOLMAN, EDDIE

H170 MOHR, Kurt: Discography *in* Shout, No. 60 (November 1970): [5–6]; additions and corrections in No. 65 (April 1971): [2] ((3, 6, 7))

HOMER AND JETHRO (musical group)

H171 [Discography] *in* Hillbilly Folk Record Journal, I/3 (July–September 1954): ? ((—))

HONEY AND THE BEES (musical group)

H172 CUMMINGS, Tony: Honey & the Bees discography *in* Black Wax, No. 6 (July 1973): 15 ((2, 3, 6, 7))

HONEYCUTT, GLEN

H173 GLENISTER, Derek: Glen Honeycutt *in* New Kommotion, No. 22 (1979): 9–13; discography p. 13 ((1, 2, 3, 7))

HOPKINS, DOC

H174 EARLE, Eugene W.: Doc Hopkins [discography] *in* Doc Hopkins [sound recording], Birch LP 1945 [1972]: included in brochure notes ((1, 2, 5, 6, 7))

HOPKINS, TED

H175 Discography *in* Hillandale News, No. 79 (August 1974): 209 ((5))

HORTON, JOHNNY

H176 [[Discography *in* Rock & Roll Performers Magazine, December 1981]]

H177 GARBUTT, Robert, and Ray Mc-CONCHIE: Johnny Horton discography *in* Goldmine, No. 58 (March 1981): 192–193 ((5))

H178 LP-Discographie *in* Country Corner, No. 46 (October 1975): [21] ((—))

H179 LEGERE, B.: [Discography] *in* Country Western Spotlight, No. 33 (January–March 1961): ? ((—))

H180 MORKE, Gerhard, et al.: Johnny Horton diskographie *in* Hillbilly, No. 49 (December 1976): 10–21 ((1, 3, 6, 7))

H181 PERKINS, Ken: Additions to previously published discographies *in* Big Beat of the 50's, No. 20 (May 1979): 62 ((—))

H182 ROKITTA, Kurt: [Discography] *in* Country Corner, No. 47 (December 1975): 10–18 ((3, 7))

HOT WATER label

H183 Hot Water label *in* Hot Buttered Soul, No. 27 (February 1974): 6 ((3))

HOUSTON, CISSY

H184   MOHR, Kurt, and Gilles PETARD:
Cissy Houston/discographie *in* Soul
Bag, XII (No. 85, October–November
1981): 17–18 ((2, 3, 7))

HOUSTON, JOE

H185   AIRLIE, Bob: Joe Houston discography *in* Rumble, III/3 (Spring 1976):
16; revised version in III/3 (Summer–
Autumn 1976): 14–16 ((—))

HOWARD, HARLAN

H186   Harlan Howard *in* Kountry Korral,
X/4 (August 1977): 13–14 ((3, 5))

HOWARD, LAKE

H187   [COHEN, Norm]: Lake Howard discography *in* JEMF Quarterly, XI/1
(No. 37, Spring 1975): 5–6 ((3, 7))

THE HUDSON BROTHERS

H188   BARNES, Ken: Charting the Hudsons
in The Rock Marketplace, No. 10
(June 1975): 36–37 [Pre-1972 recordings only, including those as the New
Yorkers] ((5))

HUDSON label

H189   [BAYLY, Ernie]: A partial listing of
Hudson records *in* Talking Machine
Review, No. 60–61 (October–Decem-
ber 1979): 1629–1630 ((3))

HUDSON-FORD (musical group)

H190   KRIEGER, Rick, and Steve LEMAN-
SKY: The Hudson-Ford Union *in*
Trans-Oceanic Trouser Press, II/3
(June–August 1975): 24–26 ((—))

HUGHES, FRED

H191   MOHR, Kurt: Fred Hughes discography *in* Shout, No. 80 (September
1972): [4–5] ((2, 3, 7))

HUGHES, FREDDIE

H192   MOHR, Kurt: Freddie Hughes discography *in* Shout, No. 80 (September
1972): [5–6] ((3, 7))

HULL label

H193   PECORARO, Joe: Hull record discography *in* Record Exchanger (No.
17): 8 ((—))

HUMBLE PIE (musical group)

H194   BETROCK, Alan: [Discography] *in*
Jamz, No. 2 (October 1971): 17
((—))

HUMPERDINCK, ENGELBERT

H195   Appendix—III [discography] *in*
SHORT, Don: Engelbert Humper-
dinck. London: New English Library,
1972: 94–96 ((5))

HUNTER, IVORY JOE

H196   Discography *in* Goldmine, No. 29
(October 1978): 9 ((5))

H197   MOHR, Kurt, and Ray TOPPING:
Discography *in* Shout, No. 100 (December 1974): 5–9; No. 101 (February
1975): 1–5; additions and corrections
in No. 107 (February–March 1976): 21
((2, 3, 5, 6, 7))

THE HUNTERS (musical group)

H198   Discografi med "The Hunters"
(England) *in* Rock 'n' Roll Inter-
national Magazine (Danish), No. 105
(April 1977): 31 ((5))

H199   HOLME, Dave: Discography *in* Rumble, III/2 (Winter 1975–6): 14–15
((—))

HURLEY, ALEC

H200   BARKER, Tony: Alec Hurley discography *in* Music Hall, No. 9 (October
1979): 44–53 ((3, 7))

HUTCHINSON, FRANK

H201   KUNSTADT, Len, and B. COLTON:
[Discography] *in* Record Research,
No. 58 (February 1964): ?; additions
in No. 64 and 66 ((7))

HUTCHINSON, LESLIE ARTHUR

H202   LYNCH, Richard C.: Mabel Mercer,
Hutch and Elisabeth Welch *in* Kastle-

musik Monthly Bulletin, V/8 (August 1980): 1, 12-13 ((—))

HYLTON, MRS. JACK

H203 Mrs. Jack Hylton and her band *in* Collecta, No. 6 (July–August 1969): 18-20 ((2, 3, 6, 7))

IAN AND SYLVIA (musical duo)

I1 Ian & Sylvia album discography *in* Goldmine, No. 53 (October 1980): 178 ((5))

IAN & THE ZODIACS

I2 Liverpool beat: Ian + Zodiacs *in* Gorilla Beat, No. 7 (1980): 10-15; discography pp. 12-15 ((5))

THE IDEALS (musical group)

I3 MOHR, Kurt: Discography *in* Shout, No. 95 (May 1974): 3-4 ((3, 5, 7))

I4 PRUTER, Robert: Discography: the Ideals *in* Goldmine, No. 33 (February 1979): 13 ((5))

THE IDLE RACE

I5 Idle Race *in* Jamz, No. 4 (May 1972): 13 ((5))

I6 Jeff Lynne/Idle Race discography *in* Trouser Press Press, No. 3 (1976): 66 ((5))

I7 LAGENFELD, Forrest: Idle Race discography *in* Goldmine, No. 61 (June 1981): 23 ((—))

I8 SCHULPS, Dave: The Idle Race rediscovered *in* Trans-Oceanic Trouser Press, II/1 (February–March 1975): 31-33 ((—))

ILES, EDNA

I9 Recordings by Edna Iles in the BIRS *in* Recorded Sound, No. 70-71 (April–July 1978): 805 ((1, 7))

IMMEDIATE label

I10 BETROCK, Alan: [Discography] *in* Trouser Press Collector's Magazine, I/1 (September–October 1978): [3] ((—))

I11 BETROCK, Alan, and Phil FOX: The Immediate story *in* The Rock Marketplace, No. 10 (June 1975): 42-44 ((5))

I12 PEARLIN, Bob: [Discography] *in* Time Barrier Express, II/8 (No. 18, August–September 1976): 18-[19] ((3))

THE IMPACTS (musical group)

I13 MOHR, Kurt: Herb Johnson and the Impacts *in* Shout, No. 95 (May 1974): 2 ((2, 3, 5, 7))

IMPERIAL label

I14 FREEMAN, Joe: More Imperial pseudonyms *in* Gunn Report, No. 79 (January–February 1981): 7-10; 14; No. 80 (March–June 1981): 15-17 ((2))

IMPERIAL ORCHESTRA
See CLARKE, LADDIE

THE IMPRESSIONS (musical group)
See also *Bibliography* Vol. 2, Jazz

I15 RICHARDSON, Clive: Discography *in* program notes for The Impressions [sound recording], Sire SASH-3717-2, 1976. ((5))

I16 Impressions discography *in* WHITE, Cliff: Jerry Butler, Curtis Mayfield, & the Impressions: the vintage years *in* Time Barrier Express, No. 23 (July–August 1977): 28-32 ((5))

THE INK SPOTS (musical group)

I17 GONZALEZ, Ferdie: Discography *in* Yesterday's Memories, III/1 (No. 9, 1976): 14-18 ((3, 5, 7))

INNES, NEIL

I18 SCHAEFER, Debbie: Neil Innes album discography *in* Goldmine, No. 49 (June 1980): 21 ((—))

THE INNOCENTS (musical group)

I19 FAULL, Trev: The Innocents *in* Instrumental Obscurities Unlimited, No. 20 (c1978): 13, 20 ((—))

I20 LAY, Rip: Innocents discography *in* Goldmine, No. 52 (September 1980): 29 ((5))

INSTANT label

I21 VERA, Billy: Instant label listing *in* Shout, No. 99 (October 1974): 3–6 ((3, 5))

THE INTERIORS (musical group)

I22 MOHR, Kurt: The Interiors *in* Shout, No. 83 (January 1973): [3–4] ((2, 3, 7))

THE INTERLUDES (musical group)

I23 SMITH, Warren L.: The Interludes *in* Yesterday's Memories, III/4 (1977): 27 ((7))

INTERNATIONAL ARTISTS label

I24 FAULL, Trev: International Artists *in* Outlet, No. 11 (May 1979): 12–14 ((—))

I25 International Artists [discography] *in* Who Put the Bomp, No. 14 (Fall 1975): 25; additions and corrections in No. 15 (Spring 1976): 44 ((—))

INTERNATIONAL NOVELTY ORCHESTRA

I26 HAYES, Jim: Listing *in* Music Hall, No. 22 (Spring 1980): 12 ((3, 7))

INTERNATIONAL POLYDOR PRODUCTION label

I27 HEBING, Alfred: [Discography] *in* Gorilla Beat, No. 12 (1981): 22–27; addenda in No. 13 (1982): 73 ((—))

INTERPHON label

I28 SHAW, Greg: Interphon discography *in* Who Put the Bomp, No. 12 (Summer 1974): 20 ((—))

THE INVICTAS (musical group)

I29 PREVOST, Greg: The history of the Invictas *in* Blitz, No. 34 (January–February 1980): 23–26; discography p. 26 ((1, 5))

IRISH GUARDS (musical organization)

I30 The Band of the Irish Guards . . . *in* Commodore, No. 9 (September 1973): 5+ ((—))

ISLAND label

I31 FAULL, Trev: Island Records *in* Outlet, No. 13 (August 1979): 12–24; No. 15 (November 1979): 24–28; No. 18 (April 1980): 28–30 ((—)) [Includes Black Swan, Sue, and Aladdin series]

ISLEY BROTHERS

I32 GONZALEZ, Fernando L.: The Isley Brothers discography *in* Goldmine (August 1981): 16–17 ((3, 5, 6))

I33 An Isley Brothers discography *in* Rock It with Aware, II/4 (1976): 25–26 ((5))

IVES, BURL

I34 [Discography] *in* Country Directory, No. 1 (November 1960): ? ((—)) [Library of Congress records only]

I35 [Discography] *in* Country Directory, No. 2 (April 1961): ? ((2, 3, 7))

I36 [Discography] *in* Disc Collector, I/2 (April–June 1951): ? ((—)) [Encyclopaedia Britannica Films records only]

I37 [Discography] *in* Disc Collector, I/3 (July–September 1951): ? ((—))

I38 NICHOLAS, J.: Burl Ives on Columbia Records *in* Record Research, No. 27 (March–April 1960), No. 29 (August 1960), No. 30 (October 1960): ? ((3, 7))

I39 SCHUMANN, E. Reinald: Schallplatten von Burl Ives *in* Hillbilly No. 4 (December 1962): 13–14, 19, 23 ((—))

IVEY, CHET "POISON"

I40 [[[Discography] *in* Soul Music (No. 32)]]

THE IVEYS (musical group)

I41 OLAFSON, Peter, and Dan MATOVINE: Iveys/Badfinger discography *in* Trouser Press Collector's Magazine, I/6 (January–April 1979): [3] ((5))

THE IVORIES (musical group)

I42 McDOWELL, Mike: The Ivories are happening! *in* Blitz, No. 28 (September–October 1978): 6–8; discography p. 8 ((1, 2, 5))

J & S-TUFF label

J1 MOHR, Kurt: J & S-Tuff label listing *in* Shout, No. 91 (December 1973): 2–5 ((3, 5))

JACK AND EVELYN (musical group)

J2 BARKER, Tony: Jack and Evelyn [O'Connor] *in* Music-Hall Records, No. 3 (October 1978): 53–55 ((3, 7))

THE JACKS (musical group)

J3 FILETI, Donn: The Jacks/Cadets *in* Yesterday's Memories, I/2 (1975): 8–9 ((7))

J4 MONDRONE, Sal: Rare sounds *in* Bim Bam Boom, I/2 (October–November 1971): 18; additions and corrections in I/3 (December 1971–January 1972): 21 ((—))

JACKSON, BENJAMIN

J5 GRENDYSA, Peter: Benjamin ("Bull Moose") Jackson discography *in* Goldmine, No. 42 (November 1979): 17–18 ((3, 7))

JACKSON, CHUCK

J6 KINDER, Bob: Chuck Jackson *in* Record Exchanger, IV/3 (No. 19): 14–15 ((—))

JACKSON, JACK

J7 WOLFE, Charles K.: Jack Jackson *in* JEMF Quarterly, IX (No. 32, Winter 1973): 145 ((3, 6, 7))

JACKSON, MILLIE

J8 DAGUERRE, Pierre: Millie Jackson discographie *in* Soul Bag, XII (No. 86, December 1981–January 1982): 22–26 ((7))

J9 MOHR, Kurt: Millie Jackson discography *in* Shout, No. 101 (February 1975): 7–9 ((2, 3, 6, 7))

JACKSON, STONEWALL

J10 KRONGARD, Rune: Stonewall Jackson disco *in* Kountry Korral Magazine (No. 2, 1980): 14–15 ((5))

JACKSON, WALTER

J11 PRUTER, Robert: Discography *in* Goldmine, No. 39 (August 1979): 22 ((5))

JACKSON, WANDA

J12 Discography *in* GARBUTT, Bob: Rockabilly queens. Toronto: Ducktail Press, 1979: 55–65 ((2, 3, 7))

J13 LAY, Rip: Wanda Jackson: the early years (1955–1963) *in* Who Put the Bomp, No. 9 (Spring 1972): 16–21; discography p. 21 [Albums only] ((5))

J14 Wanda Jackson LP disco *in* Kountry Korral, IX/2 (April 1976): 24 ((—))

J15 Wanda Jackson disco *in* Kountry Korral, IX/6 (December 1976): 21–22 ((3, 7))

J16 WOUNLUND, Jorn: Wanda Jackson disco *in* Rockville International (June–July 1974): 32–42 ((1, 2, 6, 7))

JACOBS, HOWARD

J17 WALKER, Steve: The recordings of Howard Jacobs *in* Talking Machine Review, No. 6 (October 1970): 168–169[a] ((7))

JAGUAR label

J18 MOONOOGIAN, George: Jaguar Records *in* Record Exchanger, IV/4 (No. 20): 22 ((—))

THE JAGUARS (musical group)

J19 WHITESELL, Rick, and Marv GOLDBERG: The Jaguars *in* Yesterday's Memories, III/2 (1977): 25 ((7))

JAM (musical group)

J20 OLAFSON, Peter, and Dan MARO-VINE: Jam discography *in* Trouser Press Collector's Magazine, I/6 (January–April 1979): [3] ((5))

JAMES, SONNY

J21 DAHMEN, Norbert, and E. Reinald SCHUMANN: Sonny James diskographie *in* Hillbilly, No. 59 (June 1979): 7–20 ((5, 7))

J22 Diskographie *in* Country Corner, No. 34 (April 1973): 2–7 ((—))

JAMES, TOMMY

J23 CLEE, Ken: Tommy James and Shondells discography *in* Goldmine, No. 50 (July 1980): 12 ((—))

J24 GREEN, Jim: Tommy James discography *in* Trouser Press, III/5 (No. 17, December 1976–January 1977): 22 ((—))

J25 LAUG, Steve: Tommy James & the Shondells: discography *in* Goldmine No. 18 (September 1977): 8 ((—))

JAN & ARNIE (musical group)

J26 KISKO, Frank M.: Jan & Arnie discography *in* Time Barrier Express, III/4 (No. 24, April–May 1979): 28 ((5))

JAN & DEAN (musical duo)

J27 BETROCK, Alan: &Jan&Dean&Jan& Dean& *in* The Rock Marketplace, No. 6 (July 1974): 3–7, 15, 39; addenda in No. 7 (October 1974): 43 and No. 8 (December 1974): 42 ((5))

J28 [Discography] *in* Record Finder, I/8 (October 1980): 9 ((—))

J29 Jan & Dean checklist: 45's *in* Goldmine, No. 31 (December 1978): 18 ((—))

J30 McDOWELL, Mike: Jan & Dean discography *in* Ballroom Blitz, No. 18 (February 1977): 8–9 ((5))

JANNACCI, ENZO

J31 Discografia essenziale in MOLLICA, Vincenzo: Enzo Jannacci. Poggibonsi: A. Lalli, 1979: 57–58 ((—))

JARRE, MAURICE

J32 LYNCH, Richard: The film composer on record: Maurice Jarre: part one *in* Kastlemusik Monthly Bulletin, VI/1 (January 1981): 1, 15 ((5))

J33 PECQUERIAUX, Jean-Pierre: Maurice Jarre: filmography/discography *in* Soundtrack!, No. 23 (Fall 1980): 16–17; No. 24 (Winter 1980/81): 13–16 ((5))

JASMAN label

J34 STANTON, Roy: Jasman label list *in* Shout, No. 99 (October 1974): 6 ((3, 6))

JASON CREST (musical group)

J35 Jason Crest *in* The Rock Marketplace, No. 7 (October 1974): 24; addenda in No. 8 (December 1974): 42 ((5))

JAUDAS' SOCIETY ORCHESTRA AND BAND

J36 JONES, David L.: Jaudas' Society Orchestra and Band 1915–1919 *in* New Amberola Graphic, No. 18 (Summer 1976): 4–7 ((—))

JA-WES label

J37 BAKER, Cary: Daran/Ja-Wes/DJO label listing *in* Shout, No. 83 (January 1973): [8–9]; additions and corrections in No. 95 (May 1974): 6 ((—))

JAY AND THE AMERICANS (musical group)

J38 VANCE, Marcia: Jay and the Americans discography *in* Bim Bam Boom, I/5 (April–May 1972): 12 ((3, 5))

JAY DEE label

J39 FLAM, Steve, et al.: Jay Dee records *in* Bim Bam Boom, I/2 (October–November 1971): 24; additions in I/3 (December 1971–January 1972): 21 ((—))

THE JAYHAWKS (musical group)

J40 GOLDBERG, Marv: The Jay-hawks/Vibrations *in* Bim Bam Boom, I/5 (April–May 1972): 19 ((5))

JEFFREYS, GARLAND

J41 WHITESELL, Rick: Garland Jeffreys discography *in* Goldmine, No. 57 (February 1981): 18 ((5))

JENKINS, DONALD

J42 Discography *in* PRUTER, Robert: Donald Jenkins' story *in* Record Exchanger, VI/1 (No. 28, December 1978): 14–15 ((5))

JENNINGS, WAYLON

J43 Waylon Jennings: discography *in* ALLEN, Bob: Waylon & Willie: the full story in words and pictures of Waylon Jennings & Willie Nelson. New York: Quick Fox, 1979: 122–127 ((5))

J44 ANDERL, Peter: Waylon Jennings diskographie *in* Hillbilly, No. 48 (September 1976): 8–17; No. 58 (March 1979): 22–26 ((1))

J45 GARBUTT, Bob: Waylon Jennings discography *in* Goldmine, No. 43 (December 1979): 22 ((5))

J46 MANNING, Ken: [Diskographie] *in* Country Corner (June 1981): 20–21 ((5))

J47 RAUSCHENBACH, Gunter: [Discography] *in* Country Corner, No. 48 (February 1976): [14]–16 ((5))

J48 SMITH, John L.: "I ain't no ordinary dude"—a bio-discography of Waylon Jennings *in* Journal of Country Music, VI/2 (Summer 1975): 45–95 ((2, 3, 5, 6, 7)); . . . a discographical update in VIII/2: 78–91 ((1, 2, 7))

J49 SMITH, John L.: Waylon Jennings: recording history and complete discography, 1959–1972. Des Moines, Iowa: Smith [1972]. 34 pp. ((3, 5, 7))

JENSEN, FREDERIK

J50 Frederik Jensen: den go'e gamle revy og grammofonen. Copenhagen: Andreasen, 1978. 255 pp. ((3, 4, 6, 7))

JEROME BROTHERS (musical group)

J51 ENGEL, Edward R.: Jerome Brothers discography *in* Time Barrier Express, III (No. 26, September–October 1979): 56–58 ((—))

THE JESTERS (musical group)

J52 HINCKLEY, Dave: The Jesters *in* Yesterday's Memories, II/2 (1976): 20 ((7))

JET (musical group)

J53 BETROCK, Alan: Discography *in* Trans-Oceanic Trouser Press, II/6 (February–March 1976): 15 ((5))

JETHRO TULL (musical group)

J54 Jethro Tull discography *in* Down Beat, XLIII (March 11, 1976): 16 ((—))

JEWEL label

See also *Bibliography* Vol. 2, Jazz

J55 PERIN, Jacques, and Gilles PETARD: Listing Jewel . . . *in* Soul Bag, No. 77 (1980): 23–28 ((—))

THE JEWELS (musical group)

J56 GOLDBERG, Marv, and Rick WHITESELL: The Jewels *in* Yesterday's Memories, III/2 (1977): 20 ((7))

JIM AND JESSE AND THE VIRGINIA BOYS (musical group)

See also McREYNOLDS BROTHERS

J57 Jim and Jesse and the Virginia Boys discography *in* Kountry Korral (No. 2, 1979): 18 ((—))

J58 PIETSCH, Reinhard: Jim & Jesse auf Langspielplatten *in* Country Corner, No. 45 (July 1975): 12 ((—))

J59 TAYLOR, Janet, et al.: Discography of albums by Jim & Jesse and the Virginia Boys *in* Bluegrass Unlimited, V/2 (August 1970): 7–9 ((7))

THE JIVE FIVE (musical group)

J60   MOHR, Kurt: Jive Five discography *in* Shout, No. 57 (July 1970): [5]–6 ((2, 3, 7))

THE JIVE TONES (musical group)

J61   [Discography] *in* Time Barrier Express, No. 21 (January–February 1977): [15] ((5))

J.O.B. label

See also *Bibliography* Vol. 2, Jazz

J62   J.O.B. *in* Blues Research (No. 15): 14–17 ((3, 4, 6))

JODIMARS (musical group)

J63   The Jodimars *in* Rocking Regards, No. 16 ([July?] 1979): 5–8 ((—))

JOEL, BILLY

J64   Discography *in* GAMBACCINI, Peter: Billy Joel. New York: Quick Fox, 1979: 127–128 ((5))

J65   Discography *in* MYERS, Donald M.: Headliners, Billy Joel. New York: Tempo Books, 1981: 165–167 ((5))

JOHN, ELTON

J66   Singles and albums *in* A conversation with Elton John and Bernie Taupin. New York: Flash Books; distributed by Flash Books, 1975: 110–111 ((5))

J67   GROTH, Gary, and Karen ZIMMERMANN: A consumer's guide to Elton's bootlegs; [addendum to discography in previous issue] *in* Sounds Fine *in* The Rock Collector's Marketplace, No. 10 (July 1976): 10–11 ((—))

J68   Discography *in* NEWMAN, Gerald: Elton John. New York: New American Library, 1976: 185–188 ((5))

J69   Recordings by Elton John *in* SHAW, Greg: Elton John: a biography in words & pictures. [s.l.]: Sire Books; New York: distributed by Chappell Music Co., 1976: 52–54 ((1, 5))

J70   Discography *in* TATHAM, Dick: Elton John. London: Octopus Books, 1976: 91 ((5))

JOHN, ROBERT

J71   BEACHLEY, Chris: Robert John/ Bobby Pedrick discography *in* It Will Stand, No. 21 (c1981): 7 ((5))

JOHNNIE & JACK (musical duo)

J72   Johnnie & Jack record listing *in* Country-Western Express, No. 10 [n.d.]: 17 ((—))

JOHNNY AND HIS CELLAR ROCKERS (musical group)

J73   MUYS, Piet: [Discography] *in* Rumble, II/4 (Winter 1974–75): 7 ((—))

JOHNNY AND THE HURRICANES (musical group)

J74   Johnny & the Hurricanes discography *in* Goldmine, No. 57 (February 1981): 11 ((—))

J75   Johnny & the Hurricanes; discography 45's & EP *in* Rock 'n' Roll International Magazine (Dutch), No. 107 (July–August 1977): 6 ((—))

J76   MACKENZIE, Colin: Johnny & the Hurricanes U.S./U.K. discography *in* Rumble, III/2 (Winter 1975–76): 10–11 ((5))

JOHN'S CHILDREN (musical group)

J77   BETROCK, Alan: All John's Children *in* The Rock Marketplace, No. 6 (July 1974): 32–35; discography p. 35; addendum in No. 10 (June 1975): 50 [Includes early Marc Colan and Andy Ellison solo recordings] ((5))

J78   HOGG, Brian: John's Children *in* Bam Balam, No. 2 (June 1975): 17–19; addenda in No. 5 (February 1977): 1–6 and No. 14 (September 1982): 13 ((2)) [Includes Jook]

JOHNSON, BUDDY

J79   Buddy Johnson discography *in* GRENDYSA, Peter: The Buddy Johnson story *in* Record Exchanger, VI/1 (No. 28, December 1979?): 18–23 ((5))

JOHNSON, HERB

J80   MOHR, Kurt: Herb Johnson & the Impacts *in* Shout, No. 95 (May 1974): 2 ((2, 3, 5, 7))

JOHNSON, LARRY

J81   POMPOSELLO, Tom: Living Blues interview: Larry Johnson *in* Living Blues, No. 16 (Spring 1974): 16–22; discography p. 22 ((—))

JOHNSON, ROLAND

J82   [COHEN, Norm]: McVay & Johnson discography *in* JEMF Quarterly, X/3 (No. 35, Autumn 1974): 95 ((3, 6, 7))

JOHNSON label

J83   TOPPING, Ray: Johnson label listing *in* Shout, No. 98 (September 1974): 8–9 ((3, 5))

JOHNSTON, BRUCE

J84   Bruce Johnston *in* The Rock Marketplace, No. 5 (April 1974): 18–22; discography pp. 21–22; addenda in No. 6 (July 1974): 38; No. 7 (October 1974): 43; No. 8 (December 1974): 42 [Does not include tracks with the Beach Boys] ((3, 5))

JOLSON, AL

J85   Al Jolson's recordings; an index *in* ANDERTON, Barrie: Sonny boy!; the world of Al Jolson. London: Jupiter Books, 1975: 119–133 ((—))

J86   [[JAY, Dave: Jolsonography, 2nd ed. Bournemouth, England: Barrie Anderton, 1974. 284 pp.]]

J87   Discography 1912–1950 *in* OBERFIRST, Robert: Al Jolson. San Diego: A.S. Barnes; London: Tantivy Press, 1980: [327]–337 ((—))

JONES, CASEY, AND THE GOVERNORS

J88   Casey Jones and the Governors *in* Gorilla Beat, No. 1 (1979): 24–33; discography pp. 27–33; addenda in No. 2 (1979): 21, No. 4 (1979): 39, No. 8 (1980): 46, and No. 13 (1982): 70 ((—))

JONES, DAVID

J89   CLAYTON, John: David Jones solo discography *in* Blitz, No. 27 (July 1978): 20 [Pre- and post-Monkees recordings] ((5))

JONES, EDDIE, JR.

J90   MONDRONE, Sal: Rare sounds *in* Bim Bam Boom, I/3 (December 1971–January 1972): 11 ((—))

JONES, GEORGE

J91   STRUBING, Hauke: George Jones-Langspielplatten-Disco *in* Country Corner, No. 46 (October 1975): 7–[11] ((—))

JONES, GRANPA

J92   [Discography] *in* Country Western Express, No. 21 (December 1958): ? ((—))

JONES, LINDA

J93   MOHR, Kurt: Linda Jones discography *in* Shout, No. 75 (March 1972): [3–4] ((2, 3, 7))

JONES, SPIKE

J94   MORRIS, Randy, and Ted HERING: Spike Jones—discography *in* After Beat, I/9 (June 1971): 8 ((7))

J95   SMITH, Ronald L.: Spike Jones domestic albums *in* Goldmine, No. 48 (May 1980): 147 ((—))

JONES, TOM

J96   Discography *in* JONES, Peter: Tom Jones: biography of a great star. London: Barker, 1970: 116–120; Chicago: Regnery, 1970: 157–161 ((—))

JOPLIN, JANIS

J97   Discography *in* LANDAU, Deborah: Janis Joplin, her life and times. New York: Paperback Library, 1971: 158–160 ((—))

JORDAN, ELLINGTON
See FUGI

JOSIE label

See also *Bibliography* Vol. 2, Jazz

J98   GONZALEZ, Fernando L.: The Josie label discography *in* Goldmine, No. 34 (March 1979): 36–38; additions in No. 38 (July 1979): 42 ((3, 5))

JOY DIVISION (musical group)

J99   DAVELAAR, Gerard: In concert: Joy Division *in* Gorilla Beat, No. 12 (1981): 31–37 ((1, 5, 6a))

JUANITA label

J100   TRABOSCI, Tom: [Discography] *in* Bim Bam Boom, No. 8 (December 1972): [24] ((—))

JUDD label

J101   ROBERTSON, Paul: Judd label *in* New Kommotion, No. 14 (Winter 1977): 14; addenda in No. 16 (Summer 1977): 42 ((—))

JUICY LUCY (musical group)

J102   Juicy Lucy *in* Bedloe's Island, No. 4 (Spring 1972): 12 ((2))

JULIEN, PAULINE

J103   Discographie *in* Pauline Julien. Paris: Seghers, 1974: [174] ((—)) (Collection poesie et chansons Seghers, 29)

THE JUMPING JACKS (musical group)

J104   MUYS, Piet: [Discography] *in* Rumble, II/4 (Winter 1974–75): 7–8 ((5))

JUSTICE, DICK

J105   [RUSSELL, Tony]: Dick Justice *in* Old Time Music, No. 11 (Winter 1973/4): 23 ((3, 7))

K.C. AND THE SUNSHINE BAND (musical group)

K1   MOHR, Kurt: Discographie de K.C. and the Sunshine Band *in* Soul Bag, No. 43–44 (November–December 1974): 5 ((2, 3, 7))

KALEIDOSCOPE (musical group)

K2   [Discography] *in* Zig Zag, No. 60 (May 1976): [23] ((5))

KANE, HELEN

K3   BEDOIAN, Jim: Helen Kane; a mini-discography *in* Discographer, II/3 (3rd Quarter 1971): 2-153-2-158 ((3, 7))

KAREN label

K4   WILSON, Jim: Karen label listing *in* Shout, No. 88 (August 1973): 1-[2]; additions and corrections in No. 90 (November 1973): 9; No. 92 (January 1974): [8–9] ((3, 5))

KARNES, ALFRED G.

K5   EDWARDS, J.: [Discography] *in* Disc Collector, No. 16 [n.d., 1960?]: ? ((2, 3, 7))

K6   [RUSSELL, Tony]: Alfred G. Karnes *in* Old Time Music, No. 7 (Winter 1972/3): 20 ((3, 6, 7))

KAUFMAN, IRVING

K7   Irving Kaufman: a short selection *in* Gunn Report, No. 21 (June–July 1970): 24–25 ((—))

KAZEE, BUELL

K8   [COHEN, Norm]: Discography of recordings by Buell Kazee *in* JEMF Quarterly, VI/1 (No. 17, Spring 1970): 19–22 ((1, 3, 6, 7))

K9   [Discography] *in* Folk Style, No. 1 (December 1957): ? ((—))

K10   EDWARDS, J.: [Discography] *in* Caravan, No. 17 (June–July 1959): ? ((2, 3, 7))

KEIL, FREDDY

K11   HOOKWAY, Kevin: Freddy Keil: additions to previous discographies [from issues No. 19 and 20] *in* Big Beat of the 50's, No. 21 (August 1979): 66 ((—))

KEIL ISLES (musical group)

K12 PHILLIPS, John: Additions to previously published discographies *in* Big Beat of the 50's, No. 20 (May 1979): 61; No. 21 (August 1979): 65–66 ((—))

KELLMAC label

K13 [[[Discography] *in* Shout, No. 82 (December 1972); additions and corrections in No. 92 (January 1974): 9]]

THE KENDALLS (musical group)

K14 KARLSSON, Sture: The Kendalls disco *in* Kountry Korral Magazine (No. 2, 1980): 13 ((—))

KENNY AND THE KASUALS (musical group)

K15 HOGG, Brian: [Discography] *in* Thru the rhythm: Texas rock 'n' roll *in* Bam Balam, No. 10 (November 1979): 11–12 ((5))

K16 PARKER, Richard: Kenny and the Kasuals discography . . . *in* Goldmine, No. 65 (October 1981): 176 ((5, 7))

THE KENTUCKY REVELLERS (musical group)

K17 RHODES, Roy E.: The Kentucky Revellers *in* Gunn Report, No. 56 (January–February 1976): 13 ((—)); Afterthoughts in GR 57 (May–June 1976): 5, 12 ((3, 6, 7))

KERN, JEROME. SHOWBOAT

K18 A selected discography *in* KRUEGER, Miles: Showboat, the story of a classic American musical. New York: Oxford University Press, 1977: 236–239 ((—))

KESSINGER BROTHERS (musical group)

K19 [Discography] *in* Folk Style, No. 13 [n.d., 1966?]: ? ((2, 3, 7))

K20 [Discography] *in* notes for Folk Promotions Record FP 828 [n.d.]: ? ((2, 3, 7))

KEURIS, TRISTAN

K22 Discography *in* Key Notes, No. 5 (No. 1, 1977): 25 ((—))

KICKS label

K23 GIBBON, Peter, and Tony TISOVEC: [Discography] *in* Yesterday's Memories, III/3 (1977): 27 ((7))

K24 TISOVEC, Tony: Kicks label listing *in* Shout, No. 80 (September 1972): [7] ((—))

KIDD, JOHNNY, & THE PIRATES (musical group)

K25 BRYAN, Pete: Discography *in* SMG, V/1 (October 1973): 4–5 ((—))

K26 FOX, Phil: [Discography] *in* Who Put the Bomp, No. 8 (Fall–Winter 1971): 16 ((5))

KILGORE, MERLE

K27 SWAN, Johnny: Merle Kilgore *in* Kommotion, No. 10–11 (Winter 1975–76): 30–31 ((3, 5))

KINCAID, BRADLEY

K28 Bradley Kincaid discography *in* Country & Western Spotlight, No. 12 (September 1977): 13–19; additions and corrections in No. 13 (December 1977): 33 ((2, 3, 6, 7)) [From JEMF Quarterly, No. 44]

K29 Bradley Kincaid discography *in* JEMF Quarterly, XII (No. 44, Winter 1976): 223–228 ((3, 7))

K30 COHEN, Norm: Bradley Kincaid diskographie *in* Hillbilly, No. 56 (September 1976): 15–22 ((3, 6, 7))

K31 [Discography] *in* Country Western Express, No. 21 [New series] (January 1967): 29–30 ((—))

K32 [Discography] *in* Disc Collector, No. 12 and 13 [n.d.]: ? ((—))

K33 EDWARDS, J.: [Discography] *in* Disc Collector, No. 11 [n.d.]: ? ((—))

K21 FUCHS, Walter W.: Diskographie *in* Hillbilly, No. 26 (June 1968): 19–20 ((7))

K34 Discography *in* JONES, Loyal: Radio's "Kentucky mountain boy" Bradley Kincaid. Berea, Ky.: Appalachian Center/Berea College, 1980: [171]–185 ((2, 3, 6, 7))

KING, AL
See also *Bibliography* Vol. 2, Jazz

K35 MOHR, Kurt: Discography *in* Shout, No. 95 (May 1974): 2 ((2, 3, 5, 7))

KING, B. B.
See also *Bibliography* Vol. 2, Jazz

K36 Annotated discography of B. B. King recordings, 1949–1980 *in* SAWYER, Charles: The arrival of B. B. King. Garden City, N.Y.: Doubleday, 1980; New York: Da Capo, 1982: 235–263 ((1, 5))

KING, BEN E.
See also *Bibliography* Vol. 2, Jazz

K37 BURNS, Peter: Ben E. King discography *in* Shout, No. 89 (September 1973): [5–6] ((3, 7))

KING, FREDDY

K38 BEACHLEY, Chris: Freddy King discography *in* It Will Stand, No. 27–28 (c1982): 33 ((5))

KING, REGINALD

K39 UPTON, Stuart: Reginald King and his Orchestra *in* Commodore, No. 2 (Summer 1971): 3 + ; addenda in No. 3 (Autumn 1971): 7; No. 4 (Winter 1972): 8 ((—))

KING, SID

K40 WEIZE, Richard, and Hank TAYLOR: Sid King discography *in* Not Fade Away, No. 17 (1981): 37–38 ((2, 3, 5))

KING, WINDSOR JACKSON

K41 BERGER, Ken: Windsor King discography *in* Record Exchanger, IV/1 (No. 17): 7 ((—))

KING CRIMSON (musical group)

K42 King Crimson *in* Trouser Press Collector's Magazine, IV/2 (November–December 1981): 3 ((—))

K43 SEKULOVICH, Milo: King Crimson discography *in* Aware, No. 7 (Spring 1981): 22 ((—))

K44 SLABICKY, Ihor: [Discography] *in* Trans-Oceanic Trouser Press, No. 4 (July–August 1974): 20–22 ((5))

KING label
See also *Bibliography* Vol. 2, Jazz

K45 BEZANKER, Paul: King Records 500 series *in* Paul's Record Magazine, III/5 (June 1976): 17–18; IV/1 (No. 17–18, August 1976): 84–122 ((3, 4))

K46 King 500 series numerical *in* JEMF Quarterly, IV/2 (No. 10, June 1968) to VI/1 (No. 17, Spring 1970): various paginations ((3))

K47 MARTIN, Tony: King oldies *in* Hot Buttered Soul, No. 15 (February 1973): 11 ((—))

KING label [England]

K48 FAULL, Trev: The King label *in* Outlet, No. 8 (Xmas 1978): 6–8 ((—))

THE KINGS (musical group)

K49 GOLDBERG, Marv, and Dave HINCKLEY: The Kings *in* Yesterday's Memories, III/3 (1977): 4 ((7))

KINGSTON TRIO (musical group)

K50 RUBECK, Jack A., and Benjamin S. BLAKE: Goldmine, No. 65 (October 1981): 184–185; additions and corrections in No. 67 (December 1981): 174 ((5))

THE KINKS (musical group)
See also DAVIES, RAY

K51 CLEE, Ken, and Bruce NICOLS: The Kinks discography *in* Goldmine, No. 59 (April 1981): 16, 161 ((—))

K52 HEBING, Alfred: The Kinks *in* Gorilla Beat, No. 13 (1982): 3–30; discography pp. 12–30 ((5))

K53   HOGG, Brian: The Kinks *in* Bam
       Balam, No. 3 (December 1975): 3–24;
       discography pp. 8–23; addenda in No.
       5 (February 1977): 16 ((1)) [Includes
       Dave Davies solo and cover record-
       ings. U.S., U.K., Dutch, German,
       French, Italian, and Swedish issues]

K54   Kinks compendium *in* Who Put the
       Bomp, No. 7 (Summer 1971): 7–11;
       discography pp. 10–11 ((1, 5))

K55   RICHARDSON, Ben: Kink Klassics *in*
       Trans-Oceanic Trouser Press, II/2
       (April–May 1975): 24–28 ((—))

KNAPP, ORVILLE

K56   ANDERSON, Andy: Discography—
       Orville Knapp Orchestra *in* After
       Beat, II/4 (April–May 1972): 16 ((5))

KNICKERBOCKERS (musical group)

K57   SMALL, Bill, and Ken BARNES:
       Knickerbocker discography *in* Who
       Put the Bomp, No. 12 (Summer
       1974): 13; additions and corrections in
       No. 14 (Fall 1975): 44 ((—))

KNIGHT, BAKER

K58   MILLAR, Bill: Good Knight *in* New
       Kommotion, No. 25 (1980): 42–45;
       discography (by Ray TOPPING) p. 45
       ((1, 2, 3, 7))

KNIGHT, ROBERT

K59   [MILLAR, Bill]: [Discography] *in*
       Shout, No. 94 (April 1974): 5 ((2, 5))

KNIGHT, TERRY, & THE PACK
(musical group)

K60   SHAW, Greg: Terry Knight discog-
       raphy *in* Jamz, No. 3 (February 1972):
       6–7; addendum in No. 5 (c1972): 43
       ((—))

KNOWLES, RICHARD G.

K61   BAYLY, E.: R. G. Knowles *in* Talk-
       ing Machine Review International,
       No. 48 (October 1977): 1117–1118
       ((3, 7))

K62   KELLY, A., et al.: G & T's by R. G.
       Knowles *in* Talking Machine Review,
       No. 49b [n.d.]: 1211 ((3, 7))

KNOX, BUDDY

K63   CHAPADOS, Jean-Pierre: Buddy
       Knox discography *in* Big Beat of the
       50's, No. 13 (August 1977): 45 ((—))

K64   Discography *in* TREUDE, Helmut:
       Buddy Knox: ein Rockabilly? *in*
       Country Corner, No. 55 (July 1977):
       13 ((—))

THE KODAKS (musical group)

K65   BECKMAN, Jeff: [Discography] *in*
       Big Town Review, I/3 (July–August
       1972): 56 ((3))

THE KODOKS (musical group)

K66   RUSSO, Tony: Oh gee, oh gosh, it's
       . . . the Kodoks *in* Yesterday's
       Memories, II/1 (1976): 14 ((7))

KOOB, ROGER

K67   KOOB, Roger, and Paul BEZAN-
       KER: Roger Koob discography *in*
       Paul's Record Magazine (No. 16): 9
       ((5))

K68   PEARLIN, Victor: Roger Koob group
       discography *in* Paul's Record Maga-
       zine, II/4 (October 1975): 16; addi-
       tions and corrections in II/6 (Decem-
       ber 1975): 5 ((3, 5))

K69   Roger Koob discography *in* Nostalgia
       World, No. 2 [1978]: 20 ((5))

THE KOOBAS (musical group)

K70   The Koobas *in* Gorilla Beat, No. 5
       (1979): 8–11; discography p. 11; ad-
       denda in No. 6 (1980): 46 ((5))

THE KOOL GENTS (musical group)

K71   GALGANO, Bob: El Dorados & Kool
       Gents *in* Bim Bam Boom, I/2 (Octo-
       ber–November 1971): 8 ((—))

K72   HINCKLEY, Dave: The Kool Gents
       in Goldmine, No. 35 (April 1979): 43
       ((5))

KOOPER, AL

K73   Discography *in* his Backstage passes:
       rock 'n' roll life in the sixties. New
       York: Stein and Day, 1977: 245–246
       ((—))

K74 TAMARKIN, Jeff: Discography *in* Goldmine, No. 62 (July 1981): 13 ((—))

KORNER, ALEXIS/BLUES INCORPORATED

K75 Discography *in* HOGG, Brian: Boom boom: British blue-eyed R&B *in* Bam Balam, No. 13 (August 1981): 16–18 ((5))

KOTTKE, LEO

K76 GILBUT, Jerry: Discography *in* Zig Zag, VI/6 (No. 56, 1975): 31 ((5))

KRAMER, BILLY J.

K77 CALABRO, Karen: Billy J. Kramer discography *in* Blitz, No. 35 (March–April 1980): 15 ((5))

K78 HEBING, Alfred: Billy Jay *in* Gorilla Beat, No. 11 (1981): 15–24; discography pp. 21–24; addenda in No. 13 (1982): 73 ((5)) [Includes the Dakatas]

KRISTOFFERSON, KRIS

K79 Discography *in* KALET, Beth: Kris Kristofferson. New York: Quick Fox, 1978: 94–96 ((5))

K80 RAUSCHENBACH, Gunter: Eine kleine Kristofferson-Disco *in* Country Corner, No. 42 (December 1974): 14 ((—))

KUNZ, CHARLIE

K81 BARTER, Roy: Charlie Kunz *in* Commodore, No. 5 (Spring 1972): 13 + ((—))

LABEEF, SLEEPY

L1 HAWKINS, Martin: . . . with Sleepy LaBeef *in* New Kommotion, No. 18 (Winter 1978): 46, 48; discography p. 48; addenda in No. 19 (Spring 1978): 14 ((2, 3, 7))

L2 KOMOROWSKI, Adam, and Ray TOPPING: Sleepy LaBeef *in* New Kommotion, No. 22 (1979): 4–6 ((1, 2, 3, 7))

L3 SMART, Peter: Sleepy LaBeef: a legend *in* Kommotion, No. 8 (Winter 1975): 15–16; addendum in No. 10–11 (Winter 1975–76): 26 ((—))

LABELLE, PATTI, AND THE BLUEBELLS (musical group)
See also *Bibliography* Vol. 2, Jazz

L4 [Discography] *in* Paul's Record Magazine, IV/2 (No. 13–14): 12; additions and corrections in No. 15 (January–February 1977): 41 ((5))

LAINE, DENNY

L5 BETROCK, Alan: Denny Laine *in* Jamz, No. 2 (October 1971): 10; addenda in No. 3 (February 1972): 23; No. 4 (May 1972): 34 ((—))

LAMA, SERGE

L6 Discographie *in* Serge Lama. Paris: Seghers, 1974: 156–157 ((—)) (Collection poesie et chansons Seghers, 24)

LAMAN label

L7 Laman label *in* Hot Buttered Soul, No. 27 (February 1974): 8 ((3))

LAMB label

L8 LEGERE, Will: [Discography] *in* Disc Collector, No. 16 (February 1961): ? ((—))

LAMBERT label

L9 ANDREWS, F.: The records of the Lambert Company Limited *in* Talking Machine Review, No. 27 (April 1974): 78–91; [corrections] in No. 29 (August 1974): 152–153, 162 ((5))

L10 KOENIGSBERG, Allen: In the pink: a Lambert discography *in* Antique Phonography Monthly, VI/8 (1981): 4–10; VI/9 (1981): 8–9 ((—))

L11 MANZO, J. R.: A Lambert sampler *in* New Amberola Graphic, VIII/4 (No. 32, Spring 1980): 4–7 ((—))

LAMOUR, DOROTHY

L12 LYNCH, Richard C.: A movie songbook and discography of Dorothy

Lamour *in* Kastlemusik Monthly Bulletin, VI/6 (June 1981): 1, 7-8 ((5, 7))

LAMP label

L13 GRENDYSA, Peter, and Victor PEARLIN: Discography *in* Paul's Record Magazine, III/3 (April 1976): 13; additions and corrections in III/4 (May 1976): 5, 10 ((3, 5))

LAND, NORRIS

L14 [Discography] *in* JEMF Quarterly, VII/3 (No. 23, Fall 1971): 123 +

LANDY, ART

L15 Art Landy records *in* New Amberola Graphic, No. 6 (Summer 1973): 10-[14] ((—))

LANE, JERRY MAX

L16 Jerry Max Lane disco *in* Kountry Korral, X/2 (April 1977): 37 ((—))

LANZA, MARIO

L17 The Mario Lanza discography *in* CALLINICOS, Constantine: The Mario Lanza story. New York: Coward-McCann, 1960: 251-256 ((—))

THE LARKS (musical group)

L18 BECKMAN, Jeff: The Larks *in* Big Town Review, I/3 (July-August 1972): 39 ((3, 5))

LASHWOOD, GEORGE

L19 George Lashwood discography *in* BARKER, Tony: George Lashwood in Music-Hall Records, No. 3 (October 1978): 44-50 ((3, 5, 7)); [addition] in No. 4 (December 1978): 63 ((—))

LAST, JAMES

L20 Discographie James Last *in* his James Last Story. Hamburg: R. Gloss, 1975: 302-305 ((—))

L21 Discography *in* WILLOX, Bob: James Last. London: Everest, 1976: [5-6] ((5))

LAURIE label

L22 BEZANKER, Paul: Laurie Records *in* Paul's Record Magazine, IV/1 (August 1976): 29; No. 15 (January-February 1977): 26-28 ((3, 4))

L23 CALLAHAN, Mike: Laurie Records *in* Goldmine, No. 56 (January 1981): 170-172 ((—))

L24 [Discography] *in* Time Barrier Express, No. 22 (March-April 1977): 15-19 ((—))

LAVAGNINO, FRANCESCO

L25 MARSHALL, James: Francesco Lavagnino: Filmography/discography *in* Soundtrack Collector's Newsletter, IV (No. 15, October 1978): 13-16; IV (No. 16, January 1979): 13-16 ((5))

LAVETT, BETTY

L26 [Discography] *in* Shout, No. 45 (July 1969): [7] ((3, 7))

LEAKE COUNTY REVELERS (musical group)

L27 KUNSTADT, Len, and B. COLTON: The Columbia recordings of the Leake County Revelers *in* Record Research, No. 68 (May 1965): 5 ((2, 3, 6, 7))

L28 MATHIS, R.: [Discography] *in* Disc Collector, No. 9 [n.d., 1955?]: ? ((3))

LEAMORE, TOM

L29 BARKER, Tony: Tom Leamore *in* Music-Hall Records, No. 6 (April 1979): 104-112 ((3, 7))

THE LEAVES (musical group)

L30 BARNES, Ken: Discography *in* Who Put the Bomp, No. 12 (Summer 1974): 12 ((—))

LECOR, TEX

L31 Les images d'une grande carriere: Tex Lecor *in* Tele-radiomonde, XLI (No. 43, 22–28 July 1979): 26–27

LED ZEPPELIN (musical group)

L32 Discographies individuelles *in* DISTER, Alain: Led Zeppelin. Paris: A. Michel, 1980: [185]–186 ((—))

L33 Discography *in* GROSS, Michael: Led Zeppelin's golden boy, Robert Plant. New York: Popular Library, 1975: 7–9 ((1, 5))

L34 Discography *in* YORKE, Ritchie: The Led Zeppelin biography. Toronto: Methuen; New York: Two Continents, 1976: 190–192 ((1, 7))

LEDOUX, CHRIS

L35 ROSENDAHL, Kjell: Chris LeDoux: the singin' rodeo man *in* Kountry Korral, XI/3–4 (1978): 16–18 ((5))

L36 WEIZE, Richard A.: Chris LeDoux diskographie *in* Hillbilly, No. 49 (December 1976): 41–42 ((5))

LEE, BRENDA

L37 Brenda Lee LP disco *in* Kountry Korral Magazine (No. 2, 1980): 35 ((5))

L38 GARBUTT, Bob: Brenda Lee discography *in* Goldmine, No. 47 (April 1980): 10–11 ((3, 5))

L39 GARBUTT, Bob: Brenda Lee: the early years *in* New Kommotion, No. 18 (Winter 1978): 31; addenda in No. 22 (1979): 65 ((—))

L40 Discography *in* GARBUTT, Bob: Rockabilly queens. Toronto: Ducktail Press, 1979: 67–68 ((2, 3, 7))

LEE, CURTIS

L41 BRYAN, Pete: Curtis Lee discography *in* SMG, IV/8 (March 1975): 16 ((—))

LEE, DICKIE

L42 ENGEL, Ed: The early recordings of Dickie Lee *in* Record Digest, I/16 (May 1, 1978): 12 ((5))

LEE, JACKIE

L43 SMART, Peter: Discography *in* Kommotion, No. 6 (Summer 1974): 5 ((—))

LEE, LEONARD
See SHIRLEY & LEE

LEE, LONNIE

L44 DUFF, Colin, and Frank CAMPBELL: Lonnie Lee discography *in* Big Beat of the 50's, No. 24 (June 1980): 7–9; addendum in No. 25 (September 1980): 54 ((—))

LEE, MYRON
(real name Myron Wachendorf)

L45 RUSSELL, Wayne: Myron Lee and the Caddies *in* SMG, VI/4 (October 1980): 16–18; discography p. 18 ((5))

LEE, NICKIE

L46 MOHR, Kurt: Nickie Lee discography *in* Shout, No. 60 (November 1970): [9] ((3, 7))

LEE, WILMA

L47 COGSWELL, Robert: Wilma Lee and Stoney Cooper discography *in* JEMF Quarterly, XI/2 (No. 38, Summer 1975): 89–94 ((2, 3, 5, 6, 7))

LEE label

L48 HORLICK, Dick: Lee label *in* Shout, No. 43 (April 1969): [13] ((3))

THE LEFT BANKE (musical group)

L49 FLEURY, Joseph: The Left Banke *in* The Rock Marketplace, No. 1 (May 1973): 3–5; discography p. 5 ((—))

THE LEGENDS (musical group)

L50 LEMLICH, Jeff: A history of the Legends *in* Blitz, No. 36 (May–June 1980): 18–19 [Includes Jim Sessody] ((5))

LEGGETT, ERNEST

L51 HAYES, Jim: Ernest Leggett's Orchestra/String Orchestra/Symphony Orchestra: on Sterno 78s (1930–1932) *in* Vintage Light Music, No. 14 (Spring 1978): 4 ((3, 5))

LEHRER, TOM

L52 Discography *in* WHITESELL, Rick: Tom Lehrer: forgotten but not gone *in* Goldmine, No. 23 (February 1978): 13–15 ((—))

LEIBER, JERRY, AND STOLLER, MIKE

L53 Recordings of works by Leiber and Stoller and A chronological listing of records produced by Leiber and Stoller *in* PALMER, Robert: Baby that was rock & roll. New York: Harvest, 1978: 120–131 ((5))

LEJUNE, IRY

L54 LEADBITTER, Mike: Iry Lejune *in* Old Time Music, No. 14 (Autumn 1974): 21–22 ((3, 7))

LE LURON, THIERRY

L55 Discographie *in* his Comme trois pommes. Paris: Flammarion, 1978: 259- [261] ((—))

L56 Discographie *in* MOGUI, Jean Pierre: Thierry Le Luron. Paris: Ed. Saint-Germain-des-Pres, 1971: [125–126] ((—))

LEMARQUE, FRANCIS

L57 Discographie *in* Francis Lemarque. Paris: Seghers, 1974: [185]–188 ((—)) (Collection poesie et chansons Seghers, 26)

LENNARD, ARTHUR

L58 BARKER, Tony: Arthur Lennard *in* Music Hall, No. 10 (December 1979): 65–74 ((3, 5, 7))

LENNON, JOHN

L59 Lennon's recordings *in* CONNOLLY, Ray: John Lennon, 1940–1980. London: Fontana, 1981: 177–185 ((—))

L60 John Lennon discography *in* FAWCETT, Anthony: John Lennon: one day at a time. New York: Grove Press, 1976, 1980: [188]–190 ((5, 7))

L61 John & Yoko: for the record *in* Music World, No. 81 (January 1981): 12 ((—))

L62 John Lennon/Beatles discography *in* Schwann-2 Record & Tape Guide, No. 34 (Spring–Summer 1981): 4–5 ((7))

L63 [[Discography *in* LEBLANC, Jacques: Lennon, McCartney. Paris: J. Grancher, 1981: 104–[127]]]

L64 Singles + albums *in* SIERRA I FABRA, Jordi: John Lennon. Barcelona: Teorama, 1981: 55–123 ((—))

LENO, DAN

L65 KELLY, A., et al.: Dan Leno discography *in* Talking Machine Review, No. 49b [n.d.]: 1211–1213 ((1, 3, 7))

LENORMAN, GERARD

L66 Discographie *in* CHANDET, Elisabeth: Gerard Lenorman. Paris: Seghers, 1974: 188 ((—)) (Collection poesie et chansons Seghers, 34)

LEON, JACK

L67 HAYES, Jim: Jack Leon on Piccadilly and Octacros 78s *in* Vintage Light Music, No. 15 (Summer 1978): 12–13 ((3))

LEWIS, GARY, AND THE PLAYBOYS (musical group)

L68 CLEE, Ken: Gary Lewis discography *in* Goldmine, No. 37 (June 1979): 15 ((—))

L69 GONZALEZ, Fernando L.: Gary Lewis and the Playboys discography *in* Goldmine, No. 38 (July 1979): 42 ((1, 3, 6, 7))

LEWIS, JERRY LEE

L70 Discography *in* CAIN, Robert J.: Whole lotta shakin's goin' on: Jerry Lee Lewis. New York: Dial Press, 1981: 127–141 ((5))

L71 DIVOUX, Jean-Paul: Les sessions de 1954 a 1963 *in* Big Beat, No. 15 (September 1977): 22–30 ((1, 2, 3, 7))

L72 GAMBLIN, Barrie: Jerry Lee Lewis, a post 1970 discography *in* Kommotion, No. 6 (Summer 1974): 22–23 ((—))

L73 GAMBLIN, Barrie: Jerry Lee Lewis, 1970–1974: part 3 *in* Kommotion, No. 8 (Winter 1975): 8–9 ((—))

L74 KINDER, Bob: Jerry Lee Lewis *in* Record Exchanger, IV/5 (No. 21): 11 ((—))

L75 VAN RAAY, Henk: Jerry Lee Lewis disc special. n.p.: Wim de Boer (?), 1976. 36 pp. ((1, 5)) [Albums only]

LEWIS, LINDA GAIL

L76 Discography *in* Kountry Korral (February 1973): 10–11 ((5, 7))

L77 TOSCHES, Nick: Linda Gail Lewis discography *in* Goldmine, No. 67 (December 1981): 162 ((5))

LEWIS, PETE "GUITAR"
See also *Bibliography* Vol. 2, Jazz

L78 Discography *in* Goldmine, No. 29 (October 1978): 17 ((7))

LEWIS, SMILEY

L79 LEADBITTER, Mike: Smiley Lewis— disco *in* Rockville International, No. 92 (August–September 1974): 10–12 ((2, 3, 6, 7)) [Reprinted from Rock & Roll Collector]

LEWIS BRONZEVILLE FIVE (musical group)

L80 WHITESELL, Rick: Lewis Bronzeville discography *in* Goldmine, No. 54 (November 1980): 159 ((3, 5, 6, 7))

LEWIS FAMILY

L81 LINDNER, Norbert: Lewis Family discography *in* Hillbilly, No. 57 (December 1978): 25–29 ((—))

LEYDEN, NORMAN

L82 Norman Leyden and his Orchestra, featuring Johnny Desmond *in* ED-

WARDS, Ernie, ed.: Glenn Miller alumni; a discography. Whittier, Calif.: Erngeobil Publications, 1966. 2 vols.: 1 p. in vol. 1 ((3, 7))

LEYTON, JOHN

L83 Discografi med John Leyton *in* Whole Lotta Rockin', No. 18 (1976): 15 ((5)) [Singles, EP's, and LP's issued 1960–63]

LIBERTY MUSIC SHOP label

L84 RAYMOND, Jack, and Len KUNSTADT: Exploratory discographical research of the Liberty Music Shop records *in* Record Research, No. 181–182 (April 1981): 8–9; No. 185–186 (October 1981): 9; No. 187–188 (December 1981): 9 ((2, 3, 7))

LIGGINS, JIMMY

L85 GRENDYSA, Peter: Jimmy Liggins discography *in* It Will Stand, No. 21 (c1981): 17 ((5))

LIGGINS, JOE

L86 GRENDYSA, Peter: Joe Liggins discography *in* It Will Stand, No. 21 (c1981): 16 ((5))

LIGHTFOOT, GORDON

L87 Discography *in* GABIOU, Alfrieda: Gordon Lightfoot. New York: Quick Fox, 1979: [121]–128 ((5))

L88 Gordon Lightfoot discography *in* Goldmine, No. 51 (August 1980): 180 ((—))

L89 SCHETGEN, Peter: Gordon Lightfoot discographie *in* Country Corner (June 1980): 24–26 ((5))

L90 WEIZE, Richard A.: Gordon Lightfoot diskographie *in* Hillbilly, No. 52 (September 1977): 12–16 ((—))

THE LIMELIGHTERS (musical group)

L91 Discography *in* Goldmine, No. 67 (December 1981): 175 ((—))

LIN label

L92 Discography *in* BLAIR, John: Lin
Records *in* Record Exchanger, V/1
(No. 23): 10-13 ((—))

LINDENBERG, UDO

L93 Discographie *in* his Hinter all den
Postern. Reibek bei Hamburg: Rowohlt, 1979: [158] ((5))

L94 Discographie *in* HOPPE, Ulrich: Udo
Lindenberg. Munich: Heyne, 1979:
159 ((—))

LINDSAY, REG

L95 PRICE, A. H.: [Discography] *in*
Country Western Spotlight, No. 46
(June 1964): ? ((—))

LIORET CYLINDERS Label

L96 SCOTT, Richard: Lioret Cylinders *in*
Talking Machine Review, No. 60-61
(October–December 1979): 1641
((—))

LITTLE ANTHONY AND THE
IMPERIALS (musical group)

L97 APUGLIESE, John, et al.: Little Anthony and the Imperials *in* Bim Bam
Boom, II/3 (No. 9, 1973): 53 ((3))

L98 CLEE, Ken: Little Anthony and the
Imperials discography *in* Goldmine,
No. 59 (April 1981): 12-13 ((—))

L99 Little Anthony discography *in* Record
Exchanger, No. 14 [April 1973]: 10
((—))

LITTLE CLYDE AND THE TEENS
(musical group)

L100 MOHR, Kurt: [Discography] *in*
Shout, No. 58 (August 1970): [2–4]
((3, 7))

LITTLE MARVEL label

L101 ROWLES, Peter: Little Marvel *in*
Gunn Report, No. 58 (July–August
1976): 4-5; additions in No. 59 (September–October 1976): 11 ((3))

LITTLE RICHARD
See also *Bibliography* Vol. 2, Jazz

L102 GARODKIN, John: Little Richard
special, king of rock 'n' roll. Copenhagen: Wulff, 1975. 71 pp. ((1, 4, 5,
7))

L103 Record man's platter chatter: Little
Richard *in* Mojo-Navigator Rock &
Roll News, No. 10 (November 8,
1966): 8-10; discography pp. 9-10
[Specialty recordings only] ((5))

LITTLE TICH

L104 BARKER, Tony: Little Tich discography *in* Music-Hall Records, No. 1
(June 1978): 3-7, 11 ((3, 7))

LITTLE TONY

L105 GARODKIN, John: Little Tony discografi *in* Rock 'n' Roll International
Magazine (Dutch), No. 109 (January
1978): 6 ((—))

LITTLE WONDER label

L106 BROOKS, Tim: Ever wonder about
Little Wonder: a history of Little
Wonder *in* New Amberola Graphic,
No. 28 (Spring 1979): 3-8

L107 Little Wonder *in* New Amberola
Graphic, No. 26 (Summer–Fall 1978):
14-15 ((—))

THE LIVELY ONES (musical group)

L108 DALLEY, Robert J.: Lively Ones discography *in* Goldmine, No. 53 (October 1980): 168 ((5))

LIVERBIRDS (musical group)

L109 KLITSCH, Hans Jurgen: When the
chicken rocked the Star Club . . . it
were the Liverbirds *in* Gorilla Beat,
No. 10 (1981): 58-62; discography pp.
61-62 ((5))

LIVSEY, BARBARA

L110 PRUTER, Robert: Barbara Livsey discography *in* Goldmine, No. 64 (September 1981): 183 ((—))

LLACH, LLUIS

L111 Discographie *in* his Catalogue vivre.
Paris: Lattes, 1979: 213-216 ((5))

LLOYD, MARIE

L112 BAYLEY, E.: Marie Lloyd on Pathe *in* Talking Machine Review International, No. 48 (October 1977): 1117 ((—))

L113 COOK, Richard: Marie Lloyd; note toward a discography *in* Gunn Report, No. 50 (January–February 1975): 12; No. 52 (May–June 1975): [11]–12 ((3, 7))

L114 JARRETT, Jack: Marie Lloyd *in* Record Advertiser, III/4 (May–June 1973): 11–14 ((3, 5))

LLOYDS label

L115 [Discography] *in* Shout, No. 43 (April 1969): [6–7] ((3))

LOFGREN, NILS

L116 Discography *in* Zig Zag, No. 60 (May 1976): [8] ((5))

LOGSDON, JIMMIE

L117 STRUM, Adriaan: Jimmie Logsdon discography *in* Goldmine, No. 45 (February 1980): 116 ((5))

LOMA label
See also *Bibliography* Vol. 2, Jazz

L118 TOPPING, Ray: Loma label listing *in* Shout, No. 101 (February 1975): 10–11; additions and corrections in No. 107 (February–March 1976): 21 ((—))

LOMAX, JACKIE

L119 BETROCK, Alan: Jackie Lomax *in* Jamz, No. 2 (October 1971): 11; addenda in No. 3 (February 1972): 22; No. 5 (c1972): 75 ((—))

LOMBARDO, GUY

L120 A basic discography *in* CLINE, Beverly Fink: The Lombardo story. Don Mills, Ont.: Musson Book Co., 1979: 153 ((—))

LONDON label

L121 FAULL, Trev: Great labels, part 2: London label from 9000 series *in* Instrumental Obscurities Unlimited, No. 11 (1976): 7–8 ((—))

LONDON label [Sweden]

L122 Londons EP-series RE-5000: nagot for oss over de 30!? *in* Kountry Korral, XI/5 (1978): 28–35 ((—)) [addenda, corrigenda] in XI/6 (1978): 14

LONDON label [U.S.]

L123 [[PELLETIER, Paul M.: London-American complete 78/45 r.p.m. singles: 1949–1961. London: Record Information Services. (Publication No. 8)]]

L124 [[PELLETIER, Paul M.: London-American & London-Jazz complete E.P.'s; 1954–1967. London: Record Information Services. (Publication No. 9)]]

L125 SHAW, Greg: Great labels of the 60's, part one: London *in* Kicks, No. 1 (Spring 1979): 93–97 ((—)) [Includes Parrot and Press]

L126 [[SHAW, Greg: London Records discography, part 2 *in* Kicks (1979) [Covers the Parrot 300 series and the London 900, 100 and 1,000 series]]]

LONDON PALLADIUM ORCHESTRA

L127 The London Palladium Orchestra *in* Vintage Light Music, No. 26 (Spring 1981): 10–11 ((3))

LONESOME PINE FIDDLERS
(musical group)

L128 [[Discography *in* Country Corner, No. 15: 10]]

LONG, NORMAN

L129 TAYLOR, Michael: Norman Long *in* Gunn Report, No. 26 (February–March 1971): 35 ((3))

LONG, ROBERT

L130 [[[Discography] *in* Robert Long: teksten. Aarlanderveen: Viergang, 1979: 77–[80]]]

LONG, SHORTY

L131 [[[Discography] *in* Soul Music (No. 25)]]

LOREN, DONNA

L132 HEATER, Mark, and John BLAIR: Donna Loren discography *in* Goldmine, No. 46 (March 1980): 18 ((5))

THE LOST (musical group)

L133 PREVOST, Greg: Too soon they got lost *in* Gorilla Beat, No. 10 (1981): 23–24; discography p. 24 ((5))

LOUDERMILK, JOHN D.

L134 MITCHELL, Earl: John D. Loudermilk discography *in* Big Beat of the 50's, No. 13 (August 1977): 14–16 ((4))

LOUISIANA LOU

L135 OERMANN, Robert K.: Discography *in* Old Time Music, No. 34 (Summer to Autumn 1980): 14–18 ((3))

LOUVIN, CHARLIE

L136 Charlie Louvin LP discography *in* Kountry Korral (No. 1, 1979): 9 ((—))

LOUVIN BROTHERS

L137 [Discography] *in* Country Western Express, No. 19 (April 1958): ? ((—))

L138 GARBUTT, Bob: The Louvin Brothers discography *in* Goldmine, No. 58 (March 1981): 26 ((—))

L139 WARNEWALL, Kjell: Louvin Bros. disco *in* Kountry Korral, XI/6 (1978): 20–24 ((—))

L140 WEIZE, Richard A.: Louvin Brothers diskographie *in* Hillbilly, No. 47 (June 1976): 24–31; additions and corrections in No. 48 (September 1976): 31 ((—))

LOVE (musical group)

L141 HOGG, Brian: Love *in* Bam Balam, No. 8 (December 1978): 9, 10–14; discography pp. 9, 13–14 ((5))

LOVELITE label

L142 Lovelite label *in* Hot Buttered Soul, No. 26 (January 1974): 11 ((—))

THE LOVIN' SPOONFUL (musical group)

L143 HOGG, Brian: The everlovin' Spoonful *in* Bam Balam, No. 8 (December 1978): 15–21; discography pp. 17–21; addenda in No. 10 (November 1979): 16, No. 12 (November 1980): 34, and No. 14 (September 1982): 16 ((5)) [Includes Zalman Yanovsky, the Mugwumps, and the Modern Folk Quartet]

LOWE, NICK

L144 ROSENSTEIN, Bruce: Nick Lowe (post-Brinsleys) discography *in* Trouser Press, No. 22 (October 1977): 30 ((—))

L145 WAGSTAFF, John: The story of Dai & Basher, part II: Nick Lowe *in* Gorilla Beat, No. 14 (1982): 47–57; discography pp. 48–57 ((1, 5)) [Includes Brinsley Schwarz, Kippington Lodge, and other groups Lowe has been a member of, plus solo recordings, productions, and session work]

LUCKY label

L146 GIBBON, Peter, and Tony TISOVEC: [Discography] *in* Yesterday's Memories, III/3 (1977): 27 ((7))

LUMAN, BOB

L147 SNYDER, Robert L., and Victor PEARLIN: Bob Luman discography *in* Goldmine, No. 44 (January 1980): 130–131 ((—))

L148 Bob Luman discography *in* STRUM, Adriaan: "Rockabilly-balladeer" Bob Luman *in* Record Exchanger, VI/1 (No. 28, December 1979?): 12–13 ((—))

L149 VOGEL, Manfred: Discografie *in* Country Corner, XII (No. 53, February 1977): 4–5 ((—))

LUMPKIN, HENRY

L150 [[[Discography] *in* Shout (No. 39): ?]]

LUNSFORD, BASCOM LAMAR

L151   [COHEN, Norm]: Bascom Lamar
Lunsford *in* JEMF Quarterly, IX/1
(No. 29, Spring 1973): 7 ((3, 6, 7))

L152   [Discography] *in* Country Directory,
No. 1 (November 1960): ? ((—))
[Library of Congress records only]

LUTHER, FRANK

L153   EDWARDS, J.: [Discography] *in*
Country Western Spotlight, No. 9
(July 1956): ? ((—))

L154   EDWARDS, J.: [Discography] *in*
Country Western Spotlight (Special
issue, September 1962): ? ((—))

LYMON, FRANKIE

L155   GROIA, Phil: [Frankie Lymon] and
the Teenagers *in* Bim Bam Boom, II/6
(No. 12, 1974): [17]–18 ((—))

L156   SICURELLA, Joe: [Discography] *in*
Big Town Review, I/3 (July–August
1972): 14–15 ((—))

LYMON, LEWIS

L157   SICURELLA, Joe: [Discography,
with the Teenchords] *in* Big Town
Review, I/3 (July–August 1972): 14
((3))

LYNN, BARBARA

L158   MOHR, Kurt: Barbara Lynn discography *in* Shout, No. 106 (December
1975–January 1976): 14–17; additions
and corrections in No. 108: 21 ((2, 3,
5, 6, 7))

LYNN, LORETTA

L159   EDGINTON, Richard: Loretta Lynn
record listing *in* Country & Western
Roundabout, III (No. 11, May–June–
July 1965): 18 ((—))

L160   Recordings of Loretta Lynn *in*
KRISHEF, Robert K.: Loretta Lynn.
Minneapolis: Lerner Publications Co.,
1978: [63] ((—))

L161   Loretta Lynn disco *in* Kountry
Korner, X/2 (April 1977): 9 ((—))

L162   Schallplatten (singles & LPs) *in*
Hillbilly, No. 34 (June 1970): 8–9
((—))

L163   STRUBING, Hauke: Loretta Lynn
LP-discographie *in* Country Corner,
No. 39 (May 1974): 18 ((—))

LYNN, VERA

L164   HAYES, Jim: Vera Lynn on English
78's *in* Gunn Report, No. 42 (October–November 1973) thru No. 55
(October–November 1975): various
paginations ((3))

LYNNE, JEFF

L165   Jeff Lynne/Idle Race discography *in*
Trouser Press Press, No. 3 (1976): 66
((5))

LYONS, WILLIE JAMES

L166   GOLDWASSER, Frank: Discographie
in Soul Bag, XII/81–82 (1981): 15
((—))

THE MC-5 (musical group)

M1   HEDDLE, Jim, and Mike Mc-
DOWELL: MC-5 discography *in* Ballroom Blitz, No. 20 (April 1977): 18
((5))

M2   KOENIG, John: MC-5 discography *in*
Goldmine, No. 36 (May 1979): 15
((5))

MGM label [Australia]

M3   CRISP, Dave: MGM 1951–1958 *in*
Country & Western Spotlight, No. 13
(December 1977): 31–32 ((3, 5))

McCALL, DARRELL

M4   Darrell McCall discography *in* Kountry Korral, XI/6 (1978): 28–29 ((7))

McCARTNEY, PAUL

M5   Discographie *in* DEWES, Klaus: Paul
McCartney und Wings. Bergisch Gladbach: Lubbe, 1980: 218–220 ((5))

M6   Discography *in* JASPER, Tony: Paul
McCartney and Wings. London: Octopus Books, 1977: [93] ((—))

M7   Discografie *in* MALMS, Jochen: Paul
McCartney und Wings. Munich:
Heyne, 1981: 156–159 ((5))

M8 Records by Paul McCartney/Paul & Linda McCartney/Paul McCartney & Wings *in* MENDELSOHN, John: Paul McCartney: a biography in words & pictures. London: Sire Books; New York: distributed by Chappell Music Co., 1977: 51–54 ((1, 5))

McCLUNG BROTHERS

M9 [COHEN, Norm]: McClung Bros. discography *in* JEMF Quarterly, X (No. 34, Summer 1974): 73 ((3, 7))

McCOY, CHARLIE

M10 Charlie McCoy LP discography *in* Kountry Korral (No. 2, 1979): 20 ((—))

McCOY, CLYDE

M11 LINDSLEY, Charles, et al.: Discography—Clyde McCoy *in* After Beat, I/11 (August 1971): 8–9 ((1))

McDONALD, COUNTRY JOE

See also COUNTRY JOE AND THE FISH

M12 LONG, Brian: Country Joe McDonald *in* Zig Zag, No. 59 (April 1976): [13] ((5))

McDONALD, JEANETTE

M13 BERGMAN, J. Peter: Discography *in* KNOWLES, Eleanor: The films of Jeanette McDonald and Nelson Eddy. South Brunswick, N.J.: Barnes, 1975: 396–443 ((1, 3, 5, 6, 7))

M14 Jeanette McDonald discography *in* CASTANZA, Philip: The films of Jeanette McDonald. Secaucus, N.J.: Citadel Press, 1978: 220–221 ((—))

McDONALD, SKEETS

M15 HELLBERGH, Urban: Disco *in* Kountry Korral, XIV/1 (1981): 42–45 ((—))

M16 WEIZE, Richard A., and E. Reinald SCHUMANN: Skeets McDonald diskographie *in* Hillbilly, No. 46 (March 1976): 8–11; additions and corrections in No. 48 (September 1976): 31 ((—))

McELROY, SOLLIE

M17 SBARBORI, Jack: Sollie McElroy: Flamingos: Moroccos *in* Record Exchanger, IV/5 (May 1975): 18–20 ((3))

McENERY, "RED RIVER" DAN

M18 MOERKE, Gerhard: A preliminary Red River Dan McEnery discography *in* Country & Western Spotlight, No. 24 (August 1980): 15–16 ((—))

MACEWAN, SYDNEY

M19 A selection of recordings covering a span of 39 years 1934–1973 *in* his On the high C's (a light-hearted journey): an autobiography. Glasgow: J. Burns, 1973: 324–326 ((—))

McFARLAND AND GARDNER (musical group)

M20 EDWARDS, J.: [Discography] *in* Country Western Spotlight, No. 4 (February 1956): ? ((—))

M21 EDWARDS, J.: [Discography] *in* Country Western Spotlight (Special issue, September 1962): ? ((—))

McGEE, SAM & KIRK (musical group)

M22 JOHNSON, W.: [Discography] *in* Program notes for Folkways Record FA 2379, 1964: ? ((—))

M23 LARSEN, John, and Richard A. WEIZE: Sam & Kirk McGee discography *in* Hillbilly, No. 47 (June 1976): 13–17; No. 48 (September 1976): 18–20 ((2, 3, 6, 7))

McGHEE, JOHN

M24 TRIBE, Ivan M.: A Welling and McGhee discography *in* JEMF Quarterly, XVII (No. 62, Summer 1981): 64–74 ((1, 3, 6, 7))

McGUIRE, BARRY

M25 [Discography] *in* HOGG, Brian: The Mamas and the Papas *in* Bam Balam, No. 9 (July 1979): 27–29; addenda in No. 12 (November 1980): 37 ((5))

McKAY, SCOTTY

M26   [[Discography *in* New Kommotion, No. 12 (c1976); addenda in No. 16 (Summer 1977): 42 and No. 14 (Winter 1977): 31]]

McKENZIE, SCOTT

M27   [Discography] *in* HOGG, Brian: The Mamas and the Papas *in* Bam Balam, No. 9 (July 1979): 25–26; addenda in No. 12 (November 1980): 38 ((5)) [Includes the Journeymen]

MACKENZIE, TANDY

M28   Tandy Mackenzie recordings *in* his Tandy. Norfolk Island, Australia: Island Heritage, 1975: 365–366 ((1))

McNEELY, BIG JAY

M29   MOHR, Kurt, and Norbert HESS: Big Jay McNeely discography *in* Shout, No. 105 (October–November 1975): 8–10; additions and corrections in No. 108: 21 ((2, 3, 6, 7))

McPHATTER, CLYDE

M30   Clyde McPhatter Atlantic discography *in* Big Beat of the 50's, No. 27 (May 1981): 23–25 ((5))

M31   TOPPING, Ray: Clyde McPhatter discography *in* Shout, No. 78 (July 1972): [5–10] ((2, 3, 7))

MACRAE, JOSH

M32   [Discography] *in* Country Western Express, No. 30 (August 1960): ? ((—))

McREYNOLDS BROTHERS
See also JIM AND JESSE AND THE VIRGINIA BOYS

M33   [[Discography *in* Country Corner, No. 5: 5]]

M34   NEWMAN, C.: [Discography] *in* Country News & Views, I/4 (April 1963): ?; additions in II/1: ? ((3))

MAC label

M35   Lable [sic] discografi MAC Records *in* Rock 'n' Roll International Magazine

(Danish), No. 108 (November 1977): 12 ((—))

MACK, CHARLES
See entry for MORAN, GEORGE

MACON, DAVID

M36   [Discography] *in* Country Western Express [New series], No. 2 (December 1960): ? ((—))

M37   [Discography] *in* Program notes for RBF Record RF 51, 1963: ? ((—))

M38   A discography of Uncle Dave Macon *in* JEMF Quarterly, V/2 (No. 14, Summer 1969): 47–57; V/3 (No. 15, Autumn 1969): 96–100 ((2, 3, 5, 6, 7))

M39   FUCHS, Walter W.: Uncle Dave Macon diskographie *in* Hillbilly, No. 22 (June 1967): 8–10 ((—))

M40   NICHOLAS, J.: [Discography] *in* Caravan, No. 18 (August–September 1959): ? ((3))

MACY label

M41   COMBER, Chris: [Discography] *in* Country News & Views, VI/2 (October 1967): ? ((—))

MADDOX, ROSE

M42   [[Discography *in* Country & Western Spotlight, No. 1 (December 1974): ?]]

MAEL, RON

M43   Ron & Russell at home, at work, at play *in* Trans-Oceanic Trouser Press, II/3 (June–August 1975): 18–21 ((—))

MAGIC CITY label

M44   Magic City label *in* Hot Buttered Soul, No. 29 (April 1974): 7 ((3))

MAGIC SLIM

M45   ARNIAC, Jean-Pierre: Magic Slim/ discographie *in* Soul Bag, XII/85 (October–November 1981): 7–8 ((2, 3, 7))

THE MAGIC TONES (musical group)

M46 CHANEY, Phil: The Magic Tones *in* Yesterday's Memories, II/4 (1976): 19 ((7))

MAGMA (musical group)

M47 Discographie/filmographie *in* CAUNES, Antonie de: Magma. Paris: A. Michel, 1978: [185]-187 ((—))

THE MAGNIFICENTS (musical group)

M48 Magnificents discography *in* Goldmine, No. 35 (April 1979): 34 ((5))

MAINER, J. E.

M49 DENEUMOUSTIER, Lou: J. E. and Wade Mainer [non-RCA material] *in* Disc Collector, No. 24 (May 1973): 17-24 ((—))

M50 [Discography] *in* American Folk Music Occasional No. 1 (1964): ? ((2))

M51 EDWARDS, J.: [Discography] *in* Country Western Spotlight, No. 8 (June 1956): ? ((—)) [With Wade Mainer]

M52 EDWARDS, J.: [Discography] *in* Country Western Spotlight (Special issue, September 1962: ? ((—)) [With Wade Mainer]

M53 McCUEN, Brad: [Discography] *in* Country Directory, No. 4 [n.d., 1962?]: ? ((2, 3, 7))

M54 McCUEN, Brad: J. E. and Wade Mainer [RCA recordings] *in* Disc Collector, No. 24 (May 1973): 8-15 ((3, 6, 7))

M55 WEST, H.: [Discography] *in* Disc Collector, No. 9 [n.d.]: ? ((—)) [With Wade Mainer]

MAINER'S MOUNTAINEERS (musical group)

M56 [[Discography *in* Country Corner, No. 12/13: 4]]

MAJOR LANCE

See also *Bibliography* Vol. 2, Jazz, under LANCE

M57 PRUTER, Robert, and John CORDELL: Major Lance discography *in* Time Barrier Express, No. 25 (July–August 1979): 34 ((5))

MAJOR MINOR label

M58 [Discography] *in* Matrix, No. 83 (June 1969): 7 ((—))

THE MAJORS (musical group) [ca. 1951]

M59 GROIA, Phil: The Majors *in* Bim Bam Boom, I/4 (February–March 1972): 33 ((—))

MALTAIS, GENE

M60 WARNER, Jack: Discography *in* Rockville/Roaring Sixties (March–April 1975): 20 ((—))

THE MAMAS AND THE PAPAS (musical group)

M61 HOGG, Brian: The Mamas and the Papas *in* Bam Balam, No. 9 (July 1979): 21-35; discography pp. 24-25; addenda in No. 12 (November 1980): 34-36 ((5)) [Includes the Big Three, Lamp of Childhood, Jill Gibson, and other roots and offshoots]

M62 Mamas and the Papas discography *in* Goldmine, No. 52 (September 1980): 13, 15 ((—))

MAMBO label

M63 GIBBON, Peter, and Tony TISOVEC: [Discography] *in* Yesterday's Memories, III/3 (1977): 26-27 ((7))

MAN (musical group)

M64 HILDENBRAND, Phil: Man discography *in* Trouser Press, No. 24 (December 1977): 31 ((1, 5))

MANFRED MANN (musical group)

M65 5-4-3-2-1: The Manfreds *in* Gorilla Beat, No. 8 (1980): 5-21; discography pp. 15-21; addenda in No. 9 (1981): 48 and No. 13 (1982): 72 ((5))

M66 HOGG, Brian: Manfred Mann *in* Bam Balam, No. 12 (November 1980): 22-

25; discography pp. 24–25, 29; addenda in No. 14 (September 1982): 15 ((5))

M67 Manfred Mann discography *in* Bedloe's Island, No. 5 (c1972): 15–16 ((5))

MANHATTAN TRANSFER (musical group)

M68 Manhattan Transfer discography *in* Down Beat, XLVII (March 1980): 17 ((—))

THE MANHATTANS (musical group)

M69 GROIA, Phil: The Manhattans *in* Bim Bam Boom, II/6 (No. 12, 1974): 23 ((—))

MANILOW, BARRY

M70 Barry Manilow discography *in* BEGO, Mark: Barry Manilow: an unauthorized biography. New York: Grosset & Dunlap, 1977: 131–139 ((5))

MANITAS DE PLATA

M71 Discographie de Manitas de Plata *in* his Musique aux doigts. Paris: Laffont, 1976: [323–328] ((7))

MANN, BARRY

M72 Who Put the Bomp—legendary songwriters series no. 1: Mann and Weil *in* Who Put the Bomp, No. 14 (Fall 1975): 30, 41 ((5))

MANN, CARL

M73 OLOFSSON, Claes-Hakan: Carl Mann disco *in* Kountry Korral, X/1 (February 1977): 33 ((5))

MANN, CARL [rock producer]

M74 KOMOROWSKI, Adam: Mann made hits *in* New Kommotion, No. 14 (Winter 1977): 24, 26; discography p. 26 ((—))

MANUEL, VICTOR
See VICTOR MANUEL

THE MARCELS (musical group)

M75 BRYAN, Pete: Marcels discography *in* SMG, IV/8 (March 1975): 7 ((—))

M76 SALAMON, Ed: Pittsburgh's Marcels *in* Bim Bam Boom, II/4 (No. 10, 1973): 7 ((5))

MARCHENA, PEPE

M77 Discografia de Pepe Marchena *in* GONZALEZ CLIMENT, Anselmo: Pepe Marchena y la opera flamenca y otros ensayos. Madrid: Ediciones Demofilo, [1975?]: 49–55 ((—))

MARESCA, ERNIE

M78 MASOTTI, Fred: Ernie Maresca discography *in* SMG, VI/3 (January 1978): 14 ((—))

MARGATE MUNICIPAL ORCHESTRA

M79 ADRIAN, Karlo: [Additional information to previously published material (in VLM No. 7)] *in* Vintage Light Music, No. 8 (Autumn 1976): 6 ((3, 5, 6, 7))

MARIANO, LUIS

M80 Disques *in* ALLAERT, Edith: Luis Mariano: l'artiste, l'homme. Paris: Soprode, 1972: [135]–141 ((—))

THE MARK LEEMAN FIVE (musical group)

M81 The Mark Leeman Five *in* The Rock Marketplace, No. 7 (October 1974): 37 ((5))

MARK-X label

M82 TRABOSCI, Tom: [Discography] *in* Bim Bam Boom, No. 8 (December 1972): [24] ((—))

MARLEE label

M83 LEGERE, Will: [Discography] *in* Disc Collector, No. 17 (May 1961): ? ((—))

MARLEY, BOB, AND THE WAILERS (musical group)

M84   [[[Discography] *in* BOOT, Adrian: Bob Marley, soul rebel—natural music. New York: St. Martin's Press, 1982: 93–95]]

M85   [Discography] *in* Goldmine, No. 62 (July 1981): 7 ((—))

M86   Discografia de Bob Marley & The Wailers *in* ORDOVAS, Jesus: Bob Marley. Madrid: Jucar, 1980: [214]–221 ((—))

MARMALADE label

M87   BETROCK, Alan: Marmalade singles *in* Jamz, No. 5 (c1972): 35 ((5))

MARTERIE, RALPH

M88   BRETHOUR, Ross: Discography of Ernie Marterie. Aurora, Ont.: Brethour, 1979.

MARTI, CLAUDE

M89   Claude Marti discographie *in* his Claude Marti. Choix et chansons. Paris: Seghers, 1974: [185]–186 ((—)) (Collection poesie et chansons Seghers, 27)

M90   Discographie *in* his Homme d'Oc. Paris: Stock, 1975: [245–247] ((5))

MARTIN, ASA

M91   [COHEN, Norm]: Doc Roberts, Asa Martin and James Roberts *in* JEMF Quarterly, VII/3 (No. 23, Autumn 1971): 103–   ; VII/4 (No. 24, Winter 1972): 158–162; VIII/1 (No. 25, Spring 1972): 15–17; VIII/2 (No. 26, Summer 1972): 73–76 ((2, 3, 6, 7))

MARTIN, HELENE

M92   Discographie *in* Helene Martin. Paris: Seghers, 1974: [169]–173 ((—)) (Collection poesie et chansons Seghers, 33)

MARTIN, JANIS

M93   Discography *in* GARBUTT, Bob: Rockabilly queens. Toronto: Ducktail Press, 1979: 65–66 ((2, 3, 7))

M94   KOMOROWSKI, Adam: My girl Janis *in* New Kommotion, No. 14 (Winter 1977): 6; addenda in No. 16 (Summer 1977): 42 ((3, 7))

MARTIN, JIMMY

M95   Langspielplatten *in* Hillbilly, No. 31 (September 1969): 9 ((—))

MARTIN, LLOYD

M96   Lloyd 'Skippy' Martin *in* EDWARDS, Ernie, ed.: Glenn Miller alumni; a discography. Whittier, Calif.: Erngeobil Publications, 1966. 2 vols.: 2 pp. in vol. 2 ((7))

THE MARVELETTES (musical group)

M97   [[[Discography] *in* Soul Music (No. 18)]]

M98   MOHR, Kurt: Marvelettes discography *in* Shout, No. 68 (August 1971): [2–5]; No. 69 (September 1971): [1–3, 11–12] ((2, 3, 7))

THE MARVELLOS (musical group)

M99   PRUTER, Robert: Marvellos discography *in* Time Barrier Express, III/4 (No. 24, April–May 1979): 19–20, 22 ((5))

M100   SBARBORI, Jack: Street Corner Symphony *in* Record Exchanger, IV/5 (No. 21): 29 ((—))

THE MARVELS (musical group)

M101   HINCKLEY, Dave: The Marvels *in* Yesterday's Memories, II/4 (1976): 21 ((7))

MARVIN, FRANKIE

M102   WILE, Ray: Frankie Marvin *in* Record Research, No. 93 (November 1968): 3–4 ((3, 6, 7))

THE MARYLANDERS (musical group)

M103   WHITESELL, Rick, and Marv GOLDBERG: The Marylanders *in* Yesterday's Memories, III/3 (1977): 9 ((7))

MASEKELA, HUGH

M104 Selected Masekela discography *in*
Down Beat, XLIII (May 6, 1976): 18
((—))

MATHIS, JOHNNY

M105 Johnny Mathis album discography
1956-1980 *in* Classic Wax, No. 2
(January 1981): 5 ((—))

MAXWELL, HOLLY

M106 PRUTER, Robert: Discography *in*
Goldmine, No. 28 (September 1978):
13 ((5))

MAY, BILLY

M107 Billy May and his Orchestra *in* ED-
WARDS, Ernie, ed.: Glenn Miller
alumni; a discography. Whittier,
Calif.: Erngeobil Publications, 1966. 2
vols.: 11 pp. in vol. 2 ((3, 7))

MAYALL, JOHN

M108 FARLOWE, Jesse: Mayall *in* Bedloe's
Island, No. 2 (Fall 1971): 6-7, 13; addenda in No. 3 (Winter 1972): 15-16
[Includes records by former band
members] ((—))

M109 Discography *in* HOGG, Brian: Boom
boom: British blue-eyed R&B *in* Bam
Balam, No. 13 (August 1981): 35-36;
addenda in No. 14 (September 1982):
15 ((5))

MAYE, ARTHUR LEE

M110 LAY, Rip: Arthur Lee Maye and the
Crowns *in* Big Town Review, I/1
(February–March 1972): 7 ((3))

MAYERL, BILLY

M111 NICHOLS, Michael: Brilliant
pianist—gifted composer *in* Commodore, No. 9 (Spring 1973): 7 +
((—))

MAYFIELD, CURTIS
See THE IMPRESSIONS

MAYFIELD label

M112 Mayfield label *in* Paul's Record
Magazine, IV/2 (No. 13-14, September–December 1976): 33 ((—))

MAYNARD, KEN

M113 [COHEN, Norm]: Ken Maynard *in*
JEMF Quarterly, IX (No. 38, Summer
1973): 75 ((3, 6, 7))

THE MEADOWLARKS (musical group)

M114 GOLDBERG, Marv, and Mike RED-
MOND: The Meadowlarks *in* Yesterday's Memories, III/2 (1977): 13
((7))

MEDALLION label

M115 HINZE, Michael: Medallion revisited
in Record Research, No. 144-145
(March 1977): 12-13 ((—))

MEDOFF, DAVID

M116 BENNETT, Robert J.: Discography *in*
Record Research, No. 90 (May 1968):
5 ((7))

MEEK, JOE

M117 BLAKE, Jim, and Chris KNIGHT:
Joe Meek Productions *in* Outlet, No.
2 (c1978): 15-24 ((5))

M118 HOLLIE, Jon: The Joe Meek hits list
in Outlet, No. 9 (January 1979): 6-8
((5))

THE MELLO-MOODS (musical group)

M119 GOLDBERG, Marv, and Mike RED-
MOND: Mello-Moods discography *in*
Record Exchanger, No. 16 [Fall 1973]:
13 ((3, 5))

THE MELLOWS (musical group)

M120 VANCE, Marcia: The Mellows *in* Yesterday's Memories, III/4 (1977): 6
((7))

MEL-O-DY label

M121 CALTA, Gary A.: Mel-o-dy records
(Diggin' up discographies) *in* Gold-

mine, No. 15 (March–April 1977): 8 ((—))

MERCER, MABEL

M122 LYNCH, Richard C.: Mabel Mercer, Hutch and Elisabeth Welch *in* Kastlemusik Monthly Bulletin, V/8 (August 1980): 1, 12–13 ((—))

MERCURY label [Australia]

M123 CRISP, David: Mercury & Philips *in* Country & Western Spotlight, No. 12 (September 1977): 32–35 ((—))

MERRIN, BILLY

M124 HAYES, Jim: Billy Merrin and his Commanders on Crown Records (9″ 78s) 1935–1937 *in* Vintage Light Music, No. 12 (Autumn 1977): 12–13 ((—))

MESING, RON

M125 Diskographie *in* Country Corner, XII (No. 57, December 1977): 36 ((—))

METROPOLE label

M126 HAYES, Jim: Metropole, (A) 1000 series, 1928 to 1930—continued *in* Gunn Report, No. 38 (February–March 1973): 33–35; additions and corrections in No. 39 (April–May 1973): 25–26, 28 ((3, 5))

METROPOLITAN SYMPHONY ORCHESTRA

M127 UPTON, Stuart: The Metropolitan Symphony Orchestra, conducted by Stanley Chapple: [discography of Broadcast recordings] *in* Vintage Light Music, No. 16 (Autumn 1978): 18–19 ((—))

MICKEY & SYLVIA (musical duo)

M128 WESTFALL, Bob: Mickey & Sylvia discography *in* Goldmine, No. 16 (May–June 1977): 12 ((5))

MIDAS label

M129 MOHR, Kurt: Midas label list *in* Shout, No. 86 (June 1973): [7] ((3))

MIDDLETON, ARTHUR

M130 WILE, Raymond R.: The Edison recordings of Arthur Middleton *in* New Amberola Graphic, No. 37 (Summer 1981): 10–13 ((3, 5, 7))

THE MIDNIGHTERS (musical group)
See BALLARD, HANK

MIGHTY BABY (musical group)

M131 [Discography] *in* Zig Zag, IV/1 (No. 37): [13] ((—))

MILBURN, AMOS

M132 Amos Milburn discography *in* It Will Stand, No. 3 (c1979): 5 ((—))

M133 MOONOOGIAN, George: A. Milburn discography *in* Goldmine, No. 43 (December 1979): 18 ((5))

MILLER, FRANKIE

M134 STRUBING, Hauke: Frankie Miller Disco *in* Country Corner, No. 44 (May 1975): 33–34 ((—))

MILLER, GLENN

M135 BEDWELL, Stephen F.: A Glenn Miller discography and biography. London: Glenn Miller Appreciation Society, 1956. 102 pp. ((1, 2, 3, 6, 7))

M136 FLOWER, John: Moonlight serenade: a bio-discography of the Glenn Miller Civilian Band. New Rochelle, N.Y.: Arlington House, 1972. 554 pp. ((1, 2, 3, 4, 6, 7))

M137 The RCA Victor 'airshot' LP's by Glenn Miller *in* Matrix, No. 49 (October 1963): 6+ ((—))

M138 Recordings by Glenn Miller and his orchestras *in* SIMON, George T.: Glenn Miller and his orchestras. New York: Crowell, 1974; New York: Da Capo, 1980: 451–456 ((—))

M139 Discography *in* SNOW, George: Glenn Miller & the age of swing. London: Dempsey and Squires, 1976: 127 ((—))

MILLER, JODY

M140 Jody Miller disco *in* Kountry Korral, X/2 (April 1977): 19 ((—))

MILLS, CHUCK

M141 RUSSELL, Wayne: Chuck Mills *in* New Kommotion, No. 14 (Winter 1977): 19 ((3))

MILLS BROTHERS
See also *Bibliography* Vol. 2, Jazz

M142 Discography: Mills Brothers (through 1958) *in* Classic Wax, No. 1 (October 1980): 5-9 ((2, 3, 7))

M143 Mills Brothers discography *in* GRENDYSA, Peter: The Mills Brothers: four boys and a guitar *in* Record Exchanger, V/2 (No. 24, October (?) 1977): 4-12 ((3, 7))

MILSAP, RONNIE

M144 Ronnie Milsap LP discography *in* Kountry Korral (No. 2, 1979): 22 ((—))

MILTON, BILLY

M145 PLISKIN, Barry: [Billy Milton discography] *in* Talking Machine Review, No. 62 (1980): 1676-1679, 1690 ((2, 7))

MINIT label
See also *Bibliography* Vol. 2, Jazz

M146 Minit label *in* Hot Buttered Soul, No. 28 (March 1974): 2-8 ((3))

MINSTREL SHOWS

M147 ANDREWS, Frank: Minstrels, minstrel shows & early records *in* Talking Machine Review, No. 47 (1977): "a brief discography": 1076 ((—))

MIRACLE label

M148 TOPPING, Ray: Miracle label listing *in* Shout, No. 60 (November 1970): [8] ((—))

MIRANDA, CARMEN

M149 Discografia brasileira consideracoes gerais *in* CARDOSO JUNIOR, Abel: Carmen Miranda, a cantora do Brasil. Sao Paulo: Cardoso Junior, 1978: 235-[485] ((3, 6, 7))

MIRAS LOPEZ, MANUAL

M150 Discography *in* Memorias controversivas de un musico trotamundos. Lugo: Celta, 1973: 173-174 ((—))

THE MISUNDERSTOOD (musical group)

M151 CROSS, Nigel: Misunderstood *in* Gorilla Beat, No. 15 (1982): 32-34; discography p. 34 ((5))

M152 HOGG, Brian: The Misunderstood *in* Bam Balam, No. 4 (June 1976): 9; addenda in No. 5 (February 1977): 16; No. 6 (November 1977): 23; No. 10 (November 1979): 16; No. 12 (November 1980): 37 ((1, 2))

MITCHELL, CHAD

M153 The Chad Mitchell Trio/Mitchell Trio discography *in* Goldmine, No. 50 (July 1980): 168 ((5))

MITCHELL, EDDY

M154 Albums *in* his Galas, galeres. Paris: J. Grancher, 1979: 177 ((—))

MITCHELL, JONI

M155 Joni Mitchell album discography *in* Goldmine, No. 54 (November 1980): 162 ((5))

M156 Joni Mitchell discography *in* Down Beat, XLVI (September 6, 1979): 17 ((—))

MOBY GRAPE (musical group)

M157 HOGG, Brian: Moby Grape *in* Bam Balam, No. 8 (December 1978): 3-8; discography pp. 6-7; addenda in No. 12 (November 1980): 36 ((5)) [Includes Skip Spence and Bob Mosely]

THE MOJOS (musical group)

M158 The Mojos *in* Gorilla Beat, No. 2 (1979): 38-40; discography p. 40 ((5))

MONCRIEFF, GLADYS

M159 My recordings *in* her My life of song. Adelaide: Rigby, 1971: [148–152] ((7))

MONEY, CURLEY

M160 WOUNLUND, Jorn: Curley Money discography *in* Rockville International (June–July 1974): 20 ((—))

MONEY, ZOOT

M161 [Discography] *in* HOGG, Brian: Boom boom: British blue-eyed R&B *in* Bam Balam, No. 13 (August 1981): 32–33 ((5))

M162 WILLMORE, Mike: Zoot Money discography *in* Who Put the Bomp, No. 8 (Fall–Winter 1971): 14; addenda in No. 9 (Spring 1972): 49 ((—))

MONEY label

M163 GIBBON, Peter, and Tony TISO-VEC: [Discography] *in* Yesterday's Memories, III/3 (1977): 30 ((7))

M164 Money label *in* Shout, No. 71 (November 1971): [4] ((3))

THE MONKEES (musical group)

M165 BARNES, Ken: Monkees discography *in* Who Put the Bomp, No. 16 (October 1976): 18; additions and corrections in No. 17 (November 1977): 60, 62 ((5))

M166 FAULL, Trev: The Monkees UK releases, etc. *in* Outlet, No. 22 (c1981): 32–33 ((5))

M167 HOGG, Brian: Monkees *in* Bam Balam, No. 7 (c1978): 3–9, 27; discography pp. 6–9, 27; addenda in No. 12 (November 1980): 34 ((5)) [Includes pre- and post-Monkees recordings]

M168 KOLANJIAN, Steve: The Monkees discography *in* Aware, II/5 (1977): 13–17 ((5))

M169 Monkees discography *in* Record Finder, I/8 (October 1980): 8 ((—))

THE MONKS (musical group)

M170 The first punks: the Monks *in* Gorilla Beat, No. 5 (1980): 4–7; discography p. 7 ((—))

THE MONOTONES (musical group)

M171 GONZALEZ, Fernando: Discography *in* Goldmine, No. 64 (September 1981): 7 ((3, 5))

MONROE, BILL

M172 Bill Monroe disco (MCA disco 1. Teil) *in* Country Corner, No. 41 (October 1974): 34–36; No. 42 (December 1974): 30–36 ((3, 5, 7))

M173 [Discography] *in* Disc Collector, No. 15 [n.d., 1960?]: ? ((—))

M174 McCUEN, B.: [Discography] *in* Country Directory, No. 2 (April 1961): ? ((2, 3, 7))

M175 ROSENBERG, Neil V.: Bill Monroe and his Bluegrass Boys; an illustrated discography. Nashville: Country Music Foundation Press, 1974. 122 pp. ((3, 4, 5, 6, 7))

MONROE, CHARLIE

M176 McCUEN, B.: [Discography] *in* Country Directory, No. 2 (April 1961): ? ((2, 3, 7))

M177 SPOTTSWOOD, Richard: The commercial records of Charlie Monroe *in* Bluegrass Unlimited, III/11 (May 1969): 3–6 ((2, 3, 6, 7))

M178 WEIZE, Richard: Charlie Monroe diskographie *in* Hillbilly, No. 45 (December 1975): 21–26 ((2, 3, 7))

MONROE BROTHERS

M179 McCUEN, B.: [Discography] *in* Country Directory, No. 2 (April 1961): ? ((—))

M180 McCUEN, Brad: Monroe Brothers discography *in* Bluegrass Unlimited, IV/6 (December 1969): 8 ((2, 3, 7)) [Reprinted from Country Directory, No. 2 (April 1961)]

M181 [Discography] *in* Country Western Express, No. 8 [New series]: ? ((—))

M182 [Discography] *in* Disc Collector, No. 15 [n.d.]: ? ((—))

M183 [Discography] *in* Folk Style, No. 8 [n.d.]: ? ((—))

M184 FUCHS, Walter W.: Diskographie *in* Hillbilly, No. 25 (March 1968): 15–17 ((7))

MONTANA, PATSY

M185 HEALY, Bob: [Discography] *in* Country Directory, No. 3 [n.d.]: ? ((2, 3, 7))

MONTANA SLIM

See CARTER, WILF

MONTAND, YVES

M186 Discographie *in* CANNAVO, Richard: Yves Montand: le chant d'un homme. Paris: Laffont, 1981: 297–[300] ((—))

M187 Discographie *in* Montand: de chansons en images. Paris: Brea editions: Diffusion, Weber, 1981: 99–105 ((—))

M188 Les disques de Montand *in* RE-MOND, Alain: Yves Montand. Paris: H. Veyrier, 1977: 203–204 ((—))

MONUMENT label

M189 MASOTTI, Fred, and Paul BEZAN-KER: Monument Records discography *in* Paul's Record Magazine (No. 17–18): 64–83 ((3, 5))

THE MOODY BLUES (musical group)

M190 HEBING, Alfred: The Moody Blues *in* Gorilla Beat, No. 12 (1981): 38–50; discography pp. 44–50; addendum in No. 13 (1982): 73 ((5))

MOON label

M191 DEAN, D., and Ray TOPPING: Moon label listing *in* New Kommotion, No. 14 (Winter 1977): 28 ((3, 5))

THE MOONBEAMS (musical group)

M192 The Moonbeams *in* Time Barrier Express, II/1 (October 1975): 12 ((1, 3))

THE MOONGLOWS (musical group)

M193 [[[Discography] *in* Soul Music (No. 23)]]

M194 Discography: Moonglows *in* Record Exchanger, No. 2 (March 1970): 7–10 ((2, 3, 7))

M195 GONAZALEZ, Fernando L.: The Moonglows *in* Goldmine, No. 62 (July 1981): 9, 156 ((3, 5))

M196 GOUGH, John: The Moonglows *in* SMG, VI/2 (September 1977): 19 ((5))

M197 MOHR, Kurt: Moonglows discography *in* Shout, No. 73 (January 1972): [2–3] ((2, 3, 7))

M198 The Moonglows discography *in* Rocking Regards, No. 15 (June 1979): 7–9 ((5))

M199 MUNNICH, Hartmut M.: Ergan-zungen zur Moonglows-Disco *in* Rocking Regards, No. 16 ([July?] 1979): 22 ((5))

THE MOONLIGHTERS (musical group)

M200 GONZALEZ, Fernando L.: Moon-lighters discography *in* Goldmine, No. 62 (July 1981): 9, 156 ((3, 5))

MOORE, CHARLIE

M201 BARR, Nick: Charles Moore *in* Blue-grass Unlimited, VII/7 (January 1973): 8–9 ((1, 3, 7))

M202 DEIJFEN, Lars: Charlie Moore discography *in* Kountry Korral (No. 3, 1980): 39 ((—))

M203 FINKE, Eberhard: Nicht gebuhrend gewurdigt: Charlie Moore *in* Country Corner, No. 52 (December 1976): 27–28 ((—))

MOORE, DOROTHY

M204 MOHR, Kurt, et al.: Dorothy Moore disco *in* Soul Bag, No. 83 (1981): 21–22 ((3, 7))

MOORE, JACKIE

M205 MOHR, Kurt, and Pierre DA-GUERRE: Jackie Moore discographie *in* Soul Bag, No. 83 (1981): 19–21 ((3, 7))

MOORE, LATTIE

M206 MILLAR, Bill: Lattie Moore: hillbilly haven *in* New Kommotion, No. 15 (Spring 1977): 21, 24; discography p. 24; addenda in No. 22 (1979): 65 ((3, 5))

MOORE, MERRILL

M207 [Discography] *in* Country Western Express, No. 16 (October–December 1957): ? ((—))

M208 LAFFONT, Henri: [Discography] *in* Big Beat, No. 14 (November 1976): 12 ((1, 3, 7))

MOORE-DUPREZ, MAY

M209 BARKER, Tony: Discography *in* Music-Hall Records, No. 2 (August 1978): 13–15 ((3, 7)); additions in No. 3 (October 1978): 50 ((—))

MORAN, GEORGE

M210 HAYES, Jim: George Moran & Charles Mack; "The Two Black Crows" *in* Gunn Report, No. 42 (October–November 1973): [32] ((3, 6, 7))

MORANDI, GIANNI

M211 [Discography] *in* Gianni Morandi. Rome: Petrucci, 1975: cover ((—))

MORGAN, GEORGE

M212 BINGE, Reimar: Disco *in* Country Corner, No. 46 (October 1975): 18–19, 22 ((—))

M213 WEIZE, Richard A.: Diskographie *in* Hillbilly, No. 44 (September 1975): 15–22; additions and corrections in No. 48 (September 1976): 28–29 ((—))

MORGAN, LOUMELL

M214 GRENDYSA, Peter: Loumell Morgan discography *in* Goldmine, No. 47 (April 1980): 18 ((5))

MORGAN, ROCKET

M215 [[[Discography] *in* New Kommotion (c1976); addenda in No. 14 (Winter 1977): 31]]

MORGAN, RUSS

M216 LINDSEY, John F.: Discography— Russ Morgan *in* After Beat, II/1 (October 1971): 7–9, 14–15; II/5 (June–July 1972): 14 ((—))

MORRICONE, ENNIO

M217 A filmography and discography of Ennio Morricone (cont.) part 3 in Soundtrack Collector's Newsletter, II/7 (July 1976): 13–16 ((—))

MORRIS BROTHERS

M218 [Discography] *in* Country Western Express, No. 16 (February 1957): 7 ((—))

M219 McELREA, R.: discography *in* Country News & Views, III/4 (April 1965): 9–11 ((2, 3, 7))

MORRISON, VAN
See also THEM

M220 Discografia de Van Morrison *in* Discoteca Hifi, No. 200 (November 1979): 30–32 ((5))

M221 Gloria discography *in* Gorilla Beat, No. 5 (1980): 30–32; addenda in No. 6 (1980): 46; No. 7 (1980): 16; No. 9 (1981): 48; No. 10 (1981): 45; and No. 13 (1982): 69 ((—)) [Cover recordings of the song Gloria]

M222 Van Morrison: Them and now: being a complete history of his U.S. and U.K. recordings from 1963 to the present day. Kingston, England: Rock Revelations, 1976. 32 unnumbered pages. ((5))

MORSE, LEE

M223 COLTON, Bob, and Len KUNSTADT: Lee Morse; a discography of her Perfect recordings *in* Discophile, No. 36 (June 1954): 11–13; No. 40 (February 1955): 16; No. 41 (April 1955): 15; No. 45 (December 1955): 17 ((2, 3, 6))

MOSAM SKIFFLE GROUP

M224 Discography *in* Rocking Regards, No. 15 (June 1979): 15–17 ((5))

MOTHERS OF INVENTION
  (musical group)
  See ZAPPA, FRANK

MOTOR-TRUCK DRIVING—
SONGS AND MUSIC

M225 ROSENDAHL, Kjell: Truck music on
LP *in* Kountry Korral, X/1 (February
1977): 13 ((—))

M226 SUNDGREN, Kent, and Kjell
ROSENDAHL: Truck drivin' music *in*
Kountry Korral Magazine (No. 4,
1981): 34 ((—))

MOTOWN label
See also TAMLA label

M227 CALTA, Gary: Diggin' up discographies: Motown Records: part 1 *in*
Goldmine, No. 21 (December 1977):
12; part 2 in No. 26 (May–June 1978):
16 ((—))

M228 DEPIERRO, Tom: Motown discography *in* Record Exchanger, IV/6
(No. 22): 16–17 ((6))

THE MOUNTAIN RAMBLERS
(musical group)

M229 FENTON, Mike: Discography *in* Old
Time Music, No. 22 (Autumn 1976):
16 ((5))

MOUSE AND THE TRAPS
(musical group)

M230 [Discography] *in* HOGG, Brian: Thru
the rhythm: Texas rock 'n' roll *in*
Bam Balam, No. 10 (November 1979):
12–13; addenda in No. 12 (November
1980): 36 and No. 14 (September
1982): 16 ((—))

MOUSTAKI, GEORGES

M231 Discographie *in* his Georges Moustaki.
Paris: Seghers, 1970: [189] ((—))

THE MOVE (musical group)

M232 BETROCK, Alan: Move discography
in Jamz, No. 2 (October 1971): 6; addenda in No. 3 (February 1972): 22;
No. 4 (May 1972): 35; No. 5 (c1972):
75 ((2, 5))

M233 BETROCK, Alan: The Move: roots &
offshoots *in* The Rock Marketplace,
No. 3 (October 1973): 20–24, plus unnumbered leaf of addenda; further addenda in No. 4 (December 1973) and
No. 5 (April 1974): 34 [Recordings of

predecessor and offshoot groups in-
cluding the individual members of the
Move: Roy Wood, Bev Bevan, Carl
Wayne, Chris 'Ace' Kefford, Trevor
Burton, Rick Price, and Jeff Lynne.
Does not include the Move itself nor
ELO] ((5))

M234 DAVELAAR, Gerard: Pre-Move con-
stellations *in* Gorilla Beat, No. 5
(1980): 13–15 ((5)) [Includes Keith
Powell & the Valets, Carl Wayne &
the Vikings, Mike Sheridan & the
Nightriders, Denny Laine & the Diplo-
mates, Danny King's Mayfair Set, and
Sight 'n' Sound]

M235 HOGG, Brian: The Move *in* Bam
Balam, No. 4 (June 1976): 10–15;
discography pp. 11–15; addenda in
No. 5 (February 1977): 16 and No. 12
(November 1980): 37 ((2)) [Includes
predecessor and offshoot groups]

M236 The Mods, pt. 2 *in* Gorilla Beat, No.
4 (1979): 30–39; discography pp.
34–39; addenda in No. 6 (1980): 46;
No. 8 (1980): 46; and No. 13 (1982):
72 ((—)) [Includes solo recordings by
group members. British & German
releases]

MOVING-PICTURE ACTORS
AND ACTRESSES

M237 PITTS, Michael R.: Hollywood on
record: the film stars' discography.
Metuchen, N.J.: Scarecrow Press,
1978. 411 pp. ((—))

MOVING-PICTURE MUSIC

M238 BAHN, Robert: Italian soundtrack
discography *in* RTS Music Gazette,
VIII/12 (April 1981): [4]; IX/2 (June
1981): [4]; IX/3 (July 1981): [4]; IX/4
(August 1981): [4]; IX/6 (October
1981): [6]; IX/9 (January 1982): [7]
((—))

M239 [[Discography *in* Motion picture
music. Mechelen, Belgium: Soundtrack, 1980. 155 pp.]]

M240 Discography *in* Film score: the view
from the podium. South Brunswick,
N.J.: A. S. Barnes, 1979: 245–259
((—))

M241 [[[Discography] *in* HEYMANN,
Daniele: L'annee du cinema 77. Paris:
Calmann-Levy, 1977: 253]]

M242 Gramophone records of British film music *in* HUNTLEY, John: British film music. London: Robinson, 1947; New York: Arno, 1972: 239–244 ((—))

M243 [[Discography *in* LIMBACHER, James L.: Keeping score: film music 1972: 334–425]]

M244 Recorded musical scores (a discography) *in* LIMBACHER, James L.: Film music. Metuchen, N.J.: Scarecrow, 1974: 688–828 ((—))

M245 L'elements de discographie *in* PORCILC, Francois: Presence de la musique a l'ecran. Paris: Cerf, 1969: 333–[335] ((—))

M246 PRATLEY, Gerald: Film music on records, as of July, 1951. Berkeley, 1951. pp. 73–98 ((—))

M247 SMOLIAN, Steven: A handbook of film, theater, and television music on record, 1948–1969. New York: Record Undertaker, 1970. 2 vols. ((5))

M248 Film music on records *in* THOMAS, Tony: Music for the movies. South Brunswick, N.J.: Barnes, 1973: 221–235 ((—))

MOVING PICTURES, MUSICAL

M249 [[Discography *in* GREEN, Stanley: Encyclopedia of the musical film. New York: Oxford University Press, 1981: 337–344]]

M250 [[Discography *in* MORDDEN, Ethan: The Hollywood musical. New York: St. Martin's Press, 1981: ?]]

MUD (musical group)

M251 Mud *in* The Rock Marketplace, No. 7 (October 1974): 24 ((5))

MURCO label

M252 PERIN, Jacques, and Gilles PETARD: . . . Listing Murco *in* Soul Bag, No. 77 (1980): 23–28 ((—))

MUSCANTI, JOSEPH

M253 UPTON, Stuart: Joseph Muscanti and the Commodore Grand Orchestra. West Wickham, England: Vintage Light Music, [n.d.] ((—))

MUSIC, POPULAR (SONGS, ETC.)

M254 The albums [of familiar melodies and tunes] *in* Tarakan Music Letter, II/1 (September–October 1980): 6–7 ((—))

M255 Classical pop: part II: some outstanding anthologies *in* Tarakan Music Letter, II/1 (September–October 1980): 9 ((—))

M256 CLEE, Ken: A discography collection of artists and labels. 2nd ed. Philadelphia: Stak-O-Wax, 1979. 800 pp.

M257 Diskographie *in* DIETTRICH, Eva: Tencenzen der Pop-Musik. Tutzing: Schneider, 1979: 84 ((5))

M258 ENGEL, Lyle Kenyon: Popular record directory. New York: Fawcett, 1958. 144 pp. ((—))

M259 [[GREEN, Jeff: The green book: catalog of songs categorized by subject. [Los Angeles: 87260 So. Sepulveda, #A4, Los Angeles 90045; printed by Professional Desk References, 1982] 1 vol.]]

M260 Discographies *in* KINKLE, Roger D.: The complete encyclopedia of popular music and jazz, 1900–1950. New Rochelle, N.Y.: Arlington House, 1974. 4 vols. ((4, 5))

M261 Discographies *in* KROG, Peter: Rytmisk musik. Copenhagen: Gyldeldal, 1978. ((—))

M262 [Discographical references] *in* LEDUC, Jean Marie: La pop-music. Paris: A. Michel, 1976. 2 vols. ((—))

M263 [[MURRELLS, Joseph: The book of golden discs. London: Barrie & Jenkins, 1974. 503 pp.; 2nd ed. London: Barrie & Jenkins, 1978. 413 pp.]]

M264 OSBORNE, Jerry: Popular and rock records, 1948–1978. 2nd ed. Phoenix: O'Sullivan, Woodside & Co., 1978. ((4))

M265 OSBORNE, Jerry: Record albums, 1948–1978. 2nd ed. Phoenix: O'Sullivan, Woodside & Co., 1978. ((4))

M266 Skivor *in* RASMUSSON, Ludvig: Pop & rock. Stockholm: AWE/Geber, 1977: 127–130 ((—))

M267 RICE, Jo; Tim RICE; and Paul GAMBACCINI: The Guinness book of British hit singles. 3rd ed. London: Guinness Superlatives Ltd., 1981. 352 pp. ((4))

M268 RUST, Brian, and Allen G. DEBUS: The complete entertainment discography from the mid-1890's to 1942. New Rochelle, N.Y.: Arlington House, 1973. 677 pp. Additions and corrections in Rhythm Bag, No. 4 (Spring 1977): 23-25 ((2, 3, 5, 6, 7))

M269 SOLOMON, Clive: Record hits: the British top 50 charts, 1952-1977. London: Omnibus, 1977. 270 pp. ((4))

M270 TAYLOR, Malcolm: One man's flop . . . in Big Beat of the 50's, No. 22 (November 1979): 32-33 ((—)) [The list gives a number of well-known singles with their original label and the label which purchased or leased the tracks]

M271 WHITBURN, Joel: Bubbling under the Hot 100: 1959-1981. Menomonee Falls, Wisc.: Record Research, 1982. 235 pp. ((4))

M272 WHITBURN, Joel: Top easy listening records: 1961-1974. Menomonee Falls, Wisc.: Record Research, 1975. 152 pp. ((4))

M273 WHITBURN, Joel: Top LP's: 1945-1972. Menomonee Falls, Wisc.: Record Research, 1973. 217 pp. ((4))

M274 WHITBURN, Joel: Top pop artists and singles: 1955-1978. Menomonee Falls, Wisc.: Record Research, 1979. 662 pp. ((4))

M275 WHITBURN, Joel: Top pop records: 1940-1955. Menomonee Falls, Wisc.: Record Research, 1973. 87 pp. ((4))

Music, Popular (Songs, etc.)—Brazil

M276 Discographies in VASCONCELOS, Ary: Panorama da musica popular brasiliera. Rio de Janeiro: Livararia Sant'Anna "Belle epoque," 1977. ((—))

Music, Popular (Songs, etc.)—France

M277 Discographie in MARC, Edmond: La Chanson francaise. Paris: Hatier, 1972: 108-[113] ((—))

M278 Discografie in SCHRETLEN, Ignace: Ik droom alleen wat minder. Westbroek: Harlekijn Holland, 1978: 77-78 ((—))

M279 Disques in VASSAL, Jacques: Francais, si vous chantiez. Paris: A. Michel, 1976: [327]-344 ((5))

Music, Popular (Songs, etc.)— France—Brittany

M280 Discographie in VASSAL, Jacques: La chanson bretonne. Paris: A. Michel, 1980: [180]-188 ((—))

Music, Popular (Songs, etc.)—Greece

M281 [MORRIS, Roderick Conway]: The BIRS Collection of 78 rpm commercial recordings of Greek cafe music in Recorded Sound, No. 80 (July 1981): 91-117 ((—))

Music, Popular (Songs, etc.)—Italy

M282 [[Discography in CASADEI, Raoul: Il mio libro del liscio. Rome: Casa editrice Anthropos, 1981: 111-112]]

M283 Discografia in JANNACCI, Enzo: Canzoni. Rome: Lato side, 1980: 125-[130] ((—))

Music, Popular (Songs, etc.)— Latin America

M284 Discographie in The Latin music yearbook. Diamond Bar, Calif.: Applause Publications, 1980- . ((—))

Music, Popular (Songs, etc.)— Switzerland

M285 [[Discography in BUHLER, Michel: Michel Buhler. Lausanne: P.-M. Favre, 1980. 124 pp.]]

Music, Popular (Songs, etc.)— United States

M286 Discography in BERRY, Peter E.: ". . . and the hits just keep on comin.' " Syracuse, N.Y.: Syracuse University Press, 1977: 167-276 ((5))

M287 CLEE, Ken: The directory of American 45 R.P.M. records. Philadelphia: Stak-O-Wax, 1981. 3 vols. ((—))

M288 Select discography in ROBERTS, John S.: The Latin tinge: the impact of Latin American music on the United States. New York: Oxford University Press, 1979: [234]-238 ((—))

M289 SHAPIRO, Nat: Popular music: an annotated index of American popular songs. 6 vols. New York: Adrian Press, 1964-1973. ((4, 5)) [Vol. 1: 1950-59; vol. 2: 1940-49; vol. 3:

1960–64; vol. 4: 1930–39; vol. 5: 1920–29; vol. 6: 1965–69]

M290 SYNDER, Robert L.: Cover records of the fifties; rhythm & blues songs covered by white pop artists *in* Goldmine, No. 12 (September–October 1976): 36–37 ((5))

M291 Discography *in* WHITCOMB, Ian: Tin Pan Alley: a pictorial history (1919–1939). New York: Paddington Press, 1975: 247 ((—))

M292 Discography *in* WHITE, John I.: Git along, little dogies: songs and songwriters of the American West. Urbana: University of Illinois Press, 1975: 210–214 ((3, 6, 7))

Music, Popular (Songs, etc.)— Uruguay

M293 MARTINS, Carlos: Discografia *in* CAPAGORRY, Juan: Aqui se canta: canto popular, 1977–1980. Montevideo: Arca, 1980: 134–140 ((—))

MUSIC HALLS (VARIETY-THEATERS, CABARETS, ETC.)—FRANCE

M294 [[[Discography] *in* SEVRAN, Pascal: Le Music hall francais: de Mayol a Julien Clerc. Paris: O. Orhan, 1978: 275–[278]]]

MUSIC HALLS (VARIETY-THEATERS, CABARETS, ETC.)— GREAT BRITAIN

M295 Discography of LPs *in* GAMMOND, Peter: Your own, your very own! a music hall scrapbook. London: Allan, 1971: 96 ((—))

M296 [[Discography *in* MANDER, Raymond: British music hall. Rev. ed. London: Gentry Books, 1974: 234–235]]

M297 RUST, Brian: British music hall on record. Harrow: General Gramophone Publications, 1979. 301 pp. ((3, 6, 7))

MUSICAL BROWNIES (musical group)

M298 [[PINSON, Bob: Musical Brownies discography *in* Old Time Music, No. 5 (Summer 1972): 21–22]]

MUSICAL REVUES, COMEDIES, ETC.

M299 AROS, Andrew A.: Broadway & Hollywood too. Diamond Bar, Calif.: Applause Publications, 1980. 80 pp. ((—))

M300 Discography *in* DRINKROW, John: The vintage musical comedy book. Reading: Osprey Publishing, 1974: 140–146 ((—))

M301 Discography *in* GREEN, Stanley: Encyclopaedia of the musical theatre. New York: Dodd, Mead & Co., 1976; New York: Da Capo, 1980: 478–488 ((—))

M302 HODGKINS, Gordon W.: The Broadway musical: a complete LP discography. Metuchen, N.J.: Scarecrow Press, 1980. 183 pp. ((4, 5))

M303 Discography *in* JACKSON, Arthur: The best musicals from Showboat to A Chorus Line. New York: Crown Publishers, 1977: 200–202 ((—)) [Published in Great Britain by Mitchell Beazley under the title The book of musicals in 1977; discography 200–202]

M304 KRUEGER, Miles: A discography of original-cast Capitol albums *in* American Record Guide (October 1965): 181+ ((7))

M305 KRUEGER, Miles: A discography of original-cast Columbia albums *in* American Record Guide (December 1965): 329–337 ((7))

M306 KRUEGER, Miles: A discography of original-cast Decca LP albums *in* American Record Guide (September 1965): 76–77 ((7))

M307 KRUEGER, Miles: A discography of RCA Victor LP original-cast albums *in* American Record Guide (July 1965): 1044–1046 ((7))

M308 RAYMOND, Jack: Show music on record: from the 1890s to the 1980s. New York: F. Ungar, 1981. 253 pp. ((5))

M309 A retrospective musical show discography *in* Overtures, No. 4 (November 1979): 29–30; No. 9 (September 1980): 33–34; No. 10 (November 1980): 33–34; No. 11 (January 1981): 23–24; No. 12 (March 1981): 33–34 ((—))

M310 RUST, Brian: London musical shows on records, 1894–1954. London: British Institute of Recorded Sound,

1958. 207 pp. ((4)) [Supplement issued 1959]

M311 RUST, Brian, with Rex BENNETT: London musical shows on record, 1897-1976. Harrow: General Gramophone Publications Ltd., 1977. 672 pp. ((3, 6, 7))

Musical Revues, Comedies, etc.— Denmark

M312 ANDREASEN, Axel: Ingeborg Bruhn-Bertelsen, Soffy Damaris, Ann-Sofi Norin, Erika Voigt og grammofonen; fire discografier. Copenhagen: Andreasen, 1976: 110 l. ((3, 4, 6, 7))

Musical Revues, Comedies, etc.— United States

M313 Discography in ENGEL, Lehman: The American musical theatre. New York: Macmillan, 1975: 229-241 ((—))

MYERS, J. W.

M314 LORENZ, Kenneth M.: J. W. Myers in Kastlemusik Monthly Bulletin, IV/1 (January 1979): 10-11; IV/2 (February 1979): 14-15; IV/3 (March 1979): 14-15 ((3, 7))

MYRL label

M315 TOPPING, Ray: Myrl label list in Shout, No. 101 (February 1975): 10 ((3, 5))

THE MYSTERY TREND (musical group)

M316 [Discography] in HOGG, Brian: Psychotic reaction: San Francisco begins in Bam Balam, No. 10 (November 1979): 23-24 ((5))

N.R.C. label

N1 TOPPING, Ray: NRC label listing in New Kommotion, No. 21 (1979): 12 ((3, 5))

NARMOUR AND SMITH (musical group)

N2 YOUNG, Henry: Narmour and Smith—a brief discography in JEMF Quarterly, VII/1 (No. 23, Spring 1971): 31-34 ((3, 6, 7))

NASCIMBENE, MARIO

N3 MARSHALL, James, and Enzo COCUMAROLO: Mario Nascimbene: filmography/discography in Soundtrack Collector's Newsletter, IV (No. 17, April 1979): 12-16 ((5))

NASHVILLE BRASS (musical group)

N4 BOSSINK, Bert: Discography in Rockville/Roaring Sixties (March-April 1975): 33 ((5))

THE NASHVILLE TEENS (musical group)

N5 Nashville Teens in Gorilla Beat, No. 8 (1980): 38-43; discography pp. 42-43; addenda in No. 9 (1981): 50; No. 10 (1981): 45; and No. 13 (1982): 70 ((5))

NATIONAL MUSIC LOVERS label

N6 COTTER, Dave: National Music Lovers in New Amberola Graphic, No. 16 (Winter 1976) thru No. 36 (Spring 1981): various paginations ((3, 6))

NATIONS BROTHERS

N7 [RUSSELL, Tony]: Nations Brothers (Sheldon and Marshall) in Old Time Music, No. 10 (Autumn 1973): 24 ((3, 6, 7))

THE NATURALS (musical group)

N8 KLITSCH, Hans Jurgen: Act naturally in Gorilla Beat, No. 13 (1982): 68-69; discography p. 69 ((5))

NATUS, JOSEPH

N9 LORENZ, Kenneth M.: [Discography] in Kastlemusik Monthly Bulletin, III/9 (E-46; September 1978): 11-14 ((3))

NAZARETH (musical group)

N10 Discography in Trans-Oceanic Trouser Press, No. 15 (August-September 1976): 12-15; discography p. 15; additions and corrections in No. 17 (December 1976-January 1977): 2 [Includes Dan McCafferty solo] ((—))

THE NAZZ (musical group)

N11   Nazz discography *in* Trouser Press Press, No. 3 (1976): 66 ((—))

NELSON, RICK

N12   CALLAHAN, Mike, et al.: Rick Nelson discography *in* Goldmine, No. 51 (August 1980): 19–20 ((—))

N13   FIDYK, Bernard: Ricky Nelson discography *in* New Kommotion, No. 15 (Spring 1977): 34, 36 ((3))

N14   Ricky Nelson: the Imperial years *in* New Kommotion, No. 20 (Summer 1978): 46–50; discography p. 50; addenda in No. 22 (1979): 65–66 ((1, 2, 3, 7))

NELSON, WILLIE

N15   Willie Nelson: discography *in* ALLEN, Bob: Waylon & Willie: the full story in words and pictures of Waylon Jennings and Willie Nelson. New York: Quick Fox, 1979: 116–121 ((5))

N16   Discography *in* FOWLER, Lana Nelson: Willie Nelson family album. Amarillo: Poirot, 1980: [159–160] ((—))

N17   FREDERICKS, Gene: Willie Nelson discography (1962–1978) *in* The Record Finder, I/7 (June 1979): 4 ((5))

N18   ROLLINS, Cathy, and J. J. SYRJA: Willie Nelson album discography *in* Goldmine, No. 64 (September 1981): 20 ((5))

THE NEON PHILHARMONIC

N19   LEMLICH, Jeff: Neon Philharmonic discography *in* Blitz, No. 29 (November–December 1978): 24 ((5))

NEOPHONE label

N20   ANDREWS, F.: Neophone: a catalogue of Neophone Records known to have been advertised in Britain: part 1 *in* Talking Machine Review, No. 54–55 (October–December 1978): 1397–1400 ((5))

NEPTUNE label

N21   GONZALEZ, Fernando: Neptune Records discography *in* Paul's Record Magazine (No. 16): 37–38 ((3, 5, 7))

N22   ROUNCE, Tony: Neptune label listing *in* Shout, No. 76 (May 1972): [9–10] ((3))

NESMITH, MICHAEL

N23   McDOWELL, Mike, and John CLAYTON: Michael Nesmith discography *in* Blitz, No. 28 (September–October 1978): 21–22 [Pre- and post-Monkees recordings] ((5))

NETTLES, BILL, AND HIS DIXIE BLUE BOYS

N24   [Discography] *in* Disc Collector, No. 22 [n.d., 1966?]: ? ((2, 3, 7))

N25   NETTLES, Mrs. Bill, et al.: Record listing titles A to Z *in* Country & Western Roundabout, IV (No. 14, October–December 1976): 10–12 ((—))

THE NEW BREED (musical group)

N26   [Discography] *in* HOGG, Brian: Psychotic reaction: San Francisco begins *in* Bam Balam, No. 10 (November 1979): 24; addendum in No. 14 (September 1982): 16 ((—))

NEW CHRISTY MINSTRELS (musical group)

N27   PICKLES, Tom: New Christy Minstrels discography *in* Goldmine, No. 51 (August 1980): 16 ((5))

THE NEW COLONY SIX (musical group)

N28   McDOWELL, Mike, and Jerry SCHOLLENBERGER: The history of the New Colony Six *in* Ballroom Blitz, No. 23 (November 1977): 7–11; discography pp. 10–11 ((2, 5)) [Reprinted in Blitz, No. 37 (July–August 1980): 15–18; discography p. 18 ((2, 5))]

NEW ORDER (musical group, U.S., 1975/6)

N29   KOENIG, John: New Order *in* Goldmine, No. 36 (May 1979): 15 ((5))

N30 PICKERING, Mike: New Order discography/gig guide *in* Gorilla Beat, No. 13 (1982): 46–48 ((1, 7))

NEW VICTORIA ORCHESTRA

N31 De Groot and the New Victoria Orchestra *in* Vintage Light Music, No. 24 (Autumn 1980): 6–7 ((—))

NEW YEAR HOLIDAY

N32 New Year's records *in* Record Exchanger, V/5 (No. 27, 1978): 19 ((5))

THE NEW YORKERS FIVE (musical group)

N33 MONDRONE, Sal: Rare sounds *in* Bim Bam Boom, I/3 (December 1971–January 1972): 11 ((—))

NEWBURY, MICKEY

N34 Mickey Newbury LP discography *in* Kountry Korral (No. 2, 1979): 21 ((—))

NEWHART, BOB

N35 SMITH, Ronald L.: Discography *in* Goldmine, No. 42 (November 1979): 121 ((—))

NEWMAN, ALFRED

N36 PUGLIESE, Roberto: Filmografia essenziale di Alfred Newman *in* Discoteca hi fi, No. 202–203 (January–February 1981): [38]–40 ((—))

NEWMAN, JIMMY C.

N37 MATTSSON, Soren: Jimmy C. Newman disco *in* Kountry Korral, XIV/1 (1981): 20–24 ((—))

NEWMAN, RANDY

N38 HARVEY, Steve: Randy Newman discography *in* Goldmine, No. 66 (November 1981): 19, 21 ((5))

NEWMAN, ROY, AND HIS BOYS (musical group)

N39 HEALY, R.: [Discography] *in* Country Directory, No. 4 [n.d., 1962?]: ? ((2, 3, 7))

NEWMAN BROTHERS

N40 Discography *in* TRIBE, Ivan: Georgia Crackers in the North: the story of the Newman Brothers *in* Old Time Music, No. 30 (Autumn 1978): 9–12 ((3, 7))

NEWTON-JOHN, OLIVIA

N41 [[[Discography] *in* RUFF, Peter: Olivia Newton-John. New York: Quick Fox, 1979: 93–96]]

THE NICE (musical group)

N42 BETROCK, Alan: The immediate story, vol. one: Nice discography *in* Immediate [sound recording] Sire SASH-3710-2, 1975: inside cover ((5))

NICHOLLS, BILLY

N43 BETROCK, Alan: Who is Billy Nicholls? *in* The Rock Marketplace, No. 10 (June 1975): 40–41 ((5))

NICK & THE NACKS (musical group)

N44 ENGEL, Edward R.: Out of "The night": Nick & the Nacks *in* Time Barrier Express, III/4 (No. 24, April–May 1979): 66–67 ((—))

THE NIGHTCAPS (musical group)

N45 MOONOOGIAN, George: Nightcaps discography *in* Goldmine, No. 49 (June 1980): 173 ((5))

N46 PARKER, Richard: Nightcaps discography *in* Goldmine, No. 67 (December 1981): 169 ((5))

THE NIGHTCRAWLERS (musical group)

N47 LEMLICH, Jeff: Nightcrawlers discography *in* Blitz, No. 30 (March–April 1979): 14 ((5))

NIGHTHAWK, ROBERT

N48 O'NEAL, Jim: Robert Nighthawk for United/State *in* Crazy Music, No. 11 (December 1977): 21–23 ((3, 6, 7))

NINO AND THE EBB TIDES
(musical group)

N49 PIAZZA, Mike: Nino & the Ebb Tides *in* Bim Bam Boom, No. 7 (September 1972): 12 ((3))

NIX, HOYLE

N50 SPECHT, Joe W.: Discography *in* Old Time Music, No. 36 (Summer 1981): 11 ((3))

NOLAND, TERRY

N51 [[[Discography] *in* New Kommotion, No. 11 (c1976); addenda in No. 19 (Spring 1978): 12]]

NORFOLK JAZZ QUARTET
(musical group)

N52 SEROFF, Doug: Norfolk Jazz Quartet discography *in* Goldmine, No. 40 (September 1979): 15A ((3, 7))

NORTH, FREDDIE

N53 [[[Discography] *in* Shout (No. 39)]]

NORTH CAROLINA RAMBLERS
(musical group)

N54 WILE, Ray: The Edison recordings of Posey Rorer and the North Carolina Ramblers *in* Record Research, No. 92 (September 1968): 4 ((3, 6, 7))

THE NOTATIONS (musical group)

N55 PRUTER, Robert: Notations discography *in* Goldmine, No. 32 (January 1979): 10 ((5))

NOUGARO, CLAUDE

N56 Discographie *in* Claude Nougaro. Paris: Seghers, 1974: [185]–187 ((—)) (Collection poesie et chansons Seghers, 30)

N57 Discographie in Hi-fi stereo, No. 42 (nouv. ser.)(October 1978): 225–226 ((—))

NOVELTY QUINTET

N58 [Discography] *in* Commodore, No. 4 (Winter 1971): 10 ((—))

NUCLEAR PIEROGIE (musical group)

N59 DEC, Michael: Nuclear Pierogie discography *in* Goldmine, No. 16 (May-June 1977): 19 ((5))

OAK RIDGE BOYS

O1 Oak Ridge Boys *in* Kountry Korral, X/2 (April 1977): 23 ((—))

OBJECT MUSIC label

O2 FAULL, Trev: The story of Object Music *in* Outlet, No. 15 (November 1979): 2–8; discography pp. 7–8; updates in succeeding issues ((—))

OCHS, PHIL

O3 Discography *in* ELIOT, Marc: Death of a rebel. Garden City, N.Y.: Anchor Press, 1979: [285]–293 ((5, 7))

O'CONNOR, JACK
See JACK AND EVELYN

O'DANIEL, W. LEE AND HIS LIGHT CRUST DOUGHBOYS/HILLBILLY BOYS (musical group)

O4 HEALY, R.: [Discography] *in* Country Directory, No. 3 (1962): ?; No. 4 [n.d., 1962?]: ? ((2, 3, 7))

O5 HEALY, R.: [Discography] *in* Folk Style, No. 9 [n.d.]: ? ((2, 3, 7))

O'DAY, ANITA

O6 SIXSMITH, Robert A., and Alan EICHLER: Discography *in* her High times, hard times. New York: Putnam, 1981: [299]–349 ((1, 2, 3, 5, 6, 7))

O'DAY, MOLLY

O7 TRIBE, Ivan M.: Molly O'Day, Lynn Davis, and the Cumberland Mountain Folks: a bio-discography. Los Angeles: John Edwards Memorial Foundation, 1975. 35 pp. ((2, 3, 6, 7))

O'GWYNN, JAMES LEROY

O8 Discography (USA) *in* HAWKINS, Martin: Introducing James O'Gwynn *in* Country Music Review (December 1976): 15–16 ((5))

O9 James O'Gwynn discography *in* Kountry Korral, X/5 (October 1977): 22–23 ((5))

O10 O'GWYNN, James, et al.: James O'Gwynn diskographie *in* Hillbilly, No. 55 (June 1978): 8–15 ((3, 5, 7))

OHMANN, MARTIN

O11 ENGLUND, Bjorn: [Discography] *in* Talking Machine Review, No. 44 (February 1977): 934–938 ((3, 6, 7))

O'JAYS (musical group)

O12 CUMMINGS, Tony: O'Jays diskography *in* Black Wax, No. 3 (March–April 1973): 10–12 ((2, 3, 6, 7))

O13 O'Jays discography *in* Shout, No. 98 (September 1974): 3–7 ((2, 3, 6, 7))

O'KEEFE, JOHNNY

O14 THOMPSON, Phillip: Johnny O'Keefe LP discography *in* Big Beat of the 50's, No. 20 (May 1979): 49–50 ((—))

OKEH label

See also *Bibliography* Vol. 2, Jazz

O15 HEARNE, Will Roy: [Discography, 45000 series] *in* Disc Collector, II/3 (June 1952); III/1 (January 1953); No. 9 (April 1953); No. 10 (July 1953): various paginations ((—))

O16 Okeh label—6800 series *in* Time Barrier Express, II/9 (No. 19, October 1976): 22–29 ((3))

O17 [RUSSELL, Tony]: Okeh 45000 series (45102–45116) *in* Old Time Music, No. 4 (Spring 1972): 22 ((3, 6))

O18 RUSSELL, Tony: The Asheville session list *in* Old Time Music, No. 31 (Winter 1978–1979): 5–10 ((3, 7))

OKEH MEDICINE SHOW ARTISTS (musical group)

O19 KUNSTADT, Len, and B. COLTON: [Discography] *in* Record Research, No. 58 (February 1964): ?; additions in No. 66 and 81: ? ((2, 3, 7))

OLCOTT, CHAUNCEY

O20 KUNSTADT, Len, and Bob COLTON: Discography *in* Record Research, No. 83 (April 1967): 10 ((3, 6, 7))

OLD TIME FIDDLERS' CONVENTION, UNION GROVE, N.C.

O21 [[Discography *in* AHERNS, Pat J.: Union Grove: the first fifty years. Columbia, S.C.: Aherns, 1975: 150–159]]

OLD TOWN label

O22 GONZALEZ, Ferdie, and Peter GIBBONS: [Discography] *in* Yesterday's Memories, III/4 (1977): 44–46 ((7))

O23 TOPPING, Ray: Old Town label listing *in* Shout, No. 53 (March 1970): [1–5]; No. 54 (April 1970): [1–6]; additions and corrections in No. 55 (May 1970): [6]; No. 65 (April 1971): [2] ((3))

OLOF, VICTOR

O24 UPTON, Stuart: The Victor Olof Salon Orchestra and the Victor Olof Sextet *in* Vintage Light Music, No. 29 (Winter 1982): 10–11 ((3))

OLSEN, GEORGE

O25 CAMP, George: Discography— George Olsen *in* After Beat, I/12 (September 1971): 8–10; II/3 (February–March 1972): 13 ((7))

THE OLYMPICS (musical group)

O26 HINCKLEY, Dave: The Olympics *in* Yesterday's Memories, III/2 (1977): 16 ((7))

ONE-DERFUL label

O27 TOPPING, Ray, and Kurt MOHR: One-derful label listing *in* Shout, No. 79 (August 1972): [1–3]; No. 84 (February–March 1973): [3–6]; additions and corrections in No. 92 (January 1974): 9 ((3, 5))

ONO, YOKO

O28 John & Yoko: for the record *in* Music World, No. 81 (January 1981): 12 ((1))

ONYX label

See also *Bibliography* Vol. 2, Jazz

O29 HUBBARD, Richard L.: Onyx Records—label history and listing *in* Shout, No. 92 (January 1974): 6–7 ((3, 5))

OPEN THE DOOR, RICHARD (song title)

O30 SEROFF, Doug: Open the door, Richard [song title discography] *in* Record Exchanger, IV/6 (August 1975): 10–11 ((5))

ORBISON, ROY

O31 CLEE, Ken: Roy Orbison discography *in* Goldmine, No. 41 (October 1979): 8 ((—))

O32 CLEE, Ken: Roy Orbison discography *in* Music World, No. 85 (May 1981): 34 ((—))

O33 DUFFY, Desmond, et al.: Roy Orbison disco *in* Rockville International (March–April 1974): 40 ((1, 3, 5, 7))

ORCHESTRA RAYMONDE

O34 UPTON, Stuart: Orchestra Raymonde *in* Commodore, No. 9 (Spring 1973): 3+ ((—))

ORIGINAL SOUND label

O35 SMART, Pete: Original Sound Records: part two *in* SMG, III/2 (October–November 1972): 8–11 ((—))

THE ORIGINALS (musical group)

O36 TOWNE, Steve: The Originals discography *in* Goldmine, No. 64 (September 1981): 24–25 ((5))

ORIOLE label

See also *Bibliography* Vol. 2, Jazz

O37 HAYES, Jim: Listing of 10 inch and 12 inch Oriole P100 series matrices *in* Gunn Report, No. 73 (May–June–July 1979): 19–20; No. 74 (August–September–October 1979): 16–17; No. 75 (November–December 1979): 17–19 ((3))

THE ORIOLES (musical group)

O38 Orioles discography *in* Record Exchanger, II/3 (No. 8 [Fall 1971]): 8–10; additions and corrections in III/3 (No. 14, April 1973): 23 ((5))

THE ORLONS (musical group)

O39 MOHR, Kurt: Orlons & Rosetta Hightower discography *in* Shout, No. 66 (May 1971): [6–9] ((3, 7))

OSBORNE, JIMMIE

O40 WEIZE, Richard A., and E. Reinald SCHUMANN: Jimmie Osborne diskographie *in* Hillbilly, No. 46 (March 1976): 16–18; additions and corrections in No. 48 (September 1976): 31 ((—))

OSBORNE BROTHERS (musical group)

O41 ROSENBERG, N.: [Discography] *in* Bluegrass Unlimited, I/12 (June 1967): ?; II/1 (July 1967): ? ((2, 3, 7))

O'SHEA, SHAD

O42 STIDOM, Larry: Discography: Shad O'Shea *in* Goldmine, No. 47 (April 1980): 166 ((5))

THE OSPREYS (musical group)

O43 GOLDBERG, Marv: The Ospreys *in* Yesterday's Memories, III/4 (1977): 31 ((7))

THE OTHERS (musical group)

O44 The Others *in* The Rock Marketplace, No. 7 (October 1974): 38 ((5))

OUTLAW label

O45 ADAMS, Dennis: Outlaw Records *in* New Kommotion, No. 21 (1979): 36 ((1, 3))

THE OUTLAWS (musical group)

O46 EVERS, George: Discografie *in* Rockville/Roaring Sixties (March–April 1975): 25 ((5))

THE OUTSIDERS (musical group)

O47 SMALL, Bill: Inside the Outsiders *in* Jamz, No. 5 (c1972): 57–58; discography p. 58 ((5))

OVERSTREET, TOMMY

O48 Tommy Overstreet disco *in* Kountry Korral, X/2 (April 1977): 21 ((—))

OWENS, BUCK

O49 Buck Owens and his Buckaroos disco *in* Kountry Korral, XI/3–4 (1978): 30–31 ((5))

O50 [[Discography *in* Country Corner, No. 7: 3]]

O51 [Discography] *in* Country Western Express, No. 7 [New series]: ? ((—))

O52 STRUBING, Hauke: Seine Capitol discographie *in* Country Corner, No. 38 (February 1974): 27–32 ((5))

OXFORD, VERNON

O53 CRAIG, Mike, and Richard A. WEIZE: Vernon Oxford diskographie *in* Hillbilly, No. 56 (September 1978): 25–28 ((3, 7))

O54 Vernon Oxford auf Single [und] Vernon Oxford auf Langspielplatten *in* Country Corner, No. 51 (October 1976): 7–8 ((—))

THE PACKABEATS (musical group)

P1 FAULL, Trev: The Packabeats *in* Instrumental Obscurities Unlimited, No. 20 (c1978): 14–15 ((5))

PADDY, KLAUS, AND GIBSON (musical group)

P2 SCHACHT, Janis: Paddy, Klaus & Gibson *in* The Rock Marketplace, No. 9 (March 1975): 40 ((5))

PAGANI, HERBERT

P3 [[[Discography] *in* Herbert Pagani. Paris: Seghers, 1976; 141 (Collection poesie et chansons Seghers, 40)]]

PAGE, JIMMY

P4 SCHULPS, Dave: Paging the Yardbirds *in* Trouser Press, No. 22 (October 1977): 23–28; discography p. 28 [Part 2 of a 3 part interview. Part 1 appeared in Trouser Press, No. 21 (September 1977): 10–16, and part 3 appeared in Trouser Press, No. 23 (November 1977): 17–22. The discography includes session work 1963–1974 and recordings with the Yardbirds but not Led Zeppelin] ((5))

PALETTE label
See entry for TOP RANK label

PALMIERI, EDDIE

P5 Selected Palmieri discography *in* Down Beat, XLIII (April 22, 1976): 21 ((—))

PALOS label

P6 TOPPING, Ray: Palos label listing *in* Shout, No. 53 (March 1970): [10] ((3))

PANACHORD label

P7 HAYES, Jim: Panachord 25000 series *in* Gunn Report, No. 34 (June–July 1972): 42 ((5))

PANACHORD label [Australia]

P8   CRISP, David: [Discography] *in* Country Western Spotlight, No. 40 (December 1962): ? ((—))

P9   [Discography] *in* Hillbilly Folk Record Journal, I/2 (April 1954); I/3 (July 1954): ? ((—))

PARAMOUNT label

See also *Bibliography* Vol. 2, Jazz

P10   [Discography, 3000 series] *in* Blue Yodler, No. 7 (February 1966) thru No. 15 (July 1967): various paginations ((—))

P11   HEARNE, Will Roy: [Discography, 3000 series] *in* Disc Collector, I/4 (October 1951); II/1 (January 1952): ? ((—))

THE PARAMOUNTS (musical group)

P12   LEE, Alan: [Discography] *in* Yesterday's Memories, II/4 (1976): 24 ((7))

PARKER, JOHNNY

P13   [Discography] *in* Record Research, No. 95 (February 1969): 3–10 ((3, 6, 7)) [Discographic essay]

PARKWAY label

P14   SHAW, Greg: Parkway Records discography *in* Paul's Record Magazine (No. 17–18): 56–63 ((5))

PARLOPHONE-ODEON label

P15   BAYLEY, E.: The Parlophone-Odeon "OT" series *in* Talking Machine Review, No. 56–57 (February–April 1979): 1488–1489 ((3))

PAR-O-KET label

P16   Par-o-Ket catalogue *in* Recorded Americana, No. 5 (October 1958): [6–7]; No. 6 (December 1958): [3] ((—))

PARRIS, FRED

P17   Fred Parris discography *in* Goldmine, No. 36 (May 1979): 8–9 ((3, 5))

PARRY, MAXINE

P18   [Discography] *in* Country Western Express, No. 21 (December 1958): ? ((—))

PARTON, DOLLY

P19   A selective discography *in* BERMAN, Connie: The official Dolly Parton scrapbook. New York: Grosset & Dunlap, 1978: 94–95 ((—))

P20   Dolly Parton's RCA discographie *in* Country Corner (January 1979): 25–26; (March 1979): 23–25; (April 1979): 28–29; (May 1979): 28–29; (June 1979): 33, 36 [Covers recordings made 10 Oct. 67 through 23 July 75] ((3, 5, 7))

P21   Discography *in* JAMES, Otis: Dolly Parton. New York: Quick Fox, 1978: [92–96] ((—))

P22   Discography *in* NASH, Alanna: Dolly. Los Angeles: Reed Books, 1978: 273–275 ((5))

P23   ROMIN, Ole: Dolly Parton disco *in* Kountry Korral, XI/6 (1978): 9 ((—))

PARTON, STELLA

P24   FERNQUIST, Gunnar: Stella Parton LP disco *in* Kountry Korral Magazine (No. 2, 1980): 17 ((5))

THE PASSIONS (musical group)

P25   FLAM, Steve: Insight *in* Bim Bam Boom, I/2 (October–November 1971): 15 ((—))

THE PASTELS (musical group)

P26   GOLDBERG, Marv: The Pastels *in* Yesterday's Memories, III/4 (1977): 21 ((7))

P27   GOLDBERG, Marv, and Rick WHITESELL: The Pastels *in* Goldmine, No. 35 (April 1979): 39 ((5))

PATHE label [Scandinavia]

P28   ENGLUND, Bjorn: Some notes on Pathe in Scandinavia: part 1, the acoustic era *in* Talking Machine Review, No. 47 (1977): 1060–1062 ((3, 7))

PATTEE, COL. JOHN

P29 DROCHETZ, J.: [Discography] *in*
Record Research, No. 64 (November
1964): ? ((3))

PATTERSON, RED

P30 RORRER, Kinney: Discography *in*
Old Time Music, No. 34 (Summer to
Autumn, 1980): 5–6 ((2, 3))

PATTO (musical group)

P31 RICHARDSON, Ben: Patto: a British
tragedy *in* Trans-Oceanic Trouser
Press, II/1 (February–March 1975):
34–36 ((—))

PAUL REVERE AND THE RAIDERS
(musical group)

P32 HOGG, Brian: Bits and pieces *in* Bam
Balam, No. 10 (November 1979):
14–16 ((5))

P33 Paul Revere and the Raiders discography *in* Who Put the Bomp, No. 14
(Fall 1975): 22; additions and corrections in No. 15 (Spring 1976): 44
((5))

PAULA label

P34 PERIN, Jacques, and Gilles PE-
TARD: . . . Listing Paula . . . *in* Soul
Bag, No. 77 (1980): 23–28 ((—))

PAXTON, TOM

P35 Tom Paxton discography *in* Goldmine, No. 52 (September 1980): 186
((5))

PAYNE, JOHN

P36 Partial discography *on* John Payne's
first album [sound recording] Bromfi
Records BR-1, 1974 ((—))

PEACHTREE label

P37 [[[Discography] *in* Black Wax (No. 2);
additions and corrections in No. 3
(March–April 1973): 16]]

PEARL AND THE DELTARS
(musical group)

P38 STRAITE, James: [Discography] *in*
Yesterday's Memories, II/1 (1976): 17
((—))

PEARSON, RONNIE

P39 AIRLIE, Bob: Ronnie Pearson on
Herald: 1958 *in* Kommotion, No. 9
(Spring–Summer 1975): 17–18 ((3))

PEDERSEN, HOLGER

P40 ANDREASEN, Axel: Holger Pedersen
"Gissemand" og grammofonen: en
discografi. Copenhagen: Andreasen,
1976. 63 l. ((3, 4, 7))

PEEK, PAUL

P41 DUNHAM, Bob: Paul Peek *in* New
Kommotion, No. 19 (Spring 1978):
27–31; discography pp. 30–31 ((2, 3,
7))

PEERLESS ORCHESTRA

P42 UPTON, Stuart: The Peerless Orchestra *in* Commodore, No. 3
(Autumn 1971): 13 + ((—))

PENDARVIS, PAUL

P43 LINDSLEY, Charles: Discography—
Paul Pendarvis *in* After Beat, II/5
(June–July 1972): 18 ((1))

PENDLETON, FRED

P44 [COHEN, Norm]: Fred Pendleton *in*
JEMF Quarterly, VIII/2 (No. 26,
Summer 1972): 104 ((3, 6, 7))

THE PENGUINS (musical group)
See also *Bibliography* Vol. 2, Jazz

P45 FIELDS, Tom: Penguins discography
in It Will Stand, No. 14–15 (c1980):
15 ((—))

P46 GROIA, Phil, et al.: The Penguins *in*
Bim Bam Boom, No. 7 (September
1972): 9, 57 ((3))

P47 Penguins discography *in* Record Exchanger, II/6 (No. 11 [Fall 1972]): 16
((3, 5))

PENNY, HANK

P48 KIENZLE, Rich: Hank Penny discography *in* Old Time Music, No. 28 (Spring 1978): 11-16 ((3, 5, 7))

PEOPLE (musical group)

P49 SHAW, Greg: Discography *in* Who Put the Bomp, No. 12 (Summer 1974): 29 ((—))

PERKINS, ANTHONY

P50 LYNCH, Richard C.: Tony Perkins on record *in* Kastlemusik Monthly Bulletin, VI/8 (August 1981): 4-5 ((5))

PERKINS, CARL

P51 Carl Perkins disco *in* Kountry Korral, X/2 (April 1977): 24 ((—))

P52 Carl Perkins discography *in* Kountry Korral, No. 2 (1968): 13-14 ((—))

P53 Carl Perkins LP disco *in* Kountry Korral Magazine (No. 2, 1980): [30]-31 ((—))

P54 CLEE, Ken: Carl Perkins discography *in* Goldmine, No. 49 (June 1980): 10 ((5))

P55 KOMOROWSKI, Adam: Carl Perkins discography *in* New Kommotion, No. 20 (Summer 1978): 28-29; addenda in No. 22 (1979): 66 ((1, 2, 3, 7))

P56 MAIRE, X, et al.: Discographie *in* Big Beat, No. 13 [n.d.]: 6-7, 10-11 ((2, 3, 7))

P57 SZOLKOWSKI, Roman: Carl Perkins discography *in* Time Barrier Express, III (No. 26, September-October 1979): 47-51 ((7))

P58 TREUDE, Helmut: Carl Perkins auf Langspielplatten *in* Country Corner, No. 53 (February 1977): 21 ((—))

P59 TREUDE, Helmut: Carl Perkins—country music with a coloured beat (Teil 1) *in* Country Corner, No. 52 (December 1976): 12-15 ((—))

P60 WESTFALL, Bob: Carl Perkins on disc *in* Kommotion, No. 8 (Winter 1975): 13-15; addenda in No. 9 (Spring-Summer 1975): 4-5 and No. 10-11 (Winter 1975-76): 26 ((—))

PERRET, PIERRE

P61 [[[Discography] *in* his Pierre Perret. Paris: Seghers, 1978: [183]-188 (Collection poesie et chansons Seghers, 41)]]

THE PERSIANS (musical group)

P62 CUMMINGS, Tony, and Kurt MOHR: The Persians *in* Black Wax, No. 6 (July 1973): 9 ((3, 7))

PESSIS, JACQUES

P63 Discographie *in* DAC, Pierre: Jacques Pessis. Paris: Seghers, 1977: [166]-167 ((—))

PET label

P64 MASOTTI, Fred: [Discography] *in* Paul's Record Magazine, III/4 (April-May 1976): 12 ((—))

PETER, SUE & MARC

P65 LP-Discographie *in* REBER, Peter: Peter, Sue und Marc. Bern: Edition Erpf, 1981: 53-54 ((—))

PETERSEN, PAUL

P66 JONES, Wayne: Paul Petersen discography *in* Paul's Record Magazine, III/2 (February 1976): 22-23 ((—))

PETERSON, RAY

P67 NAJMAN, Joel: Ray Peterson *in* Paul's Record Magazine, No. 15 (January-February 1977): 10-11 ((—))

PETTIS, JACK
See also *Bibliography* Vol. 2, Jazz

P68 VACHE, Warren: Jack Pettis and his Pets *in* Kastlemusik Monthly Bulletin, III/7 (E-44; July 1978): 1, 15 ((7))

THE PHANTOM BROTHERS (musical group)

P69 Beat in Germany: Phantom Brothers *in* Gorilla Beat, No. 6 (1980): 47-50; discography p. 50 ((—))

PHELPS, WILLIE, AND THE VIRGINIA RAMBLERS (musical group)

P70 [Discography] *in* Country Directory, No. 2 (April 1961): ? ((2, 3, 7))

PHILADELPHIA INTERNATIONAL label

P71 MOHR, Kurt: Philadelphia International label listing *in* Shout, No. 87 (July 1973): [5–6] ((5))

PHILLES label
See also SPECTOR, PHIL

P72 BEZANKER, Paul: Philles Records: discography *in* Paul's Record Magazine, II/6 (December 1975): 9–12; additions and corrections in III/2 (February 1976): 4 ((3, 4, 5))

P73 CALLAHAN, Mike: Philles discography *in* Goldmine, No. 47 (April 1980): 149 ((5))

P74 DALY, Mike: Philles discography *in* Mojo-Navigator Rock & Roll News, No. 13 (April 1967): 9–11 ((—))

P75 WHERRY, Nev: Philles label listing *in* Black Wax, No. 4 (May 1973): 6–8; additions and corrections in No. 5 (June 1973): 19 ((—))

P76 WHERRY, Nev: Philles label listing *in* Shout, No. 105 (October–November 1971): 16–17 ((3))

PHILLIPS, ESTHER

P77 HESS, Norbert, et al.: Esther Phillips discography *in* Shout, No. 96 (June 1974): 5–11 ((2, 3, 6, 7))

PHILLIPS, SAM C. (record producer)

P78 DANIELS, Bill: Before Sunrise: the early recordings [i.e. produced by] Sam Phillips *in* Record Exchanger, V/2 (No. 24, October (?) 1977): 16–17 ((—))

PHILLIPS INTERNATIONAL label

P79 BECKER, Robert: Phillips International *in* Record Exchanger, No. 15 [June 1973]: 12–13 ((—))

PIAF, EDITH

P80 Disques Pathe-Marconi—Columbia *in* ALLAERT, Edith: Edith Piaf, le chant d'amour. Paris: Soprode, 1973: 171–173 ((—))

P81 Discographie *in* Edith Piaf. Paris: Seghers, 1974: [175]–186 ((5)) (Collection poesie et chansons Seghers, 25)

P82 Discographie d'Edith Piaf *in* HIEGEL, Pierre: Edith Piaf. Monte Carlo: Editions l'heure, 1962: 105–107 ((—))

P83 Edith Piaf na deskach Supraphon *in* TATEROVA, Milada: Edith Piaf. Phara: Supraphon, 1969: [42] ((—))

PIANO RED (real name William Perryman)
See also *Bibliography* Vol. 2, Jazz

P84 My discography *in* Big Beat, No. 20 (May 1981): 40–46 ((2, 3, 6, 7))

PIAZZOLA, ASTOR

P85 Discographie des disques de Piazzola publies en France *in* Jazz Hot, No. 315 (April 1975): 9 ((—))

PICCADILLY label

P86 [Discography] *in* Folk Style, No. 1 (December 1957): ? ((—))

P87 HAYES, Jim: Dominion versus Piccadilly *in* Vintage Light Music, No. 14 (Spring 1978): 4–5 ((3))

PICCADILLY ORCHESTRA
See De GROOT

PICCIONI, PIERO

P88 MARSHALL, James: Piero Piccioni: filmography/discography *in* SCN; Soundtrack Collector's Newsletter, V (No. 19, October 1979): 13–16; No. 20, January 1980: 13–16 ((5))

PICKARD FAMILY

P89 Pickard Family discography *in* JEMF Quarterly, IV/4 (December 1968): 12; addenda in VI/2 (No. 18, Summer 1970): 90 ((2, 3, 6, 7))

PICKARD'S CHINESE SYNCOPATORS (musical group)

P90 Pickard's Chinese Syncopators: discography *in* Gunn Report, No. 69 (August–September 1978): 8 ((3, 7))

PICONE, VITO

P91 Vito Picone *in* Time Barrier Express, No. 21 (January–February 1977): [11] ((—))

PI DE LA SERRA, FRANCESCO

P92 Discographia *in* ESPINAS, Jose M.: Pi de la Serra. Madrid: Jucar, 1974: [157–161] ((5))

PINE RIDGE BOYS (musical group)

P93 EDWARDS, J.: [Discography] *in* Country Western Spotlight, No. 20 (October–December 1957): ? ((—))

P94 EDWARDS, J.: [Discography] *in* Country Western Spotlight (Special issue, September 1962): ? ((—))

PINK label

P95 MASOTTI, Fred: [Discography] *in* Paul's Record Magazine, III/4 (April–May 1976): 12 ((—))

THE PINK FAIRIES (musical group)

P96 KLITSCH, Hans Jurgen: The Pink Fairies *in* Gorilla Beat, No. 12 (1981): 4–21; discography pp. 19–21; addendum in No. 15 (1982): 21 ((5)) [Includes the Fairies, Mick Farren, and the Deviants]

PINK FLOYD (musical group)

P97 BETROCK, Alan: [Discography] *in* Jamz, No. 2 (October 1971): 17 ((—))

P98 HEBING, Alfred: Pink Floyd *in* Gorilla Beat, No. 15 (1982): 38–49; discography pp. 47-49 ((5))

P99 Discography *in* LEDUC, Jean Marie: Pink Floyd. Paris: A. Michel, 1973: [179]–181

P100 Discographie *in* SAHNER, Paul: Pink Floyd. Munich: Heyne, 1980: 175–184 ((5))

P101 Discografia *in* SIERRA I FABRA, Jordi: Pink Floyd, viaje al sonido. Barcelona: Musica de Nuestro Tiempo, 1976: 83–141 ((—))

P102 TAYLOR, John, and John PHILLIPS: Pink Floyd discography *in* New Haven Rock Press, V/1 (No. 19, c1973): 10 ((6a))

THE PIPES (musical group)

P103 WHITESELL, Rick: The Pipes *in* Goldmine, No. 35 (April 1979): 43 ((—))

PITNEY, GENE

P104 Discography *in* Record Finder, II (No. 21, June–July 1982): 5 ((—))

P105 LEPRI, Paul: Gene Pitney: complete discography *in* The New Haven sound: Gene Pitney *in* Music World and Record Digest Weekly News, No. 64 (September 26, 1979): 6 ((5))

PITTMAN, BARBARA

P106 STRUM, Adri: Sun—Phillips International disco *in* Rockville International (December 1973): 25 ((3))

PIXINGUINHA

P107 Discografia basica *in* ALENCAR, Edigar de: O fabuloso e harmonioso Pixinguinha. Rio de Janeiro: Livaria Editora Catedra, 1979: 93–103 ((5))

P108 Discografia *in* CABRAL, Sergio: Pixinguinha: vida e obra. Rio de Janeiro: Funarte, 1978: 76–98 [1980 ed. has discography pp. 135–163) ((3, 5, 7))

P109 Discografia *in* SILVA, Marilia T. Barboza da: Filho de ogum bexiguento. Rio de Janeiro: Funarte, 1979: [165]–169 ((7))

PLANET label
See also La Salle label in *Bibliography* Vol. 2, Jazz

P110 FAULL, Trev: Planet Records *in* Outlet, No. 3 (June 1978): 1-2 ((—))

P111 Planet discography *in* The Rock Marketplace, No. 8 (December 1974): 29 ((—))

P112   SHAW, Greg: Planet discography *in* Who Put the Bomp, No. 10–11 (Fall 1973): 34 ((—))

THE PLANTS (musical group)

P113   GOLDBERG, Marv: The Plants *in* Yesterday's Memories, II/4 (1976): 17 ((—))

THE PLATTERS (musical group)

P114   The Platters discography *in* It Will Stand, No. 17–18 (c1980–81): 8 ((—))

P115   WASSERMAN, Steve: The Platters discography *in* Bim Bam Boom, I/6 (July 1972): 11 ((3, 5))

PLAZA THEATRE ORCHESTRA

P116   Plaza Theatre Orchestra . . . *in* Commodore, No. 1 (Spring 1971): 5 + ((—))

POISON RING label

P117   BEZANKER, Paul: Discography *in* Paul's Record Magazine, IV/1 (August 1976): 20–21 ((3))

POLK label

P118   Polk 9000 numerical *in* JEMF Newsletter, II/3 (No. 6, June 1967): 61–67 ((3))

POLNAREFF, MICHEL

P119   Discographie *in* BARTHELEMY, Cecile: Michel Polnareff. Paris: Seghers, 1974: [164]–165 (Collection poesie et chansons Seghers, 23) ((—))

POOLE, BRIAN, AND THE TREMELOES (musical group)

P120   KLITSCH, Hans Jurgen: It's about time for Brian Poole & the Tremeloes *in* Gorilla Beat, No. 9 (1981): 38–47; discography pp. 44–47; addenda in No. 10 (1981): 43 ((5))

POOLE, CHARLIE

P121   Discography *in* RORRER, Clifford Kinney: Charlie Poole and the North Carolina Ramblers. Eden, N.C.: Tar Heel Printing, 1968: 18–22 ((2, 7))

P122   RUSSELL, Tony: Charlie Poole discography *in* Old Time Music, No. 32 (Spring 1979): 19–21 ((3, 7))

P123   SMITH, Andrew: A discography of Charlie Poole "reissues" *in* Country & Western Spotlight, No. 26 (February 1981): 18–21 ((2, 7))

POOVEY, JOE

P124   TOPPING, Ray, and BIG AL: Groovey Joe Poovey *in* New Kommotion, No. 18 (Winter 1978): 38; addenda in No. 19 (Spring 1982): 12 ((2, 7))

PORTER, COLE

P125   Discography of original cast and selected historical recordings of Cole Porter songs *in* KIMBALL, Robert, ed.: Cole Porter. London: Joseph, 1972: 281–283 ((5))

P126   A selected Cole Porter discography *in* SCHWARTZ, Charles: Cole Porter: a biography. New York: Dial Press, 1977; Da Capo Press, 1979: [324]–333 ((—))

PORTER, S. C.

P127   LORENZ, Kenneth M.: S. C. (Steve) Porter (ca. 1865–1936): the early years, 1897–1901 *in* Kastlemusik Monthly Bulletin, III/7 (E-44; July 1978): 12–13 ((7))

POTTER, GILLIE

P128   Good evening England, this is Gillie Potter *in* Vintage Light Music, No. 4 (Fall 1975): [12] ((—))

PRAIRIE RAMBLERS (musical group)

P129   HEALY, R.: [Discography] *in* Country Directory, No. 3 (1962): ?; corrections in No. 4: ? ((2, 3, 7))

PREFIX label

P130   [[[Discography] *in* Black Wax (No. 2); additions and corrections in No. 3 (March–April 1973): 16]] .

PRENTICE, CHARLES

P131 [Discography] *in* Commodore, No. 1
(Spring 1971): 4 ((—))

PRESLEY, ELVIS ARON

P132 AROS, Andrew A.: Elvis, his films &
recordings. Diamond Beach, Calif.:
Applause Publications, 1980. 64 pp.
((5))

P133 [[[Discography] *in* BAGH, Peter von:
Elvis!: amerikkalaisen laulajanelama
ja kuolema. Helsinki: Love kustannus,
1977: 115–119]]

P134 BANNEY, Howard: The Elvis
novelties *in* Record Exchanger, V/1
(No. 23): 28 ((—)) [Discography of
"records with Elvis's name men-
tioned in the lyrics, records with some
reference to Elvis, and Elvis novelty
albums."]

P135 BARRY, Ron: All American Elvis:
The Elvis Presley American discography. Phillipsburg, N.J.: Spectator,
1976. 221 pp. ((4, 5))

P136 Diskografi *in* BERGLIND, Sten:
Elvis: fran Vasteras till Memphis.
Stockholm: Askild & Karnekull, 1977:
171–183 ((5))

P137 BEZANKER, Paul: Elvis Presley discography *in* Paul's Record Magazine
(No. 17–18): 10–13 ((5))

P138 CARR, Roy, and Mick FARREN:
Elvis Presley: an illustrated record.
New York: Harmony Books, 1980.
191 pp. ((1, 2, 3, 6, 7))

P139 Discographie *in* Elvis Presley. Dreieich: Melzer, 1978: [106]–115 ((1, 5))

P140 Elvis Presley LP discography *in* Kountry Korral, X/5 (October 1977): 12–14
((1))

P141 ESCOTT, Colin, and Martin HAWK-
INS: 20 years of Elvis: the session file.
Maidstone, England: Hawkins, 1976.
62 pp. ((1, 2, 3, 6, 7))

P142 FAULL, Trev: Elvis: the UK singles
collection 1956–1978 *in* Outlet, No. 8
(Xmas 1978): 9–12 ((5))

P143 Discografia completa de Elvis Presley
in FRAGA, Gaspar: Elvis Presley.
Madrid: Jugar, 1974: 163–165 ((5))

P144 Diskographie *in* GRUST, Lothar
F. W.: Elvis Presley superstar.
Bergisch Gladbach: G. Lubbe, 1978:
159–190 ((5))

P145 Ny revideret plade—liste *in* HANSEN,
Mogens: Elvis—er ikke dod: et minde-
album. Copenhagen: SV Press, 1978:
79–93 ((5))

P146 HAWKINS, Martin, and Colin
ESCOTT: Elvis: the illustrated discography. London: Omnibus, 1981. 96
pp. ((1, 2, 4, 6a, 7))

P147 HOLUM, Torben; Ernst JORGEN-
SEN; and Erik RASMUSSEN: Elvis
Presley: recording sessions, 1954–1974.
Lyngby, Denmark: Elvisette, 1975. 51
pp. ((2, 3, 4, 7))

P148 Discography *in* HOPKINS, Jerry:
Elvis. London: Abacus; New York:
Simon & Schuster, 1971: [429]–444
((5))

P149 JONES, Randall: An Elvis discography *in* Record Exchanger, V/3 (No.
25, January 1978?): 16–19 ((5))

P150 JONES, Randy: The RCA recordings
of Elvis Presley: a key to the original
issues *in* Record Exchanger, V/2 (No.
24, October (?) 1977): 28 ((—))

P151 JORGENSEN, Ernst; Erik RASMUS-
SEN; and Johnny MIKKELSEN: Elvis
Presley: recording sessions. 2nd ed.
Banneringen, Denmark: JEE Publica-
tions, 1977. 112 pp. ((1, 2, 3, 4, 5,
6a, 7))

P152 KOMOROWSKI, Adam; Bill MIL-
LAR; and Ray TOPPING: Elvis: the
original versions & other notes *in* New
Kommotion, No. 17 (Autumn 1977):
4–9; addenda in No. 19 (Spring 1978):
15 and No. 22 (1979): 64 ((5))
[Original recordings that Presley's
later covers were based on]

P153 Recording sessions *in* LICHTER,
Paul: The boy who dared to rock: the
definitive Elvis. Garden City, N.Y.:
Dolphin Books, 1978: [155]–197 ((1,
2, 3, 6, 7))

P154 Movie music *in* LICHTER, Paul:
Elvis in Hollywood. New York: Simon
& Schuster, 1975: [183–185] ((—))

P155 [[[Discography] *in* MARSH, Dave:
Elvis. New York: Times Books, 1982:
239– 241]]

P156 Elvis Presley discography *in* PARISH,
James Robert: The Elvis Presley
scrapbook. New York: Ballantine
Books, 1975: 167–185; 1978 ed. has
discography pp. 177–196 ((5))

P157 PETRICK, Gary F.: Elvis tributes *in*
Goldmine, No. 56 (January 1981): 16–

18 ((—)) [Records in tribute to Presley]

P158 Presley records *in* PRESLEY, Vester: A Presley speaks. Memphis: Wimmer Brothers Books, 1978: 141–147 ((—))

P159 Die originale U.S. long play (33) albums *in* ROGALE, Jean-Yves: Le roi Elvis. Paris: Menges, 1981: 138–[141] ((5))

P160 RUSSELL, Wayne: Elvis: the early TV appearances *in* New Kommotion, No. 19 (Spring 1978): 40 ((1, 2, 7))

P161 Elvis discography *in* SHAVER, Sean: The life of Elvis Presley. [s.l.]: Timur Publishing, 1979: 286–293 ((5))

P162 Elvis Presley na deskach Supraphon *in* TATEROVA, Milada: Elvis Presley. Praha: Supraphon, 1969: [37] ((—))

P163 Los discos de Elvis Presley *in* TELLO, Antonio: Elvis, Elvis, Elvis: la rebelion domesticada. Barcelona: Bruguera, 1977: 123–125 ((5))

P164 Discographie *in* WALLRAF, Rainer: Elvis Presley: e. Biographie. Munich: Nuchtern, 1977: 134 ((—))

P165 WHISLER, John A.: Elvis Presley: reference guide and discography. Metuchen, N.J.: Scarecrow, 1981. 265 pp. ((1, 4, 5, 7))

PRESTIGE label [New Zealand]

P166 GRANT, Doug: Selected discography *in* Big Beat of the 50's, No. 24 (June 1980): 35–36 ((—))

THE PRETTY THINGS (musical group)

P167 BETROCK, Alan: Pretty Things discography *in* Jamz, No. 5 (c1972): 65, 69 ((5))

P168 The Pretty Things *in* The Rock Marketplace, No. 7 (October 1974): 33, 38; addendum in No. 8 (December 1974): 42 ((5))

P169 Rainin' in my heart: the Pretty Things *in* Bam Balam, No. 2 (June 1975): 3–6; discography pp. 4–6; addenda in No. 5 (February 1977): 15–16 ((2))

P170 SCHULPS, Dave: Pretty Things *in* Trans-Oceanic Trouser Press, No. 13 (April–May 1976): 6–11; discography p. 10 ((5))

P171 SHAW, Greg: Discography *in* The Pretty Things: the vintage years

[sound recording], Sire SASH-3717-3, 1976. ((5))

PRICE, ALAN

P172 Additions & correxions [sic] to Alan Price discography *in* II/1 (c1973): 15–16 in Rock It with Aware, II/4 [1976]: 3 ((5))

P173 SCHAFFNER, Elizabeth: Alan Price—between today and yesterday *in* Trans-Oceanic Trouser Press, II/1 (February–March 1975): 7–10, 30 ((—))

PRICE, BILL, AND THE COUNTRY PARDNERS (musical group)

P174 [Discography] *in* Country Western Express, No. 17 (January–March 1958): ? ((—))

PRICE, RAY

P175 [Discography] *in* Country News & Views, II/2 (October 1963): 8, 12–14 ((5))

P176 Discography *in* Kountry Korral (No. 3, 1979): 19–21 ((—))

P177 REHFELDT, Hans-Peter: Discographie *in* Country Corner, No. 28 (April 1971): 21–27 ((—))

PRIDE, CHARLEY

P178 Charley Pride disco *in* Kountry Korral Magazine (No. 2, 1980): 28–[29] ((5))

P179 Charley Pride discography *in* Cashbox, XLIV (No. 3, June 12, 1982): CP-16 ((5))

PRINCETON-DARTMOUTH BANDS

P180 [Untitled research] *in* Record Research, No. 125–126 (February 1974): 8–9; No. 129–130 (October–November 1974): ((3, 6, 7))

THE PRISONAIRES (musical group)

P181 MILLAR, Bill: Prisonaires *in* Bim Bam Boom, II/3 (No. 9, 1973): 52 ((3))

P182 Prisonaires discography *in* Rock 'n' Roll International Magazine (Danish), No. 108 (November 1977): [14] ((5))

P183 TOPPING, Ray: Prisonaires/Johnny Bragg discography *in* New Kommotion, No. 22 (1979): 45 ((1, 2, 3, 7)) [Includes the Marigolds]

PROBY, P. J.

P184 BUYZE, Hans: P. J. Proby albums *in* Goldmine, No. 61 (June 1981): 19 ((5))

PROCOL HARUM (musical group)

P185 BETROCK, Alan: Early Procol—Paramounts—Freedom—later Procol— + much more *in* Jamz, No. 5 (c1972): 65, 67 ((5))

P186 HEBING, Alfred: Meet me where the (Procol) Harem is *in* Gorilla Beat, No. 9 (1981): 17–25; discography pp. 22–25; addenda in No. 10 (1981): 44–45 ((5)) [Includes the Paramounts and solo recordings by Robin Trower, Matthew Fisher, and Gary Brooker]

P187 SMITH, Ronald L.: Procol Harum: the original recordings *in* Goldmine, No. 45 (February 1980): 13 ((—))

PROPHET, ORVAL

P188 FUCHS, Walter W.: Diskographie *in* Hillbilly, No. 21 (March 1967): 8 ((—))

THE PROPHETS (musical group)

P189 McELVEEN, Jerry: The Prophets and their story *in* It Will Stand, No. 10 (c1979): 4–7; discography p. 7 ((—))

PRUITT, RALPH

P190 GLENISTER, Derek, and John BURTON: The Ralph Pruitt story *in* New Kommotion, No. 17 (Autumn 1977): 11–14; discography p. 14; addenda in No. 19 (Spring 1978): 12–13 and No. 22 (1979): 66 ((1, 2, 7))

PUCKETT, GARY, AND UNION GAP (musical group)

P191 WAGENAAR, Al: Gary Puckett & Union Gap discography *in* Goldmine, No. 43 (December 1979): 24 ((—))

PUCKETT, RILEY

P192 EDWARDS, J.: [Discography] *in* Disc Collector, No. 12 [n.d.]: ? ((—))

P193 Riley Puckett (1894–1946): a discography. Bremen: Archiv fur Populare Musik, 1977: 45 pp. ((2, 3, 4, 6, 7))

PURPLE label

P194 KOLANJIAN, Steve: Purple Records discography: LPs *in* Aware Magazine, II/5 (1977): 30–31 ((5))

PYRAMID label

P195 FAULL, Trev: Pyramid Records: December 66 to March 67 *in* Outlet, No. 26 (July 1982): ? ((—))

QUEEN (musical group)

Q1 DANNA, Linda: Queen discography *in* Trouser Press, No. 16 (October–November 1971): 11 ((—))

Q2 Discografia *in* Discoteca Hifi, XX (No. 192, March 1979): 115 ((5))

Q3 Queen discography *in* PRYCE, Larry: Queen. London: Star Books, 1976: [121]–124 ((5))

Q4 VIDIGAL, Doris: Queen discography *in* Sounds Fine, No. 12 (October 1976): [7] ((—))

QUESTION MARK AND THE MYSTERIANS (musical group)

Q5 McDOWELL, Mike: The history of Question Mark and the Mysterians *in* Blitz, No. 31 (May–June 1979): 6–10; discography pp. 9–10 ((5))

QUIVER (musical group)

Q6 MUIRHEAD, Bert: Discography *in* Zig Zag, VI/7 (No. 57): 33 ((—))

R & B label

R1 GIBBON, Peter, and Tony TISOVEC: [Discography] *in* Yesterday's Memories, III/3 (1977): 30 ((7))

RA-BRA label

R2 [Discography] *in* Shout, No. 71 (November 1971): [5] ((3))

RADAR label

R3   FAULL, Trev: Complete Radar discography: singles/albums *in* Outlet, No. 11 (May 1979): 19–23 ((5))

R4   FAULL, Trev: Radar *in* Outlet, No. 3 (June 1978): 6; updated in subsequent issues ((—))

R5   McDOWELL, Mike: Radar Records discography *in* Blitz, No. 29 (November–December 1978): 13–14 ((5))

RADIANTS (musical group)

R6   PRUTER, Robert: Radiants and related groups discography/The Radiants on their own *in* It Will Stand, No. 22–23 (c1981): 6–7 ((5)) [Includes group personnel]

R7   WILSON, Jim: The Radiants/ Maurice & Mac *in* Hot Buttered Soul, No. 16 (March 1973): 7–8 ((3, 7))

RBT-ORCHESTERS

R8   SCHUTTE, Joachim: Discographie des RBT-Orchesters und der anderen Formationen des Berliner Rundfunks. Menden: Der Jazzfreund, 1977. 75 pp. ((3, 7))

THE RAG DOLLS (musical group)

R9   INGRAM, George A.: Rag Dolls discography *in* SMG, V/2 (Spring 1976): 24 ((—))

RAGTIME MUSIC

See also *Bibliography* Vol. 2, Jazz

R10   [[LOTZ, Rainer E.: Grammophonplatten aus der Ragtime-Ara. Dortmund: Harenberg, 1979. 212 pp.]]

THE RAINBOWS (musical group)

R11   PODD, Marvin H.: The Rainbows *in* Yesterday's Memories, I/4 (1975): [8] ((7))

RAINWATER, MARVIN

R12   [Discography] *in* Country Western Express, No. 19 (April 1958): ? ((—))

R13   TOPPING, Ray: Marvin Rainwater discography *in* Goldmine, No. 52 (September 1980): 25 ((1, 2, 3, 7))

RAMA label

R14   TOPPING, Ray: Rama label listing *in* Shout, No. 65 [3–6]; additions and corrections in No. 66 (May 1971): [2] ((3))

R15   TRABOSCI, Tom: Rama discography *in* Bim Bam Boom, No. 7 (September 1972): 31 ((3))

RAMBLERS DANCE BAND

R16   [Discography] *in* BULTERMAN, Jack: The Ramblers story. Bussum: Van Holkema & Warendorf, 1973: 158–159 ((—))

RAMEL, POVEL

R17   ENGLUND, Bjorn: Povel Ramel pa skiva: en diskografi. Solna: [s.n., 1973.] 1 vol. ((2, 3, 4, 6, 7))

RAMPAGE label

R18   Rampage label *in* Hot Buttered Soul, No. 26 (January 1974): 11 ((3))

THE RANCH BOYS (musical group)

R19   LARSEN, John: Discography *in* Country & Western Spotlight, No. 24 (August 1980): 20–22 ((1, 2, 3, 6, 7))

RANDY AND THE RAINBOWS (musical group)

R20   INGRAM, George: Randy and the Rainbows *in* SMG, VI/4 (October 1980): 8–10; discography p. 10 ((5))

RANEY, WAYNE

R21   LEADBITTER, Mike: Wayne Raney, Delmore Brothers, and Brown's Ferry Four *in* Old Time Music, No. 10 (Autumn 1973): 20–23 ((3, 7))

RANKIN, DUSTY

R22   [Discography] *in* Country Western Spotlight, No. 52 (December 1965): ? ((3))

RANN, GROVER

R23 Grover Rann and Harry Ayers discography *in* Old Time Music, No. 22 (Autumn 1976): 18 ((3, 7))

RARE EARTH label

R24 DELGADO, Paul: Rare Earth *in* Rock It with Aware, II/2 (1975?): 17–20; additions and corrections in II/4 [1976]: 4; II/5: 4 ((—))

THE RASCALS (musical group)

R25 GONZALEZ, Fernando, and Steve KOLANJIAN: The Young Rascals/Rascals discography *in* Goldmine, No. 56 (January 1981): 167 ((5))

THE RASPBERRIES (musical group)

R26 BETROCK, Alan, and Mike SAUNDERS: Everything about the Raspberries *in* The Rock Marketplace, No. 4 (December 1973): 3–8; discography p. 7, family tree p. 8 [Includes the Choir, Cyrus Erie, the Quick, and Eric Carmen] ((5))

R27 HOGG, Brian: Choir, Cyrus Erie, Raspberries, 'n' Quick *in* Bam Balam, No. 5 (February 1977): 3–8; addenda in No. 7 (c1978): 2 and No. 12 (November 1980): 38 ((2, 5))

THE RATIONALS (musical group)

R28 HEDDLE, Jim, and Mike McDOWELL: Rationals discography *in* Ballroom Blitz, No. 20 (April 1977): 18 ((5))

THE RATTLES (musical group)

R29 The Rattles *in* Gorilla Beat, No. 3 (1979): 3–11; discography pp. 8–11; addenda in No. 5 (1980): 12 and No. 6 (1980): 46; part II in No. 5 (1980): 16–25; discography pp. 21–23, family tree pp. 24–25; addenda in No. 8 (1980): 48 ((5))

THE RAVENS (musical group)

R30 SBARBORI, Jack: Ravens discography *in* Record Exchanger, II/4 (No. 9 [March 1972]): 15–16 ((3))

RAW label

R31 FAULL, Trev: Raw Records *in* Outlet, No. 6 (October 1978): 3–7; updates in No. 10 (March 1979): 3 and No. 11 (May 1979): 26–28 ((5))

RAZZ label

R32 FAULL, Trev: Razz Records/Tapes/Zines and trivia assoc *in* Outlet, No. 22 (c1981): 17 ((1))

REACTION label

R33 BETROCK, Alan: Reaction singles *in* Jamz, No. 5 (c1972): 35 ((5))

REAL THING label

R34 Real Thing label *in* Hot Buttered Soul, No. 27 (February 1974): 8 ((—))

REBB, JOHNNY

R35 DUFF, Colin, and Frank CAMPBELL: Discography *in* Big Beat of the 50's, No. 20 (May 1979): 7–12 ((—))

THE REBELS (musical group)

R36 SKURZEWSKI, Bob: Rebels with a cause *in* Goldmine, No. 14 (January–February 1977): 6 ((7))

R37 SKURZEWSKI, Bob: The Rockin'/Hot Toddy/Buffalo Rebels *in* Rumble, III/4 (Summer–Autumn 1976): 2–5 ((—))

REBENNACK, MAC

R38 MOHR, Kurt: Discography *in* Shout, No. 67 (June 1971): [9–10] ((2, 3, 6, 7))

RECOMMENDED label

R39 FAULL, Trev: Recommended Records *in* Outlet, No. 27 (Winter 1982): 21–22 ((—))

RED BIRD label

R40 The Red Bird nest *in* The Rock Marketplace, No. 7 (October 1974): 20–21; addendum in No. 8 (December 1974):

42; No. 10 (June 1975): 15 [Includes the Blue Cat, Tiger, Daisy, and U.S. Songs labels] ((5))

RED HOT (song title)

R41 MOONOOGIAN, George A.: "Red hot" discography *in* Goldmine, No. 32 (January 1979): 27 ((5))

RED LIGHTNIN' label

R42 STRETTON, John: The Red Lightnin' roster *in* SMG, VI/4 (October 1980): 12–14 ((—))

RED ROBIN label

R43 Red Robin discography *in* Record Exchanger, II/5 (No. 10 [May 1972]): 11–12 ((3))

REDDING, OTIS

See also *Bibliography* Vol. 2, Jazz

R44 CLEE, Ken: [Discography] *in* Music World, No. 86 (June 1981): 15 ((—))

R45 Otis Redding's albums *in* SCHIESEL, Jane: The Otis Redding story. Garden City, N.Y.: Doubleday, 1973: 139–143 ((—))

REDELL, TEDDY

R46 Teddy Redell disco *in* Kountry Korral, X/3 (June 1977): 21 ((—))

REDWING (musical group)

R47 ALLEN, Steve: Discography *in* Zig Zag, V/7 (No. 47, November 1974): 24 ((5))

REED, JERRY

R48 Discography *in* Paul's Record Magazine, No. 13–14 (September–December 1976): 3 ((5))

REEVES, DEL

R49 STRUBING, Hauke: Del Reeves—disco *in* Country Corner, No. 47 (December 1975): 7 ((—))

REEVES, GOEBEL

R50 EDWARDS, J.: [Discography] *in* Country Western Spotlight, No. 10 (August 1956): ?; No. 31 (July–September 1960): ? ((—))

R51 EDWARDS, J.: [Discography] *in* Country Western Spotlight (Special issue, September 1962): ? ((—))

R52 WEIZE, Richard, and John LARSEN: Goebel Reeves: the Texas Drifter *in* Old Time Music, No. 18 (Autumn 1975): 14–17 ((3, 6, 7))

REEVES, JIM

R53 BENSON, Charles: Jim Reeves record listing *in* Country & Western Roundabout, II/9 (November–December 1964): 16, 30; III/10 (February–March–April 1965): 12 ((—))

R54 [Discography] *in* Country News & Views, III/2 (October 1964): 9–25; additions in III/4 (April 1965): 22–23, 35 ((1, 5))

R55 [Discography] *in* Country Western Express, No. 14 (April–June 1957): ?; No. 15 [New series]: ? ((—))

R56 [Discography] *in* Country Western Spotlight, No. 22 (April–June 1958): ? ((—))

R57 DULK, Arie den, and Kurt ROKITTA: Jim Reeves *in* Country Corner, No. 60 (July 1978): 14 ((5))

R58 SCHUMANN, Reinald E.: Diskographie *in* Country Corner, No. 34 (April 1973): 16–23; No. 35 (August 1973): 22 ((—))

R59 STRUBING, Hauke: Jim Reeves erste RCA-sessions *in* Country Corner, No. 40 (July 1974): 12–16 ((4, 7))

REEVES, MARTHA

R60 Martha Reeves discography (singles) *in* CORDELL, John A.: Martha Reeves & the Vandellas *in* Record Exchanger, V/2 (No. 24, October [?] 1977): 19 ((—))

R61 Stak-O-Wax: Martha Reeves and the Vandellas *in* Goldmine, No. 61 (June 1981): 163 ((—))

REGAL ZONOPHONE label [Australia]

R62   BENSON, Charles, and John STOTEN: Australian Regal Zono-phone G. 20,000 series *in* Country & Western Roundabout, II/9 (November–December 1964) thru IV/16 (January–March 1968): various paginations ((—))

R63   CRISP, David: The Australian Regal and Regal Zonophone series numerical (1927–1958) *in* JEMF Quarterly, XIII (No. 47, Autumn 1977) thru XVII (No. 62, Summer 1981): various paginations ((3, 5, 6))

R64   CRISP, David, and Hedley CHARLES: The Regal Zonophone series—complete numerical *in* Country & Western Spotlight, No. 6 (March 1976): 5–20 [pt. 2]; No. 7 (June 1976): 41–48; No. 8 (September 1976): 15–20 ((3, 5, 6, 7))

R65   [Discography] *in* Folk Style, No. 5 (July 1959): ? ((—))

R66   [Discography, G series] *in* Hillbilly Folk Record Journal, II/1 (January 1955): ? ((—))

R67   EDWARDS, John: [Discography] *in* Country Western Spotlight, No. 16 (December 1956) and No. 19 (September 1957): ? ((—))

R68   EDWARDS, John: [Discography] *in* Country Western Spotlight (Special issue, September 1962): ? ((—))

REGAL ZONOPHONE label [England]

R69   HAYES, Jim: Regal (later Regal Zonophone) MR 1 series *in* Gunn Report, No. 32 (February–March 1972): 40–41 ((5))

R70   Regal-Zonophone singles discography *in* Jamz, No. 4 (May 1972): 49 ((—))

THE REGENTS (musical group)

R71   GONZALEZ, Fernando L.: Regents discography *in* Goldmine, No. 50 (July 1980): 25 ((5))

REGGAE MUSIC

R72   Selected discography *in* CLARKE, Sebastian: Jah music: the evolution of the popular Jamaican song. London: Heinemann Educational, 1980: [182]–186 ((—))

R73   DALKE, Roger: Ska to reggae: UK label discographies. Surrey: S.R.R., 1978– ((—))

R74   WILLIAMS, Don: Jamaica discography *in* DAVIS, Stephen: Reggae bloodlines: in search of the music and culture of Jamaica. Garden City, N.Y.: Anchor Press, 1977: 211–216 ((—))

THE REMAINS (musical group)

R75   PREVOST, Greg: Remains discography *in* Blitz, No. 35 (March–April 1980): 12 ((2, 5))

THE REMO FOUR (musical group)

R76   FAULL, Trev: The Remo Four *in* Instrumental Obscurities Unlimited, No. 20 (c1978): 15–16 ((—))

R77   Liverpool beat: Remo 4 *in* Gorilla Beat, No. 6 (1980): 11–14; discography p. 14; addendum in No. 13 (1982): 11 ((—))

R78   SCHACHT, Janis: Remo 4 *in* The Rock Marketplace, No. 9 (March 1975): 40; addendum in No. 10 (June 1975): 50 [Includes recordings with Johnny Sandon and Tommy Quickly] ((5))

RENEAU, GEORGE

R79   COHEN, Norm, and Tor MAGNUS-SON: George Reneau: a discographical survey *in* JEMF Quarterly, XV (No. 56, Winter 1979): 208–214 ((2, 3, 6, 7))

RENO, DON, AND RED SMILEY

R80   [Discography] *in* Country Western Express, No. 20 (August 1958): ? ((—))

R81   [Discography] *in* Disc Collector, No. 17 (May 1961): ? ((—))

REPARATA & THE DELRONS (musical group)

R82   ENGEL, Edward R.: Reparata & the Delrons discography *in* Time Barrier Express, No. 25 (July–August 1979): 16 ((5))

RESIA label

R83 LILIEDAHL, Karleric: Resia. Stockholm: Kungliga biblioteket, 1969. 48 l. (Nationalfonotekets diskografier, 9) ((3, 4, 6, 7))

THE RESIDENTS (musical group)

R84 FAULL, Trev: The Residents *in* Outlet, No. 20 (September 1980): 2–21; discography pp. 19–21; updates in subsequent issues ((1, 5)) [Includes details of pressings]

RETURN TO FOREVER (musical group)

R85 [Discography] *in* How can a poor man stand such times and live? [Sound recording] Rounder LP 1001 [1972] included in brochure notes. ((2, 5, 6, 7))

R86 Selected Return to Forever discography *in* Down Beat, XLIII (March 25, 1976): 14 ((—))

REX label

R87 [[[Rex cylinder records] *in* Talking Machine Review (April 1974); additions and corrections in No. 36 (October 1975): 489]]

REX label [Rhythm and blues label]

R88 TOPPING, Ray: Rex label listing *in* Shout, No. 61 (December 1970): [10] ((3, 5))

REYNOLDS, JODY

R89 KOMOROWSKI, Adam: Jody Reynolds: the king of teardrop rock *in* New Kommotion, No. 26 (1982): 22, 25–26; discography (by Ray TOPPING and Adam KOMOROWSKI): p. 26 ((1, 2, 3, 7))

RHINOCEROS (musical group)

R90 MARS, John: Rhinoceros album discography *in* Blitz, No. 37 (July–August 1980): 8 ((5))

RHYTHM ACES (musical group)

R91 VOLLMER, Al: Rhythm Aces: some notes by Al Vollmer *in* Storyville, No. 86 (December 1979–January 1980): [70]–71 ((3))

RHYTHM AND BLUES MUSIC
See also *Bibliography* Vol. 2, Jazz

R92 BECKMAN, Jeff: Teenage tenor leads [in R & B group recordings] *in* Bim Bam Boom, II/6 (No. 12, 1974): [43] ((—))

R93 CLEE, Ken: The directory of American 45 R.P.M. records. Philadelphia: Stak-O-Wax, 1981. 3 vols. ((—))

R94 CLEE, Ken: A discography collection of artists and labels. 2nd ed. Philadelphia: Stak-O-Wax, 1979. 800 pp. ((—))

R95 FERLINGERE, Robert D.: A discography of rhythm & blues and rock 'n roll vocal groups 1945 to 1965. Pittsburg, Calif.: Ferlingere, 1976. unpaged. ((2, 3, 5))

R96 GIVEN, Dave: The Dave Given rock 'n' roll stars handbook: rhythm 'n' blues artists & groups. Smithtown, N.Y.: Exposition Press, 1980. 328 pp. ((5))

R97 GONZALEZ, Fernando L.: Discofile: the discographical catalog of American rock & roll and rhythm & blues vocal harmony groups: race, rhythm & blues, rock & roll, soul: 1902–1976. 2nd ed. Flushing, N.Y.: Gonzalez, 1977. 496 pp. ((1, 3, 5, 6, 7))

R98 LEICHTER, Albert: Discography of rhythm & blues and rock & roll circa 1946–1964: a reference manual. Staunton, Va.: Leichter, 1975. 189 l.; Supplement 1. Staunton, Va., 1978. 87 l. ((5))

R99 MOHR, Kurt: Discographies [of various artists] *in* Black Wax, No. 4 (May 1973): 13; No. 6 (July 1973): 18 ((2, 3, 6, 7))

R100 MOONOOGIAN, George: The answer record *in* R & B *in* Record Exchanger, IV/6 (August 1975): 24– 25 ((—))

R101 WHITBURN, Joel: Top R & B records: 1946–1971. Menomonee Falls, Wisc.: Record Research, 1973. 184 pp. ((4))

Rhythm and Blues Music—Detroit

R102 WORTMAN, Cap: Detroit discographies *in* Goldmine, No. 15 (March–April 1977): 16 ((5))

**Rhythm and Blues Music—
New Orleans**

R103 The best selling New Orleans singles: 1946–72 and album discography *in* BROVEN, John: Walking to New Orleans: the story of New Orleans rhythm & blues. Bexhill-on-Sea, England: Blues unlimited, 1974: 228–241; Greta, La.: Pelican, 1978: 228–242 ((5))

R104 TOPPING, Ray: New Orleans rhythm & blues: label listings. Bexhill-on-Sea, England: Flyright Records, 1978. 69 pp. ((3))

**Rhythm and Blues Music—
New York City**

R105 Discographies *in* GROIA, Philip: They all sang at the corner: New York City's rhythm and blues vocal groups of the 1950's. Setauket, N.Y.: Edmond Publishing Co., 1973, 1974. 147 pp. ((2))

RICE, GLADYS

R106 WILE, Ray: The Edison recordings of Gladys Rice *in* Record Research, No. 143 (December 1976): 5–7, 10 ((3, 5, 7))

RICE, RONNIE

R107 Ronnie Rice solo discography *in* Blitz, No. 37 (July–August 1980): 18 [Member of the New Colony Six] ((5))

RICH, CHARLIE

R108 Charlie Rich LP disco *in* Kountry Korral Magazine, II (1980): [26]–27 ((—))

R109 OLOFSSON, Claes, and Bo BERGLIND: Charlie Rich disco *in* Rockville International (January– February 1974): 33–38 ((3, 5))

RICH AND RICH (musical group)

R110 BARKER, Tony: [Discography] *in* Music-Hall Records, No. 1 (June 1978): 12–13 ((3))

RICHARD, CLIFF

R111 Cliff Richard discography *in* Goldmine, No. 61 (June 1981): 21–22 ((—))

R112 Discography *in* Music Week (September 30, 1978): 12–13 ((5))

R113 NEALE, Tony: Cliff Richard U.K. discography *in* Music World, No. 3 (March 1981): 58–61 ((5))

R114 RAEBURN, Boyd: The many voices of Cliff Richard *in* Who Put the Bomp, No. 8 (Fall–Winter 1971): 18–25; discography pp. 22–24; addenda in No. 9 (Spring 1972): 48–49 [British releases only] ((5))

R115 Cliff Richard na deskach Supraphon *in* TATEROVA, Milada: Cliff Richard. Praha: Supraphon, 1970: [37] ((—))

R116 Records *in* WINTER, David Brian: New singer, new song: the Cliff Richard story. London: Hodder & Stroughton, 1967: [153]–159 ((5))

RICHARDS, KEITH

R117 [[[Discography] *in* CHARONE, Barbara: Keith Richards, life as a Rolling Stone. Garden City, N.Y.: Doubleday, 1982: [197]–198]]

RICH-R-TONE label

R118 KUYKENDALL, Pete: [Discography, 400 series] *in* Disc Collector, No. 13 (May 1960) and No. 14 (August 1960): ? ((—))

RIC-TIC label

R119 ROUNCE, Tony: Ric-Tic label listing *in* Shout, No. 72 (December 1971): [1-3] ((3))

RIDGEL'S FOUNTAIN CITIANS

R120 [NELSON, Don]: Ridgel's Fountain Citians *in* JEMF Quarterly, IX/1 (No. 29, Spring 1973): 8 ((3, 7))

RIDGLEY, TOMMY

R121 TOPPING, Ray: Tommy Ridgley discography *in* Shout, No. 63 (February 1971): [4–6] ((2, 3, 7))

RILEY, BILLY LEE

R122 Billy Lee Riley discography *in* Kountry Korral (No. 3, 1979): 38 ((—))

R123 THOMPSON, Gary, and Don EZELL: Billy Lee Riley discography *in* Goldmine, No. 28 (September 1978): 14 ((5))

R124 WESTFALL, Bob: Billy Lee Riley on disc *in* Kommotion, No. 10–11 (Winter 1975–76): 36–37 ((—))

RIM Label

R125 TOPPING, Ray, and Tim WHIT-SETT: Rim label *in* New Kommotion, No. 14 (Winter 1977): 12 ((—))

RIO label

R126 FAULL, Trev: Rio Records: from Nov 66 *in* Outlet, No. 26 (July 1982): 27–28 ((—))

RIPPERTON, Minnie

R127 CORDELL, John: Minnie Ripperton discography *in* Goldmine, No. 41 (October 1979): 11 ((5))

RITTER, TEX

R128 Discography *in* BOND, Johnny: The Tex Ritter story. [n.p.]: Chappell Music Co., 1976: 275–305 ((1, 3, 6, 7))

R129 [Discography] *in* Hillbilly Folk Record Journal, III/4 (October–December 1956): ? ((—))

R130 EDWARDS, J.: [Discography] *in* Country Western Spotlight, No. 17 (March 1957): ? ((—))

R131 EDWARDS, J.: [Discography] *in* Country Western Spotlight (Special issue, September 1962): ? ((—))

R132 TOBORG, Dick: Tex Ritter *in* Record Research, No. 108 (December 1970) thru No. 139–140 (May–June 1976): various paginations ((1, 2, 3, 7))

R133 TOBORG, Dick: Tex Ritter: the complete Capitol discography *in* Record Research, No. 163–164 (May–June 1979) thru No. 187–188 (December 1981): various paginations ((3, 5, 6, 7))

R134 WEIZE, Richard: Tex Ritter—seine Decca sessions *in* Country Corner, No. 44 (May 1975): 46 ((3, 6, 7))

RIVERS, TONY, AND THE CASTWAYS (musical group)

R135 BETROCK, Alan: Who is Tony Rivers (and the Castways) *in* The Rock Marketplace, No. 9 (March 1975): 30–32; discography p. 32; addenda in No. 10 (June 1975): 50 [Includes Harmony Grass] ((5))

THE RIVETS (musical group)

R136 Beat in Germany: the Rivets *in* Gorilla Beat, No. 7 (1980): 49–52; discography p. 52 ((—))

THE RIVIERAS (musical group)

R137 AITA, Frank: The Rivieras *in* Record Exchanger, IV/3 (No. 19): 9 ((—))

THE RIVILEERS (musical group)

R138 LUCIANI, Tom, and Steve FLAM: The Rivileers *in* Bim Bam Boom, I/5 (April–May 1972): 17 ((3))

THE RIVINGTONS (musical group)

R139 SBARBORI, Jack: Discography *in* Record Exchanger (No. 16): 21–22 ((5))

THE ROADRUNNERS (musical group)

R140 HEBING, Alfred, and Hans Jurgen KLITSCH: Liverpool beat: the Roadrunners *in* Gorilla Beat, No. 9 (1981): 4–6; discography pp. 5–6; addenda in No. 10 (1981): 43 ((5))

ROANE COUNTY RAMBLERS

R141 RUSSELL, Tony: Roane County Ramblers *in* Old Time Music, No. 8 (Spring 1973): 8 ((3, 6, 7))

ROARK, GEORGE

R142 [Discography] *in* Country Directory, No. 3 (1962): ? ((—)) [Library of Congress records]

ROBBINS, MARTY

R143 GARBUTT, Bob: Marty Robbins discography *in* Goldmine, No. 58 (March 1981): 198-199 ((5))

R144 [[Record listing *in* Record Collector, No. 4 (November 1967)]]

R145 SCHUMANN, E. Reinald: Marty Robbins diskographie *in* Hillbilly, No. 54 (March 1978): 17-21; No. 55 (June 1978): 16-33 ((1, 3, 7))

R146 STRUBING, Hauke: Langspielplatten—disco *in* Country Corner, No. 49 (May 1976): 9 ((—))

ROBBINS, SYLVIA

R147 [[[Discography] *in* Soul Music (No. 24)]]

ROBERTS, DOC

R148 [COHEN, Norm]: Doc Roberts, Asa Martin and James Roberts *in* JEMF Quarterly, VII/3 (No. 23, Autumn 1971): 103-   ; VII/4 (No. 24, Winter 1971): 158-162; VIII/1 (No. 25, Spring 1972): 15-17; VIII/2 (No. 26, Summer 1972): 73-76 ((2, 3, 6, 7))

ROBERTSON, A. C. "ECK"

R149 DAVIS, Stephen F.: A. C. "Eck" Robertson *in* Devil's Box, No. 17 (June 1972): 17-19 ((3, 6, 7))

R150 GRESS, Reinhard: Eck Robertson diskographie *in* Hillbilly, No. 52 (September 1977): 27-28 ((3, 6, 7))

ROBERTSON, TEXAS JIM

R151 BENSON, Charles: Texas Jim Robertson record listing *in* Country & Western Roundabout, I/2 (November 1962): 19-21; I/3 (February 1963): 22-23 ((—))

ROBESON, PAUL

R152 Paul Robeson na deskach Supraphon *in* Robesonova pisen zni. Praha: Osveta, 1957: [34-35] ((—))

ROBEY, SIR GEORGE

R153 RUST, Brian: George Robey: a discography *in* Recorded Sound, No. 53 (January 1974): 262-264; addenda in No. 57-58 (January–April 1975): 437 ((3, 6, 7))

THE ROBINS (musical group)

R154 GOLDBERG, Marv, and Mike REDMOND: Discography *in* Record Exchanger, III/2 (No. 13 [February 1973]): 8-9 ((—))

R155 MILLAR, Bill: Robins discography *in* Shout, No. 90 (November 1973): [1-4] ((2, 3, 5, 6, 7))

ROBISON, CARSON

R156 [Discography] *in* Disc Collector, No. 10-14, 16, 18-19 [n.d.]: ? ((—))

R157 [Discography] *in* Hillbilly Folk Record Journal, II/3 (July–September 1955): ? ((—))

R158 EDWARDS, J.: [Discography] *in* Country Western Spotlight, No. 7 (May 1956): ?; No. 20 (October–December 1957): ? ((—))

R159 EDWARDS, J.: [Discography] *in* Country Western Spotlight (Special issue, September 1962): ? ((—))

R160 MORRITT, Robert D.: Carson Robison discography *in* New Amberola Graphic, VIII/1 (No. 29, Summer 1979) thru IX/2 (No. 34, Fall 1980): various paginations ((3, 7))

ROCK MUSIC

R161 Discographies *in* BONDS, Ray: The harmony illustrated encyclopedia of rock. New York: Harmony, 1982. 288 pp. ((—)) [A revision of Logan and Woffinden, Illustrated Encyclopedia)

R162 Discographie *in* BRIERRE, Jean Dominique: Punkitudes. Paris: A. Michel, 1978: [185]-187 ((—))

R163 [[Discography *in* BROLINSON, Per Erik: Rock—Solna: Esselte studium, 1981: 234-237]]

R164 [[Discography *in* BROLINSON, Per Erik: —and roll. Solna: Esselte studium, 1981: 111-113]]

R165 CALLAHAN, Mike: The British invasion—discography *in* Goldmine, No. 44 (January 1980): 135-136 ((5)) [Records of British rock groups of the 1960's as hits in the U.S.]

R166 CALLAHAN, Mike: The reprocessed stereo blues *in* Goldmine, No. 43 (December 1979): 125 ((—))

R167 CALLAHAN, Mike: Songs from 1958 available in stereo *in* Goldmine, No. 41 (October 1979): 125 ((5))

R168 CALLAHAN, Mike: Stereo single discography *in* Goldmine, No. 42 (November 1979): 118–119 ((3)) [Single records from the late 1950's originally recorded in stereo]

R169 CALLAHAN, Mike: The story of stereo rock and roll: mono's last stand *in* Goldmine, No. 48 (May 1980): 144–145 ((—))

R170 Discographies *in* CARAMAN FOTEA, Daniela: Disco; ghid-rock. Bucuresti: Editura Muzicala, 1977: ? ((5))

R171 CLEE, Ken: The directory of American 45 R.P.M. records. Philadelphia: Stak-O-Wax, 1981. 3 vols. ((—))

R172 CLEE, Ken: A discography of artists and labels. Philadelphia: Stak-O-Wax, 1977. 2 vols. ((—))

R173 CLEE, Ken: A discography collection of artists and labels. 2nd ed. Philadelphia: Stak-O-Wax, 1979. 800 pp. ((—))

R174 COBRA: Bootlegs. n.p., 1973. ((1, 7))

R175 COBRA: Underground sounds. n.p.: Galaxy Press, 1974. ((1, 7))

R176 The complete bootlegs checklist & discography. Manchester: Babylon Books, n.d. [c1978] ((1, 7))

R177 Discographies *in* DAUFOUX, Philippe: Pop music/rock. Paris: Editions champ libre, 1972: 183–201 ((—))

R178 Discoveries *in* The Rock Marketplace: various issues [Obscurities]

R179 Discography *in* DOWNING, David: Future rock. St. Albans, England: Panther, 1976: [170]–172 ((—))

R180 Discographies *in* ENGEL, Edward R.: White & still all right. [s.l.]: Crackerjack Press, 1977– 1 vol. ((1, 3, 5))

R181 Discographies *in* Eroi a canaglie nella musica pop: Patti Smith, Lou Reed, David Bowie, Iggy Pop, Johnny Rotten. Rome: Arcana, 1979. 173 pp. ((—))

R182 FERLINGERE, Robert D.: A discography of rhythm & blues and rock 'n roll vocal groups 1945 to 1965. Pittsburg, Calif.: Ferlingere, 1976. unpaged. ((2, 3, 5))

R183 GEORGE, B., and Martha DEFOE: Volume I: International discography of the New Wave. New York: One Ten Records, 1980. [Volume II] New York: One Ten Records/Omnibus Press, 1982. 736 pp. ((2, 5))

R184 Discographies *in* GIVEN, Dave: The Dave Given rock 'n' roll stars handbook. Smithtown, N.Y.: Exposition Press, 1980. 328 pp. ((5))

R185 GOLDSTEIN, Stewart: Oldies but goodies: the rock 'n' roll years. New York: Mason/Charter, 1976. ((—))

R186 GONZALEZ, Fernando L.: Discofile: the discographical catalog of American rock & roll and rhythm & blues vocal groups. Flushing, N.Y.: Gonzalez, 1974. 200 pp. ((1, 3, 5, 6, 7))

R187 GONZALEZ, Fernando L.: Discofile: the discographical catalog of American rock & roll and rhythm & blues vocal harmony groups: race, rhythm & blues, rock & roll, soul: 1902–1976. 2nd ed. Flushing, N.Y.: Gonzalez, 1977. 496 pp. ((1, 3, 5, 6, 7))

R188 HELANDER, Brock: Rock 'n' roll to rock: a discography. [s.l.]: Helander, 1978. 240 pp. ((4, 5))

R189 HELANDER, Brock: The rock who's who. New York: Schirmer, 1982. 686 pp. ((5)) [Albums only]

R190 Discographie *in* HOFFMANN, Raoul: Rock babies: 25 ans de pop music. Paris: Seuil, 1978. ((—))

R191 Hot wacks, vol. 1 and 2. n.p.: Cobra, 1975; Underground sounds. n.p.: Galaxy Press, 1974; Hot wacks. 3rd ed. n.p.: Cobra, 1977; Hot wacks, Book V. Kitchener, Ont.: Galaxy Productions, 1978; Hot wacks, Book VI. Kitchener, Ont., 1979; Hot wacks, Book VII. Kitchener, Ont.: Blue Flake Productions, 1979; Hot wacks, Book VIII. Kitchener, Ont.: Blue Flake, 1980; Hot wacks, Book IX. Kitchener, Ont.: Blue Flake, 1981. ((1, 7)) [Coverage of bootleg recordings of rock music]

R192 HOUNSOME, Terry, and Tim CHAMBRE: Rock record. 1st ed. Southampton, 1979. 396 pp. ((4, 5))

R193 HOUNSOME, Terry, and Tim CHAMBRE: Rock record. 2nd ed. New York: Facts on File, 1981. 526 pp. ((2, 4, 5))

R194 ILIC, David: Zig Zag independent label catalog, No. 4 inset in Zig Zag, No. 116 (August 1981): 48 unnumbered pp. ((—))

R195 KIRSCH, Don R.: Rock 'n' roll obscurities (vol. 1). Tacoma, Wash.: Kirsch, 1977. [Vol. 2] 2nd ed., Tacoma, Wash.: Kirsch, 1981.

R196 KLITSCH, Hans Jurgen: Great bands, small labels. Mulheim, West Germany: Gorilla, 1979. 40 l. ((—)) [New Wave bands]

R197 Discographies in KNEIF, Tibor: Einfuhrung in die Rockmusik. Wilhelmshaven: Heinrichshofen, 1979. 151 pp. ((5))

R198 LAZELL, Barry, and Geoffrey RUST: Record business small labels catalogue 1980. London: Record Business, 1980. 47 pp. ((—)) [New Wave bands]

R199 LEICHTER, Albert: Discography of rhythm & blues and rock & roll circa 1946-1964: a reference manual. Staunton, Va.: Leichter, 1975. 189 l.; Supplement 1. Staunton, Va. 1978. 87 l. ((5))

R200 LESUER, Daniel: Les disques rares des annees 60. Volume 1. n.p.: the author(?), n.d. [c1980]. 39 pp. ((—))

R201 Ausgewahlte discografie, 1954-1975 in Let It Rock. Munich: Vienna Hanser, 1975: 217-238 ((—))

R202 Discographies in LOGAN, Nick, and Bob WOFFINDEN: The illustrated encyclopedia of rock. New York: Harmony, 1977. 256 pp.; rev. ed. New York: Harmony, 1977. 256 pp.; 3rd rev. ed. published 1982 under the same title. ((—))

R203 Discographies in LOGAN, Nick, and Bob WOFFINDEN: The New Musical Express book of rock 2. London: W. H. Allen, 1977. 553 pp. ((5))

R204 McDOWELL, Mike: Classics revisited in various issues of Ballroom Blitz and later Blitz [Obscurities] ((—))

R205 Discographies in MANRIQUE, Diego A.: De que va el rock macarra. Madrid: Los Ediciones de La Piqueta, D.L., 1977: 63-80 ((—))

R206 Notes and discographies in MARCUS, Greil: Mystery train: images of America in rock 'n' roll music. New York: Dutton, 1975: [211]-288 ((—))

R207 MARLOW, David, and Steve TAYLOR: Zig Zag small labels catalogue '80 in Zig Zag Magazine, No. 103 (July 1980): 38 pp. ((—)) [New Wave bands and labels]

R208 MOONOOGIAN, George A.: Heard it discography in Goldmine, No. 33 (February 1979): 24 ((5)) [Records reminiscent of earlier hits]

R209 Discografia in MUGGIATTI, Roberto: Rock, o grito e o mito. 2nd ed. Petropolis: Editora Vozes, 1973: 114-116 ((—))

R210 NAHA, Ed.: Lilian Roxon's rock encyclopedia. Rev. ed. New York: Grosset, 1978. 565 pp. ((5))

R211 Discographies in NITE, Norm M.: Rock on. New York: T. Y. Crowell, 1974. 675 pp.; updated ed. New York: Harper, 1982. 722 pp. Volume 2: the modern years, 1964-present. New York: Crowell, 1978.

P212 Discographie in PEELLAERT, Guy: Rock dreams. Munich: Schunemann, 1973. 356 pp. ((—))

P213 Discographies in PICART, Herve: The hard-rock. Paris: Grancher, 1980. 138 pp. ((—))

R214 PINGEL, Stefan: The "Angel" titles in Rocking Regards, No. 16 ([July?] 1979): 15-18 ((—)) [Alphabetical listing of 50's rock 'n' roll recordings whose titles include the word "angel"]

R215 PROPES, Steve: Those oldies but goodies: a guide to 50's rock collecting. New York: Collier, 1973. 192 pp. ((5))

R216 PROPES, Steve: Golden oldies: a guide to 50's & 60's popular rock & roll record collecting. Radnor, Pa.: Chilton, 1975. 185 pp. ((5))

R217 PROPES, Steve: Golden oldies: a guide to 60's record collecting. Radnor, Pa.: Chilton, 1974. 240 pp. ((5))

R218 Discographies in Rockmusik. Mainz: Schott, 1977. 210 pp. ((5))

R219 Discographies in The Rolling Stone illustrated history of rock & roll. New York: Rolling Stone Press, 1976. 382 pp. ((5))

R220   Diskografi *in* ROU JENSEN, Anders: Da graesrodderne gik grasset. Copenhagen: Swing, 1978: 100–[105] ((—))

R221   Discographies *in* ROXON, Lilian: Lilian Roxon's rock encyclopedia. New York: Grosset, 1969, 1971. 611 pp. ((5))

R222   Discographie *in* ROY, Francois: Dix ans de rock. Montreal: Editions de L'aurore, 1977: [119]–124 ((5))

R223   SHAW, Greg: The New Wave on record: England and Europe, 1975–8. Burbank: Bomp Books, 1978. 74 pp. ((5))

R224   Discographies *in* SIERRA I FABRA, Jordi: Disc-ròck-grafias. Barcelona: Teorema, 1981. 415 pp. ((5, 7))

R225   SIGG, Bernie: Diskographie *in* SCHMIDT-JOOS, Siegfried: Rock-Lexikon. Reinbek bei Hamburg: Rowohlt, 1975: [424]–428 ((5))

R226   STIDOM, Larry, and Alan LEE: Answers records *in* Goldmine, No. 18 (September 1977): 10–11 ((—)) [Answer records attempt to duplicate the success of a hit record by continuing the theme of the original]

R227   Discographie selective *in* TORGUE, Henry Skoff: La Pop-music. Paris: PUF, 1978: [109]–124 ((—))

R228   Discographie *in* URBAN, Peter: Rollende Worte, die Poesie des Rock. Frankfurt am Main: Fischer-Taschenbuch-Verlag, 1979: 304–[309] ((5))

R229   Petits discographies *in* VARENNE, Jean Michel: Les poetes du rock. Paris: Seghers, 1975: [314]–315 ((—))

R230   [[Discography *in* WOLFER, Jurgen: Die Rock und Popmusik. Munich: Heyne, 1980: 164–167]]

R231   Discographies *in* YORK, William: Who's who in rock music. Seattle: Atomic Press, 1978. 260 pp. ((5)); rev. ed. published New York: Scribner, 1982. 413 pp.

Rock Music—Argentine Republic

R232   Discografia crucial *in* GRINBERG, Miguel: La musica progresiva Argentine. Buenos Aires: Editorial Convergencia, 1977: 125–127 ((—))

Rock Music—Australia

R233   GREEN, Jim, and Dave SCHULPS: Australian discography *in* Trouser Press, III/5 (No. 17, December 1976–January 1977): 19 ((—))

R234   Discographies *in* McGRATH, Noel: Noel McGrath's Australian encyclopaedia of rock. Collingwood, Vic.: Outback Press, 1978. ((5))

Rock Music—Boston

R235   JOHNSON, David: Sounds of the sixties: Boston and New England *in* Who Put the Bomp, No. 14 (Fall 1975): 32–37; addenda in No. 16 (October 1976): 60 ((—))

Rock Music—California

R236   BLAIR, John: The illustrated discography of surf music, 1959–1965. Riverside, Calif.: J. Bee Productions, 1978. 52 pp. ((2, 3, 5))

R237   Discografia *in* ORDOVAS, Jesus: El rock acido de California. Madrid: Jucar, 1975: 221–234 ((1, 5))

R238   SHAW, Greg: An alphabetical listing of surf albums *in* Rumble, II/4 (Winter 1974–75): 11–13 ((—))

R239   SHAW, Greg: California surf instrumentals—a selective discography *in* Who Put the Bomp, No. 14 (Fall 1975): 10, 46 ((—))

R240   SHAW, Greg: Sounds of the sixties: the Bay Area *in* Who Put the Bomp, No. 12 (Summer 1974): 26–29 ((—))

R241   [[Surfin' records discography: 1956–1977. Ladd Publications: ?]]

Rock Music—California—Northern

R242   HOGG, Brian: Psychotic reaction: San Francisco begins *in* Bam Balam, No. 10 (November 1979): 17–25; addenda in No. 14 (September 1982): 16–17 ((5)) [Selected artists]

Rock Music—California— San Bernardino/Riverside

R243   BLAIR, John, and Alan OSTROFF: Rockin' in San Bernardino/Riverside *in* Kicks, No. 2 (Winter 1979): 37–41; discography pp. 40–41 ((—))

Rock Music—Canada

R244   The track record of Canadian hits *in* YORKE, Ritchie: Axes, chops & hot licks; the Canadian rock music scene.

Edmonton: M. G. Hurtig, 1971: [219]-221 ((5))

Rock Music—Chicago

R245 BAKER, Cary, and Jeff LIND: Sounds of the sixties: Chicago *in* Who Put the Bomp, No. 15 (Spring 1976): 31-36; addenda in No. 16 (October 1976): 60 ((5))

Rock Music—Connecticut— New Haven

R246 Discographies *in* LEPARI, Paul: The New Haven sound, 1946-1976. [Printed by United Print Services, 1977]: 116-120 ((5))

Rock Music—Denmark

R247 Vigtige danske rockplader *in* ELLEGAARD, Lasse: Dansk rockmusik. Copenhagen: Information, 1975: 188-[191] ((5))

R248 Discographies *in* JACOBSEN, Niels W.: Dansk rock 'n' roll. Tappernoje: Mjolner, 1980. ((5))

Rock Music—Detroit

R249 WORTMAN, Cap: Detroit discographies *in* Goldmine, No. 15 (March-April 1977): 16 ((5))

Rock Music—England

R250 Discographie *in* DISTER, Alain: Le rock anglais (de Tommy Steele a David Bowie). Paris: A. Michel, 1973: [181]-185 ((—))

R251 The encyclopedia of British rock, by the editors *in* Who Put the Bomp, No. 14 (Fall 1975) thru No. 20 (January 1979): various paginations ((5))

R252 FAULL, Trev: Beatgroup featuring the Columbia label *in* Outlet, No. 26 (July 1982): 15-16 ((—))

R253 HOGG, Brian: Boom boom: British blue-eyed R&B *in* Bam Balam, No. 13 (August 1981): 12-39; addenda in No. 14 (September 1982): 15 ((5))

R254 HOGG, Brian: British R&B remainders *in* Bam Balam, No. 6 (November 1977): 22 ((2, 5)) [The years 1963 to 1966]

R255 HOGG, Brian: Smashed! Blocked! a discography of selected U.K. pop of the sixties. East Lothian, Scotland: Hogg, 1977. 30 pp. ((2, 5))

R256 HOGG, Brian: Son of smashed! Blocked! more U.K. pop of the sixties. East Lothian, Scotland: Hogg, 1978. 20 pp. ((2, 5))

R257 MARLOW, David, and Steve TAYLOR: Small labels catalogue '80 *in* Zig Zag, No. 103 (July 1980): 38 pp. bound into issue ((—))

R258 MAY, Chris, and Tim PHILLIPS: British beat. London: Sciopack, n.d. 104 pp. ((5))

R259 SILVERTON, Pete, and Paul RAMBLI: British punk discography *in* Trouser Press, IV/6 (No. 18, February–March 1977): 16 ((—))

R260 STANTON, Roy: Catalogue of U.K. R & B releases *in* Black Wax, No. 1 thru No. 6 (July 1973): various paginations ((5))

R261 WAGSTAFF, John: A survey of UK psychedelic music *in* Gorilla Beat, No. 15 (1982): 66-79; selected discography pp. 72-79 ((5))

R262 Zig Zag cassette book 81. London: Zig Zag, 1981. 78 pp.((—)) [Independents]

Rock Music—England—Liverpool

R263 Discography *in* Who Put the Bomp, No. 15 (Spring 1975): 29

R264 HOGG, Brian: Merseybeat: the Liverpool sound *in* Bam Balam, No. 6 (November 1977): 3-9 ((2, 5)) [For groups 1963 to 1966]

Rock Music—Florida

R265 MILLER, Dick: South Florida rockabilly discography *in* Music World, No. 87 (July 1981): 18-19 ((—))

Rock Music—Germany, West

R266 Discographies *in* EHNERT, Gunter: Rock in Deutschland. Hamburg: Taurus Press, 1979. 289 pp. ((5))

R267 Discographie *in* MIGUEL, Antonio de: Rock aleman. [s.l.]: Iniciativas editoriales, 1978. ((5))

R268 Discographies *in* PEINEMANN, Steve Bernhard: Die Wut, die du im Bauch hast: politische Rockmusik. Reinbek bei Hamburg: Rowohlt, 1980. 231 pp. ((—))

R269   Discographies *in* SCHRODER, Rainer M.: Rock, made in Germany. Munich: Heyne, 1980. ((—))

Rock Music—Italy—Bologna

R270   Discographie *in* BERTRANDO, Paolo: Bologna rock. Milan: Renudo, 1980. 182 pp. ((—))

Rock Music—Kansas City

R271   HAWKINS, Martin: K. C. Rockin' *in* New Kommotion, No. 20 (Summer 1978): 42–44; discography (by Ray TOPPING): 44 ((3, 5)) [Includes Westport, Choice, R, and other local labels]

Rock Music—Mexico

R272   PHREDDIE, Phast: Discography of Mexican punk rock *in* Who Put the Bomp, No. 16 (October 1976): 8 ((—))

Rock Music—Michigan

R273   ROSEMONT, Dick: Sounds of the sixties: Michigan *in* Who Put the Bomp, No. 13 (Spring 1975): 36–42; addenda in No. 14 (Fall 1975): 42; No. 15 (Spring 1976): 44; No. 16 (October 1976): 60 ((—))

Rock Music—Michigan—Hamtramck

R274   WASACZ, Walter C.: The history of . . . . . . Hamtramck rock *in* Blitz, No. 29 (November–December 1978): 7–9; discography p. 9 [The Mutants, Panics, Quinns, Reruns, and Romantics] ((5))

Rock Music—Mississippi

R275   TOPPING, Ray, and Tim WHITSETT: Mississippi rock & blues *in* New Kommotion, No. 18 (Winter 1978): 18–21; addenda in No. 19 (Spring 1978): 14 and No. 22 (1979): 66 ((3, 7))

Rock Music—Netherlands

R276   BARNES, Ken: Discography of Dutch rock *in* Who Put the Bomp, No. 14 (Fall 1975): 18, 37 ((—))

Rock Music—New Orleans

R277   Selected New Orleans album discography *in* Goldmine, No. 57 (February 1981): 158–159 ((—))

Rock Music—New York

R278   Discographies *in* ENGEL, Edward R.: White and still all right! Scarsdale, N.Y.: Crackerjack Press, 1977. 80 pp. ((3))

Rock Music—North Carolina—Winston-Salem

R279   HOLSAPPLE, Peter: Rockin' the Camel city *in* Kicks, No. 1 (Spring 1979): 70–77; discography pp. 76–77, family tree p. 74 ((5)) [Includes the Sneakers, Chris Stamey, Alex Chilton, and others]

Rock Music—San Francisco

R280   AVERSA, John D.: San Francisco sound on 45. n.p.: American Beauty Records, n.d. 16 pp. ((5))

R281   COLONNA, Donald: The San Francisco sound: a discography of LP's. Burbank: Songs & Records International, 1975. 17 pp. ((5))

R282   HOGG, Brian: Come up the years: San Francisco grows *in* Bam Balam, No. 10 (November 1979): 32–39; addenda in No. 14 (September 1982): 16–17 ((5)) [Selected artists]

Rock Music—Scotland

R283   HOGG, Brian: Scot rock *in* Bam Balam, No. 6 (November 1977): 14–19; addendum in No. 7 (c1978): 2 ((2, 5))

Rock Music—Spain

R284   Discografias . . . *in* SIERRA I FABRA, Jordi: Historia y poder del "rock catalana." Barcelona: Musica de Nuestro Tiempo, 1977: 140–157 ((—))

Rock Music—Sweden

R285   SHAW, Greg, and Lennart PERSSON: Sounds of the sixties: Sweden *in* Who Put the Bomp, No. 16 (October 1976): 38, 57 ((—))

Rock Music—Texas

R286 HOGG, Brian: Thru the rhythm: Texas rock 'n' roll *in* Bam Balam, No. 10 (November 1979): 3–13 ((5)) [Selected artists, 1965–69]

R287 SHUTT, David: Journey to tyme: a discography & interpretive guide to Texas 60's punk/psychedelia. 2nd ed. Austin: Shutt, 1981. 116 pp. [1st ed. Austin: Shutt, n.d. [c1980]. 78 pp.] ((5))

Rock Music—United States

R288 BLACKBURN, Richard: Rockabilly: a comprehensive discography of re-issues. n.p.: Blackburn, 1975. 25 pp. ((—))

ROCK MUSICIANS—WOMEN

R289 [Discography] *in* ALESSANDRINI, Marjorie: Le rock au feminin. Paris: Michel, 1980: 209–[210] ((—))

R290 BETROCK, Alan: Girl groups: an annotated discography 1960–65. New York: Betrock, [n.d.] 28 pp. ((5))

R291 [[BETROCK, Alan: Girl groups: the story of a sound. New York: Deliah Books; distributed by Putnam Publishing Group, 1982. 175 pp.]]

R292 Discographies *in* KATZ, Susan: Superwomen of rock. New York: Tempo Books, 1978. 134 pp. ((—))

R293 [[[Discographies] *in* New women in rock. New York: Deliah/Putnam, 1982]]

THE ROCKATEENS (musical group)

R294 SMART, Peter: The Rockateens *in* Rumble, III/4 (Summer–Autumn 1976): 12–13 ((—))

ROCKIN' label

R295 LEADBITTER, Mike, and Dick HORLICK: Rockin' label listing *in* Shout, No. 92 (January 1974): 7–8 ((3, 6))

R296 ROTANTE, Anthony, and Paul SHEASTLEY: Rockin'—a King label *in* Record Research, No. 144–145 (March 1977): 7 ((3))

RODEO label [Australia]

R297 [[Discography] *in* Country & Western Spotlight, No. 1 (December 1974)]]

R298 LEGERE, Will: [Discography] *in* Disc Collector, No. 14 (August 1960); No. 16 (February 1961); No. 17 (May 1961): ? ((—))

RODGERS, JESSE

R299 Jesse Rodgers Australian discography *in* Country & Western Spotlight, No. 27 (May 1981): 21 ((7))

R300 PARIS, Mike: Yesterday's winner is a loser today *in* Old Time Music, No. 15 (Winter 1974/5): 5–8 ((3, 6, 7))

RODGERS, JIMMIE

R301 BOND, Johnny: The recordings of Jimmie Rodgers: an annotated discography. Los Angeles: John Edwards Memorial Foundation, 1978. 76 pp. ((2, 3, 4, 6, 7))

R302 CRISP, David: Jimmie Rodgers 78 R.P.M. Australian discography *in* Country & Western Spotlight, No. 29 (November 1981): 23–27 ((3, 6))

R303 [Discography] *in* Hillbilly Folk Record Journal, I/4 thru III/2 (October–December 1954 thru March–June 1956): ? ((2, 3, 7))

R304 EDWARDS, J.: [Discography] *in* Country Western Spotlight, No. 21 (January–March 1958): ? ((2, 3, 7))

R305 EDWARDS, J.: [Discography] *in* Country Western Spotlight (Special issue, September 1962): ? ((2, 3, 7))

R306 McELREA, R.: [Discography] *in* Country News & Views, IV/4 (April 1966): ? ((2, 3, 7))

R307 [[The Jimmie Rodgers discography *in* PARIS, Mike: Jimmie the kid: the life of Jimmie Rodgers. London: Eddison Press: Old Time Music Magazine, 1977: [171]–196]]

R308 The recordings of Jimmie Rodgers *in* PORTERFIELD, Nolan: Jimmie Rodgers. Urbana: University of Illinois Press, 1979: 379–429 ((1, 2, 3, 6, 7))

R309 SCHUMANN, Reinald: Jimmie Rodgers aufnahmen *in* Hillbilly, No. 2 (June 1962): 6–9 ((7))

RODGERS, RICHARD

R310 [[Discography] *in* Richard Rodgers: fact book, with supplement. New York: Lynn Farnol Group, 1968: [553]–564]]

ROGAN, J. MACKENZIE [Lt. Col., conductor of Coldstream Guards Band]

R311 TANNER, William C.: Around the bandstand *in* Commodore, No. 5 (Spring 1972): 11 + ((—))

ROGERS, LEE

R312 MOHR, Kurt: Lee Rogers *in* Shout, No. 95 (May 1974): 2–3 ((2, 3, 5, 7))

ROHLAND, PETER

R313 Discographie *in* Peter Rohland: 1933–1966. Russelsheim: Edition Venceremos, 1976: 65–69 ((5))

THE ROKES (musical group)

R314 SORGE, Claudio: Ravin' Rokes *in* Kicks, No. 1 (Spring 1979): 47–50; discography pp. 49–50 ((—))

ROLF, ERNEST

R315 LILIEDAHL, Karleric: Ernst Rolf. Stockholm: Kungliga biblioteket, 1970. 71 l. ((3, 4, 6, 7)) (Nationalfonotekets diskografier, 501)

ROLFE, B. A.

R316 WILE, Ray: Discography *in* Record Research, No. 107 (October 1970): 3–6 ((3, 7))

ROLLER COASTER label

R317 Roller Coaster label listing *in* Gorilla Beat, No. 2 (1979): 22 ((—))

ROLLIN' ROCK label

R318 Rollin' Rock Records diskografi *in* Whole Lotta Rockin', No. 9 (February 1974): 25–26 ((—))

THE ROLLING STONES (musical group)

R319 [[Discography] *in* BAS-RABERIN, Philippe: Les Rolling Stones. Paris: A. Michel, 1972: [180]–186]]

R320 BEACH, Tom: The reel Stones *in* Trans-Oceanic Trouser Press, II/3 (June–August 1975): 4–8 ((1, 6))

R321 BEACH, Tom, and James KARNBACH: Sessionography, the Stones, in the studio, 1962–1981 *in* DALTON, David: The Rolling Stones; the first twenty years. New York: Knopf, 1981: 189–191 ((7))

R322 Discography *in* CARR, Roy: The Rolling Stones: an illustrated record. New York: Harmony Books, 1976: 104–107 ((1, 5))

R323 Discografie *in* CASAMONTI, Ivano: Rolling Stones. Milan: Gammalibri, 1980: 149–166 ((1, 5))

R324 Discographie *in* CONSTANTIN, Philippe: Les Rolling Stones. Paris: Nouvelles editions polaires, 1972: 110–115 ((7))

R325 Discography *in* DALTON, David: Rolling Stones. New York: Amsco Music Publishing Co., 1972: 348–351 ((—))

R326 FREEPORT FATS: Ephemera: installment 1: the Rolling Stones *in* New Haven Rock Press, III/2 (early summer 1971): 19 ((1, 5))

R327 GEIGER, Barry: The Rolling Stones: oddities, rarities & balderdash *in* Trouser Press, No. 23 (November 1977): 23–25 ((1, 5))

R328 HOGG, Brian: The Rolling Stones *in* Bam Balam, No. 11 (June 1980): 19, 31–39; discography pp. 19, 37–39; addenda in No. 12 (November 1980): 30–31 ((1, 5))

R329 Discography *in* JASPER, Tony: The Rolling Stones. London: Octopus Books, 1976: [83]–89 ((5))

R330 KARNBACH, James, and David DALTON: Discography *in* DALTON, David: The Rolling Stones. New York: Quick Fox, 1979: 123– [127] ((5))

R331 Stonographie *in* LEBLANC, Jacques: Rolling Stones. Paris: A. Michel, 1978: n.p. ((1, 7))

R332 Rolling Stones discography *in* LUCE, Philip C.: The Stones. London; New

York: Allan Wingate-Baker Ltd.,
1970: 108-109 ((—))

R333   MILES: The Rolling Stones: an illustrated discography. London: Omnibus
Press, 1980. ((1, 5, 7))

R334   Discografie *in* OETS, Pim: De Rolling
Stones. Bussum: Centripress, 1974:
119-126 ((5))

R335   STEELE, Nanette: The Rolling
Stones: bootlegs and rare records: a
catalog. Copenhagen: Rolling Stones
Fan Club, 1975. 52 unnumbered pp.
((1, 7))

ROMEO label

See also Banner label in *Bibliography*
Vol. 2, Jazz

R336   The Romeo 5000 series numerical *in*
JEMF Quarterly, VI/2 (No. 18, Summer 1970) thru VII/1 (No. 22, Summer 1971): various paginations ((3, 6,
7))

ROMERO, CHAN

R337   RUSSELL, Wayne: Chan Romero and
the Valens sound *in* Kommotion, No.
9 (Spring–Summer 1975): 20 ((3))

THE RONETTES (musical group)

R338   BOELENS, Milou: Ronettes discog-
raphy *in* Rock 'n' Roll International
Magazine (Danish), No. 107 (July–
August 1977): extra 4 ((5))

R339   NEWMAN, Ralph M.: Ronnie Spector and the Ronettes *in* Bim Bam
Boom, III/1 (No. 13, August–September 1974): 12-13 ((5))

RONN label

R340   PERIN, Jacques, and Gilles PE-
TARD: . . . Listing Ronn . . . *in* Soul
Bag, No. 77 (1980): 23-28 ((—))

RONSTADT, LINDA

R341   Linda Ronstadt discography *in* BER-
MAN, Connie: Linda Ronstadt, an il-
lustrated biography. London: Carson
City, Nev.: Proteus, 1979: 116-117
((—))

R342   Discography *in* CLAIRE, Vivian: Linda Ronstadt. New York: Flash Books,
1978: 71-72 ((5))

R343   Discography *in* KANAKARIS,
Richard: Linda Ronstadt, a portrait.
Los Angeles: L.A. Pop Publishers,
1977: 1. 24-27 ((5))

RORER, POSEY

R344   WILE, Ray: The Edison recordings of
Posey Rorer and the North Carolina
Ramblers *in* Record Research, No. 92
(September 1968): 4 ((3, 6, 7))

ROSA, NOEL

R345   Musicografia e discografia de Noel
Rosa *in* FOREIS, Henrique: No tempo de Noel Rosa. Rio de Janeiro:
Liveria F. Alves Editora, 1977:
217-229 ((5, 7))

ROSS, DIANA

R346   [[Discography *in* BROWN, Geoff:
Diana Ross. London: Sidgwick &
Jackson, 1981: 136-141]]

R347   Discography of Diana Ross and the
Supremes *in* Billboard (March 20,
1976): D-63 ((—))

ROSSI, TINO

R348   Discographie *in* TRIMBACH, Gerard:
Tino Rossi. Paris: Editions Delville,
1978: 155-160 ((—))

ROTA, NINO

R349   LATORRE, Jose Maria: Nino Rota:
filmography/discography *in* Soundtrack Collector's Newsletter, No. 13
(March 1978): [13-17] ((5))

ROUGH TRADE label

R350   FAULL, Trev: Rough Trade *in*
Outlet, No. 14 (October 1979): 2-9;
continually updated in subsequent
issues ((—))

ROULETTE GOLDEN GOODIES label

R351   MARTIN, Tony: Roulette Golden
Goodies listing: 45 RPM hit single
series *in* SMG, III/3 (December 1972–
January 1973): 4-6 ((—))

ROUNDER label

R352   The Rounder list *in* Old Time Music, No. 34 (Summer–Autumn 1980): [12–13] ((—))

THE ROUTERS (musical group)

R353   COWLEY, Mike, et al.: The Routers *in* Rumble, II/4 (Winter 1974–75): 14–15 ((5))

ROXY MUSIC (musical group)

R354   Roxy Music discography *in* Trouser Press Press, No. 3 (1976): 65 [Includes solo work by Brian Ferry, Andy MacKay, Phil Manzanera, Eddie Jobson, and Rik Kenton] ((—))

ROY, HARRY

R355   BARTER, Roy: a tribute *in* Commodore, No. 1 (Spring 1971): 11 + ((—))

ROYAL, BILLIE JOE

R356   McNUTT, Randy, and Billie Joe ROYAL: Billy Joe Royal, 1962–1980 *in* Goldmine, No. 65 (October 1981): 181 ((3))

ROYAL COURT THEATRE

R357   UPTON, Stuart: Royal Court Theatre *in* Commodore, No. 12 (Winter 1973–74): 5 ((—))

THE ROYAL TEENS (musical group)

R358   INGRAM, George: Royal Teens discography *in* Goldmine, No. 38 (July 1979): 16 ((5))

R359   Royal Teens *in* Rock 'n' Roll International Magazine (Danish), No. 107 (July–August 1977): 23 ((—))

R360   SMART, Peter: The Royal Teens *in* SMG, III/8 (October–November 1973): 2–3; additions in III/11 (March 1974): 11 ((—))

THE ROYALS (musical group)

See also *Bibliography* Vol. 2, Jazz

R361   TOPPING, Ray: Royals discography *in* Shout, No. 62 (January 1971): [5–

7]; additions and corrections in No. 65 (April 1971): [1] ((2, 3, 7))

THE ROYALTONES (musical group)

R362   IFILL, James: The Royaltones *in* Yesterday's Memories, I/3 (1975): 27 ((7))

R363   [[SMART, Peter: Discography *in* Rumble, I/3; additions and corrections in II/4 (Winter 1974–75): 17]]

ROYCROFT label

R364   BLACKER, George R.: Roycroft label *in* Record Research, No. 117 (August 1972): 4–5 ((3))

ROZSA, MIKLOS

R365   JURTSCHAK, Jordan: [Miklos Rozsa discography] *in* RTS Music Gazette, VIII/4 (August 1980): [8]; VIII/5 (September 1980): [8]; VIII/6 (October 1980): [8] ((5))

R366   PUGLIESE, Roberto: Film discografia essenziale di Miklos Rozsa *in* Discoteca, XVIII (No. 174, September 1977): 20 ((—))

RUBY label

R367   SHORT, Larry, and Derek GLENISTER: The story of Ruby Records *in* New Kommotion, No. 16 (Summer 1977): 30–33; discography p. 33 ((—))

RUDD, AUSTIN

R368   BARKER, Tony: Austin Rudd *in* Music-Hall Records, No. 6 (April 1979): 113–117 ((5))

RUDNIGGER, WILHELM

R369   [[[Discography] *in* his Sachn zum Lachn. Klangenfurt: Carinthia, 1978: 82–85]]

RUFF, RAY

R370   KOMOROWSKI, Adam: Ruff country *in* New Kommotion, No. 15 (Spring 1977): 5; addenda in No. 16 (Summer 1977): 42; No. 17 (Autumn 1977): 38; and No. 19 (Spring 1978): 12 ((—))

RUFFIN, RIFF

R371 PEARLIN, Victor: Discography *in* Music World and Record Digest Weekly News, No. 61 (September 5, 1979): 9 ((3))

THE RUMBLERS (musical group)

R372 DALLEY, Robert: Rumblers discography *in* Goldmine, No. 54 (November 1980): 12 ((5))

THE RUMBLES (musical group)

R373 RICHARD, Doug: They're back: the Rumbles *in* Blitz, No. 36 (May–June 1980): 8–11; discography p. 11 ((5))

RUSH, TOM

R374 Tom Rush album discography *in* Goldmine, No. 44 (January 1980): 142 ((5))

RUST label

R375 BEZANKER, Paul: Rust Records *in* Paul's Record Magazine, IV/1 (August 1976): 30; IV/2 (No. 13–14): 52–53; additions and corrections in No. 15 (January–February 1977): 40 ((4))

R376 [Discography] *in* Time Barrier Express, No. 22 (March–April 1977): 20 ((—))

RUSTICHELLI, CARLO

R377 COCUMAROLO, Enzo, and James MARSHALL: Carlo Rustichelli filmography/discography *in* SCN (Soundtrack Collector's Newsletter): No. 10: ?; No. 11 (August 1977): [13–16] ((5))

THE RUTLES (musical group)

R378 FULK, Marty: Rutles discography (Cleveland releases only) *in* Full Blast, I/1 (Winter 1979): 35–37 ((7))

RYAN, PAUL and BARRY

R379 FLEURY, Joseph: The Ryan discography *in* Jamz, No. 5 (c1972): 63, 90 ((5))

RYDELL, BOBBY

R380 BRUNNER, Tony: Bobby Rydell discography *in* Goldmine, No. 39 (August 1979): 12 ((—))

R381 ENGEL, Ed: Discography *in* Paul's Record Magazine, III/5 (June 1976): 8–9; additions and corrections in IV/1 (August 1976): 4 ((5))

RYDER, MITCH

R382 CSERNITS, Bill, and Mike Mc-DOWELL: Mitch Ryder discography *in* Ballroom Blitz, No. 24 (January 1978): 15–16 ((5))

R383 Mitch Ryder discography *in* Time Barrier Express, III (No. 26, September–October 1979): 30 ((7))

SABLON, JEAN

S1 Discographie *in* his De France ou bien d'ailleurs. Paris: R. Laffont, 1979: 275–[285] ((—))

SADDLER, REGGIE

S2 HOOK, John: Reggie Saddler/Janice discography *in* It Will Stand, No. 19 (c1981): 6 ((5))

SAHM, DOUG
See SIR DOUGLAS QUINTET

SAILOR (musical group)

S3 ROBBINS, Ira: Sailor: hard rock at its most sublime *in* Trouser Press, No. 15 (August–September 1976): 16–17; discography p. 17 ((5))

THE SAINTS (musical group)

S4 FAULL, Trev: The Saints *in* Instrumental Obscurities Unlimited, No. 20 (c1978): 12 ((—)) [Not to be confused with the 1970's Australian punk group]

THE SALON ORCHESTRA

S5 CLIFFE, Peter: The Salon Orchestra *in* Vintage Light Music, No. 18 (Spring 1979): 1 ((—))

S6 HAYES, Jim: The Salon Orchestra (and Victor Salon Orchestra) on English HMV *in* Vintage Light Music, No. 20 (Autumn 1979): 13 ((3, 5))

SALVATION ARMY

S7 HINDMARCH, Alan W.: Salvation Army bands *in* Vintage Light Music, No. 15 (Summer 1979): 8-9 ((—))

SALVO label

S8 FAULL, Trev: Little known UK labels #1—Salvo 1962 only *in* Outlet, No. 26 (July 1982): 9 ((—))

SAM AND DAVE (musical duo)

S9 SPERRAZZA, Gary: Sam & Dave discography *in* Time Barrier Express, III (No. 26, September–October 1979): 16 ((7))

S10 SPERRAZZA, Gary, and Mike McDOWELL: Sam and Dave discography *in* Blitz, No. 27 (July 1978): 12; addenda in No. 28 (September–October 1978): 26 ((5))

SAN ANTONIO label

S11 LEGERE, Will: [Discography] *in* Disc Collector, No. 16 (February 1961): ? ((—))

SANDBERG, SVEN-OLOF

S12 LILIEDAHL, Karleric: Sven-Olof Sandberg. Stockholm: Kungliga Biblioteket, 1971. 72 l. ((2, 3, 4, 6, 7))

SANDERS, SONNY

S13 PRUTER, Robert: Sonny Sanders discography *in* Goldmine, No. 48 (May 1980): 21 ((5))

SANDLER, ALBERT

S14 UPTON, Stuart: Albert Sandler and his Orchestra *in* Commodore, No. 10 (Summer 1973): 2+; additions and corrections in No. 11 (Autumn 1973): 6 ((—))

THE SANDMEN (musical group)

S15 GOLDBERG, Marv, and Rick WHITESELL: The Sandmen *in* Goldmine, No. 35 (April 1979): 41 ((5))

SANSU label

S16 CHURCHILL, Trevor, and Jim WILSON: Sansu label listing *in* Black Wax, No. 6 (July 1973): 14 ((3, 5, 6))

SANTANA, CARLOS

S17 Indice discografico *in* SIERRA I FABRA, Jordi: Santana: el fuego latino. Barcelona: Musica de Nuestro Tiempo, 1977: 105–112 ((—))

SAR label

S18 TOPPING, Ray: SAR label listing *in* Shout, No. 97 (July 1974): 6-8 ((3, 5))

SARDE, PHILIPPE

S19 DEMARY, Tom, et al.: Philippe Sarde filmography/discography *in* SCN (Soundtrack Collector's Newsletter), No. 11 (August 1977): [17]; No. 12 (November 1977): [13–15] ((—))

SARG label

S20 Selected Sarg discography *in* FROST, David M.: The Sarg Records story *in* Record Exchanger, V/2 (No. 24, October (?) 1977): 13–14, 26 ((5))

SARONY, LESLIE

S21 BADROCK, Arthur: A discography of Leslie Sarony's recordings for the Crystalate Company *in* Collecta, No. 23 (January 1975): 8-14 ((3, 6, 7))

S22 BARTER, Roy: The two Leslies [on Regal Zonophone records] *in* Vintage Light Music, No. 12 (Autumn 1977): [15]-16 ((—))

S23 Discography *in* Memory Lane, VIII (No. 29, Winter 1975): 20-24 ((7))

S24 HAYES, Jim: The imperial Leslie Sarony *in* Commodore, No. 3 (Autumn 1971): 12 ((—))

SAUNDERS, LITTLE BUTCHIE

S25 NEWMAN, Ralph M.: Discography *in* Bim Bam Boom, No. 7 (September 1972): 18 ((3, 6))

SAVAGE ROSE (musical group)

S26 BYERS, Dave: Savage Rose discography *in* Goldmine, No. 64 (September 1981): 171 ((5))

SAYLES, JOHNNY
See also *Bibliography* Vol. 2, Jazz

S27 PRUTER, Robert: Discography *in* Goldmine, No. 42 (November 1979): 115 ((5))

SCEPTER label

S28 Scepter singles listing *in* Shout, No. 106 (December 1975–January 1976): 10–13; No. 107 (February–March 1976): 10–12; additions and corrections in No. 108: 21 ((5))

SCHIFRIN, LALO

S29 JURTSHAK, Jordan: Lalo Schifrin film/discography *in* RTS Music Gazette, VIII/2 (June 1980): [6] ((—))

SCHONBERG, IB

S30 ANDREASEN, Axel: Ib Schonberg og grammofonen; en discografi. Copenhagen: Andreasen, 1974: 57 l. ((3, 4, 6, 7))

SCHULZE, KLAUS

S31 Klaus Schulze discography *in* Trouser Press, No. 23 (November 1977): 33 [Solo, plus Tangerine Dream, Ash Ra Temple, and Cosmic Couriers] ((—))

SCOTT, JACK

S32 LE GUYADER, Tanguy: Jack Scott French discography *in* Goldmine, No. 59 (April 1981): 23 ((5))

S33 SMART, Peter: Jack Scott discography *in* Kommotion, No. 8 (Winter 1975): 2–6; addenda in No. 9 (Spring–Summer 1975): 5 and No. 10–11 (Winter 1975–76): 26 ((3, 5))

S34 THOMPSON, Gary: Jack Scott is back *in* Goldmine, No. 12 (September–October 1976): 33 ((5))

SCRUGGS, EARL
See FLATT, LESTER

THE SEARCHERS (musical group)

S35 KOLANJIAN, Steve, and Aware Magazine: The Searchers discography *in* Goldmine, No. 61 (June 1981): 15–17 ((5))

S36 Rock retrospective: The Searchers *in* Rock It with Aware Magazine, II/3 (1976?): 7–9 ((5)); additions & correxions [sic] in II/4 [1976]: 4 ((—)); additions . . . in II/5 (1977): 4 ((—))

THE SEEDS (musical group)

S37 BARNES, Ken: Discography *in* Who Put the Bomp, No. 12 (Summer 1974): 10; additions and corrections in No. 14 (Fall 1975): 44 ((—))

S38 HOGG, Brian: The Seeds *in* Bam Balam, No. 1 (February 1975): 3–7; discography pp. 5–6; addenda *in* No. 2 (June 1975): 8; No. 5 (February 1977): 15; No. 7 (c1978): 9; and No. 12 (November 1980): 38 ((—))

SEELEY, BLOSSON

S39 Blosson Seeley; a discography *in* Discographer, I/2 (4th Quarter 1967): 1–153 ((3, 7))

SELF, RONNIE

S40 TOPPING, Ray: Ronnie Self discography *in* New Kommotion, No. 18 (Winter 1978): 11; addenda in No. 22 (1979): 66 ((2, 3, 7))

SENTAR label

S41 PRUTER, Robert: Discography *in* Goldmine, No. 37 (June 1979): 16 ((5))

S42 Sentar label *in* Paul's Record Magazine, IV/2 (No. 13–14, September–December 1976): 33 ((—))

THE SERENADERS (musical group)

S43 MONDRONE, Sal: Rare sounds *in* Bim Bam Boom, I/1 (August–September 1971): 13 ((—))

S44 MOONOOGIAN, G. A.: The Serenaders *in* Goldmine, No. 46 (March 1980): 147 ((5))

SERVINO, DEL, AND THE BOWTIES (musical group)

S45 VANCE, Marcia, and Ed ENGEL: Del Servino and the Bowties: discography *in* Paul's Record Magazine, III/2 (February 1976): 9 ((3))

SERVAT, GILLES

S46 Discography *in* his Gilles Servat. Paris: Seghers, 1975: [189] ((—))

SESTA, DON

S47 HAYES, Jim: Don Sesta on English 78's *in* Commodore, No. 13 (Spring 1974): 8 + ((—))

SETTERS, JILSON

S48 [Discography] *in* Country Directory, No. 1 (November 1960): ? ((—)) [Library of Congress records only]

S49 Jilson Setters discography *in* Devil's Box, XXI/1 (March 1978): 45 ((1, 2, 3, 6, 7))

7 TO 11 label

S50 GIBBON, Peter, and Tony TISOVEC: [Discography] *in* Yesterday's Memories, III/3 (1977): 27 ((7))

SHAD label

S51 Shad label *in* Paul's Record Magazine, IV/2 (No. 13–14): 54 ((—))

THE SHADOWS (musical group)

S52 HENDRICK, Tom: Spotlight on the Shadows *in* Who Put the Bomp, No. 8 (Fall–Winter 1971): 28–33; discography p. 33 ((—))

SHADOWS OF KNIGHT (musical group)

S53 SAUNDERS, Mike: Shadows of Knight discography *in* Jamz, No. 3 (February 1972): 9 ((—))

SHADWELL, CHARLES

S54 The Coventry Hippodrome Orchestra conducted by Charles Shadwell *in* Commodore, No. 2 (Summer 1971): 4 ((—))

SHAKIN' STEVENS & THE SUNSETS (musical group)

S55 HOLLIE, Jon: Shakin' Stevens & the Sunsets recording list *in* SMG, III/3 (December 1972–January 1973): 7 ((—))

S56 HOOS, Willem: L.P. discography *in* Rockville International (December 1973): 12 ((—))

THE SHAMROCKS (musical group)

S57 KLITSCH, Hans Jurgen: The Shamrocks *in* Gorilla Beat, No. 12 (1981): 61–63; discography p. 63; addendum in No. 13 (1982): 73 ((—))

SHA NA NA (musical group)

S58 Discography *in* Goldmine, No. 37 (June 1979): 13 ((—))

SHAND, JIMMY

S59 [Discography] *in* PHILLIPS, David: Jimmy Shand. Dundee: D. Winter and Son, 1976: 132–133 ((—))

THE SHANGRI-LAS (musical group)

S60 COHEN, Mitch: Shangri-las discography *in* Who Put the Bomp, No. 15 (Spring 1976): 10 ((5))

S61 UNDERWOOD, Barry K.: A Shangri-las discography *in* SMG, IV/1 (June 1974): 5–6 ((—))

SHANNON, DEL (real name Charles Westover)

S62 BARNES, Ken: Del Shannon *in* The Rock Marketplace, No. 10 (June 1975): 3–7, 15; discography p. 7 ((1, 5))

S63   Del Shannon *in* Who Put the Bomp, No. 7 (Summer 1971): 22, 30 ((5))

S64   Del Shannon discography *in* Music World and Record Digest Weekly News, No. 53 (July 11, 1979): 6 ((—))

S65   FAULL, Trev: Del Shannon discography *in* UK London and Stateside labels: 1960–1966 *in* Outlet, No. 2 (c1978): 4–7 ((3, 5))

S66   GARDNER, Graham: Del Shannon discography *in* Goldmine, No. 67 (December 1981): 20 ((5))

S67   HOLLIE, J.: Continuing the Del Shannon discography from 1966 to 1978 *in* Outlet, No. 3 (June 1978): 13–16 ((5))

S68   HOLLIE, Jon: "Singles disco" *in* New Rockpile, No. 11 (Summer 1974): [17] ((3))

S69   HOLLIE, Jon, and Barry LAZELL: Del Shannon discography (U.S. and U.K. releases) *in* SMG, IV/8 (March 1975): 2–3; IV/11 (June 1975): 7–9 ((—))

S70   McDOWELL, Mike: The search: the Del Shannon story, part 1 *in* Blitz, No. 41 (November–December 1981): 8–11; discography p. 11; part 2: the further adventures of Charles Westover in No. 42 (March–April 1982): 16–20; album discography p. 20 ((1, 5))

SHARPE, RAY

S71   KOMOROWSKI, Adam, and Dick GRANT: Razor sharp *in* New Kommotion, No. 26 (1982): 4–14; discography (by Ray TOPPING and Adam KOMOROWSKI): 13–14 ((1, 2, 3, 7))

S72   TOPPING, Ray: Ray Sharpe discography *in* New Kommotion, No. 15 (Spring 1977): 12; addenda in No. 16 (Summer 1977): 42 and No. 22 (1979): 66 ((1, 2, 3, 7))

THE SHA-WEES (musical group)

S73   GOLDBERG, Marv, and Dave HINCKLEY: The Shaw-wees [sic] *in* Yesterday's Memories, III/3 (1977): 6 ((7))

THE SHELLS (musical group)

S74   [[[Discography] *in* Soul Music (No. 25)]]

S75   STIERLE, Wayne: Shells discography *in* Bim Bam Boom, II/3 (No. 9, 1973): 50 ((3))

SHEPARD, JEAN

S76   [Discography] *in* Country Western Express, No. 18 (March 1958): ? ((—))

SHEPHERD, BILL

S77   [Discography] *in* Old Time Music, No. 30 (Autumn 1978): 15 ((3, 7))

SHEPHERD, HAYS

S78   COLTMAN, Robert: A 90's murder mystery: 'The peddler and his wife' *in* Old Time Music, No. 30 (Autumn 1978): 13–15 ((3, 7))

THE SHEPPARDS (musical group)

S79   PRUTER, Robert: Sheppards discography *in* Time Barrier Express, IV/1 (No. 27, April–May 1980): 73–74 ((5))

THE SHIELDS (musical group)

S80   HINCKLEY, Dave: The Shields *in* Yesterday's Memories, III/2 (1977): 3 ((7))

THE SHIRELLES (musical group)

S81   GONZALEZ, Fernando L.: Shirelles discography *in* Paul's Record Magazine (No. 17–18): 21–[24] ((1, 3, 5, 7))

SHIRLEY & LEE (SHIRLEY GOODMAN AND LEONARD LEE)
See also *Bibliography* Vol. 2, Jazz

S82   [[[Discography] *in* Shout, No. 106 (December 1975–January 1976); additions and corrections in No. 108 (April–May 1976): 21]]

SHOCK label

S83   Shock label *in* Hot Buttered Soul, No. 42 (November 1975): 4 ((3))

THE SHOES (musical group)

S84 Shoes discography *in* Goldmine, No. 50 (July 1980): 17 ((5))

SHORES, BILL

S85 WOLFE, Charles: Five years with the best; Bill Shores and North Georgia fiddling *in* Old Time Music, No. 25 (Summer 1977): 4-8 ((3, 6, 7))

SIFFER, ROGER

S86 Discographie *in* his Alsace/Elsass. Paris: J. C. Lattes, 1979: 213-[214] ((—))

SILVER label

S87 [[[Discography] *in* New Kommotion, No. 13 (c1976); addenda in No. 16 (Summer 1977): 42]]

SILVER SPOTLIGHT label

S88 United Artists reissue line: the 'Silver Spotlight' series *in* SMG, III/5 (April-May 1973): 6-9 ((—))

SILVERSTEIN, SHEL

S89 Shel Silverstein—discographie *in* Country Corner, No. 58 (February 1978): 22 ((5))

SILVERTONE label
See also *Bibliography* Vol. 2, Jazz

S90 [Discography] *in* Disc Collector, No. 15 (November 1960) thru No. 17 (May 1961): ? ((—))

SIMMONS, LUKE

S91 GIBSON, Garth: Luke Simmons discography *in* Country & Western Spotlight, No. 8 (September 1976): 12-13 ((—))

SIMON, PAUL

S92 BETROCK, Alan: 'Not so' simple Simon *in* The Rock Marketplace, No. 10 (June 1975): 18-19, 31; discography p. 31 [Early recordings only, including compositions and productions, as well as recordings as Tom & Jerry and Jerry Landis]

S93 Appendix *in* COHEN, Mitchell S.: Simon & Garfunkel: a biography in words & pictures. [s.l.]: Sire Books; New York: distributed by Chappell Music Co., 1977: 51-55 ((5))

S94 FRIEDMAN, Ken: Simon & Garfunkel; the early years *in* Goldmine, No. 12 (September-October 1976): 7 ((—))

S95 Simon and Garfunkel—C.B.S. records *in* LEIGH, Spencer: Paul Simon—now and then. Liverpool: Raven Books, 1973: 97-104 ((5))

S96 Discografia *in* SANCHEZ VIDAL, Agustin: Simon & Garfunkel. Madrid: Jucar, 1975: 203-208 ((1, 5))

SIMS, GERALD

S97 PRUTER, Robert: Discography *in* Goldmine, No. 31 (December 1978): 26 ((5))

SIMS label

S98 MASOTTI, Fred: An incomplete Sims label listing *in* Kommotion No. 10-11 (Winter 1975-76): 41-42 ((—))

SINATRA, FRANK

S99 CAMP, Jack: Frank Sinatra recordings with Tommy Dorsey's Orchestra *in* After Beat, I/5 (February 1971): 5, 10 ((7))

S100 [[[Discography] *in* GOLDSTEIN, Norm: Sinatra. New York: Holt, Rinehart, and Winston, 1982]]

S101 HAINSWORTH, Brian: Songs by Sinatra, 1939-1970. Bramhope, Leeds, England: Hainsworth, 1973. 92 pp. ((1, 3, 6))

S102 LONSTEIN, Albert L.: The compleat Sinatra. Ellenville, N.Y.: Cameron Publications, 1970. 383 pp. ((1, 2, 3, 4, 6, 7))

S103 LONSTEIN, Albert L.: The revised compleat Sinatra. Ellenville, N.Y.: S. M. Lonstein, 1979. 702 pp. ((1, 2, 3, 4, 5, 6, 7))

S104 O'BRIEN, Ed, and Scott SAYERS, Jr.: The Sinatra sessions: 1939-1980. Dallas: Sinatra Society of America, 1980. 125 pp. ((1, 3, 7))

S105 PLEASANTS, Henry: Frank Sinatra: a great vocal artist retires *in* Stereo

Review, XXVII/5 (November 1977):
59–74 ((7))

S106   RIDGWAY, John: The Sinatrafile.
Pt. 1. Non-commercial. Pt. 2. Com-
mercial. Birmingham: John Ridgway
Books, 1977. 2 vols. ((1, 4, 7))

S107   Sinatra as a recording artist *in*
SHAW, Arnold: Sinatra: retreat to
the romantic. London: Allen, 1968
[369]–384 ((—))

SINGERS—FRANCE

S108   Discographie *in* HAMON, Andre-
Georges: Chantres de toutes les
Bretagnes: 20 ans de chanson
bretonne. Paris: L. Picollec, 1981:
516–529 ((—))

SINGERS, WOMEN

S109   Discographies *in* GARBUTT, Bob:
Rockabilly queens. Toronto: Ducktail
Press, 1979: 55–78

SINGERS UNLIMITED (musical group)

S110   The Singers Unlimited—discographie
in Program notes for Friends [Sound
recording] MPS 5D 064-D99444, 1977
((7))

THE SINGING DOVES (musical group)

S111   MONDRONE, Sal: [Cliff Butler and
the Singing Doves] *in* Bim Bam
Boom, I/3 (December 1971–January
1972): 11 ((—))

SINHO

S112   [[Discography] *in* ALENCAR, Edigar
de: Nosso Sinho do Samba. Rio de
Janeiro: FUNARTE, 1981: 151–157]]

SINKS, EARL

S113   [[[Discography] *in* New Kommotion,
No. 13 (c1976); addenda in No. 16
(Summer 1977): 42]]

SIR DOUGLAS QUINTET

S114   CORTESE, Bob: The Doug Sahm/Sir
Douglas Quintet discography *in* Music
World, No. 86 (June 1981): 52 ((—))

S115   HOGG, Brian: Thru the rhythm:
Texas rock 'n' roll *in* Bam Balam,
No. 10 (November 1979): 9–11 ((5))

SIRE label

S116   Sire records discography *in* Bomp!,
No. 20 (January 1979): 21 ((—))

SIXTY MINUTE MAN (song title)

S117   MOONOOGIAN, George, and Chris
BEACHLEY: 60 minute man & asso-
ciated records discography *in* It Will
Stand, No. 20 (c1981): 7 ((5))
[Covers and sequels to the Dominoes'
recording]

SKAGGS, RICKY

S118   Ricky Skaggs discography *in* Bluegrass
Unlimited (January 1977): 17 ((—))

THE SKILLETLICKERS (musical group)

S119   Discographie *in* Country Corner, No.
23 (March–April 1970): 11–12 ((—))

S120   NOBLEY, Robert: The Skilletlickers
Bluebird discography *in* Devil's Box,
No. 14 (April 1971): 12–13 ((3, 7))

SKILONDZ, ANDREJEWA VON

S121   ENGLUND, Bjorn: Andrejewa von
Skilondz *in* Talking Machine Review,
No. 39 (April 1976): 616–619; additions in No. 43 (December 1976): 865
((3, 6, 7))

SKIP BIFFERTY (musical group)

S122   Skip Bifferty *in* The Rock Marketplace, No. 7 (October 1974): 24 ((5))

S123   TELL, Pontus von: From the chosen
few to a bunch of blockheads *in*
Gorilla Beat, No. 10 (1981): 35–42;
discography p. 42; No. 11 (1981):
39–48; discography pp. 47–48; addendum in No. 13 (1982): 72 ((5)) [In-
cludes Heavy Jelly, Graham Bell,
Lindisfarne, and other related groups]

THE SKY ROCKETS (musical group)

S124   WAANDERS, Dick: Sky Rockets discografie *in* Rock and Roll Inter-

national Magazine (Dutch), No. 2 (October–November 1975): 19 ((5))

THE SKYLINERS (musical group)

S125 GONZALEZ, Fernando, and Ken CLEE: Discography *in* Goldmine, No. 64 (September 1981): 9 ((3, 5))

SLADE (musical group)

S126 Slade discography *in* Bedloe's Island, No. 5 (c1972): 7 ((2))

THE SLICKEE BOYS (musical group)

S127 BUDNOVITCH, George: The Slickee Boys *in* Gorilla Beat, No. 13 (1982): 31–43; discography pp. 40–43; family tree p. 36 ((2, 5)) [Includes related groups, e.g., the Nurses and Africa Korp]

S128 FAULL, Trev: The Slickee Boys *in* Outlet, No. 16 (January 1980): 5–8; discography pp. 7–8 ((5))

THE SLITS (musical group)

S129 MALLON, Cathy: Slits discography *in* Goldmine, No. 58 (March 1981): 195 ((—))

SLOAN, P. F.

S130 GARI, Brian, and Alan BETROCK: P. F. Sloan *in* The Rock Marketplace, No. 8 (December 1974): 3–7; discography p. 7; addenda in No. 9 (March 1975): 46; No. 10 (June 1975): 15, 50 [Includes Sloan as performer, writer, and producer, as well as recordings of collaborator Steve Barri] ((5))

S131 HOGG, Brian: The Mamas & the Papas *in* Bam Balam, No. 9 (July 1979): 31–35; addenda in No. 12 (November 1980): 31 and No. 14 (September 1982): 15–16 ((5))

SMALL FACES (musical group)

S132 BETROCK, Alan: The original Small Faces discs *in* Jamz, No. 3 (February 1972): 30; addenda in No. 4 (May 1972): 34 ((5))

S133 BETROCK, Alan: Small Faces discography *in* The Immediate story—vol. 2; the Small Faces [Sound recording] 1975: inside cover ((5))

S134 Discography *in* Aware, No. 7 (Spring 1981): 24–27 ((5))

S135 HOGG, Brian: Small Faces *in* Bam Balam, No. 6 (November 1977): 24–27; addendum in No. 14 (September 1982): 13 ((2, 5)) [Includes Steve Marriott and Jimmy Winston solo]

S136 The mods, part VI. Tough kids: Small Faces *in* Gorilla Beat, No. 7 (1980): 4–9; discography pp. 6–9; addenda in No. 8 (1980): 45 and No. 9 (1981): 48 ((5))

S137 SILVERTON, Pete: All or nothing: the Small Faces story *in* Trouser Press, No. 22 (October 1977): 10–15; discography p. 15 ((5))

SMECK, ROY

S138 WILE, Ray: The Edison recordings of Roy Smeck *in* Record Research, No. 142 (September 1976): 7 ((3, 6, 7))

SMILEY, RED

S139 [Discography] *in* Country Western Express, No. 20 (August 1958): ? ((—))

S140 [Discography] *in* Disc Collector, No. 17 (May 1961): ? ((—))

SMITH, CONNIE

S141 Connie Smith record listing *in* Country Record Exchange, II (No. 12, February 1968): 4–5 ((—))

SMITH, FIDDLIN' ARTHUR

S142 [[Discography *in* Country Corner, No. 4: 38]]

S143 Discography *in* Devil's Box, XI/4 (December 1977): 73–80 ((2, 3, 6, 7))

S144 JOHNSON, W.: [Discography] *in* Program notes for Folkways LP FA 2379, 1964: ? ((—))

SMITH, HOBART

S145 Hobart Smith *in* Devil's Box, No. 22 (September 1973): 20–21 ((—))

SMITH, HUEY

S146   MOHR, Kurt: Huey Smith discography *in* Shout, No. 70 (October 1971): [4–8] ((2, 3, 7))

S147   Slim, Almost [pseud.]: Huey 'Piano' Smith Discography *in* Goldmine, No. 73 (June 1982): 16–17 ((—))

SMITH, JOSEPH C.

S148   JONES, David L.: [Discography] *in* New Amberola Graphic, VII/4 (No. 28, Spring 1978): 9–11 ((7))

SMITH, MARVIN

S149   PRUTER, Robert: Marvin Smith discography *in* Goldmine, No. 50 (July 1980): 167 ((5))

SMITH, MAYBELLE

See also *Bibliography* Vol. 2, Jazz

S150   MOHR, Kurt: Big Maybelle discography *in* Shout, No. 74 (February 1972): [1–5]; additions in No. 75: [6] ((2, 3, 7))

SMITH, PATTI

S151   Patti's discs *in* ROACH, Dusty: Patti Smith: rock & roll madonna. South Bend, Ind.: And Books, 1979: 93 ((5))

SMITH, RAY

S152   Discography *in* R-O-C-K (February 1981): 44–45 ((—))

S153   GORDON, Ray: Discography—Ray Smith—45's *in* Goldmine, No. 40 (September 1979): 20A ((—))

S154   KOMOROWSKI, Adam: Ray Smith *in* New Kommotion, No. 22 (1979): 20–27; discography pp. 26–27 ((1, 2, 3, 7))

S155   Ray Smith Fan Club: Ray Smith discography *in* Mean Mountain Music, IV/1 (1979): [14] ((—))

S156   SMART, Peter: Ray Smith *in* Kommotion, No. 10–11 (Winter 1975– 76): 43–45 ((1, 7))

SMITH, WALTER

S157   RUSSELL, Tony: Alias Walter Smith *in* Old Time Music, No. 17 (Summer 1975): 15–17 ((3, 6, 7))

SMITH, WARREN

S158   ALESINA, Mac: Discographie *in* Big Beat, No. 10 (March–April–May 1974): 13 ((5))

S159   KOMOROWSKI, Adam: Warren Smith *in* New Kommotion, No. 22 (1979): 48–53; discography pp. 52–53 ((1, 2, 3, 7))

S160   THOMAS, Peter: Releases on the Sun label [and] selected album discography *in* Big Beat of the 50's, No. 29 (October 1981): 18–19 ((7))

S161   TREUDE, Helmut: Discographie [Warren Smith] *in* Country Corner, No. 54 (May 1977): 5–6 ((—))

S162   Warren Smith discografi *in* Kountry Korral (October 1973): 11 ((—))

THE SMOKE (musical group)

S163   MARTUCCI, Mark, and Hans Jurgen KLITSCH: The Shots, Chords Five, The Smoke *in* Gorilla Beat, No. 10 (1981): 4–11; discography pp. 9–11; addendum in No. 13 (1982): 71 ((5))

S164   The Smoke *in* The Rock Marketplace, No. 7 (October 1974): 24 ((5))

SMOTHERS BROTHERS

S165   SMITH, Ronald L.: The comedy albums *in* Goldmine, No. 40 (September 1979): 7A ((—))

SNOW, HANK

S166   BENSON, Charles: Hank Snow record listing *in* Country & Western Roundabout, I/1 (August 1962): 13–16; I/2 (November 1962): 15–16, 22; I/3 (February 1963): 17–21; I/4 (May 1973): 26–27 ((—))

S167   [Discography] *in* Country Western Spotlight, No. 19 (June–September 1957): ? ((—))

S168   [Discography] *in* Disc Collector, No. 21 [n.d., 1966?]: ? ((3))

S169   Discography [1936–1947 only] *in* Hank Snow, the yodeling/singing ranger, vol. 1 [Sound recording] Country Music History LP 102: Program note insert ((3, 6, 7))

S170   FUCHS, Walter W.: Hank Snow diskographie *in* Hillbilly, No. 33 (March 1970): 39 ((—))

S171   [Song index] *in* Hillbilly, No. 9 (March 1964): 5-10 ((—))

SNYDER, HARRY

S172   LEICHTER, Al: Harry Smith discography *in* Goldmine, No. 48 (May 1980): 11 ((5))

SOLID HIT label

S173   Solid Hit label *in* Hot Buttered Soul, No. 27 (February 1974?): 9 ((3))

THE SOLITAIRES (musical group)

S174   GOLDBERG, Marv, and Mike RED-MOND: Solitaires discography *in* Record Exchanger (No. 16 [Fall 1973]): 9 ((3, 5))

SOMERS, WILLIAM DEBROY

S175   BARTER, Roy: The dance band scene *in* Commodore, No. 9 (Spring 1973): 13 + ((—))

SOMMERS, JOANNIE

S176   WRIGHT, Frank: Joannie Sommers discography *in* Goldmine, No. 64 (September 1981): 22 ((5))

SONGS, AMERICAN

S177   Selected discography *in* Program notes for . . . and then we wrote . . . American composers and lyricists sing, play and conduct their own songs [Sound recording] New World Records NW 272, 1977: 4 ((—))

S178   Selected discography *in* Program notes for Brother, can you spare a dime?; American songs during the Great Depression [Sound recording] New World Records NW 270, 1977: 6 ((—))

S179   Selected discography *in* Program notes for Come Josephine in my flying machine: inventions and topics in popular song 1910–1929 [Sound re-

cording] New World Records NW 233, 1977: 5-6 ((—))

SONGS, HUMOROUS

S180   HOGG, Brian: Sonics *in* Bam Balam, No. 4 (June 1976): 20–21; addenda in No. 12 (November 1980): 38 ((2))

S181   ROGERS, Michael C.: Break-in recordings: a discography *in* Record Exchanger, V/2 (No. 24, October(?) 1977): 24–26 ((—))

SONNY AND PHYLLIS (SONNY THREATT AND PHYLLIS BROWN)

S182   DAVIS, Jim: Sonny & Phyllis discography *in* It Will Stand, No. 11 (c1981): 5 ((—))

SONS OF THE PIONEERS (musical group)

S183   EDWARDS, J.: [Discography] *in* Country Western Spotlight, No. 13 (November 1956): ? ((—))

S184   EDWARDS, J.: [Discography] *in* Country Western Spotlight (Special issue, September 1962): ? ((—))

S185   Discography *in* GRIFFIS, Ken: Hear my song: the story of the celebrated Sons of the Pioneers. Los Angeles: John Edwards Memorial Foundation, 1974: 82–124 ((1, 3, 4, 6, 7))

S186   HEARNE, W. R.: [Discography] *in* Disc Collector, I/2 (March–June 1951): ? ((3))

THE SOPWITH CAMEL (musical group)

S187   [Discography] *in* HOGG, Brian: Psychotic reaction: San Francisco begins *in* Bam Balam, No. 10 (November 1979): 21 ((5))

THE SORROWS (musical group)

S188   HOGG, Brian: The Sorrows *in* Bam Balam, No. 11 (June 1980): 20–22 ((5))

S189   Sorrows *in* Gorilla Beat, No. 1 (1979): 3–8; addenda in No. 2 (1979): 21; No. 4 (1979): 29; No. 8 (1980): 48; and No. 13 (1982): 72 ((5))

SOUCHON, ALAIN

S190   [[[Discography] *in* his Alain Souchon. Paris: Seghers, 1979: [145–146] (Collection poesie et chansons Seghers, 42)]]

SOUL CITY label
See also *Bibliography* Vol. 2, Jazz

S191   FAULL, Trev: Soul City records *in* Outlet, No. 15 (November 1979): 29–32 ((—))

S192   LYNSKEY, Phil: Soul City listing *in* Shout, No. 108 (April–May 1976): 17–19 ((5))

SOUL CLOCK label

S193   Soul Clock label *in* Hot Buttered Soul, No. 36 (December 1974): 7 ((3))

SOUL MUSIC—ENGLAND

S194   STANTON, Roy: Catalogue of soul & R & B records issued in the U.K. *in* Shout, No. 105 (October–November 1975): 28–34; No. 106 (December 1975–January 1976): 33–36 ((5))

SOUL MUSIC—UNITED STATES

S195   A short list of recordings *in* RIEDEL, Johannes: Soul music, black and white: the influence of black music on the churches. Minneapolis: Augsburg Publishing House, 1975: 158–159 ((—))

SOUL POWER label

S196   PERIN, Jacques, and Gilles PETARD: . . . Listing Soul power . . . *in* Soul Bag, No. 77 (1980): 23–28 ((—))

S197   Soul Power label *in* Hot Buttered Soul, No. 26 (January 1974?): 4 ((3))

SOUNDS INCORPORATED
(musical group)

S198   FAULL, Trev: Sounds like . . . Sounds Incorporated *in* Instrumental Obscurities Unlimited, No. 14–15 (March 1977): 13–16; discography p. 16 ((—))

SOUSA BAND

S199   The Sousa Band on records *in* BERGER, Kenneth Walter: The march king and his band. New York: Exposition Press, 1957: [88]–95 ((—))

S200   Selected discography *in* [SMART, James]: Program notes for The Sousa and Pryor bands [Sound recording] New World Records NW 282, 1976: 6 ((—))

S201   SMART, James R.: The Sousa Band, a discography. Washington, D.C.: Library of Congress, 1970. 123 pp. ((3, 4, 6, 7))

SOUTH GEORGIA HIGHBALLERS
(musical group)

S202   [RUSSELL, Tony]: South Georgia Highballers *in* Old Time Music, No. 7 (Winter 1972/3): 20 ((3, 6, 7))

SOUTHERN MELODY BOYS
(musical group)

S203   EDENS, George C., Jr.: Southern Melody Boys *in* Old Time Music, No. 13 (Summer 1974): 13–15 ((3, 6, 7))

THE SOUVENIRS (musical group)

S204   GOLDBERG, Marv: The Souvenirs *in* Yesterday's Memories, III/2 (1977): 26 ((7))

SOVINE, RED

S205   Red Sovine—Langspielplatten (Auswahl) *in* Country Corner, No. 52 (December 1976): 6 ((—))

THE SPANIELS (musical group)

S206   LEE, Alan, and Donna HENNINGS: The Spaniels *in* Yesterday's Memories, II/2 (1976): 6–7 ((3, 7))

SPARK label

S207   HORLICK, Dick: Spark discography *in* Bim Bam Boom, III/1 (No. 13, August–September 1974): 31 ((3))

SPARKS (RON & RUSSEL MAEL)

S208   Ron & Russel Mael/Sparks discography *in* Trouser Press Press, No. 3 (1976): 67 ((5))

SPEARS, BILLIE JOE

S209   Billie Joe Spears disco *in* Kountry Korral, X/2 (April 1977): 14 ((—))

SPECIALTY label

See also *Bibliography* Vol. 2, Jazz

S210   LEADBITTER, Mike, et al.: Specialty label singles listing: 1946–1964: 500 & 300 series. N. Weedon, England: Terance Courtney, n.d. 22 pp. ((3, 5))

S211   Specialty discography *in* Record Exchanger, No. 4 (August–September 1970): 18–19 ((—))

S212   Specialty listing *in* Rockville International, No. 94 (October 1974): bound in between p. 10 and 19 ((—))

SPECTOR, PHIL (record producer)

See also PHILLES label

S213   BEACH, Keith A.: Phil Spector discography *in* Goldmine, No. 55 (December 1980): 12–14 ((5))

S214   BETROCK, Alan: Spector-cles *in* The Rock Marketplace, No. 4 (December 1973): 18–22; discography p. 22, plus unnumbered leaf of addenda; addenda in No. 5 (April 1974): 34; No. 6 (July 1974): 38; No. 7 (October 1974): 43; No. 8 (December 1974): 42 [Includes Philles Records, Trey Records, the Teddy Bears, and other Spector productions and compositions] ((3, 5))

S215   CALLAHAN, Mike: The story of stereo rock and roll: Phil Spector—the pre-Philles years *in* Goldmine, No. 46 (March 1980): 141–142 ((—))

S216   Discography *in* FINNIS, Rob: The Phil Spector story. London: Rockon, 1975: 128–143 ((5))

S217   Listing of instrumental Spector discs *in* SMART, Peter: The "other" Phil Spector *in* Rumble, IV/1 (Spring 1977): 13–14 ((—))

S218   Discography *in* WILLIAMS, Richard: Out of his head: the sound of Phil Spector. London: Abacus, 1974: 140–151 ((5))

SPECTOR, RONNIE

S219   Ronnie Spector discography *in* Goldmine, No. 34 (March 1979): 13; additions in No. 36 (May 1979): 4 ((5))

S220   Trmmings: Ronnie Spector *in* The Rock Marketplace, No. 6 (July 1974): 19–20 ((5))

SPEDDING, CHRIS

S221   SCHULPS, Dave: This guitar for hire—Chris Spedding *in* Trouser Press, No. 19 (April–May 1977): 12–16; discography p. 16; addenda in No. 21 (September 1977): 36 (Includes Battered Ornaments, Sharks, solo and session work] ((5))

THE SPIDERS (musical group)

S222   GOLDBERG, Marv: The Spiders *in* Yesterday's Memories, III/3 (1977): 13 ((7))

SPORT label

S223   Sport label *in* Hot Buttered Soul, No. 31 (June 1974?): 7 ((3))

SPOT label

S224   TOPPING, Ray: Spot label listing (West Coast) *in* Shout, No. 63 (February 1971): [12] ((7))

SPRAGUE, CARL T.

S225   [Discography] *in* Disc Collector, I/4 (October–December 1951): ? ((—))

S226   WEIZE, Richard A.: Notes to: Carl T. Sprague, the first popular singing cowboy [Sound recording] Folk Variety LP FV 12001, 1973: Program note insert ((3, 6, 7))

SPRINGSTEEN, BRUCE

S227   Discography *in* GAMBACCINI, Peter: Bruce Springsteen. New York: Quick Fox, 1979: [125]–127 ((5))

S228   Discography *in* WHITESELL, Rick: Bruce Springsteen: greetings from Asbury Park *in* Goldmine, No. 22 (January 1978): 8–9 ((1, 5))

SQUARE DANCE MUSIC

S229 MYHR, Peter: Tips om square dans skivor *in* Kountry Korral, XIV/2 (1981): 31 ((—))

J. H. SQUIRE CELESTE OCTET

S230 The J. H. Squire Celeste Octet *in* Vintage Light Music, No. 16 (Autumn 1978): [9–12] ((—))

S231 THORNE, Roger: J. H. Squire Celeste Octet *in* Commodore, No. 5 (Spring 1972): 2 ((—))

THE SQUIRES (musical group)

S232 HINCKLEY, Dave: Don and Dewey . . . the Squires *in* Yesterday's Memories, III/2 (1977): 5 ((7))

STACKHOUSE, HOUSTON

S233 O'NEAL, Jim: Living Blues interview: Houston Stackhouse *in* Living Blues, No. 17 (Summer 1974): 13–17 ((—))

STAFFORD, TERRY

S234 Terry Stafford discography *in* Goldmine, No. 56 (January 1981): 23–24 ((5))

STAG label

S235 CUMMINGS, Tony, and Ray TOPPING: Stag label listing *in* Black Wax, No. 5 (June 1973): 7–9 ((3, 5))

STAINED GLASS (musical group)

S236 SHAW, Greg: Discography *in* Who Put the Bomp, No. 12 (Summer 1974): 29 ((—))

STAMPLEY, JOE

S237 Joe Stampley LP discography *in* Kountry Korral (No. 2, 1979): 24 ((—))

THE STANDELLS (musical group)

S238 DALLEY, Robert J.: The Standells discography *in* Goldmine, No. 60 (May 1981): 168 ((5))

S239 McDOWELL, Mike: Standells discography *in* Blitz, No. 39 (March–April 1981): 12 ((5))

S240 SHAW, Greg: Standells discography *in* Who Put the Bomp, No. 12 (Summer 1974): 7 ((—))

STANLEY, RALPH

S241 DEIJFEN, Lars: Ralph Stanley and the Clinch Mountain Boys LP-disco *in* Kountry Korral, XIV/1 (1981): 47–49 ((—))

STANLEY BROTHERS (musical group)

S242 [Discography] *in* Country News & Views, II/3 (January 1964): 12–19 ((3, 5, 7))

S243 [Discography] *in* Country Western Express, No. 22 (April 1959): ? ((—))

S244 [Discography] *in* Country Western Express, No. 21 [New series] (January 1967): 5–8 ((—))

S245 [Discography] *in* Disc Collector, No. 16 [n.d., 1961?] ? ((2, 3, 7))

S246 [Discography] *in* Disc Collector, No. 20 (n.d., 1965?]: ? ((2, 3, 7))

S247 PIETSCH, Reinhard: Stanley Brothers diskographie *in* Hillbilly, No. 51 (June 1977): 13–27 ((3, 6, 7))

S248 The Stanley Brothers—LP Disco *in* Kountry Korral, XIII/4 (1980): 35 ((—))

STANTON, BARRY

S249 DUFF, Colin, and Frank CAMPBELL: Barry Stanton discography *in* Big Beat of the 50's, No. 26 (February 1981): 7–8 ((—))

STARCHER, BUDDY

S250 WEIZE, Richard A.: Buddy Starcher diskographie *in* Hillbilly, No. 53 (December 1977): 18–22 ((3, 6, 7))

STAR-CLUB, HAMBURG

S251 Plattenverzeichnis *in* BECHMANN, Dieter: Star-Club. Reinbeck bei Hamburg: Rowholt, 1980: 264–265 ((5))

STAR-CLUB label

S252   Star-Club discography *in* Bomp!, No. 19 (October–November 1978): 26–27 ((5))

STARDALE label

S253   THOMPSON, Gary: Discography: The Starday [sic] label *in* Goldmine, No. 31 (December 1978): 11 ((1, 5))

STARDAY label

S254   BOOTHROYD, John: The Starday catalogue *in* Country & Western Spotlight, No. 7 (June 1976): 18–25 ((—))

S255   [Discography] *in* Disc Collector, No. 14 (August 1960) thru No. 16 (February 1961): ? ((—))

STARLIGHT, BILLY

S256   CRISP, David L.: Billy Starlight discography *in* Country & Western Spotlight, No. 8 (September 1976): 31–32 ((—))

THE STARLIGHTERS (musical group)

S257   LEE, Alan: [Discography] *in* Yesterday's Memories, II/4 (1976): 24 ((7))

STARR, EDWIN

S258   Edwin Starr discography *in* It Will Stand, No. 16 (c1980): 5 ((5))

STATESIDE label

See entry for TOP RANK label

STATUS QUO (musical group)

S259   Preserving the Status Quo *in* The Rock Marketplace, No. 4 (December 1973): 29–31; discography p. 31 [Includes the Spectres and Traffic Jam] ((5))

S260   ROBBINS, Ira: The pinkies that destroyed the world *in* Trans-Oceanic Trouser Press, II/3 (August 1975): 21–23 ((—))

S261   Discography *in* SHEARLAW, John: Status Quo. London: Sidgwick & Jackson, 1979: 149–151 ((7))

S262   Status Quo discography *in* Trouser Press Press, No. 3 (1973): 67; addenda in No. 19 (April–May 1977): 26 [Includes Spectres and Traffic Jam] ((5))

STEDEFORD, MARJORIE

S263   BARNES, Terry: Marjorie Stedeford, a disco-biography *in* Memory Lane, XIII (No. 50, Spring 1981): 16–18 ((—))

STEELE, TOMMY

S264   REFF, Morten: Diskographie *in* R-O-C-K (May 1981): 51–54 ((—))

STEELY DAN (musical group)

S265   RAY, Larry: Steely Dan discography *in* Goldmine, No. 62 (July 1981): 164–165; additions and corrections in No. 65 (October 1981): 17 ((5))

S266   Steely Dan discography *in* Down Beat, XLII (September 11, 1975): 15 ((—))

STEEMAN, STEPHANE

S267   JOIRIS, Jean-Claude: Discographie tres complete pour eventuels collectionneurs *in* his Encore des memoires. Brussels: Rossel, 1976: 207–210 ((5))

THE STEREOS (musical group)

S268   [[[Discography] *in* Soul Music (No. 31)]]

STERLING label

S269   WEIZE, Richard A., and Gerhard MORKE: Sterling label *in* Hillbilly, No. 49 (December 1976): 21 ((—))

STERNO label [England]

S270   [Discography] *in* Folk Style, No. 4 (February 1959): ? ((—))

STERNO label [U.S.]

S271   Sterno label *in* Record Research, No. 173–174 (June 1980): 14 ((3))

STEVENS, DODIE

S272   Discography *in* Goldmine, No. 30 (November 1978): 15 ((5))

STEVENS, ERNEST L.

S273   WILE, Ray: The Edison recordings of Ernest L. Stevens, piano *in* Record Research, No. 163-164 (May-June 1979): 10-11 ((3, 5))

S274   WILE, Ray: Edisonia: Ernest L. Stevens: the Quartet, the Dance Orchestra, and the nom-de-plume, Franz Falkenburg *in* Record Research, No. 171-172 (March 1980): 14, 24 ((7))

S275   WILE, Ray: Edisonia: Ernest L. Stevens Trio *in* Record Research, No. 165-66 (August 1979): 9 ((7))

STEWART, AL

S276   Discography *in* Trans-Oceanic Trouser Press, II/6 (February-March 1976): 15 ((5))

STEWART, BILLY

S277   PRUTER, Robert: Billy Stewart discography *in* It Will Stand, No. 17-18 (c1980-81): 20 ((5, 6a))

STEWART, DAVE

S278   GALLANTER, Bruce: Do the egg with Dave Stewart! *in* Trouser Press, No. 19 (April-May 1977): 17-18; discography p. 18; addenda in No. 21 (September 1977): 36 [Includes Uriel, Egg, and Hatfield and the North] ((5))

STEWART, JOHN

S279   BLAKE, Benjamin S.: John Stewart discography *in* Goldmine, No. 35 (April 1979): 29 ((5))

S280   WESTFALL, Bob: Discography *in* SMG, III/6 (June-July 1973): 4 ((—))

STEWART, ROD
See also FACES (musical group)

S281   Rod Stewart—a discography *in* BURTON, Peter: Rod Stewart: a life on the town. London: New English Library, 1977: 91-93 ((5))

S282   Rod Stewart, Steampacket & the Shotgun Express *in* The Rock Marketplace, No. 7 (October 1974): 37 [Pre-1968 recordings only] ((5))

STIFF label

S283   FAULL, Trev: The Stiff story, part 1/ Stiff discography: August 1976-December 1977 *in* Outlet, No. 1 (c1978): 9-18; the continuing saga of a record company called Stiff, part 2 in No. 2 (c1978): 11-13; continually updated in subsequent issues ((—))

S284   Stiff discography *in* Record World presents Stiff records ([20] pp.) *in* Record World, XXXV (No. 1642, December 23, 1978): 14 [As a specially numbered supplement; p. 64 of regular issue] ((—))

S285   Stiff Records *in* Bomp!, No. 20 (January 1979): 19 ((5))

STILLS, STEPHEN

S286   Discografia *in* discoteca Hifi, No. 201 (December 1979): 40-42 ((2, 5))

STOCKARD, OCIE, AND THE WANDERERS (musical group)

S287   [Discography] *in* Record Research, No. 65 (December 1964): ? ((2, 3, 7))

S288   HEALY, R.: [Discography] *in* Disc Collector, No. 18 [n.d.]: ? ((2, 3, 7))

STONE, LEW

S289   BARTER, Roy: Lew Stone *in* Commodore, No. 2 (Summer 1971): 13 + ((—))

S290   [Discography] *in* TRODD, Kenith: Lew Stone: a career in music. London: Joyce Stone, 1971: Recorded music p. 47; discography pp. 48-96; reissues on microgroove pp. 117-119; recorded programmes & interviews with Lew Stone pp. 120-122 ((1, 3, 6, 7))

STONEMAN, ERNEST V.

S291   COHEN, Norm, and Gene EARLE: An Ernest V. Stoneman discography *in* JEMF Quarterly, XVI (No. 57, Spring 1980): 36–49 ((2, 3, 4, 6, 7))

S292 [Discography] *in* Record Research, No. 23 (June–July 1959): ? [Edison records only] ((3, 7))

S293 Ernest V. Stoneman discography *in* JEMF Newsletter, III/1 (No. 7, September 1967): 23–28; III/2 (No. 8, December 1967): 46–53; additions and corrections in IV/1 (No. 9, March 1968): 25–27 ((3, 4, 6, 7))

S294 WILE, Ray: The Edison records of Ernest V. Stoneman *in* Record Research, No. 110 (May 1971): 5 ((3, 7))

THE STONEMANS (musical group)

S295 The Stonemans LP's *in* Kountry Korral, No. 4 (1969): 7–8 ((—))

STONEWAY label

S296 [[Discography] *in* Country & Western Spotlight, No. 2 (March 1975)]]

THE STOOGES (AND IGGY POP)

S297 McDOWELL, Mike, and Jim HEDDLE: The Stooges' discography *in* Ballroom Blitz, No. 22 (September 1977): 27 ((5))

STOVALL, VERN

S298 Vern Stovall: singel och Lp disco *in* Kountry Korral, XIV/1 (1981): 15 ((—))

STRANGE, TOMMY

S299 RUSSELL, Wayne: Tommy Strange *in* New Kommotion, No. 15 (Spring 1977): 15 ((3))

THE STRANGERS (musical group)

S300 GOLDBERG, Marv, and Mike REDMOND: The Strangers and the King label *in* Yesterday's Memories, I/3 (1975): 25 ((3, 7))

S301 MOHR, Kurt: Strangers discography *in* Shout, No. 93 (February 1974): 10 ((2, 3, 6, 7))

STRATTON, EUGENE

S302 Eugene Stratton discography *in* Music Hall, No. 12 (April 1980): 116 ((3, 7))

STRAWBS (musical group)

S303 GILBERT, Jerry: Discography *in* Zig Zag, VI/2 (1975): 40 ((—))

S304 KRIEGER, Rick, and Steve LEMANSKY: Strawbs *in* Trans-Oceanic Trouser Press, II/1 (February–March 1975): 20–22, 36 ((—))

STRIPLING BROTHERS

S305 [COHEN, Norm]: Stripling Brothers (Charles and Ira) *in* Devil's Box, No. 18 (September 1972): 15–18 ((3, 7)) [Reprinted from JEMF Newsletter]

S306 EARLE, Eugene, and Graham WICKHAM: Stripling Brothers discography *in* JEMF Newsletter, IV/1 (No. 9, March 1968): 21–22; additions in IV/2 (No. 10, June 1968): 83 ((3, 6, 7))

STUART, AMBROSE

S307 "Uncle Am" Stuart discography *in* JEMF Newsletter, IV/2 (No. 10, June 1968): 43–44 ((3))

STUDIO ONE label

S308 FAULL, Trev: Studio One: 2000 series, 1967 *in* Outlet, No. 16 (January 1980): 34–37 ((—))

SUE label [England]

S309 [[PELLETIER, Paul M.: Sue complete singles, E.P.'s & LP's: 1963–1968. London: Record Information Services. (Publication No. 10)]]

S310 WILSON, Jim, and Barry LAZELL: U.K. Sue label listing *in* SMG, V/1 (October–December 1975): 6–13; additions in V/2 (Spring 1976): 24; V/3 (Summer 1976): 17 ((5))

SULLIVAN, EDDIE

S311 PRUTER, Robert: Eddie Sullivan discography *in* Goldmine, No. 59 (April 1981): 19 ((5))

SULLIVAN, NIKI

S312 Niki Sullivan discography *in* Goldmine, No. 28 (September 1978): 11
((1))

SUMAC, YMA

S313 LEONARD, Maurice: The legendary
Sumac *in* Records and Recording,
XXIII/2 (No. 266, November 1979):
32-35 ((—))

SUMMER, DONNA

S314 Discographie *in* HOPPE, Ulrich:
Donna Summer. Munich: Heyne,
1980: 159 ((—))

SUMMERS, GENE

S315 Gene Summers *in* New Kommotion,
No. 15 (Spring 1977): 33; addenda in
No. 16 (Summer 1977): 42 and No. 22
(1979): 66 ((2, 3, 7))

S316 Gene Summers discography *in* Rock
and Roll International Magazine
(Dutch), No. 1 (September 1975): 7
((5))

SUN, JOE

S317 DAHMEN, Norbert: Joe Sun discography *in* Hillbilly, No. 61 (January
1980): 26-27 ((7))

SUN label

See also *Bibliography* Vol. 2, Jazz

S318 BECKER, Robert J.: Sun Records *in*
Record Exchanger, III/2 (No. 13
[February 1973]): 13-14 ((—))

S319 Appendices *in* ESCOTT, Colin:
Catalyst: the Sun Records story.
London: Aquarius Books, 1975:
117-152 ((—))

S320 ESCOTT, Colin, and Martin HAW-
KINS: The complete Sun label session
files. Bexhill-on-Sea, East Sussex:
Swift Record Distributors, 1978. 64
pp. ((1, 2, 3, 6, 7))

S321 Discographies *in* ESCOTT, Colin, and
Martin HAWKINS: Sun Records: a
brief history of the legendary label.
London: Quick Fox, 1980: 159-176
((3))

S322 Sun Record Company discography *in*
Mean Mountain Music, IV/1 (1979):
15-21 ((3)) [Includes numerical listings of Sun, Flip, and Sam C. Phillips
International labels]

SUNBEAM label

S323 Discography *in* Paul's Record Magazine, IV/2 (No. 13-14): 4; additions
and corrections in No. 15 (January-
February 1977): 4 ((—))

THE SUNNYSIDERS (musical group)

S324 VULPUS, Dieter: [Discography] *in*
Country Corner, No. 29 (August
1971): 46-47 ((—))

SUNRISE label

S325 CHRISTIE, K., and E. WADIN:
[Discography] *in* Disc Collector, No.
14 (August 1960) thru No. 18 (August
1961): various paginations ((—))

SUPER label

S326 Rhode Island Rock!?! *in* The Rock
Marketplace, No. 7 (October 1974): 30
((—))

SUPERTONE label

S327 [Discography, 2000 series] *in* Disc Collector, II/1 (January 1952) and II/2
(April 1952): ? ((—))

S328 HEARNE, Will Roy: [Discography,
9000 series] *in* Disc Collector, No. 15
(November 1960) thru No. 17 (May
1961): ? ((—))

THE SUPREMES (musical group) [male]

S329 ARDIT, Dave, and Steve PETRYS-
ZYN: Discography *in* Bim Bam
Boom, II/3 (No. 11, 1973): 18 ((—))

THE SUPREMES (musical group)
[not Motown group]

S330 MOONOOGIAN, George, and Jim
COTE: Supremes discography *in*
Record Exchanger, IV/1 (No. 17): 20
((—))

THE SURFARIS (musical group)

S331 DALLEY, Robert J.: Surfaris discography *in* Goldmine, No. 51 (August 1980): 23; additions and corrections in No. 64 (September 1981): 185 ((—))

SUTCH, SCREAMIN' LORD (DAVID SUTCH)

S332 HOLLIE, Jim: Screamin' Lord Sutch; British disco *in* Whole Lotta Rockin', No. 18 (1976): 16 ((5))

S333 Screamin' Lord Sutch *in* Gorilla Beat, No. 14 (1982): 4–13; discography pp. 10–13 ((5))

SUTHERLAND BROTHERS BAND AND QUIVER

S334 SCHULPS, Dave: Tales from the Quiverlands *in* Trouser Press, No. 14 (June–July 1976): 19–21; discography p. 21 [Includes the groups on their own and Tim Renwick sessions] ((—))

SUTTON, RANDOLPH

S335 ALLCORN, Roy, and Jim HAYES: Randolph Sutton discography *in* Gunn Report, No. 39 (April–May 1973): [30]–34 ((3))

THE SWALLOWS (musical group)

S336 GOLDBERG, Marv, and Mike REDMOND: The Swallows *in* Yesterday's Memories, I/4 (1975): [11] ((7))

SWAN label

S337 BEZANKER, Paul: Swan Records *in* Paul's Record Magazine, No. 15 (January–February 1977): 19–25, 38 ((4))

THE SWEET (musical group)

S338 FLEURY, Joseph: Will success spoil the Sweet? *in* The Rock Marketplace, No. 2 (July 1973): 3–6; discography p. 6; addendum in No. 5 (April 1974): 34 ((5))

THE SWEET INSPIRATIONS (musical group)

S339 Sweet Inspirations/disco *in* Soul Bag, XII (No. 85, October–November 1981): 15–17 ((2, 3, 7))

SWIFT JEWEL COWBOYS (musical group)

S340 RUSSELL, Tony: Chuck wagon swing: the story of the Swift Jewel Cowboys *in* Old Time Music, No. 32 (Spring 1979): 5–15; discography p. 10 ((3, 7))

THE SWINGING BLUE JEANS (musical group)

S341 SCHACHT, Janis: Merseybeat revisited: part 2 *in* The Rock Marketplace, No. 10 (June 1975): 48–49 [Includes group personnel, 1958–1974] ((5))

SWINGTIME label

S342 PEARLIN, Victor: Swingtime Records discography *in* Paul's Record Magazine (No. 17–18): 51–55 ((3, 4))

SYLVA, MARGUERITE

S343 STONE, Robert B.: Neglected Edison Diamond Disc artists: IV, Marguerite Sylva *in* New Amberola Graphic, VIII/4 (No. 32, Spring 1980): 8–9, 7 [sic] ((5))

S344 WILE, Raymond R.: The Edison recordings of Marguerite Sylva *in* New Amberola Graphic, IX/2 (No. 34, Fall 1980): 4–5 ((7))

SYLVESTRE, ANNE

S345 EVANS, Colin: Barbara and Anne Sylvestre *in* Recorded Sound, No. 79 (January 1981): 11–22 ((—))

SYMBOL label

S346 MOHR, Kurt: Symbol label listing *in* Shout, No. 104 (August 1975): 1–3 ((3, 5))

SYNCOPATERS (musical group)

S347 GOLDBERG, Marv: The Syncopaters—discography *in* Goldmine, No. 49 (June 1980): 175 ((—))

SYNDICATE OF SOUND (musical group)

S348 SHAW, Greg: Discography *in* Who Put the Bomp, No. 12 (Summer 1974): 29 ((—))

T. REX
See BOLAN, MARC

TALMY, SHEL

T1 BETROCK, Alan: The Shel Talmy story *in* The Rock Marketplace, No. 8 (December 1974): 18–21, 29; discography p. 29; addenda on p. 28 and in No. 9 (March 1975): 46; No. 10 (June 1975): 50 ((5))

T2 HOGG, Brian: Shel Talmy & Planet *in* Bam Balam, No. 11 (June 1980): 12–17; addenda in No. 12 (November 1980): 39 and No. 14 (September 1982): 14 ((5))

TAMLA label
See also MOTOWN label

T3 CALTA, Gary: Tamla records *in* Goldmine, No. 16 (May–June 1977): 11 ((—))

TAMLA-MOTOWN label [England]

T4 PELLETIER, P. M.: Tamla-Motown, Part 1: 1959 to 1970. London: Record Information Services, 1976. 41 pp. (Publication No. 7) Part Two: 1971–1975. London: Record Information Services, 1977. 41 pp. (Publication No. 13) ((5))

TANGERINE DREAM (musical group)

T5 [Discography] *in* Zig Zag, No. 44 (August 1974): 43 ((5))

TANGO (DANCE)

T6 ETCHEGARAY, Natalio P.: Guia minima para una discografia del tango evolucionista (escuela decareana) *in* Buenos Aires Tango y los demas, No. 20 (June 1978): 13–20 ((3,7))

T7 Discographie *in* FLEOUTER, Claude: Le tango de Buenos Aires. Paris: Lattes, 1979: 127–[128] ((—))

TARLTON, JIMMIE
See listing for DARBY, TOM

TATE, HOWARD

T8 HUGHES, Rob: Howard Tate discography *in* Shout, No. 105 (October–November 1975): 2–3; additions and corrections in No. 108 (April–May 1976): 20–21 ((2, 3, 5, 6, 7))

TAYLOR, CARMEN

T9 MOHR, Kurt: Carmen Taylor discography *in* Shout, No. 91 (December 1973): 9–10 ((2, 3, 7))

TAYLOR, HOUND DOG
See also *Bibliography* Vol. 2, Jazz

T10 DIEUDONRE, Jean-Claude: Discographie *in* Big Beat, No. 16 (June 1978): 29 ((2, 7))

TAYLOR, VERNON

T11 RUSSELL, Wayne: Vernon Taylor *in* New Kommotion, No. 15 (Spring 1977): 14 ((2, 3, 7))

TAYLOR, VINCE

T12 LABAT, Marc: Vince Taylor discography *in* Kicks, No. 2 (Winter 1979): 47–48 ((5))

TEDDY & THE TWILIGHTS
(musical group)

T13 HORNER, Charlie, and Steve APPLEBAUM: Discography *in* Yesterday's Memories, III/1 (No. 9, 1976): 20–23 ((5))

TEE GEE label

T14 [Discography] *in* Bim Bam Boom, No. 8 (December 1972): [24] ((—))

TEEM Label

T15 [[[Discography] *in* Soul Music (No. 31)]]

TEEN BEAT label

T16   Teen Beat EP's *in* Gorilla Beat, No. 6
      (1980): 23 ((—))

THE TEEN QUEENS (musical group)

T17   MOHR, Kurt: Teen Queens discog-
      raphy *in* Shout, No. 34 (October
      1968): [9] ((2, 3, 7))

TEENAGE HEAD (musical group)

T18   MARS, John: Teenage Head discog-
      raphy *in* Blitz, No. 42 (March–April
      1982): 42 ((2, 5))

THE TEENAGERS (musical group)

T19   GROIA, Phil: The Teenagers *in* Bim
      Bam Boom, II/6 (No. 12, 1974):
      [17]–18 ((—))

T20   SICURELLA, Joe: [Discography] *in*
      Big Town Review, I/3 (July–August
      1972): 14–15 ((—))

THE TEENCHORDS (musical group)

T21   SICURELLA, Joe: [Discography] *in*
      Big Town Review, I/3 (July–August
      1972): 14 ((3))

TELEFUNKEN label
      See also *Bibliography* Vol. 2, Jazz

T22   ENGLUND, Bjorn: Telefunken.
      Stockholm: Kungliga Biblioteket,
      1975. 46 l. ((3, 4, 5, 6, 7)) (National-
      fonotekets diskografier, 17)

TELEVISION PROGRAMS—THEMES

T23   GELFAND, Steve: Classified dis-
      cography of 45 rpm television theme
      recordings *in* Goldmine, No. 40 (Sep-
      tember 1979): 25A–26A ((—))

THE TEMPTATIONS (musical group)

T24   SBARBORI, Jack: Discography *in*
      Goldmine, No. 53 (October 1980):
      15–16 ((3, 5))

10cc (musical group)
      See also GOULDMAN, GRAHAM

T25   [BETROCK, Alan]: Discography *in*
      Zig Zag, No. 44 (August 1974): 17–18
      ((5)) [Reprinted from Rock Market-
      place, No. 5]

T26   BETROCK, Alan: 10cc's please! *in*
      The Rock Marketplace, No. 5 (April
      1974): 3–7; discography pp. 7 and 35;
      addenda in No. 6 (July 1974): 38; No.
      10 (June 1975): 50 [Includes Hotlegs,
      the Mockingbirds, the Mindbenders
      (without Wayne Fontana), and Gra-
      ham Gouldman as solo performer,
      writer, and producer] ((5))

T27   THOM, Mike: 10cc discography *in*
      Full Blast, I/1 (Winter 1979): 16–30
      ((7))

TENNESSEE RAMBLERS (musical group)

T28   WOLFE, Charles K.: Tennessee Ram-
      blers: ramblin' on *in* Old Time Music,
      No. 13 (Summer 1974): 5–12 ((3, 6,
      7))

**THE TENNEVA RAMBLERS
(musical group)**

T29   WEIZE, Richard A.: Sessions *in*
      Country Corner, No. 34 (April 1973):
      25 ((2, 3, 6, 7))

TERRY, DEWEY

T30   HESS, Norbert: Don Harris & Dewey
      Terry discography *in* Shout, No. 102
      (April 1975): 5–10 ((2, 3, 6, 7))

TETRA label

T31   BEZANKER, Paul: Tetra label *in*
      Paul's Record Magazine, III/2 (Feb-
      ruary 1976): 22 ((3, 4))

TEX, JOE
      See also *Bibliography* Vol. 2, Jazz

T32   MOHR, Kurt: Joe Tex discography *in*
      Shout, No. 54 (April 1970): [6–10];
      No. 55 (May 1970): [1–4]; additions
      and corrections in No. 56 (June 1970):
      [6] ((2, 3, 6, 7))

THEM (musical group)
      See also MORRISON, VAN

T33   BETROCK, Alan: Them *in* Trans-
      Oceanic Trouser Press, II/5 (Novem-
      ber–December 1975): 8–10 ((5))

T34 BETROCK, Alan: Them discography *in* Jamz, No. 5 (c1972): 67 ((5))

T35 HOGG, Brian: Them *in* Bam Balam, No. 12 (November 1980): 26–29; discography pp. 28–29 ((5))

THIN LIZZY (musical group)

T36 Thin Lizzy discography *in* Trouser Press, No. 19 (April–May 1977): 7; addenda in No. 21 (September 1977): 36 ((5))

13th FLOOR ELEVATORS (musical group)

T37 Discography *in* HOGG, Brian: Thru the rhythm: Texas rock 'n' roll *in* Bam Balam, No. 10 (November 1979): 5–6 ((—))

THOMAS, B. J.

T38 PRESLEY, Norm: B. J. Thomas discography *in* Goldmine, No. 67 (December 1981): 17 ((—))

THOMAS, JAMO

T39 MOHR, Kurt: Jamo Thomas discography *in* Shout, No. 72 (December 1971): [4–5] ((2, 3, 7))

THOMAS, KID

T40 Discographie Kid Thomas *in* Big Beat, No. 13 [n.d.]: 19 ((2, 7))

THOMAS label

T41 WILSON, Jim, and Bob FOSTER: Thomas label listing *in* Shout, No. 89 (September 1973): [7–8] ((3))

THOMPSON, ERNEST

T42 KUNSTADT, Len, and B. COLTON: [Discography] *in* Record Research, No. 56 (November 1963): ?; additions in No. 58: ? ((2, 3, 7))

THOMPSON, HANK

T43 [Discography] *in* Country Western Spotlight, No. 22 (April–June 1958): ? ((—))

T44 MORKE, Gerhard, and E. Reinald SCHUMANN: Hank Thompson diskographie *in* Hillbilly, No. 61 (January 1980): 13–23 ((1, 3))

THOMPSON, HAYDEN

T45 THOMPSON, Gary: Hayden Thompson discography *in* Goldmine, No. 41 (October 1979): 16 ((5))

THOMPSON, UNCLE JIMMIE

T46 [Discography] *in* Record Research, No. 80 (November 1966): ?; additions in No. 81: ? ((2, 3, 7))

THOMS, SHIRLEY

T47 [Discography] *in* Country Western Spotlight, No. 37 (March 1962): ?; additions in No. 81: ? ((2, 3, 7))

THORNDIKE PICKLE DISH CHOIR (musical group)

T48 SILVERSTONE, Dean: Complete discography of Thorndike Pickle Dish Choir *in* Goldmine, No. 54 (November 1980): 10 ((5))

THE THRASHERS (musical group)

T49 MOHR, Kurt: Charmers/Thrashers discography *in* Shout, No. 87 (July 1973): [3–4] ((2, 3, 7))

THE THREE CHUCKLES (musical group)

T50 GOLLENDER, Walt: Chuckles discography *in* Record Exchanger, III/2 (No. 13 [Fall 1973]): [21] ((—))

THE THREE FLAMES (musical group)

T51 GRENDYSA, Peter: The Three Flames discography *in* Goldmine, No. 47 (April 1980): 17 ((3, 5, 7))

THE THREE FRIENDS (musical group)

T52 BERGER, Ken, and Glenn SLADE: The Three Friends *in* Record Exchanger, IV/5 (No. 21): 23–24 ((5))

THREE SHARPS AND A FLAT
(musical group)

T53 WHITESELL, Rick: The Three
Sharps and a Flat discography *in*
Goldmine, No. 46 (March 1980): 11
((3, 5, 7))

THE THREE TOBACCO TAGS
(musical group)

T54 EDWARDS, J.: [Discography] *in*
Country Western Spotlight, No. 18
(April–June 1957): ? ((—))

T55 EDWARDS, J.: [Discography] *in*
Country Western Spotlight (Special
issue, September 1962): ? ((—))

THE THUNDERBIRDS (musical group)

T56 LEE, Kevin: The local scene, starring
the Thunderbirds *in* Big Beat of the
50's, No. 13 (August 1977): 29–32
((—))

THE TIDAL WAVES (musical group)

T57 The Tidal Waves discography *in*
Ballroom Blitz!, No. 25 (March 1978):
[29] ((5))

TIEKEN, FREDDIE

T58 BAKER, Cary: Freddie Tieken discography *in* Goldmine, No. 62 (July
1981): 16 ((5))

TILLOTSON, JOHNNY

T59 U.S. Cadence/U.K. London discography *in* SMG, IV/11 (June 1975):
10–12 ((7))

TIME label

T60 Discography *in* Paul's Record Magazine, IV/2 (No. 13–14): 54–55 ((—))

TIMELY label

T61 TISOVEC, Tony: Timely label listing
in Shout, No. 63 (February 1971):
[1–2]; additions and corrections in No.
65 (April 1971): [2] ((3))

TIMELY TUNES label

T62 HEALY, Bob: [Discography] *in* Disc
Collector, No. 15 (November 1960)
and No. 16 (February 1961): ? ((—))

T63 WADIN, Eric: [Discography] *in*
Country Western Spotlight, No. 42
(June 1963): ? ((—))

TIMES SQUARE label

T64 FITZGERALD, Dave, and Nick
LATZONI: Times Square discography
in Record Exchanger, V/4 (No. 26,
1978): 16–17 ((—))

TINY TIM

T65 [Discography] *in* Record Finder, II/12
(March 1981): 5 ((—))

T66 TORTELLI, Joseph: Tiny Tim album
discography *in* Goldmine, No. 65 (October 1981): 191 ((—))

TIOMKIN, DIMITRI

T67 LYNCH, Richard C.: Dimitri
Tiomkin *in* Kastlemusik Monthly Bulletin, VII/2 (February 1982): 1, 8–9
((5))

T68 PUGLIESE, Roberto: Filmodiscog-
rafia essenziale di Dimitri Tiomkin *in*
Discoteca hi fi, No. 202–203 (January–
February 1981): [38]–40 ((—))

THE TITANS (musical group)

T69 GOLDBERG, Marv: The Titans *in*
Yesterday's Memories, III/2 (1977): 22
((77))

TODDLIN' TOWN label

T70 MOHR, Kurt: Toddlin' Town label
list *in* Shout, No. 86 (June 1973):
[5–7]; additions and corrections in No.
92 (January 1974): 9 ((3))

THE TOKENS (musical group)

T71 ENGEL, Ed: Both sides now *in* Bim
Bam Boom, III/1 (No. 13, August–
September 1974): 19 ((—))

T72 WOODWARD, Rex: Tokens discography *in* Goldmine, No. 65 (October
1981): 24 ((5))

TOLLIE label

T73 SHAW, Greg: Tollie discography *in* Who Put the Bomp, No. 12 (Summer 1974): 20 ((—))

TOMORROW (musical group)

T74 BETROCK, Alan: [Discography] *in* Jamz, No. 2 (October 1971): 16; addenda in No. 5 (c1972): 43 ((—))

T75 KLITSCH, Hans Jurgen: 4 jolly little dwarfs and the band that was Tomorrow *in* Gorilla Beat, No. 15 (1982): 10–16; discography p. 16 ((5)) [Includes the In Crowd, Four Plus One, and Keith West solo]

T76 Tomorrow *in* Bam Balam, No. 2 (June 1975): 9–11; addenda in No. 5 (February 1977): 16 ((—)) [Includes Four Plus One, the In Crowd, and Keith West]

T77 Tomorrow *in* The Rock Marketplace, No. 7 (October 1974): 22 [Includes Four Plus One, the In Crowd, Keith West, and Mark Wirtz] ((5))

TOMPALL & THE GLASER BROTHERS (musical group)

T78 MATTSSON, Soren: Tompall & the Glaser Brothers LP'n *in* Kountry Korral, XIII/4 (1980): 22–25 ((—))

TON STEIN SCHERBEN (musical group)

T79 KORBIK, Mike: Anarchistic rock music from the German underground *in* Gorilla Beat, No. 6 (1980): 18–21; discography pp. 20–21 ((5))

THE TONICS (musical group)

T80 Whisky [sic] & Tonics *in* Gorilla Beat, No. 10 (1981): 25–35; discography pp. 29–35 ((5)) [Includes the Ravers]

TOOMEY, WELBY

T81 Discography of recordings by Welby Toomey *in* JEMF Quarterly, V/2 (No. 14, Summer 1969): 66–67; additions and corrections in VI/2 (No. 18, Summer 1970): 90 ((2, 3, 6, 7))

TOP RANK label

T82 [[PELLETIER, Paul M.: Top Rank/Stateside/Triumph/Palette complete singles & EP's: 1959–1974. London: Record Information Services. (Publication No. 5)]]

T83 [[PELLETIER, Paul M.: Top Rank/Stateside complete LP's: 1959–1974. London: Record Information Services. (Publication No. 6)]]

TORCH, SIDNEY

T84 UPTON, Stuart: Sidney Torch and his Orchestra *in* Commodore, No. 14 (Summer 1974): 2 +; No. 15 (Autumn 1974): 11 + ((—))

THE TORNADOS (musical group)

T85 BLAIR, John: Discography *in* Goldmine, No. 44 (January 1980): 129 ((5))

T86 FAULL, Trev: [Tornados discography] *in* Instrumental Obscurities Unlimited, No. 14–15 (March 1977): 17–20 ((5)) [Includes solo and backing work]

T87 NEHLS, Rudiger: The (Hollywood) Tornados *in* Rocking Regards, No. 19 (March 1981): 13 ((—))

TORONTO BAND (musical group)

T88 Discography *in* BERGMEIER, H.J.P.: The Toronto Band: Dave Caplan's Toronto Band, New York, Dave Caplan's Toronto Band, from Canada. Johannesburg, South Africa: H.J.P. Bergmeier, 1979.

TOURS, FRANK

T89 The Plaza Theatre Orchestra conducted by Frank Tours from the Plaza Theatre, London *in* Commodore, No. 1 (Spring 1971): 5 + ((—))

TOWER OF POWER (musical group)

T90 Selected Tower of Power discography *in* Down Beat, XLVII (February 1980): 23 ((—))

THE TOYS (musical group)

T91   INGRAM, George A.: Toys discography *in* SMG, V/2 (Spring 1976): 23–24 ((—))

TRAFFIC (musical group)

T92   Traffic discography *in* Down Beat, XLII (January 30, 1975): 14 ((—))

TRAMMELL, BOBBY LEE

T93   WESTFALL, Bob: A discography of one of the wildmen of rock and roll *in* Kommotion, No. 4 (Winter 1974): 16–17; addenda in No. 9 (Spring–Summer 1975): 4 and No. 10–11 (Winter 1975–76): 26 ((5))

THE TRENIERS (musical group)

T94   BRADY, Barry: Treniers discography *in* The Big Beat of the 50's, No. 21 (August 1979): 7–11 ((—))

T95   BRADY, Barry: Treniers discography *in* Crazy Music, No. 11 (December 1977): 42–44 ((—))

TRIP label

T96   HOLLIE, Jon: Trip label listing *in* SMG, III/2 (October–November 1972): 2–4 [A reissue label. Original label of issue is noted] ((—))

TRI-PHI label

T97   CALTA, Gary: Tri-Phi *in* Goldmine, No. 30 (November 1978): 9 ((—))

T98   TOPPING, Ray: Tri-Phi label listing *in* Shout, No. 75 (March 1972): [6–7] ((3))

TRIUMPH label

See entry for TOP RANK label

THE TROGGS (musical group)

T99   Discography *in* Who Put the Bomp, No. 8 (Fall–Winter 1971): 84; addenda in No. 9 (Spring 1972): 59 ((—))

T100   HOGG, Brian: The Troggs *in* Bam Balam, No. 7 (c1978): 11–15; discography pp. 12–15; addenda in No. 12

(November 1980): 39 ((5)) [Includes solo recordings]

T101   RICHARD, Mike: The Troggs discography *in* Goldmine, No. 50 (July 1980): 23–24 ((5))

T102   ROBBINS, Ira, and Dave SCHULPS: The Troggs—banned again *in* Trans-Oceanic Trouser Press, II/4 (September–October 1975): 19–21 ((—))

T103   SHAW, Greg: Discography *in* The Troggs: the vintage years. [Sound recording] Sire SASH-3714-2, 1976. ((5))

T104   Trogglodynamites *in* Gorilla Beat, No. 6 (1980): 24–33; discography pp. 28–33; addenda in No. 7 (1980): 17; No. 8 (1980): 46–47; and No. 13 (1982): 71 ((5)) [Includes solo recordings by band members]

T105   Troggs discography *in* Trouser Press, No. 3 (1976): 68; addenda in No. 19 (April–May 1977): 26 [Includes solo recordings by Reg Presley, Ronnie Boyd, and Chris Britton] ((5))

TRUMPET label

T106   FAULL, Trev: Trumpet label full discography: 1951–1956 *in* Outlet, No. 26 (July 1982): 5–6 ((—))

T107   STROLPER, Darryl: Trumpet discography *in* Goldmine, No. 44 (January 1980): 127 ((1))

THE TRU-TONES (musical group)

T108   LEE, Alan: [Discography] *in* Yesterday's Memories, II/4 (1976): 24 ((7))

TUBB, CARRIE

T109   WATTS, Len: Carrie Tub *in* The Hillandale News, No. 93 (December 1976): 59–62 ((5))

TUBB, ERNEST

T110   BARTHEL, Norma: Ernest Tubb discography (1936–1969) Roland, Okla., 1970. 36 pp. ((—))

T111   [Discography] *in* Disc Collector, No. 10–11 [n.d.]: ? ((—))

TUCKER, TANYA

T112   Tanya Tucker Diskographie *in*
GLODEK, Bernd: Tanya Tucker: ein
Phanomen *in* Country Corner (January 1979): 12 ((—))

THE TUMBLEWEEDS (musical group)

T113   [Discography] *in* Country Western
Spotlight, No. 22 (April–June 1958): ?
((—))

THE TUNE WRANGLERS (musical group)

T114   HEALY, B., and G. WHITE: [Discography] *in* Record Research, No. 69
(July 1965): 5; additions in No. 78: ?
((2, 3, 7))

TURA, WILL

T115   Mijn volledige diskographie *in* his Will
Tura: mijn prive fotoalbum. Brussels:
Hoste, 1977: 2 unnumbered pages
((5))

TURBO label

T116   CUMMINGS, Tony, and Ray TOPPING: Turbo listing *in* Black Wax,
No. 6 (July 1973): 4–5 ((3, 5))

THE TURKS (musical group)

T117   GOLDBERG, Marv, and Dave
HINCKLEY: The Turks *in* Yesterday's Memories, III/2 (1977): 18
((7))

TURNER, TITUS

T118   [[[Discography] *in* Soul Music (No.
30)]]

THE TURTLES (musical group)

T119   HOGG, Brian: The Turtles *in* Bam
Balam, No. 9 (July 1979): 14–20; discography pp. 17–20; addenda in No.
12 (November 1980): 39 ((5))

THE TWEEDS (musical group)

T120   DUFFEY, Jim: Tweeds discography *in*
Goldmine, No. 51 (August 1980): 163
((—))

THE TWILIGHTS (musical group)

T121   HORNER, Charlie, and Steve
APPLEBAUM: Teddy and the Twilights *in* Yesterday's Memories, III/1
(No. 9, 1976): 23 ((7))

T122   MOHR, Kurt: Twilights discography
in Shout, No. 88 (August 1973): [4]
((2, 3, 5, 7))

TWILLEY, DWIGHT

T123   HOGG, Brian: Dwight Twilley Band
in Bam Balam, No. 5 (February 1977):
10–11 ((2, 5))

T124   THOM, Mike: Dwight Twilley Band
discography *in* Full Blast, I/1 (Winter
1979): 31–34 ((7))

THE TWIST (dance step)

T125   The Twist on wax: an era preserved *in*
Nostalgia World, No. 3 (March 1979):
13 ((—))

TWITTY, CONWAY

T126   Conway Twitty disco *in* Kountry Korral, IX/6 (December 1976): 23–24
((5)); X/2 (April 1977): 10 ((—))

T127   Conway Twitty LP discography *in*
Kountry Korral (No. 2, 1979): 29
((—))

T128   Discography *in* Billboard, XC/19
(May 13, 1978): CT-12 ((5))

T129   STRUBING, Hauke: MCA [Decca]
disco *in* Country Corner, No. 48 (February 1976): [46]; No. 50 (July 1976):
37; No. 51 (October 1976): [46–47]
((3, 5, 7))

T130   THOMPSON, Gary: Discography
(through 1962) *in* Goldmine, No. 27
(January–April 1978): 15 ((5))

T131   WOUNLUND, Jorn: Conway Twitty
on wax *in* Rockville International, No.
95 (November–December 1974): 9–10,
12–15 ((5))

THE TWO BLACK CROWS
(musical group)

T132   HAYES, Jim: George Moran and
Charles Mack; the Two Black Crows
in Gunn Report, No. 42 (October–
November 1973): [32] ((3, 6, 7))

TYLER, T. TEXAS

T133 [Discography] *in* Disc Collector, III/1 (January–March 1953): ? ((—))

TYRANNOSAURUS REX
See BOLAN, MARC

THE UGLY DUCKLINGS (musical group)

U1 MARS, John: Ugly Ducklings discography *in* Blitz, No. 39 (March–April 1981): 16 ((5))

U2 PREVOST, Greg: The Ugly Ducklings: an interview with Dave Bingham *in* Kicks, No. 2 (Winter 1979): 29–30; discography p. 30 ((5))

U3 Ugly Duckling discography '66–'80 *in* Goldmine, No. 48 (May 1980): 17 ((5))

THE UGLY'S (musical group)

U4 BETROCK, Alan: [Discography] *in* Jamz, No. 3 (October 1971): 16; addenda in No. 3 (February 1972): 22 ((5))

THE UNDERTAKERS (musical group)

U5 SCHACHT, Janis: Undertakers *in* The Rock Marketplace, No. 9 (March 1975): 38 ((5))

UNDERWOOD, IAN

U6 Selected Underwood discography *in* Down Beat, XLIV (May 19, 1977): 20 ((—))

UNITED DAIRIES label

U7 FAULL, Trev: United Dairies *in* Outlet, No. 27 (Winter 1982): 2–4; discography p. 3 ((—))

UNITED STATES RECORD COMPANY label

U8 BLACKER, George: Eli was an operator!: part 2: continued from issue 149–150 *in* Record Research, No. 151–152 (January 1978): 12

URIAH HEEP (musical group)

U9 [[[Discography] *in* OTT, Markus: Uriah Heep. Bergish Gladbach: Lubbe, 1980: 151–152]]

V-DISCS
See also *Bibliography* Vol. 2, Jazz

V1 SEARS, Richard S.: V-Discs: a history and discography. Westport, Conn.: Greenwood Press, 1980. 1,166 pp. ((1, 2, 3, 4, 5, 6, 7))

THE VAGRANTS (musical group)

V2 KAYE, Lenny: Vagrants discography *in* Goldmine, No. 62 (July 1981): 22 ((—))

V3 ROBBINS, Wayne: The Vagrants *in* Jamz, No. 3 (February 1972): 9–12; discography p. 12; addenda in No. 4 (May 1972): 35 ((—))

THE VALENTINES (musical group)

V4 GOLDBERG, Marv, and Rick WHITESELL: The Valentines *in* Yesterday's Memories, III/4 (1977): 17 ((7))

V5 GROIA, Phil: Carl Hogan, the Valentines *in* Bim Bam Boom, No. 7 (September 1972): 39 ((3))

VALLEE, RUDY

V6 CAMP, Jack: Discography—Rudy Vallee *in* After Beat, II/3 (February–March 1972): 6, 8 ((7))

VALLI, FRANKIE

V7 ENGEL, Edward R.: The end of an era: Frankie Valli & the Four Seasons *in* The Time Barrier Express, No. 23 (July–August 1977): [10]–24; discography (by Engel and Joe SICURELLA): 18–24 ((—))

V8 ENGEL, Ed, and Paul BEZANKER: Frankie Valli on record *in* Paul's Record Magazine, IV/2 (No. 13–14): 38–42; additions and corrections in No. 15 (January–February 1977): 41–42 ((5))

V9 Frankie Vallie/the Four Seasons—album discography *in* Record World, XXXI (No. 1541, January 8, 1977): Special section [12] ((5))

VAN DER GRAAF GENERATOR (musical group)

V10 CHILDS, Andy: Discography *in* Zig Zag, VI/7 (No. 57): 25 ((1))

V11 FORMAN, Bill: Peter Hammill's songs for the new depression *in* Trouser Press, No. 21 (September 1977): 17–19; discography p. 19 [Includes Peter Hammill solo] ((—))

V12 Pete Hammill/Van Der Graaf Generator discography *in* Trouser Press, IV/3 (No. 21, September 1977): 19 ((—))

VAN DYKE, CONNIE

V13 MOHR, Kurt: Discography *in* Shout, No. 95 (May 1974): 3 ((2, 3, 7))

THE VAN DYKES (musical group)

V14 MOHR, Kurt: Discography *in* Shout, No. 53 (March 1970): [7–9] ((3, 7))

VAN LOAN, JOE

V15 SBARBORI, Jack: Joe Van Loan discography *in* Record Exchanger, IV/1 (No. 17): [11] ((1, 3, 5))

VANCE, DUDLEY

V16 Dudley Vance *in* Devil's Box, No. 20 (March 1973): 10 ((3))

VANDA, HARRY

V17 Vanda & Young: then, now & in between *in* The Rock Marketplace, No. 3 (October 1973): 6–7; addenda in No. 8 (December 1974): 42 ((5))

VANDO label

V18 Vando label *in* Paul's Record Magazine, IV/2 (No. 13–14, September–December 1976): 33 ((—))

VANILLA FUDGE (musical group)

V19 TAMARKIN, Jeff: Vanilla Fudge discography *in* Goldmine, No. 66, (November 1981): 21 ((—))

VARSITY label

V20 [Discography] *in* Folk Style, No. 6 (February 1960) and No. 9 [n.d.]: ? ((—))

VAUCAIRE, CORA

V21 Discographie *in* COSTAZ, Gilles: Cora Vaucaire. Paris: Seghers, 1973: [159]–162 (Collection poesie et chansons Seghers, 27) ((—))

VEE, BOBBY (real name Robert Thomas Velline)

V22 CLEE, Ken: Bobby Vee discography *in* Goldmine, No. 58 (March 1981): 14–15 ((—))

V23 McDOWELL, Mike: Bobby Vee be true to yourself *in* Blitz, No. 34 (January–February 1980): 12–16; discography (by McDowell and Frank ROSSI) pp. 15–16 ((1, 5))

VEE-JAY label

V24 CALLAHAN, Mike: Vee-Jay discography *in* Goldmine, No. 60 (May 1981): 13, 15, 16–18, 162–163 ((5))

V25 FLAM, Steve: The Vee-Jay story *in* Bim Bam Boom, I/4 (February–March 1972): 19–21 ((3))

THE VELOURS (musical group)

V26 [[[Discography] *in* Soul Music (No. 19)]]

V27 HINCKLEY, Dave: The Velours *in* Yesterday's Memories, II/3 (1976): 18–19 ((—))

THE VELVATONES (musical group)

V28 [[[Discography] *in* Soul Music (No. 28)]]

VELVET UNDERGROUND (musical group)

V29 HOGG, Brian: Velvet Underground *in* Bam Balam, No. 14 (September 1982): 3–9; discography pp. 7–9 ((5))

V30 MACLISE, Walter: Buried treasure *in* What Goes On, No. 2 (June 1979): 3–7; discography pp. 6–7 ((1))

V31   MILSTEIN, Philip: Covering up . . . *in* What Goes On, No. 2 (June 1979): 8–10 ((5)) [Velvets' songs recorded by other artists]

V32   VIGLIONE, Joe, and Philip MILSTEIN: Boots of Velvet *in* What Goes On, No. 2 (June 1979): 13 ((1))

THE VELVETS (musical group)

V33   GERULSKI, Joe: Velvets discography *in* Paul's Record Magazine (No. 16): 22 ((3))

VENT label

V34   FOSTER, Bob, and Jim WILSON: Vent label listing *in* Hot Buttered Soul, No. 22 (September 1973): 10 ((3))

THE VENTURES (musical group)

V35   DALLEY, Robert J.: The Ventures discography *in* Goldmine, No. 62 (July 1981): 15–16; additions and corrections in No. 64 (September 1981): 185; No. 65 (October 1981): 17 ((5))

V36   Ventures discography *in* Record Finder, II/12 (March 1981): 3 ((—))

V37   The Ventures: '60–'65 *in* The Rock Marketplace, No. 10 (June 1975): 20–22; discography p. 22 ((5))

VERA, BILLY

V38   VERA, Billy: Billy Vera discography *in* Shout, No. 85 (April 1973): 2–4 ((2, 3, 7))

THE VERSATILES (musical group)

V39   MOHR, Kurt: Discography *in* Shout, No. 95 (May 1974): 2 ((5, 7))

VIAN, BORIS

V40   [[[Discography] *in* Boris Vian de A a Z. Paris: Obliques, 1976: 22–44]]

V41   [[[Discography] *in* Boris Vian, sa vie, son oeuvre. Paris: Centre Georges Pompidou, 1978: 46–47]]

THE VIBRANAIRES (musical group)

V42   GOLDBERG, Marv, and Mike REDMOND: The Vibranaires *in* Yesterday's Memories, I/3 (1975): 21 ((7))

V43   McCUTCHEON, Lynn E.: The Vibranaires *in* Bim Bam Boom, I/2 (October–November 1971): 10 ((—))

THE VIBRATIONS (musical group)

V44   GOLDBERG, Marv: The Jay Hawks/ Vibrations *in* Bim Bam Boom, I/5 (April–May 1972): 19 ((5))

VIBY, MARGUERITE

V45   ANDREASEN, Axel: Marguerite Viby og grammofonen (1929–1965) en discografi. Copenhagen: Andreasen, 1974. 54 l. ((3, 4, 6, 7))

VICKERS, CHARLES

V46   Discography *in* Shout, No. 45 (July 1969): [7] ((3))

VICTOR label
See also *Bibliography* Vol. 2, Jazz

V47   BRYAN, Martin: Victor 8-inch records *in* New Amberola Graphic, No. 22 (Summer 1977): 3–7; No. 23 (Fall 1977): 5–9 ((5))

V48   COLEMAN, B. L., and Dave G. COTTER: The Victor purple label series *in* Talking Machine Review, No. 1 (December 1969): 28–31 ((—))

V49   [Discography] *in* Blue Yodler, No. 18 (February 1968): ? [23500 series] ((—))

V50   HEALY, Bob: Victor 23500 series *in* Country News & Views, II/3 (January 1964): 32; III/1 (July 1964): 18–19; IV/1 (July 1965); V/3 (January 1967); VI/2 (October 1967): ? ((—))

V51   HEARNE, Will Roy: [Discography] *in* Disc Collector, No. 11 (November 1959) thru No. 15 (November 1960): ? [4000 series] ((—))

V52   KRUEGER, Miles: The 60000 purple-label personality series (10") Victor Talking Machine Company series *in* American Record Guide (February 1967): 537–540 ((5))

V53 Victor 60000 series *in* New Amberola Graphic, No. 7 (Fall 1973): 3–10 ((3, 6, 7))

V54 Victor 70000 series *in* New Amberola Graphic, No. 9 (Spring 1974): 5–12 ((3, 6, 7)) [An index to both 60000 and 70000 discographies appears in New Amberola Graphic, No. 10 (Summer 1974): 5–6]

VICTOR label [Canada]

V55 TENNYSON, J. R.: Canadian Victor 21600 series *in* New Amberola Graphic, No. 13 (Spring 1975) thru No. 24 (Winter 1977): various paginations ((5))

V56 TENNYSON, J. R.: Canadian Victor 235000 series (12-inch series) *in* New Amberola Graphic, No. 24 (Winter 1977): 13 ((5))

VICTOR LIGHT OPERA COMPANY

V57 WARNER, Larry: The early sound of the American musical theatre: the "Gems" series of the Victor Light Opera Company *in* Kastlemusik Monthly Bulletin, IV/6 (June 1979): 1, 10–12 ((—))

VICTOR MANUEL

V58 Discografia *in* VAZQUEZ-AZPIRI, Hector: Victor Manuel. Madrid: Jucar, 1974: [167–168] ((—))

VICTOR SALON ORCHESTRA
See SALON ORCHESTRA

VICTORY label

V59 BADROCK, Arthur, and Jim HAYES: 7" Victory research *in* Gunn Report, No. 67 (March–April 1978): 11–12; No. 68 (June–July 1978): 15–16; No. 69 (August–September 1978): 21–22; No. 70 (October–December 1978): 7–8; No. 71 (January–February 1979): 7–8; No. 72 (March–April 1979): 6–8; No. 73 (May–June–July 1979): 6–7; No. 74 (August–September–October 1979): 20–21; No. 75 (November–December 1979): 13–14 ((3))

VIGLIETTI, DANIEL

V60 Discografia *in* BENEDETTI, Mario: Daniel Viglietti. Madrid: Jucar, 1974: 189–193 ((5))

VIGNEAULT, GILLES

V61 Livres et disques de Gilles Vigneault *in* BARBRY, Francois-Regis: Passer l'hiver: Francois-Regis Barbry interroge Gilles Vigneault. Vendome: Editions du Centurion, 1978: 153–156 ((—))

THE VILONS (musical group)

V62 OSTROWSKI, Bob: [Discography] *in* Bim Bam Boom, I/6 (July 1972): 29 ((3))

VIN label

V63 [[[Discography] *in* Soul Music (No. 13)]]

V64 Vin label *in* Shout, No. 67 (June 1971): [11] ((3))

VINCENT, GENE

V65 [Discography] *in* Big Beat, No. 11/12 [n.d.]: 28–29 ((5, 7))

V66 Discography *in* FINNIS, Rob, and Bob DUNHAM: Gene Vincent and the Blue Caps. London: Finnis and Dunham, 1974: 44–47 ((2, 3, 4, 5, 7))

V67 PAUL, Fred: Gene Vincent discography *in* Record Exchanger, II/6 (No. 11 [Fall 1972]): 19 ((—))

V68 ROWBOTHAM, Cliff: Gene Vincent on record A–Z *in* Not Fade Away, No. 6 (March 1975): 12–18 ((—))

V69 SIMONS, Paul: [Discography] *in* Big Beat of the 50's, No. 31 (May 1982): 19–24 ((5))

V70 WEISER, Ron: Ahead of his time: Gene Vincent's influence in rock & roll *in* Who Put the Bomp, No. 9 (Spring 1972): 9–14; discography pp. 12–14 ((—))

V71 WILKES, Richard T.: Gene Vincent on disc (pt. 3) *in* Kommotion, No. 6 (Summer 1974): 9–11 ((—))

THE VIOLENTS (musical group)

V72 FAULL, Trev: Please don't hit me cos I'm with the Violents *in* Instrumental Obscurities Unlimited, No. 20 (c1978): 9–11; discography pp. 10–11 ((—))

THE V.I.P.'s (musical group)

V73 HOGG, Brian: The V.I.P.'s with Mike Harrison *in* Bam Balam, No. 14 (September 1982): 33–35 ((5)) [Includes Art]

VIRGIN label

V74 Virgin discography *in* Trouser Press Collector's Magazine, II/1 (September–October 1979): [4–5]; II/2 (November–December 1979): [1] ((—))

THE VIRTUES (musical group)

V75 FAULL, Trev: The Virtues discography 53–65 *in* Instrumental Obscurities Unlimited, No. 18–19 (Winter 1977): 13–14 ((—))

VITO AND THE SALUATIONS (musical group)

V76 GONZALEZ, Fernando: Discography *in* Goldmine, No. 64 (September 1981): 7 ((3, 5))

VOCALION label

See also *Bibliography* Vol. 2, Jazz

V77 WOLFE, Charles K.: Early country music in Knoxville *in* Old Time Music, No. 12 (Spring 1974): 19–37 ((3, 7))

THE VOGUE (musical group)

V78 KORBIK, Mike: En Vogue *in* Gorilla Beat, No. 15 (1982): 57–60; discography p. 60 ((5))

VOGUE label [England]

V79 PELLETIER, Paul: British Vogue V 9000 singles listing *in* Shout, No. 105 (October–November 1975): 18–19; No. 106 (December 1975–January 1976): 17–19; No. 107 (February–March 1976): 16–18 ((3, 5))

VOKES, Howard

V80 FINKE, Eberhard: Howard Vokes; Pennsylvania's king of country music *in* Country Corner, No. 56 (October 1977): 5–6 ((2, 7))

V81 Howard Vokes disco *in* Kountry Korral (April 1971): 6–7 ((2, 3, 7))

THE VONTASTICS (musical group)

V82 MOHR, Kurt: Vontastics discography *in* Shout, No. 57 (July 1970): [8–9]; additions and corrections in No. 60 (November 1970): [1] ((7))

V83 PRUTER, Robert: Windy City soul: the Vontastics *in* Goldmine, No. 22 (January 1978): 20 ((5))

WADER, HANNES

W1 Diskographie *in* HiFi Stereophonie, XV/11 (November 1976): [1280] ((—))

WAGONER, PORTER

W2 STRUBING, Hauke: Auf Langspielplatten *in* Country Corner, No. 44 (May 1975): 75 ((—))

W3 STRUBING, Hauke: Diskografisches (1): Porter Wagoner: seine fruhen Singles *in* Country Corner, No. 54 (May 1977): 4; No. 55 (July 1977): 9 ((3))

THE WAILERS (musical group)

W4 SMART, Peter: Wailers discography *in* Rumble, III/3 (Spring 1976): 14–15 ((—))

WAITS, TOM

W5 O'BRIEN, Peter: Discography *in* Zig Zag, No. 62 (July 1976): [11] ((5))

W6 Waits discography *in* Down Beat, XLIII (June 17, 1976): 16 ((—))

WAKEMAN, RICK

W7 Rick's albums *in* WOODING, Dan: Rick Wakeman: the caped crusader. London: Hale, 1978: 189 ((5))

WALKER, JOHN V.

W8   [COHEN, Norm]: John V. Walker *in*
JEMF Quarterly, VIII/4 (No. 27,
Autumn 1972): 139 ((3, 6, 7))

WALKER, PHILLIP

W9   PERIN, Jacques: Phillip Walker/dis-
cographie *in* Soul Bag, XII (No. 86,
December 1981–January 1982): 11–14
((7))

WALKER'S CORBIN RAMBLERS
(musical group)

W10   WARD, Edward: Discography *in*
Devil's Box, XIII/1 (March 1979):
35–36 ((2, 3, 6, 7))

WALLS, VAN

W11   GRENDYSA, Peter: Play it, Mr.
Van!! *in* Disc-O-Graph, II/9 (December 1977): 21–22 ((3, 7))

WALSH, DOCK

W12   EARLE, E.: [Discography] *in* Program notes for Folk Legacy Record
FSA-24, 1965: ? ((2, 3, 6, 7))

W13   KUNSTADT, Len, and B. COLTON:
[Discography] *in* Record Research,
No. 62 (August 1964): ?; corrections
in No. 64: ? ((2, 3, 6, 7))

W14   TITTERINGTON, K.: [Discography]
in Blue Yodler, No. 14 (1967): ? ((2,
3, 6, 7))

WAND label

W15   Wand singles list *in* Shout, No. 108
(April–May 1972): 9–12 ((5))

WANLS, SHIRLEY

W16   PRUTER, Robert: Shirley Wanls discography *in* Goldmine, No. 67 (December 1981): 172 ((5))

WARING, FRED

W17   GOTTLIEB, R. E. : Waring's Penn-
sylvanians—Victor record discography
in Record Research, No. 119–120
(December 1972–January 1973): 8–9;
No. 121 (March 1973): 8–9; No. 122
(June 1973): 4–5 ((3, 7))

WARNER, TEX, AND THE
WESTERNAIRES (musical group)

W18   Diskographie *in* Hillbilly, No. 59
(June 1979): 22 ((7))

WARNER'S SEVEN ACES (musical group)

W19   Warner's Seven Aces: a discography
in Storyville, No. 94 (April–May
1981): 132–148 ((2, 3, 7))

WARWICK, DEE DEE

W20   MOHR, Kurt: Dee Dee Warwick discography *in* Shout, No. 79 (August
1972): [4–6] ((2, 3, 7))

WASHINGTON D.C.'s (musical group)

W21   Washington DC's *in* Gorilla Beat, No.
4 (1979): 12–14; discography pp.
13–14; addenda in No. 6 (1980): 46
((—))

WATKINS, BILL

W22   LIGON, Peggy: Cincinnati rockabilly,
part 1: Bill Watkins *in* New Kommotion, No. 21 (1979): 53–54; discography p. 54 ((2, 3, 7))

WATSON, DOC

W23   WHITTAKER, H. Lloyd: Discography *in* Bluegrass Unlimited, V/5
(November 1970): 6–7 ((1, 2, 7))

WATTERS, CYRIL

W24   [Discography] *in* Commodore, No. 5
(Spring 1972): 8+ ((—))

W25   EDWARDS, John: [Discography] *in*
Disc Collector, No. 14 (August 1960):
? ((—)) [Reprinted in Country Western Spotlight, Special issue, September
1962] ((—))

WATTS, WILMER

W26   [COHEN, Norm]: Wilmer Watts *in*
JEMF Quarterly, IX/3 (No. 31,
Autumn 1973): 96 ((3, 6, 7))

W27   Wilmer Watts discography of known
issued recordings *in* JEMF Quarterly,
V/4 (No. 16, Winter 1969): 139–140
((3, 6))

WAYNE, ALVIS

W28 STRUM, Adri: Alvis Wayne disco *in* Rockville International (March–April 1974): 22 ((—))

WAYNE, GARNER

W29 Garner Wayne record listing *in* Country & Western Roundabout, IV (No. 15, March–June 1967): 10, 28 ((—))

WAYNE, GAYLOR

W30 STRUM, Adriaan: Gaylor Wayne discography *in* Goldmine, No. 50 (July 1980): 163 ((5))

WEA labels [England]

W31 FAULL, Trev: The WEA freebies list (play it again Sam!) *in* Outlet, No. 11 (May 1979): 18 ((—))

WEATHER REPORT (musical group)
See also *Bibliography* Vol. 2, Jazz

W32 Discografia essenziale *in* Discoteca Hifi, XX (No. 192, March 1979): 108 ((5))

WEAVER, DENNIS

W33 Dennis Weaver disco *in* Kountry Korral, X/2 (April 1977): 27 ((—))

WEBER, MAREK, AND HIS ORCHESTRA

W34 GARNER, Clive: Marek Weber and his Orchestra *in* Vintage Light Music, No. 2 (Spring 1975): 6–8 ((—))

WEEDON, BERT

W35 FAULL, Trev: Bert Weedon is back *in* Instrumental Obscurities Unlimited, No. 14–15 (March 1977): 21–23 ((5))

WEEKS, ANSON

W36 CAMP, J. H.: Anson Weeks discography *in* After Beat, I/2 (November 1970): 5 ((5))

WEEL, LIVA

W37 ANDREASEN, Axel: Liva Weel og grammofonen: en discografi. Copen-

hagen: Andreasen, 1973. 84 pp. ((3, 5, 6, 7))

WEINERT, ERICH

W38 [[[Discography] *in* BARAKOW, Margot: Erich Weinert. Berlin: Berliner Stadtbibliothek, 1978]]

WELLING, FRANK

W39 TRIBE, Ivan M.: A Welling and McGhee discography *in* JEMF Quarterly, XVII (No. 62, Summer 1981): 64–74 ((3, 7))

WELLS, JEAN

W40 BERNHOLM, Jonas, and Tony CUMMINGS: Jean Wells *in* Shout, No. 49 (November 1969): [2–4] ((2, 3, 6, 7))

WELLS, JUNIOR
See also *Bibliography* Vol. 2, Jazz

W41 ARNIAC, Jean-Pierre: Discographie de Junior Wells *in* Soul Bag, XI/75–76 (1980): 16–19; ROBS, Gerard: Disco additions in No. 77 (1980): 22 ((2, 3, 7))

WELLS, KITTY

W42 . . . Decca LP med Kitty Wells *in* Kountry Korral (April 1973): 12 ((—))

W43 [Discography] *in* Country News & Views, II/4 (April 1964): 6–15 ((3, 5, 7))

WELLS, MARY

W44 JANCIK, Wayne: Mary Wells discography *in* Goldmine, No. 52 (October 1980): 19 ((5))

W45 TOWNE, Steve, and Chris BEACHLEY: Mary Wells discography *in* It Will Stand, No. 24–25 (c1981): 7 ((5))

WELSH, ELISABETH

W46 LYNCH, Richard C.: Mabel Mercer, Hutch and Elisabeth Welch *in* Kastlemusik Monthly Bulletin, V/8 (August 1980): 1, 12–13 ((—))

WELZ, JOEY

W47 WESTFALL, Bob: Joey Welz discography *in* Kommotion, No. 10–11 (Winter 1975–76): 50 ((5))

WERICH, JAN

W48 Diskograficky soupis *in* CINIBUS, Josef: Gramofonova deska a Jan Werich: Praha: Statni hudebni vydavatelstvi, 1964: 31–37 ((5))

WEST, CLINT

W49 Clint West discography *in* Rock 'n' Roll International Magazine (Danish), No. 108 (November 1977): [17] ((—))

WEST, HEDY

W50 Diskographie *in* FINKE, Eberhard: Hedy West: Stammgast in Deutschland *in* Country Corner (April 1979): 17, 32 ((—))

WEST, MAE

W51 LYNCH, Richard C.: Mae West on records *in* Kastlemusik Monthly Bulletin, VII/7 (July 1982): 1, 7 ((7))

WEST, SONEE

W52 GLENISTER, Chris: The Sonee West story *in* New Kommotion, No. 21 (1979): 30–32; discography pp. 31–32 ((1, 2, 3, 7))

WEST, SPEEDY

W53 [COHEN, Norm]: Speedy West *in* JEMF Quarterly, IX/2 (No. 30, Summer 1973): 82–83 ((3, 6, 7))

WESTFIELD, FRANK

W54 UPTON, Stuart: Frank Westfield's Orchestra *in* Commodore, No. 4 (Winter 1971): 5+ ((—))

WESTMORELAND, ROBERT LEE

W55 ROWE, Mike: Rare post-war records *in* Blues Unlimited, No. 113 (May–June 1975): 13 ((7))

WESTON, RANDY

See also *Bibliography* Vol. 2, Jazz

W56 Randy Weston on LP *in* Different Drummer, I/5 (February 1974): 30 ((—))

WHEELER, ONIE

W57 Onie Wheeler disco *in* Kountry Korral, X/5 (October 1977): 17 ((—))

THE WHEELS (musical group)

W58 MONDRONE, Sal: Wheels discography *in* Bim Bam Boom, II/3 (No. 9, 1973): 37 ((3))

WHEN IN LOVE (song title)

W59 [Discography] *in* Time Barrier Express, No. 21 (January–February 1977): 19 ((5))

WHIDDEN, JAY

W60 WALKER, Steve: The Jay Whidden discography *in* Talking Machine Review, No. 4 (June 1970): 112–116; No. 5 (August 1970): [125]–129; No. 6 (October 1970): [156]; additions and corrections in No. 8 (February 1971): 232 ((2, 3, 6, 7))

WHIRLIN label

W61 Discography *in* Record Exchanger, II/5 (No. 10 [May 1972]): [14–17] ((—))

THE WHISPERS (musical group)

W62 SBARBORI, Jack: Whispers discography *in* Time Barrier Express, III/4 (No. 24, April–May 1979): 63–64 ((5))

WHIT label

W63 PERIN, Jacques, and Gilles PETARD: . . . Listing Whit . . . *in* Soul Bag, No. 77 (1980): 23–28 ((—))

WHITE, EDNA

W64 WILE, Raymond R.: The Edison recordings of Edna White, trumpet *in* Record Research, No. 144–145 (March 1977): 5 ((7))

WHITE, JOHN

W65 DANIEL, Harlan, and Tony RUS-
SELL: John White *in* Old Time
Music, No. 11 (Winter 1973/4): 20–21
((3, 7))

WHITE CYLINDER label

W66 ANDREWS, Frank: White Cylinders
in Talking Machine Review, No. 24
(October 1973): 243–246 ((5))

WHITLEY, RAY

W67 VAUGHN, Gerald F.: Discography *in*
his Ray Whitley, country-western
musicmaster and film star. Newark,
Del.: Vaugh, 1973: 9–11 ((3, 7))

WHITMAN, SLIM

W68 [Discography] *in* Country News &
Views, V/1 (July 1966): ? ((—))

W69 [Discography] *in* Country Record Exchange, I (No. 9, October 1967): 5–8
((—))

W70 [[Discography *in* Country & Western
Spotlight, No. 2 (March 1975); No. 4
(September 1975)]]

W71 [[[Discography] *in* GIBBLE, Kenneth
L.: Mr. Songman: the Slim Whitman
story. Elgin, Ill.: Brethren Press,
1982]]

W72 Discography *in* JINKERSON, Jr.,
Bob: A taste of country: Slim Whitman *in* Goldmine, No. 23 (February
1978): 23 ((—))

W73 WEIZE, Richard A.: Slim Whitman
diskographie *in* Hillbilly, No. 36 (December 1970): 18–19; No. 37 (March
1971): 36–38 ((—))

WHITSETT, TIM

W74 TOPPING, Ray, and Tim WHIT-
SETT: Tim Whitsett discography *in*
New Kommotion, No. 14 (Winter
1977): 12; addenda in No. 16 (Summer 1977): 42 and No. 22 (1979): 64
((2, 3, 7))

WHITTER, HENRY

W75 COHEN, Norm, and Eugene EARLE:
Henry Whitter discography *in* JEMF
Quarterly, XI/2 (No. 38, Summer
1975): 62–66; addenda in XII/2 (No.

42, Summer 1976): 53 ((2, 3, 5, 6,
7))

W76 GRAYSON, C. B.: Discography *in*
Old Time Music, No. 35 (Winter
1980–Spring 1981): 13–14 ((2, 3, 6,
7))

W77 OLESEN, Keith: Henry Whitter,
pioneer *in* Record Collector's Journal,
I/6 (December 1975): 8 ((3, 7))

THE WHO (musical group)

W78 [[Discography *in* ARNAIZ, Jorge: Los
Who. Madrid: Jucar, 1980:
[181]–193]]

W79 [[Discography *in* BARNES, Richard:
The Who, maximum R. & B.: an illustrated biography. New York: St. Martin's Press, 1982]]

W80 HANEL, Ed: The Who: the illustrated discography. London: Omnibus, 1981. 176 pp. ((1, 3, 5, 6a, 7))
[Includes releases from over 11 coun-
tries]

W81 Discography *in* HERMAN, Gary: The
Who. New York: Macmillan, 1971:
152–159; London: Studio Vista, 1971:
108–112 ((5))

W82 HOGG, Brian: The Who *in* Bam
Balam, No. 11 (June 1980): 3–12; discography pp. 8–12; addenda in No. 12
(November 1980): 39 ((1, 5, 6a)) [In-
cludes covers and productions]

W83 Discographie *in* REINS, Sacha: Les
Who. Paris: Nouvelles editions
polaires, 1974: [117–121] ((5))

W84 Discographie solo *in* REINS, Sacha:
The Who. Paris: Grancher, 1979:
[101]–106 ((5))

W85 ROBBINS, Ira: Who discography *in*
Trans-Oceanic Trouser Press, No. 3
(June 1974): 15–20; No. 5 (October–
November 1974): 29–30 ((1, 7))

W86 ROBBINS, Ira, and John VISNAS-
KAS: The Who: definitive discography and guide to collecting, 1975
ed. Trouser Press Press No. 2 [In-
cludes solo recordings by Roger
Daltrey, Pete Townsend, Keith Moon,
and John Entwhistle, plus cover recordings by other artists] ((1, 5, 6a))

W87 SHAW, Greg: Ephemera #3: the Who
in New Haven Rock Press, III/3 (No.
13, Fall 1971): 24–25 ((1))

W88 Discografia *in* SIERRA I FABRA,
Jordi: The Who, su leyenda y "Tom-

my.'' Barcelona: Musica de nuestro
tiempo, 1976: 81-122 ((—))

W89 TAYLOR, Barry: The compleat Who
in Jamz, No. 5 (c1972): 36, 39 ((1, 5,
6a))

W90 The Who discography in Cash Box,
XL/21 (October 7, 1978): [40] ((—))

W91 The Who discography in Gorilla Beat,
No. 2 (1979): 6-10, 41; addenda in
No. 3 (1979): 34; No. 4 (1979): 39;
No. 5 (1980): 12; No. 6 (1980): 46;
No. 7 (1980): 18; No. 9 (1981): 48;
and No. 13 (1982): 71 ((—))

W92 Discography in The Who—ten great
years. San Francisco: Straight Arrow
Publishers, 1975: 82-85 ((5))

W93 [[[Discography] in WICKS, Ted,
comp.: A decade of the Who. London: Fabulous Music, 1977: 238-239]]

WIGWAM (musical group)

W94 GOTT, Ronn: Wigwam, bam! in
Trouser Press, No. 16 (October-
November 1976): 25-26; discography
p. 26 ((5))

WILBURN BROTHERS

W95 STRUBING, Hauke: The Wilburn
Brothers discographie in Country Corner, No. 38 (February 1974): 15-18
((—))

WILLIAMS, BILLY

W96 MOORE, David: Billy Williams:
towards a discography in Gunn
Report, No. 69 (August-September
1978): 10; No. 71 (January-February
1979): 21; No. 73 (May-June-July
1979): 23-24; No. 78 (September-October 1980): 15-16; No. 80 (March-
June 1981): 9, 18 ((2, 3))

WILLIAMS, BUDDY

W97 BENSON, Charles: Buddy Williams
record listing in Country & Western
Roundabout, II/5 (August 1963): 19,
33 ((—))

W98 [[Discography in Country & Western
Spotlight, No. 3 (June 1975); No. 4
(September 1975); No. 5 (December
1975)]]

W99 [Discography] in Country News &
Views, IV/2 (January 1965): ? ((3,
7))

W100 [Discography] in Country Western
Spotlight, No. 47 (September 1964): ?
((—))

W101 WATSON, Eric: Buddy Williams in
Country Music Times (Australia),
VI/7 (August 1972); VI/8 (October
1972): 25-27 ((7))

WILLIAMS, CHARLES

W102 [Discography] in Commodore, No. 4
(Winter 1971): 13 + ((—))

WILLIAMS, DOC

W103 BINGE, Reimar: Discographie in
Country Corner, No. 25 (July-Oc-
tober 1970): 5-8 ((5))

W104 [COHEN, Norm, and Barbara
KEMPF]: A preliminary Doc &
Chickie discography in JEMF
Quarterly, X/1 (No. 33, Spring 1974):
7-13 ((3, 7))

W105 SCHUMANN, E. Reinald: Doc
Williams diskographie in Hillbilly, No.
50 (March 1977): 11-14 ((3, 7))

WILLIAMS, DON

W106 Discography in Kountry Korral, X/2
(April 1977): 16 ((—))

WILLIAMS, GARY

W107 Gary Williams diskographie in Hillbilly, No. 52 (September 1977): 18-22
((1, 5, 7))

WILLIAMS, HANK

W108 [[Discography in Country Corner, No.
4: 12]]

W109 [Discography] in Country News &
Views, I/3 (January 1963): ? ((—))

W110 [Discography] in Country Western
Spotlight, No. 18 (April-June 1957): ?
((—))

W111 [Discography] in Country Western
Spotlight, No. 28 (October-December
1959): ? ((—))

W112 [Discography] *in* Hillbilly Folk Record Journal, I/2 (March–June 1954): ? ((—))

W113 [Discography] *in* Hillbilly Folk Record Journal, III/3 (July–September 1956): ? ((—))

W114 GONZALEZ, Fernando L.: Hank Williams discography *in* Goldmine, No. 37 (June 1979): 8–10; additions and corrections in No. 39 (August 1979): 5 ((3, 5, 6, 7))

W115 HEAD, Mike: Hank Williams on the air *in* New Kommotion, No. 21 (1979): 35 ((1, 2, 3, 7)) [Health and Happiness shows (1949) and AFRS transcriptions of Opry shows (1950–51)]

W116 Discography *in* MOORE, Thurston, ed.: Hank Williams, the legend. Denver: Heather Publications, 1972: 60–62 ((—))

W117 RIVERS, Jerry: Discography *in* CARESS, Jay: Hank Williams; country music's tragic king. New York: Stein and Day, 1979: 234–247 ((—))

W118 Hank Williams discography *in* RIVERS, Jerry: Hank Williams, from life to legend. Denver: Heather Enterprises, 1967: 34–39 ((—))

W119 Schallplatten von Hank Williams *in* Hillbilly, No. 6 (July 1963): 8–9 ((—))

W120 SCHUMANN, E. Reinald: Hank Williams Tribut-diskographie *in* Hillbilly, No. 54 (March 1978): 28–29 ((—))

W121 [[Singles by Hank Williams *in* Country Singin' and Pickin' News, III/8 (January 1958): 29–31]]

W122 VOKES, H.: [Discography] *in* Disc Collector, No. 9 (1955): ? ((—))

WILLIAMS, HANK, JR.

W123 ENGELS, Ernst: Hank Williams Jr.: disco *in* Country Corner, No. 55 (July 1977): 10 ((5))

WILLIAMS, JIMMY

W124 MOHR, Kurt: Jimmy Williams discography *in* Black Wax, No. 57 (June 1973): 6 ((2, 3, 5, 7))

WILLIAMS, MARC

W125 LARSEN, Johnny, and Richard A. WEIZE: Marc Williams *in* Hillbilly, No. 46 (March 1976): 12–13 ((2, 3, 6, 7))

WILLIAMS, OTIS

W126 Otis Williams and the Charms *in* Time Barrier Express, II/8 (No. 18, August–September 1976): 11–12 ((3))

WILLIAMS, PAUL "HUCKLEBUCK"

W127 GRENDYSA, Peter: Paul 'Hucklebuck' Williams discography *in* Goldmine, No. 43 (December 1979): 115 ((5))

WILLIAMS, TEX

W128 GRIFFIS, Ken: Tex Williams discography *in* JEMF Quarterly, XV (No. 53, Spring 1979): 10–19 ((1, 3, 7))

WILLIAMSON, SONNY BOY

W129 FAULL, Trev: Blues *in* Outlet, No. 17 (March 1980): 24–26 ((2, 7))

WILLIS, CHICK

W130 WILLIS, Chick, and Joel DUFOUR: Discographie/Chick Willis *in* Soul Bag, No. 83 (1981): 16 ((3, 7))

WILLIS, CHUCK

See also *Bibliography* Vol. 2, Jazz

W131 PEARLIN, Victor: Chuck Willis: discography *in* Paul's Record Magazine, II/6 (December 1975): 16–17 ((3))

THE WILLOWS (musical group)

W132 MOHR, Kurt, et al.: Discography *in* Shout, No. 37 (November 1968): [8–9] ((2, 3, 6, 7))

W133 VANCE, Marcia, and Phil GROIA: The Willows *in* Bim Bam Boom, I/6 (July 1972): 16 ((3))

WILLS, JAMES ROBERTS (known as Bob Wills)

W134 ANDERSON, I.: [Discography] *in* Disc Collector, No. 9, 11–12 (1955?): ? ((—))

W135 [[Discography *in* Country Corner, No. 18: 3]]

W136 HATCHER, Danny: Bob Wills *in* Journal of Country Music, III/3–4 (Fall and Winter 1973): 114–134 ((3, 5, 6, 7))

W137 HEALY, Bob: More from Bob Healy *in* Record Research, No. 125–126 (February 1974): 13 ((3))

W138 HEALY, Bob, et al.: [Discography] *in* Record Research, No. 79 (October 1966) thru No. 83 (April 1967): ?; additions in No. 84: ? ((1, 2, 3, 7))

W139 PINSON, Bob: The Bob Wills recordings: a comprehensive discography *in* TOWNSEND, Charles R.: San Antonio Rose: the life and music of Bob Wills. Urbana: University of Illinois Press, 1976: 337–376 ((1, 3, 6, 7))

WILLS, JOHNNY LEE

W140 [RUSSELL, Tony]: Making Western swing *in* Old Time Music, No. 15 (Winter 1974/5): 11–12 ((—))

WILSON, BRIAN
See also THE BEACH BOYS

W141 Brian Wilson's greatest flops *in* The Rock Marketplace, No. 7 (October 1974): 6–7 [Productions other than the Beach Boys] ((3, 5))

WILSON, JACK

W142 [Discography] *in* Commodore, No. 3 (Autumn 1971): 6; No. 4 (Winter 1971): 15+ ((—))

WILSON, JACKIE

W143 CORDELL, John A.: Jackie Wilson discography *in* Time Barrier Express, III/4 (No. 24, April–May 1979): 31–32 ((—))

WILSON, LES

W144 GIBSON, G.: [Discography] *in* Country Western Spotlight, No. 5 (March 1956): ? ((—))

WINCHESTER label

W145 Winchester label *in* Paul's Record Magazine, IV/2 (No. 13–14, Septem-

ber–December 1976): 33; additions and corrections in No. 15 (January–February 1977): 40 ((—))

WINDY CITY label

W146 Windy City label *in* Paul's Record Magazine, IV/2 (September–December 1976): 33 ((—))

WING label

W147 GIBBON, Peter, et al.: Discography: the Wing label *in* Goldmine, No. 26 (May–June 1978): 31 ((3, 5))

WINLEY label

W148 GROIA, Phil: The Paul Winley story *in* Bim Bam Boom, II/3 (No. 9, 1973): 57 ((—))

WINTERS, JONATHAN

W149 SMITH, Ronald L.: Jonathan Winters albums of original material *in* Goldmine, No. 44 (January 1980): 20 ((—))

WINWOOD, STEVE

W150 TAMRAKIN, Jeff, et al.: Steve Winwood album discography *in* Goldmine, No. 64 (September 1981): 15, 173 ((—))

WISEMAN, MAC

W151 [Discography] *in* Country Western Express, No. 16 (October–December 1957): ? ((—))

W152 WEIZE, Richard A.: Mac Wiseman diskographie *in* Hillbilly, No. 57 (December 1978): 10–20 ((3, 7))

WONDER, STEVIE

W153 [[[Discography] *in* DRAGONWAGON, Crescent: Stevie Wonder. New York: Flash Books, 1977: 93–[95]]]

W154 [[[Discography] *in* ELSNER, Constanze: Stevie Wonder. London: Everest, 1977: 329–351]]

W155 Stevie Wonder discography *in* FOX-CUMMING, Ray: Stevie Wonder.

London: Mandabrook Books, 1977:
122–123 ((5))

W156 Discography *in* HASKINS, James:
The story of Stevie Wonder. New
York: Lothrop, Lee & Shepard Co.,
1976: 121–123 ((—))

WOOD, RON

W157 DEBENEDETTO, Nick: Wizzo
disco *in* Trans-Oceanic Trouser Press,
II/1 (February–March 1975): 28–30
((—))

WOODHULL'S OLD TYME MASTERS (musical group)

W158 RCA Victor discography *in* JEMF
Quarterly, XII/2 (No. 42, Summer
1976): 62 ((3, 6, 7))

WOODIE, EPHRAIM

W159 [RUSSELL, Tony]: Ephraim Woodie
and the Henpecked Husbands *in* Old
Time Music, No. 8 (Spring 1973): 13
((3, 6, 7))

WOOLEY, SHEB

W160 STIDOM, Larry: Sheb Wooley discography *in* Goldmine, No. 65 (October
1981): 179 ((5))

THE WOOLIES (musical group)

W161 McDOWELL, Mike: The Woolies:
keeping the spirit of punk rock alive
in Ballroom Blitz, No. 19 (May 1977):
3–4 ((—))

WORLD RECORDS label

W162 78 rpm discs on L.P. *in* Talking
Machine Review, No. 59 (August
1979): 1576, 1585, 1595 ((—))

WORLD WIDE label

W163 STANTON, Roy: World Wide
Records label list *in* Shout, No. 99
(October 1974): 2 ((3))

WORLE, JIMMY

W164 WEIZE, Richard: Jimmy Worle-Dis-
cographie *in* Country Corner, No. 37
(December 1973): 35–36 ((7))

WORTHY label

W165 [Discography] *in* Time Barrier Express, No. 22 (March–April 1977): 29
((1))

WRAY, LINK

W166 FAULL, Trev: [Link Wray discog-
raphy] *in* Instrumental Obscurities Unlimited, No. 18–19 (Winter 1977): 3–4
((5))

W167 MILLAR, Bill: Link Wray discography *in* Goldmine, No. 56 (January
1981): 165 ((2, 3, 7))

W168 WESTFALL, Bob: The Wray Family
on disc *in* Kommotion, No. 8 (Winter
1975): 9–12; addendum in No. 10–11
(Winter 1975–76): 26 ((5)) [Includes
Vernon and Doug Wray]

W169 WESTFALL, Bob, and Cub KODA:
Wray Family discography *in* Time
Barrier Express, III (No. 26, Sep-
tember–October 1979): 36–38 ((7))

WRIGHT, EDYTHE

W170 CAMP, Jack: Discography—Edythe
Wright *in* After Beat, II/5 (June–July
1972): 6–7 ((7))

WRIGHT, HAROLD

W171 MONDRONE, Sal: Rare sounds *in*
Bim Bam Boom, I/4 (February–
March 1972): 23 ((3))

WRIGHT, O. V.

W172 MOHR, Kurt, and Pierre DA-
GUERRE: Soul portrait: O. V.
Wright *in* Soul Bag, XII/80 (1981):
25–27 ((2, 7))

WYNETTE, TAMMY

W173 Tammy Wynette LP discography *in*
Kountry Korral (No. 2, 1979): 23
((—))

XTC (musical group)

X1   KOLANJIAN, Steve, and David
DASCH: X-plaining XTC *in* Aware,
No. 8 (Winter 1981–82): 28–33 ((5))

XX label (FLYRIGHT RECORDS)

X2   FAULL, Trev: Little known UK label #2: XX *in* Outlet, No. 26 (July 1982): 25–26 ((—))

YARDBIRDS (musical group)

Y1   HINMAN, Doug: Ephemera #4: the Yardbirds *in* New Haven Rock Press, IV/1 (No. 15, c. early 1972): 4–5 ((—))

Y2   . . . of the Yardbirds *in* The Rock Marketplace, No. 6 (July 1974): 16–18; addenda in No. 8 (December 1974): 42 [Includes Keith Relf solo recordings] ((5))

Y3   RICHARDSON, Ben: Discography *in* Trans-Oceanic Trouser Press, No. 6 (December 1974–January 1975): 20–23; II/1 (February–March 1975): 37–38 ((1))

Y4   The Yardbirds *in* Bam Balam, No. 1 (February 1975): 13–19; discography pp. 15–19; addenda in No. 2 (June 1975): 8; No. 5 (February 1977): 15–16; No. 6 (November 1977): 23; and No. 14 (September 1982): 13 ((1, 2))

Y5   The Yardbirds *in* Gorilla Beat, No. 3 (1979): 3–11; discography pp. 8–11; addenda in No. 4 (1979): 39; No. 5 (1980): 12; No. 6 (1980): 46; and No. 8 (1980): 46 ((—))

Y6   Yardbirds discography *in* Jamz, No. 4 (May 1972): 7–8 [Includes Keith Relf solo] ((5))

Y7   Yardbirds discography *in* Trouser Press Collector's Magazine, I/4 (March–April 1979): 5 ((5))

YELVINGTON, MALCOLM

Y8   HAWKINS, Martin: Malcolm Yelvington *in* New Kommotion, No. 22 (1979): 39–40; discography p. 40 ((1, 2, 3, 7))

YES (musical group)

Y9   [[Discography *in* HEDGES, Dan: Yes: the authorized biography. London: Sidgwick & Jackson, 1981: 140–145]]

YORK BROTHERS (musical group)

Y10   [Discography] *in* Hillbilly Folk Record Journal, II/2 (March–June 1955): ? ((—))

YOUNG, FARNON

Y11   [LP's] *in* Country Corner, No. 44 (May 1975): 92, 94 ((—))

YOUNG, GEORGE

Y12   Vanda & Young: Then, now & in between *in* The Rock Marketplace, No. 3 (October 1973): 6–7; addendum in No. 8 (December 1974): 42 ((5))

YOUNG, NEIL

Y13   Discography *in* DUFRECHOU, Carole: Neil Young. New York: Quick Fox, 1978: 123–126 ((5))

YOUNG, VANDER

Y14   BAKER, Glenn, and Ken BARNES: The Vander Young discography *in* Bomp, No. 18 (February 1978): 65 ((5))

THE YOUNG RASCALS (musical group)
See THE RASCALS

THE YOUNG TYRANTS (musical group)

Y15   PREVOST, Greg: The history of the Young Tyrants *in* Blitz, No. 39 (March–April 1981): 17 ((1, 5))

THE YOUNGSTERS (musical group)

Y16   HINCKLEY, Dave: The Youngsters *in* Yesterday's Memories, III/2 (1977): 24 ((7))

YUPANQUI, ATAHUALPA

Y17   Discografia *in* LUNA, Felix: Atahualpa Yupanqui. Madrid: Jucar, 1974: [145]–150 ((7))

ZAPPA, FRANK

Z1   Vollstandige Diskografie *in* Alla Zappa. Zurich: Painting Box Press, 1976: [60–62] ((5))

Z2   Discographie *in* DISTER, Alain: Frank Zappa et les Mothers of Invention. Paris: A. Michel, 1975: [173]–178 ((1, 5))

Z3   Diskografie *in* KAISER, Rolf-Ulrich: Frank Zappa. Hoorn: West Friesland, 1971: 159–160 ((—))

Z4   [Discography] *in* KAISER, Rolf-Ulrich: Zapzapzappa. Cologne: Kinder der Geburtstagspress, 1968: unnumbered page ((—))

Z5   OBERMANN, Norbert: Zappalog. 2nd ed. Los Angeles: Rhino, 1982. 127 pp. ((1, 2, 4, 5, 7))

Z6   SLATER, Peter R.: Golden decade of Mother's records [with] "Mothers/ Zappa discography" *in* Goldmine, No. 14 (January–February 1977): 5 ((—))

Z7   Album chronology, singles . . . *in* WALLEY, David: No commercial potential, then and now. New York: Dutton, 1980: 181–184 ((—))

ZERO, RENATO

Z8   Discografia *in* GRANETTO, Luigi: Renato Zero. Rome: Lato side, 1981: 89–91 ((5))

Z9   Discografia *in* SALVATORI, Dario: Renato Zero. Rome: Gremese, 1980: [91] ((5))

ZIEGFELD FOLLIES

Z10   WARNER, Larry: The original Ziegfeld Follies on records *in* Kastlemusik Monthly Bulletin, II/12 (E-37, December 1977): 1, 14–15 ((7))

ZIEGLER, LULU

Z11   ANDREASEN, Axel: Lulu Ziegler og grammofonen: en discografi. Copenhagen: Andreasen, 1976. 47 l. ((3, 4, 6, 7))

THE ZODIACS (musical group)

Z12   BEACHLEY, Chris: The Gladiolas/ Zodiacs *in* Yesterday's Memories, I/3 (1975): 16 ((7))

THE ZOMBIES (musical group)

Z13   KOLTEC, W. T.: The Zombies *in* Jamz, No. 4 (May 1972): 9–12; discography p. 12 [Includes Colin Blunstone solo] ((5))

Z14   OLAFSON, Peter, and Alan BETROCK: Zombies discography *in* Trouser Press Collector's Magazine, I/3 (January–February 1979): [4] ((5))

ZONOPHONE label
See also REGAL ZONOPHONE labels

Z15   CRISP, David L.: Discography [EE series 1927–1933] *in* Devil's Box, XII/2 (June 1978): 27–29; XII/3 (September 1978): 24–26 ((3, 5, 6))

Z16   CRISP, David L.: Zonophone 'EE' series 1927–1933 *in* Country & Western Spotlight, No. 10 (March 1977): 29–36 ((3, 5, 6)) [Australian series]

Z17   [Discography] *in* Folk Style, No. 3 (November 1958): ? [English T series] ((—))

Z18   EDWARDS, John: [Discography] *in* Country Western Spotlight, No. 13 (May 1960) thru No. 15 (November 1960): ? ((—)) [Reprinted in Country Western Spotlight (Special issue, September 1962): ? [Australian EE series] ((—))]

Z19   RUST, Brian: (British) Berliner, G & T and Zonophone 7-inch records *in* Talking Machine Review, No. 63–64 (Autumn 1981): 1726–1758 ((2, 3, 7))

Z20   Zonophone 5-inch (12.5 cm) discs *in* Talking Machine Review, No. 32 (February 1975): 299–309; additions in No. 43 (December 1976): 864 ((3))

THE ZOOKS (musical group)

Z21   McDOWELL, Mike: Exploring the orange rooftops of your mind with the Zooks *in* Blitz, No. 27 (July 1978): 23–24; discography p. 24 ((1, 5))

PERIODICALS CITED

After Beat
American Folk Music Occasional
American Record Guide
Anschalage
Aware Magazine

Ballroom Blitz
Bam Balam
Bedloe's Island
Big Beat
Big Beat of the 50's
Big Town Review
Billboard
Bim Bam Boom
Black Wax
Blitz
Blue Yodler
Bluegrass Unlimited
Blues Link
Blues Research
Bomp!
Buenos Aires Tango
Bulletin de la Phonotheque Nationale

Caravan
Cashbox
Classic Wax
Collecta
Commodore
Country & Western Roundabout
Country & Western Spotlight
Country Corner
Country Directory
Country Music Review
Country Music Times
Country News & Views
Country Record Exchange
Country Roundup
Country Singin' & Pickin' News
Country Western Exchange

Country Western Express
Crazy Music

Devil's Box
Diapason
Different Drummer
Disc Collector
Disc-O-Graph
Discographer
Discophile
Discoteca hi fi
Down Beat

Film Music Notebook
Folk Style
Footnote
Full Blast

Goldmine
Gorilla Beat
Gunn Report

Hifi Stereo
HiFi Stereophonie
Hillandale News
Hillbilly
Hillbilly Folk Record Journal
Hobbies
Hot Buttered Soul

Instrumental Obscurities Unlimited
It Will Stand

JEMF Quarterly
Jamz
Jazz Freund

Jazz Hot
Jazz Press
Journal of Country Music

Kastlemusik Monthly Bulletin
Keynotes
Kicks
Kommotion
Kountry Korral

Matrix
Mean Mountain Music
Memory Lane
Memory Mail
Mojo-Navigator Rock & Roll News
Music-Hall Records
Music Memories & Jazz Report
Music Week
Music World
Music World and Record Digest Weekly News

New Amberola Graphic
New Haven Rock Press
New Kommotion
New Rockpile
Nostalgia World
Not Fade Away

Old Time Music
Outlet
Overtures

Paul's Record Magazine

RSVP
RTS Music Gazette
R & B Magazine
Record Advertiser
Record Collector
Record Collector's Journal
Record Exchanger
Record Finder
Record Research
Recorded Americana

Recorded Sound
Records and Recording
Rhythm Bag
R-O-C-K
Rock and Roll International Magazine
    (Danish and Dutch magazines)
Rock It with Aware
Rock Marketplace
Rocking Regards
Rockville International
Rockville/Roaring Sixties
Rumble

SMG
Schwann-2 Record and Tape Guide
Shout
Soul Bag
Soul Music
Sounds Fine
Soundtrack Collector's Newsletter
Stereo Review
Street Singer
Strictly Cash
Stormy Weather
Storyville

Talking Machine Review
Talking Machine Review International
Tarakan Music Letter
Tele-radiomonde
Time Barrier Express
Trans-Oceanic Trouser Press
Trouser Press
Trouser Press Collectors Magazine
Trouser Press Press

What Goes On
Whiskey, Women, and . . .
Who Put the Bomp
Whole Lotta Rockin'

Yesterday's Memories

Zig Zag

INDEX

Note: References are to entry numbers, not page numbers. Only authors', compilers', and editors' names and series titles have been indexed.